J. Harris.

An Introduction to the
OLD TESTAMENT

EXPLORING TEXT,
APPROACHES AND ISSUES

JOHN GOLDINGAY

IVP Academic

An imprint of InterVarsity Press
Downers Grove, Illinois

InterVarsity Press
P.O. Box 1400, Downers Grove, IL 60515-1426
ivpress.com
email@ivpress.com

InterVarsity Press® is the book-publishing division of InterVarsity Christian Fellowship/USA®, a movement of
students and faculty active on campus at hundreds of universities, colleges and schools of nursing in the United
States of America, and a member movement of the International Fellowship of Evangelical Students. For
information about local and regional activities, visit intervarsity.org.

Cover design: Cindy Kiple
Interior design: Beth McGill
Images: Abstract background: © viktor_vector/iStockphoto

ISBN 978-0-8308-4090-8 (print)
ISBN 978-0-8308-9908-1 (digital)

Printed in the United States of America ∞

Library of Congress Cataloging-in-Publication Data
Goldingay, John.
  An introduction to the Old Testament : exploring text, approaches & issues / John Goldingay.
     pages cm
  Includes index.
  ISBN 978-0-8308-4090-8 (casebound : alk. paper)
  1. Bible. Old Testament—Textbooks. 2. Bible. Old Testament—Introductions. I. Title.
  BS1194.G635 2015
  221.6'1—dc23

                                                                                                    2015026991

P   23   22   21   20   19   18   17   16   15   14   13   12   11   10   9   8   7   6   5   4   3   2   1

Y   34   33   32   31   30   29   28   27   26   25   24   23   22   21   20   19   18   17   16   15

Contents

Preface

In this introduction to Old Testament study my aim is to help you study Scripture for yourself. I spend little time telling you what the OT says or what scholars say. I focus more on giving you background material, noting approaches to interpretation, raising questions and suggesting approaches to questions. My goal is to provide you with a workbook, based on the material I use with my students and on my discovery of what works with them. After the introduction (part one) the main structure of the book follows the Jewish community's division of the OT into the Torah (part two), the Prophets (part three) and the Writings (part four); then the conclusion to the book (part five) looks back over the whole. Full information on other books that I refer to also comes in the conclusion. The five parts are divided into self-contained two-page spreads, each of which has a number (101, 102, and so on). You can open the book at any point and be able more or less to understand that spread. You don't need to read the entire introduction before plunging into the study that starts in part two, or to read part two before part three. There is also considerable material on my webpage to supplement the material in this book (see "Web Resources," which follows this preface).

I have implied already that it's more important to help people read the Bible for themselves than to tell them what the Bible says. The Reformation displaced the pope as the person who decided what the Bible means, but it's easy to replace the pope with pastors or professors, in which case you're no better off. My aim in this book is to help you study the Bible for yourself. I am told that there is a joke in Latin America: Catholics don't read the Bible because they think it's too hard to understand; Protestants don't read it because they're sure they already understand it. My experience is that Protestants in the United States are inclined to the alleged Catholic attitude. They assume that they need to be told what the Bible says by an expert. I believe that you can get to understand it. Further, there are limits to what anyone can teach you. Learning requires active involvement, thinking things out, ideally articulating things to other people and arguing things out, and applying things. It's a process that involves an interaction between experience and study and prayer.

I am grateful to Gillian Cooper, my Old Testament colleague at St. John's Theological College, Nottingham, England, who got me to join in rethinking our aims and methods in teaching Old Testament in a way that bears this fruit twenty-five years later; to Robert Hubbard for accidentally sowing in my thinking the idea of writing this book and for commenting on much of the material; and to generations of students at St John's Theological College and Fuller Theological Seminary, Pasadena, California, for questions that stimulated much of what I have thought and written, among them especially Kathleen Scott, who liked the course so much that she married me and has commented with insight on the material, though she wishes there were more of the jokes that come in my lectures but that Americans don't understand.

Biblical translations are my own from the Hebrew, Aramaic or Greek except where otherwise indicated.

Web Resources

To supplement the material in this book, there is material at johngold ingay.com under the "OT Introduction" tab. This site includes more background material and more material suggesting implications for our own day. You're welcome to print out and copy any of it. There are references to this web material throughout the book in the form of the phrases "see or see further 119 or 245 or 363 or 442 or 507." These particular numbers refer to spreads at the end of each of the five parts of the book where you will find a list of the web material relating to each part of this book. The numbering of the web material resumes from the numbering at the end of each of the five parts of the book. The material also includes responses to many of the questions that students have asked when they have studied with me.

If you find you have questions that are not covered there, you're welcome to email me with them at johngold@fuller.edu. I'll answer as many as I can each week, and I'll add these questions and responses to the main body of questions and answers on the website. If that process stops, it means I've died or gone gaga.

I expect I shall think of things to add to the web material as time goes by, and there is much more material under other tabs on that webpage. But this book itself is self-contained. While a few of the questions I suggest you think about involve looking at things on the web, otherwise you don't need access to the web in order to read the Bible, use this book and do the study I am suggesting.

Part One INTRODUCTION

1 | 01 | Approaching the Old Testament

The "Old Testament" is the Christian term for the collection of scrolls in Hebrew and Aramaic that the Jewish community accepts as its Scriptures, and to which it often refers as the "Torah [or Law], the Prophets and the Writings," or "Tanak" for short (from the initial letters of the three Hebrew nouns "Torah," "Nebi'im," "Ketubim"). Scholars often refer to them as the "Hebrew Bible." The books were written at different times between about the eighth century and the second century B.C. We don't know when they became a defined collection, when they became the "Scriptures." From a Christian viewpoint, it's significant that as far as we can tell, it's the collection of Scriptures that Jesus and his first followers would have recognized; most of the books are quoted in the NT.

Nearly half the OT comprises narratives telling the story of the world's creation and then the story of Israel over the centuries. Incorporated into the first part of this narrative are substantial swathes of instructions about how Israel should live. The OT goes on to include a collection of works preserving the messages of some prophets and a collection of poetic and prose works offering teaching about sensible ways to live everyday life and examples of praise and prayer for people to use.

The OT refers to other historical records, prophets and teachers that are not included in the OT; we have examples of such works from other Middle Eastern peoples contemporary with Israel. The ones in the OT are the examples that Israel preserved as having permanent significance for the people of God. There are also many other Jewish works from the centuries just before or just after Christ, some of which came to be used in the church along with the works in the OT. They are referred to as the "Apocrypha" (the "hidden" books) or as the "Deuterocanonical Writings." The latter of these two terms is clumsier but more appropriate. The word "canon" means "ruler," and "deutero" means "second"; the OT (the Torah, the Prophets and the Writings) are the primary canon, and these are a second canon. As far as we know, these books never were regarded as Scripture by the Jewish community, and they are not quoted in the NT. (The NT does quote from Enoch, which is not part of most versions of the Apocrypha, though the Ethiopian Church did come to recognize it, perhaps because it is quoted in the NT.) See further 118.

What's the appropriate way to go about studying the OT? It's tricky discussing that question at this point because you can really answer it only by getting involved in doing the study. So what I am doing here is giving you conclusions that I have come to.

1. I read these books as the church's Scriptures, the canon or ruler for my thinking and life. As we often put it, they are "the Word of God." I therefore need to study them self-critically. Where they say something different from what I'm inclined to think, I assume that I'm the one who's wrong. As people often put it, I accept the authority of the Scriptures.

2. In addition, they are works of literature, the products of Israel's history, created through human processes, emerging from their Middle Eastern context. So I seek to understand them as human, historical, contextual documents, and not read into them meanings that would be alien to their writers and their first readers. That principle includes not reading NT ideas into them. Their being human and contextual doesn't mean that they are limited because they came into being before the modern age and before Jesus, that they are bound to contain mistakes. It does mean that we have to understand them in their context.

3. In this connection, I use the methods of biblical criticism, not to criticize the text, but to understand it. Over time, "biblical criticism" came to be understood as criticizing the Bible, but it started off as a commitment to asking questions about the way church leaders and scholars interpreted the Bible, so as to let the Bible speak for itself. It's that use of biblical criticism that interests me.

4. Because most church leaders and scholars in the West have been middle-aged white men, being critical also includes seeking to study the OT from perspectives other than those of middle aged white men. Since I'm one of those, do read books about the OT by other kinds of people.

Students sometimes ask how I got interested in the OT. There are some jokey or superficial answers to the question. My theology degree program required Greek, whereas Hebrew was optional; but I had already studied Greek, so I could fit in Hebrew. The OT came first in the program; if church history had come first, I would have fallen in love with that instead. Further, I undertook my undergraduate study at a time when scholarly OT study was going through what seemed a positive and confident phase, and OT study felt exciting in that respect. More seriously, I had two outstanding OT mentors: John Baker, who modeled how you could undertake university academic study of the OT and also be a priest, and Alec Motyer, a seminary teacher and priest who was a great preacher on the OT.

Yet these considerations from years ago are not the reasons why I am passionate about the OT now. My enthusiasm issues from my ongoing involvement with it. I love the stories about Israel's ancestors, about the leaders in Judges, about Jonah and Esther. I love the boldness of the prayers and praises of the psalms. I love the way the prophets confront Israel with challenges to faith and to faithfulness. I love the courage with which Job and Ecclesiastes raise questions. Indeed, it's the facing of questions that I love as much as anything. The OT is relentlessly realistic about human beings and about life, but it never steps away from staying in conversation with God about such matters.

I also continue to be enthusiastic about getting at the OT's own meaning in its context. I want to see things through the eyes of Genesis or Isaiah or Lamentations. My Christian faith will sometimes enable me to perceive things in the OT that I might otherwise miss; it will give me ways into the OT. But I want to see what's there, and I want the OT to correct my Christian assumptions when they need correction. And I've proved for myself that when I can work out what these books would mean for the Israelites for whom they were written, there's a good chance that I can find my way to what it might mean for me.

I make the assumption that where the OT says something scandalous, it's more likely to be right than I am. I sometimes get the impression that students assume that a professor's job is to reassure them that the Bible says nothing different from what they believe already. After all, the students are good Christian people, and they ought to be able to trust their worldview and presuppositions. I think that it's wiser to assume that we are decisively shaped by the culture in which we live, and that we are likely to be quite wrong in some of our beliefs and presuppositions. Thus, when I see the Bible saying something different from what I think, that's a moment when studying the Bible becomes especially interesting. So you won't find this book doing much to make the OT more comfortable to read.

Is this passion of mine simply my peculiarity, like my enthusiasm for jazz? There are two sorts of reasons for Christians to see if they can share this involvement. One is that Jesus and the NT writers shared it. For them, the OT simply was the "Scriptures," given for them to benefit from and be shaped by (2 Tim 3:14-17). It was vital for them to see that their faith was in keeping with these Scriptures. The other is that as a consequence the church accepted them and has passed them on to us as part of the church's heritage and rule for life and thinking.

The trouble is that the OT isn't what we would expect. We would expect God's revelation to be nice, so that its stories would give us examples of people living good lives with God. But the Bible makes clear at many points that to be the Word of God, Scripture does not have to be nice or to make us feel good. We would expect biblical history to give us examples of people living faithful lives and to make it very clear what was their message. Joshua, Judges and Samuel don't do so. So we may have to change our views on what God would want to give us and ask why God wanted to give us what he did. It is these nasty stories (e.g., the Levite's concubine) as well as the nice stories (e.g., Hannah) that are designed to change our thinking, our lives and our relationship with God.

READING THE OLD TESTAMENT
AS THE WORD OF GOD IN ITS
OWN RIGHT

1. The NT encourages us to get wisdom for life from the OT. These writings are able to teach us and train us in righteousness (2 Tim 3:14-17).

2. However, it's not true that the NT lies hidden in the OT, and that the OT is revealed in the NT. The OT tells us how God really related to people and really spoke to them. God did so in ways that were designed for them to understand; they were not obscure. The NT then tells us that the OT is the inspired and authoritative Word of God, which we should therefore take with absolute seriousness. It doesn't need decoding.

3. The OT thus isn't a sneak preview of Jesus. Jesus isn't all God has to say; God has lots of other things to say, and he has said lots of them in the OT. If we narrow the OT down to what the NT says, we miss these things. It is the case that lenses provided by the NT sometimes help us see things that are there in the OT. But if we want to understand what God wants us to understand from the OT, we do best not to think too much about the NT because that tends to narrow our perspective.

4. It's not true that the OT God is a God of wrath, and the NT God a God of love. In both Testaments, God is one who loves to love people, but who is prepared to be tough when necessary.

5. It's not true that the OT offers a partial or incomplete or imperfect revelation. Or rather, there is one thing that the OT doesn't tell you but the NT does. That thing is (amusingly) the fact that some people are going to hell. Neither hell nor heaven comes in the OT. But the NT does also tell you that it's possible to enjoy resurrection life: that because Jesus rose, we will rise.

6. It's not true that the OT is a religion of law, and the NT a religion of grace. Because of this misunderstanding I don't follow the practice of referring to the opening books of the OT as the "Law." I rather keep the

Hebrew word "Torah" (which means "teaching"). In both Testaments, God relates to people on the basis of grace but then expects them to live a life of obedience.

7. It's not true that the OT is a book of stories about people who are meant to be examples to us. You only have to read the stories to see this point. Both Testaments are books of stories about what God did through people, often despite who they were not because of who they were. If anyone is an example to us in the OT, it's God (see Lev 19:2), not even people such as Abraham, Moses or David.

8. One aspect of the wisdom that the NT expects us to get from these books is that they show how Israel went wrong (see 1 Cor 10:1-13). We can easily make the same mistakes that Israel made. The Israelites failed to enter into God's real rest (Ps 95); we could do the same (Heb 3–4).

9. It's not true that you can do whatever you like to your enemies in the OT. "Loving your neighbor" includes loving your enemy; your enemies usually are the people who live near you, who attack you or defraud you. Of course, in the NT there's no event like Joshua slaughtering the Canaanites; but the NT doesn't disapprove of such acts by OT heroes such as Joshua (see, e.g., Heb 11).

10. The OT is the record of how God spoke to the people of God and acted in their lives, and acted in the affairs of the nations. We can discover from it more about what God is like and what God says to us and how God may be involved in our world.

11. So the OT is designed to transform our lives. The way it does so is by setting our lives in the context of the story of what God had been doing with Israel, seeing us in a relationship with God (of praise, protest, trust, repentance and testimony), setting our thinking in the context of an argument as it encourages us to face questions, and thus rescuing us from the limitations of what we believe already. The OT is there to help the people of God live concretely, worshipfully, wisely and hopefully. It's to help us see what God is like and to live with God.

THE BOOKS IN THE OLD TESTAMENT

In most English Bibles the *content* follows the Hebrew Bible, but the *order* follows the Greek Bible, called the "Septuagint," which is mostly a translation from the Hebrew made in the third and second centuries B.C. and also includes the Second Canon or Apocrypha (see 118). So here are two lists of the works that appear in the two versions, in the two different orders. In the Greek/English list, in square brackets I also include the books in the Second Canon (though there's some variation in different versions of the Second Canon). In this book, partly because we are following the content of the Hebrew Bible, we will also follow its order: first the Torah, then the Prophets, then the Writings.

Hebrew Bible	Greek and English Bibles
The Torah Genesis, Exodus, Leviticus, Numbers, Deuteronomy	**The Pentateuch and First History** Genesis, Exodus, Leviticus, Numbers, Deuteronomy, leading into Joshua, Judges, Ruth, Samuel, Kings
The Former Prophets Joshua, Judges, Samuel, Kings	
	The Second History (These come in the Writings in the Hebrew Bible) Chronicles, 1 and 2 Esdras (two versions of Ezra–Nehemiah), Esther (a longer version) [Judith, Tobit, Maccabees] [Another work also known as 2 Esdras, an apocalypse, also appears in the Latin Bible]

Hebrew Bible	Greek and English Bibles
	The Poetic Books (These come in the Writings in the Hebrew Bible) Psalms, Proverbs, Ecclesiastes, Song of Songs, Job [Psalm 151, Odes, including the Prayer of Manasseh, Wisdom, Ben Sira]
The Latter Prophets Isaiah, Jeremiah, Ezekiel, the Twelve Shorter Prophets	**The Prophets** Isaiah, Jeremiah, Lamentations, Ezekiel, Daniel (a longer version), the Twelve Shorter Prophets [Baruch, Epistle of Jeremiah]
The Writings Psalms, Job Proverbs The Five Scrolls (Song of Songs, Ruth, Lamentations, Ecclesiastes, Esther) Daniel, Ezra, Nehemiah, Chronicles	

The Latter Prophets in Hebrew are thus approximately the same as the Prophets in Greek and English. In the Hebrew Bible Joshua through Kings are the Former Prophets (former in order, not time).

Although the Jewish community uses the order in the first column and the Christian community the order in the second column, quite likely both orders originally came from the Jewish community. But it's worth remembering that the question of order (and of exactly which books belong) would not be so much of an issue in the centuries before the invention of the codex (that is, something like a book) in Christian times, for which you would need to put the books in an order. When the Scriptures took the form of individual scrolls, it wouldn't mean so much.

The two orders do suggest complementary ways of seeing the message that issues from the collection of books. The Jewish order broadly moves from past to future to present. The Christian order broadly moves from past to present to future.

1 | 05 | HOW DID OLD TESTAMENT BOOKS GET WRITTEN?

My wife, Kathleen, is writing a novel. The story takes place in NT times, so she does lots of research into what was going on and what life was like in places such as Jerusalem and Rome, but the story itself then comes out of her head. Actually, she might say that it comes *to* her rather than coming *from* her; she transcribes what comes. In due course she will edit the story, so that its eventual published form will be different from what she is writing at the moment. Something analogous will happen to this book that I am writing. Publishers in the United States like to edit books for authors, so there will be phrases in this book that I didn't write. In my own writing I am sometimes starting from scratch, sometimes taking up an outline that I use in class and expanding it, so that the paragraphs will never have been in written form before. Elsewhere in this book I shall sometimes reuse sections from lectures that I have written out. So books come into existence in different ways.

How did people write books in the Bible's world? Things that the writers say and comparisons with other works from the Middle Eastern world suggest that the Holy Spirit's inspiration of the biblical authors did not issue in their writing books in ways different from the ones that were customary in their culture. For instance, biblical laws, proverbs, psalms and poems are similar in form to those of other Middle Eastern writings. Evidence within the Bible tells us something of the ways their authors went about writing, and this study confirms that they wrote in similar ways to other peoples. The Holy Spirit's involvement inspired them to write great (inspired, authoritative) examples of these forms of literature, but the human processes whereby they came into being were the same as those for other peoples.

What can we tell from the OT books themselves about how they got written?

1. Some books look as if they were written from scratch, like Kathleen writing her novel. It seems this was true of short stories such as Jonah, Ruth and Esther. We cannot get behind them to sources or earlier versions or raw

materials. It has been suggested that the Torah was written from scratch in the Persian period, without the use of earlier sources or versions.

2. Some books were based on ones that already exist; they are new editions of those earlier books. Chronicles is an example. Chronicles' story of Israel from David to the fall of Jerusalem is based on the story in Samuel–Kings; or possibly both are based on some other version of the story that no longer exists, but this possibility doesn't affect the point. We know that it is so because many sections of Chronicles are word-for-word the same as a section of Kings, or differ only in small ways. There are theories of this kind about the origin of the Torah; that is, that the Torah as we know it may have come into existence through an author writing the story, which later was supplemented by extra materials of various kinds.

3. Some books are a kind of collage. We can see how Ezra–Nehemiah combines materials that the compiler has derived from various sources: lists of people who returned from exile and who took part in rebuilding Jerusalem's walls, copies of correspondence between the Jerusalem authorities and the Persian court, first-person accounts by Ezra and Nehemiah of things that they did, and third-person accounts of the temple rebuilding and other events, accounts apparently written by other people. Someone then assembled these materials and put them together. There have been similar "fragmentary" theories about the origin of the Torah; that is, that it issued from the compilation of pieces that had never before been brought together.

4. Joshua–Judges–Samuel–Kings also has something of the nature of a collage, but in addition there are indications that it went through more than one edition.

5. About a century after the four Gospels were written, the theologian Tatian interwove them to produce the *Diatessaron*, a "harmony" of the Gospels, as Matthew and Luke had produced their Gospels by conflating earlier versions of the story. The dominant view of the Torah's origin has been such a "documentary" or "source" theory; four earlier documents were combined to produce it.

OLD TESTAMENT STORY AND
OLD TESTAMENT HISTORY

The OT as a whole tells a story. One could think of it as a story with six acts and a number of scenes. (A much more detailed version of the story can be found in "How to Read the Bible"; see 119.)

1. (a) God created the world, but things went wrong.

   (b) God almost destroyed the world, then started it off again; but it went wrong again.

2. (a) God called a particular family through which to bring the world blessing and promised that it would become a great people with its own land.

   (b) The people did grow, but they had to take refuge in Egypt, and they ended up as serfs there, so God had to rescue them from Egypt, proving himself greater than the king of Egypt.

   (c) God appeared to them at Sinai and laid down his expectations for many areas of their life.

   (d) On the way to their land they frequently rebelled, and God decided that this entire generation could not go into the land.

3. (a) The next generation did occupy the land and divided it among their clans.

   (b) The subsequent generations became more and more wayward religiously and socially. In addition, they couldn't hold their own in relation to other peoples.

   (c) They therefore asked to have a king like other peoples. Saul, David and Solomon were the first kings. David and Solomon built the temple in Jerusalem.

4. (a) The nation then split into two, Ephraim in the north and Judah in the south. Ephraim was especially disloyal to Yahweh and was conquered by Assyria. (On the names Israel, Ephraim and Judah, see 116.)

(b) Judah wasn't much more loyal than Ephraim was, and it was conquered by Babylon; Jerusalem and its temple were destroyed.

5. (a) Persia replaced Babylon as superpower and allowed the Judahites to restore the temple, though many stayed abroad rather than returning to Jerusalem.

(b) Ezra brought the Torah to Jerusalem and sought to reform Jerusalem in light of it.

(c) Nehemiah came to Jerusalem to rebuild its walls and joined Ezra in this work.

6. (a) Greece replaced Persia as superpower, then its empire fell apart. The Seleucid Empire, based in Syria, and the Ptolemaic Empire, based in Egypt, took turns controlling Judah.

(b) The Seleucids sought to impose pagan worship in Jerusalem. The Judahites rebelled, and Yahweh rescued them, so that they were then independent until the Romans arrived.

Such is the outline of the OT story. But sometimes we may suspect that this story wasn't designed to be history as it actually happened (the creation story is the obvious example). Some archaeological discoveries mesh with the story. For instance, they indicate that someone destroyed the great city Hazor in Galilee in the time of Joshua, and that there was substantial development of settled life in Canaan in the period to which the book of Judges refers. Some archaeological discoveries don't mesh with the OT's own story. For instance, they do not suggest that Jericho was there to be destroyed in Joshua's day. Some events in the story feature in Middle Eastern or Greek records and histories. For instance, Assyria, Babylon and Persia had their own records of some of their actions in relation to Ephraim and Judah. But most of the events don't feature there; virtually nothing does before about the eighth century B.C. There are thus varying scholarly views about how historical the OT story was designed to be and actually was.

Thinking about these questions is complicated by the existence of different scholarly views on when different parts of the OT were written. In the course of this book we will come back to these questions at appropriate points, especially in connection with the accounts of creation, of Israel's ancestors, of the exodus and of Israel's emergence in Canaan.

1200	1260 The exodus (Moses)	
	1220 The entry into the land (Joshua)	
		Israel in conflict with,
	1125 The judges (e.g., Deborah)	**e.g., Philistines**
1100		
	1050 Saul	
	1010 David	
1000		**Israel**
	970 Solomon	**independent**
	930 Division into two kingdoms: northern	
	Israel (Ephraim), southern Judah	
900		
	850 Elijah and Elisha	
800		
	Jonah, Amos, Hosea, Micah, Isaiah ben Amoz	**Assyria**
	722 Ephraim falls to Syria; Ephraimites exiled	**in control**
700		
	Jeremiah, Nahum, Habbauk, Zephaniah	
	622 Josiah's reform	**Babylon**
600	Ezekiel	**in control**
	587 Jerusalem falls to Babylon; Judahites exiled	
	Lamentations, Obadiah, Isaiah 40–55	
	539 Babylon falls to Persia; Judahites free to	
	return, rebuild temple	**Persia**
500	Haggai, Zechariah, Isaiah 56–66	**in control**
	Joel, Malachi	
	458 Ezra brings Torah to Jerusalem	
	445 Nehemiah rebuilds walls	

Here are some things to note from this timeline.

1. I haven't given any dates for events in Genesis, because Genesis itself doesn't give hard dates and neither is there information from elsewhere in the ancient Middle East that helps us with dating.

2. People sometimes get the impression that the exile in 587 is the closing event of OT times, but actually the exile is not much more than half way through the story from Moses to the end of the OT period. The OT story continues for over four more centuries in telling of the restoration of Judah after the exile, and of events in the Persian and Greek periods, though we do lack a continuous account of that story of the kind that Exodus to Kings gives for the earlier part of the story.

3. In the way Israel's story unfolds, a key factor is the rise of the great empires of Assyria, Babylon, Persia and Greece. A grasp of this sequence of empires is key to understanding why Israel's story unfolds as it does and to understanding the messages of the different prophets.

FACT AND TRUTH IN THE OLD TESTAMENT

I f the OT is wholly reliable as a guide to who God is, who we are and how we may relate to God, must it be factual at every point in order to be really the Word of God? Views on the factual nature of the OT belong at various points on a spectrum. At one end is the conviction that the whole OT narrative is literally factual. God created the world in six days; all Israel's ancestors were involved in the exodus; Jonah was swallowed by a fish. In the middle is the conviction that the OT story is basically reliable history, but none of those specific elements need be factual. There are more and less conservative versions of that view. At the other end of the spectrum is the view that the OT is basically an imaginative story created in late OT times. Again, there are more and less radical versions of that view (maybe David and Ezra existed, maybe they didn't). My guess is that most scholars who view the OT as Scripture take some version of the middle view. But there are evangelical scholars who take the first or the last view.

There are no grounds within Scripture or outside Scripture for saying that the whole of Scripture is factual. Responding to the challenge of biblical criticism in the late nineteenth century, B. B. Warfield made the inspiration of Scripture the basis for believing that the history in Scripture is factually inerrant. But this inference is not based on Scripture. When the Bible describes biblical narrative as inspired, its point is that it therefore speaks beyond its original context (it speaks to us) and it is effective (it does things to us), not that it's necessarily factually accurate at every point. It's the best possible human history. Inerrancy is not a scriptural doctrine, but rather a nineteenth-century one.

On the other hand, there are both theological and critical grounds for doubting whether it is simply a made-up story. For the story to "work," it needs to be basically factual. The authors of the exodus story would hardly have thought that their story made sense if there was no exodus and the story issued from their imagination.

We can trust God's providence to have ensured that Scripture's narrative is accurate enough. Yet this trust does not give grounds for expecting it to be inerrant. God did not need to provide us with an inerrant Bible, just with a Bible that is approximately accurate. So if its history seems to be not quite accurate, we needn't worry. It's still God's inspired Word, able to speak to us and do things to us—the nonfactual as well as the factual parts. It doesn't matter if we don't know where fact stops and fiction starts. The basis of our assurance that the OT is God's Word is not that we can show that it's history or that we know who wrote it, but that Jesus gave it to us and that it speaks to us. We don't believe in Jesus because of the authority of Scripture; we believe in Scripture's authority because we know that Jesus is God's Son. I trust the OT because I trust Jesus, not the other way round.

We might expect God's revelation to be like Joseph Smith's tablets, or Moses' tablets or prophecy—given directly from heaven. Scripture itself tells us that the opposite is the case. Most of Scripture is things such as psalms, letters and proverbs. That is, the Scriptures look like the ordinary human writings of the culture. As far as narrative is concerned, Luke 1:1-4 tells us how a biblical author goes about writing history: the same as anyone else.

What is history like when written by a traditional society? There are no Middle Eastern historical works to compare the OT narratives with, but there are Mediterranean ones, such as the work of the Greek historian Thucydides. He brings together (1) historical narratives; (2) traditional stories; (3) products of imagination—stories and speeches; (4) evaluation. We would expect that the kind of "history" that the Holy Spirit inspired would be the kind that people such as Thucydides wrote; and it is what we find in books such as Samuel and Kings. They include historical material, but we can't always tell which elements are historical. Yet that's not a problem because the whole of each book is inspired by the Holy Spirit, not just the historical bits. The OT story is true, and it has a historical basis, but it is more than merely a factual account of the event.

In seeking to discover what God wanted to say through the OT and what God wants to say to us through it, we can read it as it is without fretting about where lies the boundary between the history and elaboration, because we know it is true even where it is not factual.

WHEN THE OLD TESTAMENT IS
PARABLE NOT HISTORY

In 108 we considered the nature of the great "historical" narratives that provide the framework for the OT as a whole. Their story needs to be basically factual because its message is about something that happened. If it didn't happen, there is no gospel. We have noted that these inspired narratives can incorporate imaginative and other nonfactual elements, but they still have a factual base. Yet God also inspired fictional stories such as Jesus' parables. Some messages are best communicated through parables. Parables are true but not factual. It could also be an open question whether some entire biblical books are parable not history, or are a mixture. And it could be that God leaves us to work out whether we are to take particular stories as history or parable.

Jesus sometimes explains to people that he's about to tell a parable, but other times he expects them to work it out (e.g., Lk 15:11–16:31). How might he expect them to do so? Among the features of his stories that put us on the track of their being parable not history are (1) humor and irony; (2) exaggeration (things are larger than life); (3) "stock" characters; (4) schematic structure; (5) numerical schemes; (6) formulaic neatness and closure. The Gospels as a whole are not formulaic, ironic or exaggerated. The parables are fictions within a basically historical story. They are supportive of it because they help to explain what it means. They are also supported by it because without the factual Gospel story the parables would just be interesting stories that provide us with no basis for believing in their truth.

This insight about the Gospels and the parables transfers to the OT. While the great OT narrative needs to be basically historical for it to work, OT stories such as Ruth, Esther and Jonah have features of the same kind as the parables (humor, exaggeration and so on), which points to their being like the parables. They are Spirit-inspired, true parables, as are some elements in other books such as Genesis 1–11 and the stories in Daniel. They are true but not very factual (I say "not very factual" because I suspect that they usually have a factual kernel somewhere, but it may not be the most vital thing about them).

Realizing that these stories are parables rather than history helps us to take them really seriously as the Word of God because we know that the Holy Spirit specially inspired them to portray the way God deals with us. They aren't mere history. In her book *Poetic Justice*, Martha Nussbaum has suggested something of the importance of fiction in a way that helps us see why the Holy Spirit would inspire fiction in the Bible.

1. By its nature, history records only things that once happened. Fiction tells of the kind of things that happen to people in such a way as to invite us into the stories and wonder about ourselves.

2. History records things that happened. Fiction expresses a vision of how things could be or should be, or a sharpened version of how things are. It invites us to imagine the world differently.

3. History traditionally focuses on national events and "important" people. Fiction characteristically deals with ordinary people living ordinary lives, or with issues as they affect ordinary people.

4. Fiction portrays human beings with human hopes, fears, needs and desires, realized in specific social situations. Readers learn both from the similarities and the differences in the context.

5. The factual nature of history invites us to relate to it objectively. Fiction invites us to involve ourselves in it emotionally and in our inner world. It invites response. It is disturbing.

6. In particular, fiction invites us to engage with real individual people and communities that exist and matter in their own right and not only as part of a larger historical process or purpose.

7. Outside the Bible (in the ancient world and the modern world) fiction has always been a major serious way of engaging with fundamental theological, philosophical and moral issues.

These considerations show why the idea that the Bible includes fictional stories fits the Bible's nature.

READING THE OLD TESTAMENT
PREMODERNLY, MODERNLY AND
POSTMODERNLY

Those points about how OT books got written, about the "mixed" nature of OT history, and about the importance of parable or fiction can be seen in light of premodern, modern and postmodern ways of thinking and reading.

1. **In the premodern era,** readers assumed that the people named in the books' headings wrote them. Moses wrote the Torah, Joshua wrote Joshua, Samuel wrote 1 Samuel, David wrote Psalms, Solomon wrote Proverbs, Ecclesiastes and Song of Songs, Isaiah wrote all of Isaiah, Jeremiah wrote all of Jeremiah. Readers could use these convictions as keys to understanding the books.

2. Readers could therefore feel that the Bible came from important people who had lived lives close to God and could speak reliably about God's ways, and were people who lived close to the events and could therefore speak reliably about them.

3. Readers could also take for granted that the stories related events that happened, just as they happened. So you could add up the years that people lived and come to, say, 4004 B.C. as the date when the world was created.

4. Readers assumed that the OT talked about Jesus in prophecy and type.

5. **In the modern era,** readers took nothing for granted. Everything had to be proved. So biblical critics asked about the evidence for those assumptions about authorship and concluded that it wasn't very good. For example, the Torah issued from the interweaving of several versions of the story that came from different centuries, all later than Moses. Conservative critics sought to use modern methods to show that it was still possible to maintain the premodern assumptions.

6. If the books were written by anonymous authors, readers could feel that the Bible emerged through the Holy Spirit's inspiring ordinary people like us, and not just through great heroes.

7. When readers didn't take anything for granted in investigating the books' background, their work had the possibility of providing evidence regarding OT history that did not depend on faith.

8. They assumed that the OT talked about the events of its day, not about Jesus.

9. **In the postmodern era,** readers begin from the fact that it's impossible to prove very much in the modern way. The twentieth-century consensus on questions of authorship and OT history collapsed, and no other consensus has emerged. One reason is that the nature of the material is such that it does not yield the information that we are looking for. We are asking questions that it will not answer.

10. This doesn't mean that readers go back to premodern views, because the data that led to the modern theories are still there. We can know that Moses didn't write the Torah, that Isaiah didn't write all of Isaiah and so on. But we have no other grand theories to put in the place of the traditional ones.

11. In the postmodern era Christians can combine premodernity and modernity in a new way. We read the books as they are, trusting them. We seek to do so with open eyes; we do not revert to what premodern tradition said they say. In this sense, we approach them critically. We use whatever keys seem to unlock aspects of the text, trying different ones until we find one that opens the lock without forcing it. We practice what has been called "believing criticism."

12. Sometimes the historical approaches of modernity open the lock; sometimes they don't.

13. We assume that in the OT God was speaking to Israel about the affairs of its day, but this doesn't preclude God speaking about the future, nor does it preclude God's speaking being significant for Christian faith.

14. The postmodern approach doesn't claim to support or prove the idea that the OT is God's Word. When used by Christians, this approach presupposes that the OT is God's Word, partly on the basis of Jesus having given the OT (see 108), partly in order to give it the chance to prove it as we let it loose among us.

The boundaries of the land of Israel often changed, but its heartland is the mountain chain the bulk of which is now known as the West Bank or Judea and Samaria or Palestine. It averages twenty miles or so east to west, stretches about fifty miles north and south of Jerusalem, and ascends to 3,000 to 4,000 feet (1,000 meters). The rain falls chiefly on the western slopes, so that side is the most fertile land; the eastern slopes get very dry. Before David's day, Jerusalem was just a village; the key cities were Hebron in the south, Shechem in the north. After the fall of Samaria in 722 B.C., the Assyrians moved people from other parts of their empire here; and after the reestablishment of the Judahite state after the exile, the relationship between Samaria and Judah often was tense, both politically and religiously.

North, west and south of this chain is a semicircle of plains, well watered in the north but drier the farther you go south. Apart from Jerusalem, the great cities are here. It was mostly here that the Canaanites lived; hence early Israel emerged more in the mountains, where there was scope to settle. The northern plain is the scene of the great battles in the OT.

Further north is another mountainous area. The traditional northern boundary of the land is Dan; from Dan to the traditional southernmost town, Beersheba, is 150 miles. Farther south than Beersheba is desert. To the east is the deep valley of the River Jordan, emptying into the Dead Sea, one thousand feet below sea level. West to east, from the Mediterranean to the Jordan, is fifty to eighty miles. Beyond the Jordan the mountains rise again. The Torah recounts how, when the Israelites approached Canaan from the east, some of the clans settled there. To the far northeast is Mount Hermon; to its south are the fertile regions of Bashan and Gilead. Through Bashan runs a road from Damascus and the north and east, on its way to the Mediterranean and Egypt. It's the route that Israel's ancestors will have taken (the Jordan fords are named after Jacob's daughters), as later will Judahites going into exile and returning.

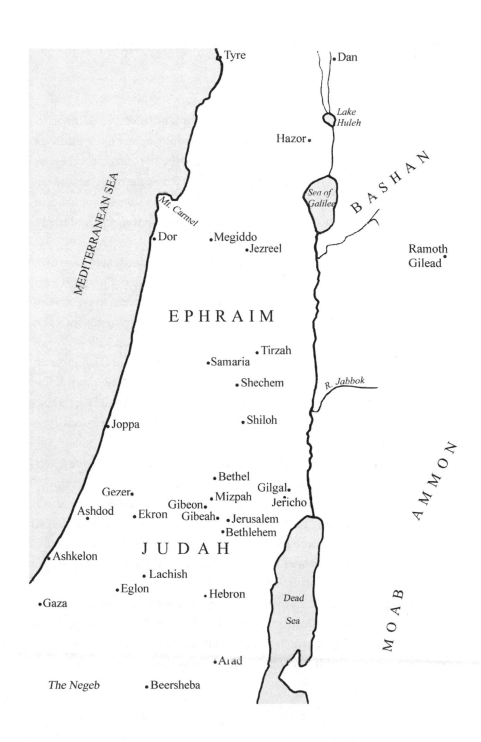

TYRE
• Dan

Lake Huleh

Hazor •

MEDITERRANEAN SEA

Mt. Carmel

B A S H A N

Sea of Galilee

• Dor
• Megiddo
• Jezreel

Ramoth Gilead •

E P H R A I M

• Tirzah
• Samaria
• Shechem

R. Jabbok

• Joppa

• Shiloh

A M M O N

• Bethel
Gezer •
• Mizpah
Gibeon •
• Gilgal
• Jericho
Ashdod •
• Ekron
Gibeah •
• Jerusalem
• Bethlehem

J U D A H

• Ashkelon

• Lachish
• Eglon
• Hebron

Dead Sea

M O A B

• Gaza

• Arad

The Negeb
• Beersheba

Canaan sits at a crossroads of geography and history; perhaps its location is why God placed his chosen people there. To the south are Egypt and the countries of Africa, from which the OT describes the Israelites as coming to Canaan. For much of the OT story Egypt was a major regional power if not a superpower, the land of oppression where Israel locates the beginnings of its story but a place of refuge in the exile and henceforth a major Jewish center.

To the east, beyond the area immediately across the Jordan, is desert. To the east and northeast of the desert are the Tigris and Euphrates Rivers and the centers of the great Middle Eastern superpowers: Assyria, then Babylon, then Medo-Persia. It is this Mesopotamian plain that is the background to the stories of the garden of Eden, the flood and the tower of Babel, and it was from this direction that God brought Abraham and Sarah to Canaan. It was Assyria that put an end to Ephraim, Babylon that destroyed Jerusalem and took people into exile there, and Medo-Persia that facilitated Judah's restoration and controlled it for two centuries until the Greeks arrived.

To the west are the Mediterranean and the countries of Europe, the direction from which the Philistines came to settle in the coastal plains of Canaan at about the same time that the Israelites were establishing themselves in the mountains. From this same direction, toward the end of the OT story, Greece took over from Medo-Persia as the superpower that controlled Judah (then the Romans later came from the same direction, but that's another story).

Isaiah 19:23-25 is an illuminating passage to look at in light of the map. The prophecy looks forward to a day when there will be a metaphorical highway between Egypt, which will be God's people, Assyria, which will be God's handiwork, and Israel, which will be God's possession.

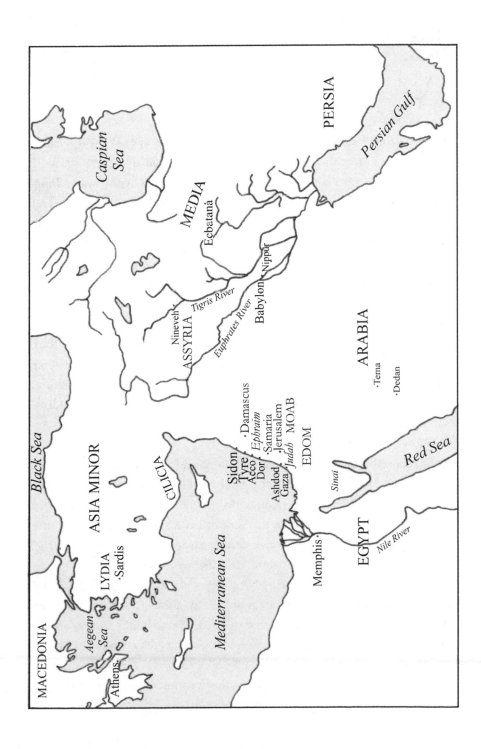

Caspian Sea

PERSIA

Persian Gulf

MEDIA

Ecbatanà

Black Sea

Nineveh

ASSYRIA

Tigris River

Euphrates River

Babylon Nippur

ARABIA

·Tema

·Dedan

MACEDONIA

ASIA MINOR

LYDIA

·Sardis

Aegean Sea

Athens·

CILICIA

Mediterranean Sea

Sidon
Tyre
Acco
Dor

Ashdod
Gaza

·Damascus

Ephraim
Samaria
Jerusalem
Judah MOAB

EDOM

Sinai

Red Sea

Memphis·

EGYPT

Nile River

13 How Did the Old Testament Come to Be the Old Testament?

We don't know when the Torah, the Prophets and the Writings came to count as the Scriptures. It used to be said that the "Synod of Jamnia" in A.D. 90 made the decisions. The so-called synod was a long-running set of discussions at Jamnia (modern Yavneh, near Tel Aviv) among the leadership of the Jewish people during the half-century following the fall of Jerusalem in A.D. 70. The focus of these debates lay on discussing the framework of the Jewish people's life now that the temple had been destroyed. These discussions did include some debate concerning the status of some of the books in the Scriptures, but the debates don't imply the making of decisions about what should be in the Scriptures. If anything, they presuppose that the Scriptures are long-established; thus these scholars are making slightly theoretical points, like Martin Luther when he sought to downgrade NT books such as James and Revelation. The Jamnia theory was attractive because it provided a way of avoiding saying that we don't know when the scriptural canon was finalized. Actually, we don't know.

On some theories, the Jewish community made decisions on this matter some centuries later. On another theory, the de facto decision was taken after Jerusalem's deliverance from Antiochus Epiphanes in 164 B.C., when the book of Daniel was included in the Scriptures on the basis of the way this deliverance had proved that the visions were a true revelation from God. The expression "de facto" is important. Discussion of when the Torah, the Prophets and the Writings finally became Scripture has been confused by talk in terms of "the closing of the canon," the assumption that at some point there must have been a meeting that decided, "These books and no others are the Scriptures." More likely the development of a collection of books that the community recognized as normative Scriptures was a gradual one, and at some stage, without anyone deciding that it should be so, no more books were added. Perhaps 164 B.C. was indeed the last occasion when a book was added, and perhaps a Jewish meeting five hundred years later did declare the canon closed; but we do not know.

Given that we have no information on when the Torah, the Prophets and the Writings (and no other writings) became Scripture, there are two sorts of argument for recognizing them as the definitive OT. One is that in accepting Jewish Scriptures at all, the church is recognizing its continuity with and its dependence on the Jewish people, and it is appropriate that it should let the Jewish community itself be the body that determines what these Scriptures are. It is not the church's job to decide on the Jewish Scriptures. The other, related consideration is that if we were able to ask Jesus, Peter or Paul what books were in the Scriptures, then the Torah, the Prophets and the Writings are as near as we can get to knowing what would be their answer to that question.

Could the church (or Judaism) today decide to add to the Scriptures or, for that matter, to take away from them? Three points must be made. First, it would be inappropriate to think of adding writings from a later period, because theologically the reason why the OT and NT are the Scriptures lies in their relationship with the story of how God brought about the world's redemption in the process that came to a climax with Christ. They issue from and they witness to that process. Subsequent works may be just as true and edifying, but they do not have that significance. Second, suppose that we discovered another prophecy by Isaiah or another letter by Paul. Could we add that to the Scriptures? A related consideration is that determining what books should count as Scripture was also part of the process whereby God brought about the world's redemption. There likely were other prophecies and epistles that were accepted as having come from God, but the Scriptures were not designed to include all such inspired works. To seek to add to the collections that Judaism and the church established in OT and NT is to imply that they were. Third, yes, it would be perfectly possible to add books to the OT. You simply have to convene a meeting of an authoritative body representing all Jewish groups and all Christian groups and get them to agree on the matter. Good luck.

For our main knowledge of the text of the OT we are indebted to the work of Jewish scholars who saw that it was preserved over the centuries. But if it was copied by hand for centuries, how sure can we be that it didn't get altered a lot?

There are admittedly many little differences between translations of the OT. Here is the beginning of Psalm 89 in two different translations:

I will sing of the LORD's loyal love forever. (CEB)

I will sing of your steadfast love, O LORD, forever. (NRSV)

Where the CEB has "loyal love" and the NRSV has "steadfast love," these are simply different ways of translating the Hebrew word *ḥesed*. But further, in the CEB the psalm is talking *about* God, in the NRSV the psalm is talking *to* God. Why that little difference?

All printed Hebrew Bibles have the same text in them, which makes for a differentiation over against the NT. There are many Greek manuscripts of the NT, which all differ in tiny ways. So in chapter after chapter editors have to make up their mind which manuscript is likely to be the nearest to what the NT author wrote. As a result, editions of the Greek NT all diverge slightly from each other.

With the OT, the situation is otherwise. For a thousand years after Christ, Jewish scholars took care of the Hebrew Bible, and this care included trying to make sure of holding on to traditions about matter of detail in the text such as the accents on words. The word for "tradition" is *masorah*, so these scholars are called the "Masoretes." About A.D. 1000 this work came to a climax when these scholars agreed on the right text of the Hebrew Bible, which is thus called the "Masoretic Text" (MT). The oldest and thus most authoritative example of the Masoretic Text is the Aleppo Codex (named thus because it was long in Aleppo in Syria), but a third of it is missing. The oldest complete copy in existence is one made by Samuel ben Jacob in Egypt about 1009. And it is this manuscript that appears in any modern Hebrew Bible. The manuscript itself is now in the Russian National Library in St. Petersburg; the city used to be called "Leningrad," so the manuscript is known as the Leningrad Codex (a codex is a manuscript that is in the form of a book rather than a scroll).

Only a very few older manuscripts of the Hebrew Bible survived the Masoretes' work in determining what they believed was the true text. That fact raises two questions, one practical and one theoretical. The practical one arises from the fact that there are passages in the OT that don't seem to make sense, which leads one to wonder whether the text had been altered. The theoretical one is whether the text might have been altered even when it does make sense. Where could we go from here with regard to these two questions?

Long before the Masoretes' time, the OT had been translated into other languages such as Greek, Latin, Aramaic and Syriac, and one possibility is to translate these translations back into Hebrew and see whether the Hebrew text that they might have used is different from the MT. It is this process that produces the NRSV version of the opening of Psalm 89; it follows the Greek translation, the Septuagint. At other points, translators have simply guessed at what the text might have been. The marginal notes in modern translations usually tell you where they have thus "corrected" the MT.

The fact that our oldest copy of the Hebrew OT is only a thousand years old explains the importance in this connection of the discovery beginning in 1947 of the "Dead Sea Scrolls" at Qumran, a Jewish monastery by the Dead Sea. This discovery gave us a cache of manuscripts of OT books or parts of books that were a thousand years older than the MT and thus much nearer to the writing of the books. There are many small differences in the Qumran manuscripts from the MT, like those between translations such as the Septuagint and the MT. Indeed, sometimes their text corresponds to one that had been hypothesized by that process of translating back into Hebrew from a text such as the Septuagint. But all are matters of detail. There is nothing that makes a significant difference to our understanding of the OT. The differences are more like the differences between one modern translation and another.

OLD TESTAMENT TRANSLATIONS AND
THE NAME OF GOD IN TRANSLATIONS

All the recognized modern translations of the Bible are more or less accurate, though they have different philosophies of translation (e.g., whether to be more word for word or more phrase for phrase). In addition, they may be more or less inclined to correct the Masoretes' work. I like the NRSV and the TNIV for study and preaching because they are fairly word for word and use gender-inclusive language (i.e., they do not use "men" when the biblical writers would have meant "men and women"). I also like the Jerusalem Bible and the New Jerusalem Bible because they keep the name of God instead of replacing it with "LORD" or "GOD." The background of that practice is as follows.

Most modern translations replace the name of God, "Yahweh," by the ordinary words "LORD" or "GOD" (in small capitals). Only when translations have the words "Lord" or "God" (not in small capitals) does their wording mean that the text has the actual words for "Lord" or "God" rather than the name "Yahweh." This practice, begun in ancient times, of replacing the name by one of these words avoided giving the impression that Israel's God was just a weird Israelite God with a strange name, and it safeguarded against taking Yahweh's name in vain. Over against these advantages are some disadvantages.

- It's often significant that the OT uses God's actual name—for example, when the text says "Yahweh is God" (as opposed to, say, Marduk being God).

- It was a privilege to be invited to call God by name, part of being invited into a relationship with God. It seems a shame to refuse the invitation and thereby distance ourselves from God, as odd as refusing to use the name "Jesus."

- Like the name "Jesus" (which means "savior"), the name "Yahweh" is not just a label. It has a meaning. Yahweh explained to Moses that it defines Israel's God as one who is always with his people in ways that are needed by changing situations ("I am who I am," "I will be what I will be," "I will be with you"). It's a shame to lose what the name stands for.

- Using the particular word "Lord" instead of that name "Yahweh" introduces into OT faith a patriarchal, authoritarian cast that it does not otherwise have. The name encourages a personal relationship, but the title "Lord" encourages a distanced, subordinating relationship.

In the nineteenth century the American Standard Version of the Bible, a revision of the King James Version, restored the use of the name, though it spelled it as "Jehovah." This traditional pronunciation implies a misunderstanding. In the Hebrew Bible, scribes eventually incorporated in the text a reminder to say "Lord" (or "God") not "Yahweh."

It worked as follows. Most of the Bible is written in Hebrew; the exceptions are the middle parts of Daniel and Ezra, which are written in Aramaic, a sister language. Other closely related languages include Ugaritic (an older Canaanite language) and Akkadian (the contemporary language of Babylonia). Written Semitic languages such as Hebrew don't have vowels. Readers are expected to be able to work them out (it's a little like the modern-day language of text messaging). It is still the case with modern Hebrew. This system works when you are used to speaking the language, but not when this ceases to be so. Jewish scholars therefore devised systems of dots and dashes to indicate vowels for the sake of people who were less familiar with Hebrew. The Masoretes incorporated these in the text, on the basis of their knowledge of how the text should be read. When they came to the name of God, the copyists put the vowels of the words for "Lord" (*ʾădōnāy*) or "God" (*ʾĕlōhîm*) into the consonants *yhwh* in order to remind people to use the substitute words "Lord" or "God." It is this substitution that produces the name "Jehovah," which is a non-word; it combines the consonants of *yhwh* and the vowels of *ʾădōnāy*.

Because Jews gave up using the name, we are not absolutely sure about its pronunciation, but "Yahweh" is our best guess as to the way the people who wrote the OT would have pronounced it. The basis for thinking that "Yahweh" is the right pronunciation is some comments in early church writers about what Jews had told them regarding the pronunciation.

(On OT translations, see further 119.)

ISRAELITES, HEBREWS, JEWS;
ISRAEL, JUDAH, EPHRAIM

The names for peoples in the OT and the NT cause confusion.

Israel	(1) The ancestor Jacob. (2) The people descended from Jacob's twelve sons. (3) After Solomon's day, the people who belonged to the northern state—the majority of the people as a whole. "Israel" is then set over against "Judah," which denotes the southern clans. But the OT also refers to the northern state as "Ephraim" (the name of the biggest of the northern clans), and it is less confusing if one follows this practice. Ephraim (Israel in the sense of the northern state) went out of existence with the fall of Samaria in 722; (4) The people of God. In this sense, the people of Judah can constitute Israel.
Hebrews	(1) In the OT, more a sociological entity than an ethnic one; it suggests people from ethnic minorities, without proper status. It thus does not refer to Israelites in particular. (2) In NT times, Hebrew-speaking Jews as opposed to Greek-speaking Jews.
Judah	(1) One of Jacob's sons. (2) One of the twelve clans, which traced its origins back to Judah the man. (3) After Solomon's day, the southern state (of which Judah was the biggest clan). (4) After the exile, a province of the Persian Empire, known in Aramaic as "Yehud."
Jew	A shortened version of the word *yĕhûdî*, which denotes a member of the clan or province of Judah/Yehud. As Judah/Yehud became the heart of Israel in the Second Temple period, *yehudim* ("Jews") became a term for all members of the people of Israel and became a regular term for members of this religious community rather than members of an ethnic group. But the term *yehudim* hardly occurs in the OT. There, *yehudim* would exclude most Israelites.
Judea	A Roman province, which included Judah, Samaria and Idumea. (In Ezra's and Jesus' time the Judahites/Judeans saw the Samarians/Samaritans as insufficiently loyal to Yahweh, but the Samaritans, at least, returned the compliment; they accepted only the Torah, not the Prophets and the Writings, and saw the Judeans as too liberal.)

Thus, we conclude that the people of God in the OT are "Israelites." It's confusing to call them "Hebrews" or "Jews." Here is an overview:

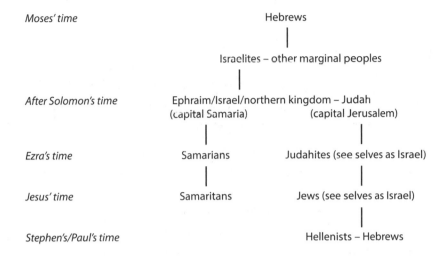

Moses' time	Hebrews
	Israelites – other marginal peoples
After Solomon's time	Ephraim/Israel/northern kingdom – Judah
	(capital Samaria) (capital Jerusalem)
Ezra's time	Samarians Judahites (see selves as Israel)
Jesus' time	Samaritans Jews (see selves as Israel)
Stephen's/Paul's time	Hellenists – Hebrews

Some other names that cause confusion:

1. "Canaanites" is a general-purpose word for the peoples of Canaan, the area where Israel came to live, but it doesn't denote a specific group—it's rather like the term "America," which can denote the United States or refer to the Americas more broadly. Something similar is true about "Amorites" (see 234).

2. "Hittites" usually denotes not people from the great Hittite Empire in Turkey but members of a smaller people in Canaan.

3. Chaldeans or Kaldeans were people from southeast Mesopotamia who gained control of Babylon in OT times, so that "Chaldeans" comes to denote "Babylonians."

4. Jerusalem and Zion are both terms for Israel's capital, but in origin "Jerusalem" is more a political term, and it is the name one would see on signposts if there were any. "Zion" is more a religious term—it refers to Jerusalem as the place where the temple is.

NEW TESTAMENT LENSES FOR LOOKING
AT THE OLD TESTAMENT

I want to understand the OT in its own right, yet a Christian perspective
does sometimes help one to see what's there in the OT. The NT itself
looks at the OT with a range of lenses. A lens enables you to see things; different lenses bring different things into focus.

1. Christians are most familiar with the Jesus lens. Jesus' birth involved an
   odd sequence of events; the OT helps Matthew understand them (see Mt
   1:18–2:23). Jesus experiences opposition and rejection from his own
   people, but this reaction is not surprising when considered in light of the
   people's treatment of God and of God's prophets in the OT. Jesus' death
   somehow sorts out relationships between God and us, but how does it do
   so? The institution of sacrifice in the OT helps us to understand how it
   does so. In the OT, God spoke in many different ways, and you may not
   be able to see how they fit together, but now God has spoken in his Son,
   who helps you see how they fit together (Heb 1:1). He brings not a new
   revelation, but a focused embodiment of the old revelation.

2. The NT uses the church lens. "You are a chosen race, a kingly priesthood, a
   holy nation, a people to be [God's] possession . . . , you who once were no
   people but now are God's people, who were not shown mercy but now have
   been shown mercy" (1 Pet 2:9-10). Nearly all the terms in this description
   come from Exodus 19:6 and Hosea 1–2. How are members of the church to
   cope with wrongful treatment by other people? By following Jesus' example,
   which he received from Isaiah 53; so Isaiah 53 is not only a passage of which
   he was a fulfillment, but also a passage of which they are called to be a fulfillment (1 Pet 2:21-25). First Corinthians 10 and Hebrews 3–4 similarly
   look back to the OT for a reminder of how easily the people of God can lose
   their place with God; Israel's story is instructive for the church.

3. The NT thus gets much of its understanding of what it means to be the
   church from what the OT says about Israel. The implication is not that
   the church replaces Israel, but the emergence of the church as a body

semi-separate from Israel does raise the question how the church should understand Israel, and the Israel lens is one with which the NT looks at the OT to find the answer to this question (see, e.g., Rom 9).

4. The NT uses the mission/ministry lens. How is Paul to understand his commission as an apostle? He understands it in the terms Jeremiah used for his commission (Gal 1:15; cf. Jer 1:5). Specifically, how is he to understand his commission to bring the gospel to the Gentile world? In Isaiah 49:6 God's servant sees himself as having such a commission, and Paul applies these words to himself (Acts 13:47).

5. How are we to understand the dynamics of our relationship with God and God's relationship with us? In Matthew 5:3-12 Jesus outlines an answer, in which practically every line takes up phrases from the OT, mostly from Isaiah and Psalms. Jesus makes a new creative whole out of the elements that he takes from the Scriptures, but it is from there that he gets his raw materials for an understanding of spirituality. The NT uses the spirituality lens. Paul's exhortations about praise and prayer in Ephesians 5 and 6 likewise assume that the Psalms are a place where Christians will learn to pray.

6. How am I to become mature as a man or woman of God? Paul reminds Timothy that he has been nurtured on the OT Scriptures and that they provide the answer to this question (see 2 Tim 3:14-17). Elsewhere as an example: How should we treat our enemies? The OT says it is by feeding them (Rom 12:20).

7. How are we to understand the world of the nations and the superpowers? In the NT this question comes into prominence in Revelation, where the significance of Babylon (i.e., Rome) is a key issue. It has been said that there is not a single actual quotation from the OT in Revelation, but there is hardly a verse that would survive if you removed the OT allusions. And the world lens is of great importance to Revelation's reading of the OT.

A whole series of questions (how shall we think of Jesus, of the church, of Israel, of mission and ministry, of our relationship with God, of the world) provide lenses with which to ask questions about the OT and open up aspects of the OT. Christians sometimes assume that *the* point about the OT is its prophecies of Jesus. This assumption does not come from the NT.

From the second century A.D. onwards, churches in different areas treated as Scripture a broader collection of scrolls than just the Torah, the Prophets and the Writings. As far as we know, these works were not recognized as Scripture by the Jewish community, and they are not quoted by Jesus or the NT authors.

Some questioning of these books' status in the church goes back to Jerome, who produced a new translation of the OT for the church (the translation that came to be called the "Vulgate") around A.D. 400 and noted that these other books came only in the Greek or Latin Bible and not in the Hebrew Bible. But the questioning became a formal issue only in the sixteenth century, when Martin Luther declared that these "Apocrypha" had only a secondary authority, as edifying reading but not as having theological authority. In response, at the Council of Trent the Roman Catholic Church affirmed that they were fully part of Scripture. Luther was followed by John Calvin and the Anglican reformers, but the Westminster Confession later declared that these books "are of no authority in the Church of God."

Our main copies of the books in the Second Canon are in Greek or Latin, but some were originally written in Hebrew. And although all of them were written after about 300 B.C., some are older than the latest books in the OT. And while some of them raise theological questions, it's often felt that the OT books also do so. Further, some of the books in the Second Canon seem ethically questionable; it would then seem doubtful whether one can say that they are edifying.

Theologically, three features of the Second Canon stand out. First, it talks more about what happens after death than the OT does, and in this respect it parallels the NT. The account of martyrdoms in 2 Maccabees 7 emphasizes the resurrection of the martyrs. The theme recurs in 2 Maccabees 12:39-45, where Judas's faith in the resurrection makes him want to pray for God to forgive men who have died in battle but who have disobeyed the Torah (this passage about prayer for the dead was one that made the Second Canon stick in Luther's gullet). Second, Wisdom and Ben Sira bring together wisdom and

Torah, whereas the OT wisdom books keep them separate. Third, the Second Canon assumes that the story of the Maccabean crisis, of God's deliverance and of events in the decades that followed belongs in the context of the Scriptures that tell of God's activity from the beginning through to the time of Ezra and Nehemiah. The Books of Maccabees take up the story again three centuries later. The Second Canon thus again compares with the NT, which generates narrative about historical events and implies the conviction that God has again acted in a way that takes up Israel's story (see further 507).

The following are the books that most often appear in the different versions of the Second Canon.

1–2 Maccabees: Two accounts of Antiochus's persecution of the Jewish community in the 160s B.C.

3 Maccabees: An account of an earlier persecution and deliverance at the end of the third century B.C.

4 Maccabees: An exhortation to live by reason rather than emotion, appealing to the Maccabean story.

Wisdom of Solomon: A book of teaching in the tradition of Proverbs and Ecclesiastes.

Ecclesiasticus or Ben Sira or Sirach: Another wisdom book of this kind, not to be confused with Ecclesiastes.

Judith: The story of a Jewish widow who beheads one of Nebuchadnezzar's generals, Holofernes.

Tobit: The story about a faithful exiled Ephraimite and his restoration from blindness.

Greek Esther: An expanded version of Esther's story, making explicit God's involvement.

Greek Daniel: A version of Daniel with several further stories and expressions of praise and prayer.

Greek Jeremiah: A version of Jeremiah amplified by the book of Baruch and the Letter of Jeremiah.

1 Esdras: A Greek version of material about the temple from Chronicles, Ezra and Nehemiah.

2 Esdras: An apocalypse reflecting on the fall of Jerusalem in A.D. 70.

The Prayer of Manasseh: A prayer designed to suggest his repentance reported in 2 Chronicles 33.

Psalm 151: Testimony attributed to David in connection with his anointing and his defeat of Goliath.

1 | 19 | WEB RESOURCES

See the note on web resources at the beginning of this book.

120 AN OLD TESTAMENT GLOSSARY

Explanations or definitions of hundreds of terms in the Old Testament and terms used by scholars (and used in this book).

121 HOW TO READ THE BIBLE

A brief introduction to the Bible as a whole, more basic than this book.

122 INTRODUCTION: FURTHER RESOURCES

a. How Translations Emend the Text

b. Which Is the Best Translation of the Old Testament?

c. Large Numbers in the Old Testament

d. Death and Afterlife in the Old Testament

e. Death and Afterlife in the New Testament

f. Satan in the Old Testament

g. Satan's Fall

h. The Soul

123 (Anything else I dream up after this book is published)

Part Two THE TORAH

2 | 01 | THE TORAH
The Five Books

The Torah comprises the first five books of the Bible: Genesis, Exodus, Leviticus, Numbers, Deuteronomy. Indeed, another Hebrew word for the Torah is "Chumash," which means "five," and in English the Torah is often called the "Pentateuch," meaning "five scrolls." These scrolls begin with stories about God creating the world, and then they tell of God's involvement with Israel's ancestors and with Israel itself as a nation of serfs in Egypt. God rescues them from there and meets with them at Sinai, then leads them to the edge of a country that is to be their own, to fulfill promises that he made to their ancestors. While the story is thus a gospel story, a good news story, it also incorporates substantial teaching from God and from Moses about the lifestyle that God expects of this people.

What the Torah is not. (See further 245.)

1. It's not law. We have noted that the word "Torah" means "teaching" rather than "law." Within the story it tells are vast swathes of instructions concerning Israel's life, and sometimes the Torah calls these "laws"; but "law" is a misleading term for the Torah as a whole.

2. It's not a veiled anticipation of Jesus. It's a transparent and direct portrayal of the real relationship between God and Israel. It includes no prophecies of the Messiah.

3. It's not a revelation of a God of wrath. From the beginning, it's a revelation of a God of love, though this God is like any parent in properly getting angry with his children from time to time.

4. It's not just a collection of dusty stories that need to have happened as it says but are irrelevant to us. According to 1 Corinthians 10, they are frighteningly relevant to us.

The Torah and the Former Prophets. To separate the five books of the Torah from the ones that follow (Joshua, Judges, Samuel, Kings) is to do something artificial. To begin with, it's only with Joshua that the good news story about Israel's origins comes to a kind of end, when the Israelites arrive in their country. The book called "Joshua" relates the fulfillment of God's promise to Abraham about his people having a country of their own. So if Genesis through Deuteronomy is a Pentateuch, Genesis through Joshua is a Hexateuch, a six-scroll work. Further, the ending of the story in Joshua is only a kind of end, because this sixth book also emphasizes that Israel's gaining possession of its country is incomplete, and the story continues in Judges, Samuel and Kings. Only because the books that then follow go in another direction do we know that 2 Kings does constitute an end. So Genesis through Kings is one long story, a little like the nine seasons of a long-running television series. Each season and each episode is complete in itself, yet each needs to be seen in light of the whole. (For outlines of Genesis to Joshua and Genesis to Kings as chiasms, see 245.)

The Five Books. Separating off the first five books is thus a little risky (as is separating off some seasons of television series), though it had happened long before Christ. Among the books appended to the OT in some churches (the "Apocrypha" or "Deuterocanonical Writings"; see 507) is a book called "Ecclesiasticus" or "Ben Sira" or "Sirach." Its prologue, which carries a date equivalent to 132 B.C., refers to "The Law and the Prophets and the others that followed them," which presupposes that the first five books are already separate from the books that come afterwards. Why might that separation have happened? One possible reason is that within the narrative from Genesis through Kings, the period of Moses has great importance; the books from Joshua through Kings often are looking back to it. Another reason is that the teaching of Moses is foundational for the life of the people of God in the later period.

The Five Books unfold as follows:

Genesis: How Yahweh created the world and related to it, and how Yahweh made promises to Abraham.

Exodus: How Yahweh delivered the Israelites from serving Egypt so as to serve Yahweh, initially at Sinai.

Leviticus: What this service looks like in terms of worship and holiness of life.

Numbers: How Yahweh took Israel from Sinai to the edge of its promised land.

Deuteronomy: Moses' final sermon to Israel on the edge of the land.

2 | 02 | THE TORAH
Not Really Five Books

The outline in 201 indicates that each of the Five Books has some unity, but the fivefold division obscures some of the dynamic of the story as a whole. More than one of the books divides into more than one part that could have stood on its own. And none of the books is complete on its own; each leads into the next in a way that means you can't stop when you come to the end. They are, again, like the seasons of a television series that end with a cliffhanger to make sure you come back next season.

1. Genesis divides into two parts, and each forms a coherent whole.

    a. Genesis 1–11 tells the story of God's relationship with the world.

    b. Genesis 12–50 tells of God's promises to Israel's ancestors.

2. Exodus likewise divides into two parts.

    a. Exodus 1–18 tells of God's deliverance of Israel from Egypt and its journey to Sinai.

    b. Exodus 19–40 is the first part of the story of God's revelation at Sinai. It includes God's instructions for making a sanctuary and for the ordination of some priests to serve God there; it then recounts the making of the sanctuary.

3. Leviticus follows seamlessly from Exodus 19–40 in that it describes how sacrifices are to be offered in the sanctuary; then it relates the ordination of the first priests to serve there.

4. Numbers in due course follows seamlessly from Leviticus in that it begins with God's final instructions at Sinai concerning the journey to Canaan. It then goes on:

    a. Numbers 10–21 relates Israel's journey toward Canaan.

    b. Numbers 22–36 tells of events as Israel waits to cross into the land.

5. Deuteronomy continues the account of the time Israel spent in the

steppe land of Moab, east of the Jordan, as it waits to enter the land.

So we will look at the Five Books as follows (for an expanded version called "The Torah: A Story in Six Acts," see 245):

1. Genesis 1–11: The beginning.

2. Genesis 12–50: God's promises to Israel's ancestors.

3. Exodus 1–18: Yahweh commandeers his son Israel from the control of Pharaoh.

4. Exodus 19—Leviticus—Numbers 10: Israel at Sinai.

5. Numbers 10–36: Israel's journey to the promised land.

6. Deuteronomy: Moses' last sermon.

Another noteworthy aspect of the way the story works is that the amount of space it allocates to different episodes bears no relationship to the way chronological time is unfolding.

1. Genesis 1–11 covers several thousand years (millions of years on our reckoning).

2. Genesis 12–50 covers several centuries.

3. Exodus 1–18 covers at least several decades.

4. Exodus 19—Leviticus—Numbers 10 covers less than a year.

5. Numbers 10–36 covers thirty-nine years.

6. Deuteronomy covers one month.

There can be varying reasons why chronological time and narrative space in a story are different. A particular event or time may be worth exploring because some incidents or events bring out important facts or make it possible to discuss significant issues. The noteworthy feature of the chronological outline of the Torah is that the attention given to the time at Sinai and to the time spent on the edge of Canaan is out of all proportion to the rest of the space allocation. So while the Torah is not really a book of "law" (this word, as we have noted, gives a wrong impression), it is indeed a book of teaching or instruction about how Israel is to live its life.

The Questions It Might Raise and Answer for Israel

T he Torah answers some questions Israelites might ask or should ask.
What was Israel's relationship with the rest of the world? Genesis 1–11
opens up this question. The Israelites might wonder how they relate to other
nations, and how their God relates to them. There are several moments
when they might ask these questions.

1. There is the high point of their achievement as a nation in the time of
   David and Solomon (about 1000–950 B.C.). By this time they have not
   only consolidated possession of Canaan and put both the Canaanites
   and the Philistines in their place; they have also turned themselves into
   a player on the Middle Eastern political scene, with an area of influence
   (you might almost call it an empire) stretching some way beyond their
   promised land.

2. Another moment is when Ephraim and Judah have in turn been put in
   their place by Assyria and Babylon (in 722 B.C. and 587 B.C.) and no
   longer exist as nations; indeed, many of their people have been exiled.

3. Another moment is when Judah exists as a colony of the Persian Empire
   in the shadow of other colonies surrounding it, such as Samaria and
   Ammon (about 500 B.C. and onward).

Genesis 1–11 gives people ways of thinking about their relationship with
the nations of the world and about their God's relationship with these nations. Yahweh is these nations' creator and sovereign. They too live their lives
within Yahweh's purview. Yahweh has a purpose for them. The transition to
Yahweh's promise to Abraham in Genesis 12 makes explicit that Yahweh
wants the nations to find his blessing. Israel cannot ignore the nations, or
assume to be more important than they are, or fear to be simply subject to
the whim of the nations.

Did this land really belong to Israel? Genesis 12–50 opens up this
question. In 722 B.C. the northern nation of Ephraim collapsed under attack

from Assyria; many of its people were transported, and other people were brought there from different parts of the Assyrian Empire. Ephraim's collapse would raise the question of whether the land of Canaan was really Israel's possession. Judah's collapse in 587 B.C., when many Judahites were transported to Babylon, would raise this question again.

One can imagine the Judahite community then listening to the story of God's promises to their ancestors and being challenged by these stories to believe that those promises still hold. This decimated community, rather pathetic remains of the Israel that had been so significant in the time of David and Solomon, might wonder whether it was destined ever to be a thriving community again. Whether or not they wondered about the question is not just a matter of our imagination; Isaiah 40–55 makes explicit that it did so. Genesis 12–50 would invite it to believe that this destiny still held.

What kind of people was Israel, and what kind of God was theirs? Exodus 1–18 opens up this question, reminding the Israelites that they started off as a mere bunch of state serfs, and a bunch of people whose spiritual insight was not very marked. Yet Yahweh designated them "my son" (Ex 4:22-23) and declined to accept Pharaoh's intention to hold on to this son. The contrary intentions of Pharaoh and Yahweh set up a conflict between the two parties. The question is, who will turn out to be the king who holds actual power? The story establishes that Yahweh exercises kingly power in Egypt as much as anywhere else, and that it is Yahweh whom Israel serves as son.

The story's having this significance suggests that it matters that the story is basically factual. The story defines who God is in the sense that it describes Yahweh as the God who kept the covenant, listened to the Israelites cry out of their serfdom and acted in power to defeat Pharaoh. It also demonstrates who God is in the sense that it provides the basis for believing statements about Yahweh such as that Yahweh is faithful, caring and powerful. If the story is not basically factual, then the definition of Yahweh's nature disappears. Yahweh might still be one who kept the covenant commitment, listened to the Israelites' cry and defeated Pharaoh, and the one who is faithful, caring and powerful, but the basis that the story provides for believing these things has disappeared.

THE TORAH

Looking at It Historically

S o it matters that the Torah relates the historical events on which Israel's faith is based. This statement is true in varying ways and to varying degrees in connection with the different questions that I have suggested that the Torah would have answered for the Israelites. In these connections, they would have an interest in looking at the Torah historically. But it is fine if the Torah is more like a movie based on fact than like a totally factual documentary, and describing the Torah as narrative or story rather than simply history releases us from having to ask which we are reading at any given moment.

There is another sense in which we can seek to look at the Torah historically. The Torah is a story addressed to an audience.

It begins, for instance, with two accounts of how God brought the world and humanity into being, two stories having significant differences. The significant differences are not the small-scale ones such as the possible implication in Genesis 1 that God created the first man and woman together and the statement in Genesis 2 that God formed one after the other, or the way Genesis 1 describes that creation of humanity as the last act of creation, whereas Genesis 2 describes the shaping of the man as the first act. More significant differences are the way Genesis 1 is interested in the whole cosmos and includes a description of the creation of sun, moon and stars on day four, whereas Genesis 2 is not very interested in anything outside the earth itself. Another difference is that Genesis 2 emphasizes the good-and-bad-knowledge tree, whereas Genesis 1 does not refer to it. These differences point to the different historical contexts of the stories in which they come. Genesis 1 helps Israel form an understanding of creation that resists views held by their Babylonian overlords in the time of the exile, such as the idea that the planets and stars determine what happened on earth. The stress on the good-and-bad-knowledge tree, on the other hand, might suggest a context when Israel was focusing on gaining wisdom for its life as a nation (and perhaps was inclined to learn from the insight of other peoples), and urges Israel that "awe in relation to Yahweh is the beginning of knowledge" (Prov 1:7).

Asking about the historical contexts in which the Torah was coming into being and/or the historical context in which it was being read helps us to see some of its significance. Here are some ways in which the history may interconnect with the Torah:

1220: The Israelites' entry into Canaan fulfills promises in Genesis and implements commissions in Deuteronomy.

1100s: The Israelites' life in the period before they had kings fits the social context of the instructions in Exodus 21–23; 33–34 (though there's little indication that Israel actually lived by the Torah in that period).

1000–722: The Israelites' life becomes more urban and temple focused; the concerns of Leviticus and Deuteronomy speak to this kind of social context.

700s: Prophets such as Hosea protest Ephraim's ignoring of the Torah in its worship and community life; Ephraim falls to Assyria.

622: A reformation undertaken by King Josiah seeks to implement some of the requirements of Deuteronomy. It is the moment when Deuteronomy becomes a living force in Judah's life.

587: After prophets such as Jeremiah and Ezekiel protest Judah's continuing to ignore the Torah in the conduct of its worship and life, Judah falls to Babylon.

500s: The fall of Jerusalem introduces a time for rethinking, and the Torah speaks of the possibility of restoration after downfall.

400s: Ezra comes from Babylon as a teacher of the Torah. He and Nehemiah seek to get Jerusalem to base its life on the Torah.

160s: Antiochus Epiphanes bans the worship in the temple prescribed by the Torah; members of the Jewish community rebel and reinstate worship in accordance with the Torah.

2 | 05 | THE TORAH
Expectations at the Edge of the Promised Land

Gods's rescuing the Israelites from the overlordship of Pharaoh is a great act of liberation. They are "free at last" (as the spiritual puts it). Does being free mean being able to do whatever you like?

Whereas the Torah's framework is expressed in indicatives, its content is dominated by imperatives. It instructs Israel on matters such as how to worship, how neighbors should relate to one another when there is conflict in the community, how to treat the needy and how to safeguard family life. It might not surprise us that the Torah covers such topics. It doesn't instruct Israel on matters that we might have expected, such as how to have a personal prayer life, how to find God's will for your life or how to have a successful marriage.

It does instruct Israel on topics that we find surprising, such as how to make war and how to distinguish between food that is permissible to eat and food that is not. For Israel, the question of how to make war was one of recurrent importance. God did not tell Israel that it mustn't make war, but God did place constraints around Israel's war making that would be the despair of the modern general. For any people, the question of food is important in the sense that most cultures have convictions about what it is proper to eat and what is improper, and there is often a close tie between eating and worship. God took such instincts and made them part of Israel's discipleship.

They are thus part of the way God shaped the community into which Jesus would be born. The opening of Luke's Gospel illustrates the point. What makes Jesus who he is? One factor is the family that brings him up. Luke portrays Mary and Joseph as part of a community shaped by the Torah. His broader family includes Elizabeth and Zechariah, the parents of John the Baptizer, who contributed to preparing the way for Jesus; they are part of a Torah-shaped community. Their broader community includes Simeon and Anna, who welcomed Jesus in the context of the temple and its worship; they too are part of a Torah-shaped community.

In expounding Yahweh's expectations, Exodus, Leviticus and Deuteronomy cover many parallel topics, but they approach them in different ways. This difference applies to a question such as the rules concerning how Israelite families are to treat their servants (I avoid the word *slaves* because it gives a misleading impression). Understanding the Torah's expectations, like understanding the Torah's story, will be helped by considering the historical context of its teaching. In this connection, it's worth bearing in mind the key moments and transitions in Israel's history noted in 204, which will have affected the development of the Torah and will have been the context in which Israel listened to the Torah.

A related question raised by the Torah is, what kind of people are these Israelites when God has brought them out of Egypt? The stories in the middle of Exodus and Numbers give an unflattering answer. They always needed to face how easily they could ignore God's expectations and fall into rebellion and mistrust.

That portrayal of Israel coheres with the portrayal of humanity with which the Torah begins. It tells of God creating the world and planting an orchard, which the first human couple is to "serve." Things go wrong as they ignore God's single prohibition upon their life and get thrown out of the garden. One of their sons murders the other, and trouble spreads in the community and then extends to relationships between heavenly beings other than God and the human victims of their sexual advances. God concludes that the creation project has failed and must be abandoned in its present form. But God exempts one family from the destruction that is to follow and gives them instructions on how to survive a great inundation that is to flood the world. They are to take with them examples of the various animal species, so that they can form the starting point for a new world after the disaster. God makes a new commitment with the new humanity, a covenant, but they perform no better than the first humanity: relations again go wrong within the family, within society and in relation to God, which leads to God's scattering humanity over the face of the earth. It is the background to Israel's own story.

2 | 06 | READING GENESIS 1–11
The Story of the Beginning

Reading Genesis 1–11 and thinking about the questions suggested below will take several hours, but undertaking such reading is key to learning about the OT. There are no shortcuts. There is material relating to some of the issues raised by the reading in the following sections, and more at 245.

Note that in the questions and elsewhere I sometimes use the expressions "Genesis 1" and "Genesis 2" as shorthand for "Genesis 1:1–2:3" and "Genesis 2:4-25." You can see from the contents of Genesis 1:1–2:3 that the opening verses of Genesis 2 are really the closing verses of the first chapter. The chapter divisions in English Bibles are not part of the original text; they were added to the text in about the thirteenth century to make it easier for professors to refer to specific passages (the Hebrew Bible had divisions into chapters, sections and verses, but they had no numbers and so didn't facilitate reference). The system is most often credited to Stephen Langton, a professor in Paris who was subsequently archbishop of Canterbury. Sometimes the chapter divisions are made in an illuminating way, sometimes in a way that obscures the text. In general, the English chapter divisions, which now also appear in printed Hebrew Bibles, do not correspond to the older Hebrew chapter or section divisions, though ironically in this particular case the Hebrew tradition agrees that a new chapter starts at what we call Genesis 2:1, so neither is very helpful.

1. Read Genesis 1:1–2:3 as if you are reading it for the first time. What would strike you about it?

2. What words and themes recur? What emphases do these suggest?

3. How does the chapter work as a story? What is its structure? Where is its own highpoint? (There are two possible right answers to this last question.)

4. Then read Genesis 2:4–3:24, forgetting Genesis 1:1–2:3 for the moment. What is the message of this story?

5. Now compare Genesis 2:4–3:24 with Genesis 1:1–2:3. What are the simi-

larities and differences in what the stories have to say about God, about the manner of God's creation, about the world, about humanity, about man and woman, about anything else they talk about, about their message, and about how they would have brought good news or challenge to their readers?

6. What are the similarities and differences about the manner in which the stories are told (as opposed to the content of the stories)? Are they same kind of story? How are they different?

7. Read Genesis 4:1-26. In its mode of storytelling, does it compare more with Genesis 1:1–2:3 or with Genesis 2:4–3:24? What are the similarities and differences?

8. What do you think would have been the message of Genesis 4:1-26 to its hearers in Israel? How did it bring them good news or challenge?

9. In its understanding of God, of human beings and of sin, how does Genesis 4:1-26 compare with Genesis 1:1–2:3 and Genesis 2:4–3:24?

10. What understanding of the relationship of men and women and of husbands and wives do Genesis 1, Genesis 2, Genesis 3 and Genesis 4 suggest? Do the different chapters imply that men should exercise authority over women or husbands over wives? How does the teaching of a passage such as 1 Timothy 2:8-15 in the NT correspond to that of these chapters?

11. Read Genesis 5–11. Can you see patterns recurring in Genesis 1–11 as a whole? What words recur? What do these suggest is the pattern or structure of the whole?

12. What is God like, according to Genesis 1–11? And how does God relate to us as human beings?

13. What are human beings like, according to Genesis 1–11 (leave sin for the next question)?

14. What understanding of sin does Genesis 1–11 imply? Look for the words for sin, the action or inaction that is sinful, the effects of sin, who is involved in sinning, and what attitude God takes toward sin. Ask these questions concerning each of these sections: Genesis 2:4–3:24; 4:1-24; 6:1-4; 6:5-13; 8:20–9:17; 9:18-27; 11:1-9. You could also think about Genesis 1:1–2:3, where sin isn't mentioned: in light of the content of that chapter, what would count as sin?

GENESIS 1 AND OTHER MIDDLE
EASTERN CREATION STORIES

The first-discovered and most famous of the Old Babylonian creation
stories is *Enuma Elish* ("When on High"). This title is the story's opening
words (in Israel's world some of the first words of a book could be used as
its title: Genesis is *Bereshit*, "In the Beginning"; Exodus is *Shemot*, "Names";
Leviticus is *Wayyiqra'*, "And He Called"; Numbers is *Bemidbar*, "In the Wilderness"; Deuteronomy is *Devarim*, "Words").

Enuma Elish may have originated in Joshua's time. So did the Babylonians
gain their knowledge of creation from a story written by Moses? But Babylon
was a more sophisticated culture than Israel and not one likely to be interested in learning from Israel. Further, we know of no contact between Israel
and Babylon in this period. Was *Enuma Elish* the source of the Israelite
creation story? Reading the Babylonian story makes clear that Israel did not
simply copy its creation story from the Babylonian one. The differences from
the Babylonian story are at least as noteworthy as the similarities. Yet there
are similarities, and it is unlikely that they are coincidental. You can read
Enuma Elish (see 245) and ask yourself what seems similar to Genesis 1 and
what seems different.

Here are some responses of mine to those questions.

1. The basic order of events in *Enuma Elish* parallels Genesis 1, and there
   are similarities in points of detail. For example, the name Tiamat may
   be etymologically related to the Hebrew word *tәhôm* ("deep"; Gen 1:2),
   and humanity is created to serve the gods. (In other Mesopotamian creation stories humanity is created from clay [cf. Gen 2:7], and other
   stories refer to a tree of life and water of life.)

2. Both documents assume that behind the human and physical world
   there are ultimate personal realities. Their worldview is theistic. But in
   Enuma Elish the ultimate realities (Apsu, Tiamat, Mummu) are still tied
   with the material. There is no real concept of beginning, since matter
   itself is eternal. And the ultimate realities are not the gods. The gods

come from the ultimate realities; they are not eternal, they are material.

3. *Enuma Elish* thus makes no clear distinction between gods and human beings. Both are made from matter. Both multiply by means of biological reproduction. The life of the gods reflects that of human beings: they marry, procreate, enjoy (?) family life, eat and drink, and die. They quarrel; disunity on earth is mirrored in disunity in heaven. The gods can be perplexed, fooled and frustrated. They are harsh and malicious, and they rejoice in evil. Evil is a permanent supernatural reality; there is no morality in heaven except the morality of violence. In contrast, in Genesis, sin, conflict and trouble are not ultimate realities. They derive from the failure of created beings. God is one; God is not material; God has no beginning (birth) or end (death); God is independent of the natural order and thus cannot be manipulated; God is not humanlike (in the sense of being involved in marriage, eating, etc.). God is good and gracious.

4. In *Enuma Elish* Marduk predetermines earthly events, which guarantees the stability of the cosmos. In Genesis there is a personal will of God being worked out, but events are not predetermined. God has a personal relationship with human beings. God is boss (as it has been put), but you can knock at his door.

5. In *Enuma Elish* Marduk's greatness reflects that of Babylon and the leadership of Babylon in Mesopotamia. *Enuma Elish* is thus a political document and also a social document: it expresses a vision of society. Genesis 1 has a parallel function. It introduces Israel's history, which the Israelites regard as the history that God is especially involved in. But it does not itself refer to Jerusalem or the temple. The connection of creation and ongoing history is peculiar to Genesis.

6. In *Enuma Elish* humanity is made through the recycling of trash; the creation of humanity is an afterthought. In Genesis the creation of humanity is a highpoint (Gen 1) or the center (Gen 2) of the story. Genesis has a positive theology of humanity's role in the world and a positive theology of marriage.

It was when Judahites were taken into exile in Babylon in the sixth century B.C. that Israel came into direct contact with Babylonian culture and thus potentially with the Babylonian creation story. Babylon was now the leading culture in the Middle Eastern world, and *Enuma Elish* was recited each year at the New Year festival in Marduk's temple to honor Marduk and Babylon, to which the story of creation is subservient. The story explains how the obscure god of Babylon, Marduk, came to be king of the gods, and therefore how Babylon came to be the capital of its world.

We know from Isaiah 40–55 that it was tempting for Judahites to believe that the Babylonian gods were the real thing. The outward form of Babylonian religion, with its images of the god and its processions, was more impressive than the outward form of Israelite religion, and the contrast would be more obvious now that the Babylonians had destroyed Yahweh's temple. Genesis 1 and Isaiah 40–55 are parallel expositions of the real truth about God, the gods and creation, coming from the same historical context, though they go about their exposition in different ways. Isaiah 40–55 emphasizes the sovereign creative acts that God is about to undertake in enabling exiled Judahites to go back to Jerusalem and in transforming the city. Genesis emphasizes the sovereign creative acts that God undertook at the beginning. It says to the Judahites, "You know that Babylonian creation story? It's stupid. Let me tell you the real story."

One can see specific ways in which Genesis 1 confronts Babylonian beliefs and also buttresses Israelite beliefs and practices. The picture in Genesis 1 of God doing a week's work and then having a day off declares that the Israelites' distinctive structuring of the week is not just their peculiarity; it reflects the pattern of God's working. It can seem odd that God created the sun and moon only on day four of that week's work; for Babylonians, sun and moon were the entities that ruled people's lives. Genesis puts sun and moon in their place and underscores the point by the extra throwaway phrase, "and the stars"; the Babylonians attributed to the stars a key role in governing what happened on earth. The cool and systematic logic and organization of the week of creation in Genesis 1 contrast with the chaotic nature of the process that the Babylonian story describes.

If Genesis 1 can be seen against a historical context in this way, is the same true of Genesis 2–4? Although Genesis 1 comes first in the order of the Torah narrative, interpreters usually have seen Genesis 2–4 as the older story. In other words, there once was a version of Genesis that began with Genesis 2, and Genesis 1 was put in front of it. (There is an analogy with the Gospels, where Mark is the oldest Gospel but Matthew was put in front of it, perhaps because Matthew is easier to understand.) Interpreters have particularly looked at Genesis 2–4 against the background of the history of Israel in the time of David and Solomon, and there are many ways of doing so (see 245). These approaches comprise a rich collection of ideas concerning the possible historical, cultural and religious background of Genesis 2–4 and the chapters' original significance for their readers. The problem is that there are too many of them—too many theories about the chapters' background and their consequent significance for their first readers. They cannot all be true. While all of them might be illuminating observations on ways the chapters could be read in different contexts, they cannot all be statements about the chapters' meaning in their actual historical context. While all are plausible accounts of what that meaning might have been, we do not have a basis for adjudicating between them.

Asking after the historical origins of the opening chapters of Genesis thus produces mixed results. It works better with Genesis 1 than with Genesis 2–4. This realization doesn't mean that we are prevented from understanding Genesis 2–4; it simply means that we cannot do so on the basis of setting them in a precise historical context. And Genesis 2–4 is more typical of our situation in relation to the Torah than Genesis 1. It's appropriate to ask, "What would this story mean to an Israelite community?" but we cannot usually locate that community in a particular historical context.

GENESIS 1–4

Patriarchalism as a Contemporary Context

Patriarchy is the assumption that some human beings properly exercise authority and control over other human beings, and specifically that men exercise authority and control over women. We have little indication within the OT that Israel was concerned about such issues in the way they have become a focus of attention in Western culture over the past century or so. On the other hand, there are many stories, rules and sayings in the Torah and elsewhere that suggest less directly that the issues were around in the culture. In the late twentieth century, among the approaches to Scripture that developed in the West was feminist interpretation. Its original concern was to expose the way the Bible had been subject to patriarchal interpretation—that is, the way the Bible had been read in a fashion that supported patriarchy. But it also found approval of patriarchy within the text itself.

What happens when we read Genesis 1–4 in light of the Western concern with this question?

1. Genesis 1 sees men and women as together created in God's image and commissioned on that basis to exercise authority in the world. It contains no indication that there is any exercise of authority by one human being over another—specifically, men over women. Because its authors often are assumed to have been men and specifically priests, it might be thought unlikely that they meant to make such a statement. Yet it is what they said.

2. Genesis 2 has been seen to imply that men are designed to exercise authority over women. But the fact that the man was created first does not imply superiority; it might be more logical to infer that the Mark 2 version of a human being would be superior to the Mark 1 version. Describing the woman as designed to help the man does not imply inferiority; the OT often uses the word "help" to describe God. The man names the animals, which may be a sign of authority over them; he does not name the woman in the way he names the animals.

3. In Genesis 3:1-7 the serpent's approaching Eve might as easily imply her superiority or authority as imply her subordination or inferiority; both the man and the woman fail in agreeing to disobey God's instructions.

4. Genesis 3:16 does describe the exercise of rule of men over women, or at least husbands over wives. It may refer either to the sexual relationship between men and women or to a more general authority of men over women. Either way, hierarchy or control or patriarchy begins not as an aspect of the way humanity was created but rather as an aspect of what resulted from human disobedience.

5. The context in Genesis 3:14-19 indicates that in general God wills the results of human disobedience, such as patriarchy. But even where God declares that these consequences are his direct intention (e.g., "I will give you great pain in connection with pregnancy; in pain you will have children"), we do not infer that we must simply submit to them. We fight against the pain involved in motherhood. It would imply that we can fight against patriarchy.

6. In Genesis 4 the story of Lamech shows how violence and oppression become more prevalent in the life of humanity, and Lamech's accumulating wives is an aspect of this degeneration.

7. In 1 Timothy 2 we see a reflection of issues in the church, where some people are teaching a rejection of marriage (1 Tim 4:3). Over against this teaching, Genesis shows that marriage and children were integral to God's purpose for womanhood. So the community of women should not reject this central aspect of its vocation. Being saved (1 Tim 2:15) then perhaps means being saved from God's wrath and entering into life at the End as the outcome of living a certain style of life, a life that involves continuing in faith, love and holiness, with propriety (cf. 1 Tim 4:16). Such a life fulfills our vocation, the reason for God's creating us; and for women, having children is part of that life and vocation, so that women are saved through childbirth. This is not to say that every woman has to have children; like Genesis, 1 Timothy is talking about womanhood in general.

Genesis 1–11 and History
Views on a Spectrum

In 108-9 we have looked in general terms at the question of the relationship between the OT's historical nature and its truth. For many people in a Western cultural context, Genesis 1–11 raises this question especially sharply. Some important questions in reading Genesis are then the following. Did God really create the world in seven days? Was Eve really formed from Adam's rib? Did a serpent really speak? Where did Cain get his wife? Did Methuselah really live nearly a thousand years? Did God really flood the whole planet? Did the animals really go into the ark two by two?

We can perhaps characterize views on the historical nature of the opening chapters of Genesis by placing writers at one or another place on a spectrum between "It happened as it says" and "It's pure fiction."

It happened as it says.

Francis Schaeffer, *Genesis in Space and Time*—it's factual history

Derek Kidner, *Genesis*—it's a parabolic presentation of actual events

Karl Barth, *Church Dogmatics* III.1, and Gerhard von Rad, *Genesis*—it's saga

Alan Richardson, *Genesis*—it's simply parable

Rudolf Bultmann, *Existence and Faith*, and William Dever, *What Did the Biblical Writers Know?*—it's myth

Rabbi Lawrence Schiffman, "Losing Faith"—"It's like a microcosm of human relations between a man and a woman, about people and God, and about good and evil"

It's pure fiction.

At one end of the spectrum, Francis Schaeffer emphasizes the importance of the fact that God really acted in the world, "in space and time," and he wants no compromise with that principle.

The writers at the other end of the spectrum see the stories as expressing the way things always are in human life and between God and humanity, in the manner of Jesus' parables or the statements about God's relationship with the world that appear in the psalms. In other words, to say the stories are not factual is to say that they are true, but true as permanent truths rather than historical truths. For instance, Genesis 2 is a true story about the fact that when a man and a woman find each other, there is paradise (Dever, *What Did the Biblical Writers Know?* p. 98).

In between are authors who believe that in some sense the text is making factual, historical statements (God's creating the world was a historical event; God created a good world, and humanity chose to ignore God's instructions and acted in a way that had disastrous consequences for everyone who came after; and so on), but that we should not take the stories as giving a literal account of these events.

The "in between" view seems to me to be right. The stories are talking about things that happened, but they are full of symbolism: a tree that gives life, a tree that conveys wisdom, a talking snake. When we come across such motifs elsewhere in Scripture, they are symbols that we are not invited to take as having literal reference. A number of these symbols reappear in Revelation at the other end of the Bible from Genesis, as well as elsewhere in prophecy. When the Holy Spirit inspired the account of the end time in Revelation, it did not involve giving the author further hard facts that the author could not otherwise have access to; rather, it involved inspiring a narrative about real future historical events that is expressed in theological symbols but has virtually no concrete facts. It is not surprising if the same is true about the Holy Spirit's inspiring the account of the beginning in Genesis, where the same symbolism already appears. In both contexts the authors use such symbols to describe realities to which the author had no access.

To put it another way, Genesis 1–11 is parabolic history, a picture account of events. This fact doesn't mean that we don't take every detail of these stories seriously; all of it is inspired by the Holy Spirit and is there for a purpose. It does mean that we don't try to get literal history from it.

In his commentary on Genesis, Derek Kidner makes a comparison with the story in 2 Samuel 12:1-4. In that passage Nathan tells David a parable about a man who has many sheep and another man who has one small lamb. The first man makes the second man surrender his lamb in order to feed a visitor. The story is not implying that there actually was a rich sheep owner, a poor man, a visitor and a meal; it is a parabolic way of telling the story of David, Bathsheba and Uriah in order to communicate with David.

Similarly, the creation stories are not saying that creation actually took six days, or that the sun and the moon did not come into existence until day four, or that the first sin involved a talking snake; rather, it is a parabolic account of events at the beginning designed to communicate with Israelites. The 2 Samuel 12 story is history in the sense that it speaks of real people and events (David, Uriah, Bathsheba), but it does so in pictures. Genesis 1–11 is history in the sense that it speaks of real people and events (God, creating, orderliness, goodness, expectations not met, God's design not being realized), but it does so in pictures. It speaks of God's historical intention and God's historical act of creation, but its story takes parabolic form. We cannot know anything that we would have seen in the news from it. You cannot ask, for instance, where Cain got his wife from; to do so is to treat the parable as the kind of allegory in which every detail has something corresponding to it in the literal events that the parable represents.

If Genesis 1–11 is parabolic, when does the Torah make a transition from parabolic history to literal history? In the long narrative work to which the Torah belongs, Genesis through Kings, the chapter that corresponds most closely to literal history is the very last, the account of the destruction of Jerusalem in 2 Kings 25, which is arguably the most literal piece of history in the entire Bible. There is also hardly a chapter on which fewer sermons have been preached. History, on its own, does not preach. It needs to have its significance written into its telling in order for it to preach. Thus much of the scriptural narrative combines historical reference with symbolism, interpretation and devices to communicate its significance. (A small example is the description of Abraham's home as "Ur of the Chaldeans." The Chaldeans were not in Ur in Abraham's day, but the description underscores for later readers that God called Abraham from the Chaldean Babylon that they know, the great imperial power of the last years of Judah.)

So the Torah's narrative does not make a transition at some point from parabolic narrative to literal narrative. Throughout, it combines in varying proportions history with symbolism or interpretation or communication devices. One could place the Scriptures as a whole on another spectrum in this connection according to the extent to which they tell a straight story and the extent to which they incorporate symbolism, interpretation and communication devices. Even 2 Kings 25 is interpreted by the last verse in 2 Kings 24 (part of the same chapter in the old Hebrew chapter divisions).

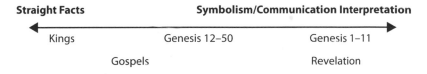

Rabbi Schiffman, in the comments quoted on the previous spread, goes on to relate how he spoke in the terms he uses there to a TV interviewer who was making a program about Adam and Eve. The interviewer turned off his recorder at that point to speak about his puzzlement because "everybody else I interviewed is talking about—Where is Eden? Was there really one human being in the beginning?" Now, I have suggested that the Genesis story does not seem to speaking merely about how things always are between us and God; it is offering an explanation of how they came to be as they are. But it's an explanation in symbols, not in literal facts. Once again the parallel with Revelation holds. Revelation is talking about how things will indeed be when God creates the new heavens and the new earth. But it depicts it in symbols. What it will actually look like is a different question.

A subset of the question concerning Genesis and history is the relationship between Genesis and scientific understandings of how the world as we know it came into being. For this question, see 245.

READING GENESIS 12–50

God's Promises to Israel's Ancestors

The second of the six "acts" into which we divide the Torah tells the story of Israel's ancestors. They used to be referred to as the "patriarchs," but the word "patriarchal" now has negative connotations, so "ancestors" is a better word. Furthermore, "ancestors" can include the matriarchs such as Sarah, Rebekah and Rachel as well as the patriarchs, and the matriarchs have a significant place in the story.

Genesis 12–25. The narrative begins with God's summons of Abraham, Sarah and their broader household from Babylonia to Canaan. Notwithstanding Sarah's infertility, God promises to turn this family unit into a great people. Further, notwithstanding the Canaanites' presence, God promises that the country will become the possession of Abraham and Sarah and their family (though God later notes that this transfer of ownership will need to be delayed because it would not be fair simply to take the country away from the Canaanites when they do not deserve to be so deprived). The way God will bless the family and turn it into a great nation will lead to the world's seeking the same blessing. God's original intention to bless the whole world will thus find realization. The story of Abraham and Sarah develops the theme of how implausible God's promises are, but these promises begin to find some fulfillment. The household is able to live in the country, and Abraham and Sarah eventually have a son.

Genesis 26–36. Their son Isaac and his wife, Rebekah, then become the focus. Their story too focuses on their children, because having children is of key significance for the fulfillment of God's purpose to bless them and through them to bless the nations. Esau is the marginally older of their twin sons, so he would be the senior son, but in the OT God often reverses such human conventions. So in this case God makes Jacob the son through whom God's purpose will be fulfilled. Another pattern within the OT is that many of the people whom God uses are morally reprehensible. In this case, Esau is a more honorable person than Jacob, but it is Jacob the deceiver that God uses. Jacob is eventually renamed "Israel," and Israelites reading his story would be continually given food for thought by the character of their ancestor. In turn, Esau is the ancestor of Edom, Israel's southeastern neighbor, and his featuring in the story would remind Israel of its relationship with this other member of its broader family (as would the story's also including Lot, the ancestor of Israel's other eastern neighbors, Moab and Ammon).

Genesis 37–50. The last section of the book tells the story of Jacob, his wives Leah and Rachel, and their servants Bilhah and Zilpah, who had become de facto secondary wives of Jacob. The Isaac and Rebekah section of the book has already described the process whereby Jacob thus had twelve sons. This last section of Genesis focuses on them. As a result of bad relations among the sons, one of them ends up as a slave in Egypt, but this facilitates a course of events whereby Jacob, his wives and his sons are also able to move to Egypt when there is a famine in Canaan. Later, the twelve Israelite clans trace their origin to Jacob's twelve sons, so that here the history of the relationships between the sons would illumine the interrelationships between those later clans. (The "clans" are often referred to as "tribes," but since they are related, "clans" is a more appropriate term.)

Read Genesis 12–50.

1. What do you discover about God from the stories? What is God's nature or character? Does God always behave in the same way, or does God change? Does God do or say anything surprising?

2. How does God relate to the women in the stories? What do you think of these women's stories? What issues are raised by what you find? Do you discover anything about womanhood?

3. How does God relate to other ethnic groups (people outside of the "chosen line"), and how do the chosen people relate to these other people?

4. How do the families work in these stories? What are their problems? How do their stories throw light on problems in our families? How does God relate to these families?

5. How does God relate to the main four men in the stories, Abraham, Isaac, Jacob and Joseph? What does Genesis imply about the men themselves? What issues are raised by what you find?

GENESIS 12–50
How Genesis Portrays Marriage

The marriages and families in Genesis are quite dysfunctional in nature, so it is encouraging to see God nevertheless at work through them. Western readers may also be puzzled or horrified at some of the stories' assumptions about marriage and family. The stories may be less puzzling for readers in traditional societies—for instance, in Africa, where some assumptions are similar.

Translations use the words "husbands" and "wives," but the equivalent Hebrew words imply that the husband is "master" or "owner" and the wife is "mastered" or "owned," and the OT usually prefers the ordinary words for "man" and "woman." Thus "his wife" is literally "his woman"; "her husband" is "her man." The OT doesn't imply that a wife is her husband's property, except in the sense that every wife belongs to her husband and every husband belongs to his wife. Nor does it suggest that a husband controls his wife or gives her orders. Abraham has to ask Sarah if he may describe her as his sister in Egypt; nor are Rebekah and Rachel women whom their husbands can mess with.

The stories show how marriages are arranged by negotiation between the man, the woman and the families, though there is no set pattern about how this negotiation is conducted. In the case of ordinary people, it doesn't seem that a man or woman would be married off unwillingly, though this happens later in Israel in the case of royal marriages because marriage is subordinate to politics.

Genesis gives no information on the process whereby a marriage happens, though Genesis 2:24 may tell us the essence of it. It means leaving one's household of birth, having sex with a person and thus forming a new social unit ("one flesh" isn't a mere redescription of the sexual act; it is an indication that the couple forms a new social unit, as when we say that someone "is my own flesh and blood"). Admittedly, Genesis 2:24 is puzzling because Genesis usually assumes that it is the woman not the man who leaves her parents; while the couple forms a new unit, it will usually be within the husband's broader family. Perhaps the point in Genesis 2:24 lies there; the fact that the man will still live within the broader ambit of his extended family means that it is important that there is a sense in which he leaves his parents and forms that new unit with his wife, in their own tent or later their own house.

Genesis 1–2 further presupposes that the essence of marriage is that the couple has a shared vocation of subduing the world and serving the ground. The essence of marriage is not that the two have a close personal friendship. Romantic love does appear in the Isaac story and the Jacob story, but the focus in understanding marriage does not lie here. Genesis 2:18 does not suggest that Adam is lonely; his problem is that he is alone and cannot generate people who will help him fulfill his vocation. The OT does have a vision for a romantic relationship, but this comes in Song of Songs, not Genesis.

The stories of Israel's ancestors reflect how marriage doesn't work out in the way one would expect in light of Genesis 1 and Genesis 2. Couples often cannot have children and often experience conflict. In fulfillment of the declaration in Genesis 3, "'To love and to cherish' becomes 'To desire and to dominate'" (Kidner, *Genesis*, p. 71). The stories work with the reality of patriarchy and androcentrism. They mostly speak of God relating to the male leader of the family and speak more about sons than about daughters. They take for granted the practice of prostitution, which issues from men's desire for sex outside marriage and from the need for women to find a way of surviving when, for instance, they have been thrown out by their husbands. They take for granted that a man may take more than one wife, usually because his first wife cannot have children (though in later contexts in the OT men such as kings do so because multiplication of wives and children is a status symbol). They take for granted the distinction between primary wives and secondary wives. (Translations often refer to these as "concubines," but this term can be misleading. A secondary wife is just as much a wife, but she has a lower status, perhaps in connection with her children's inheritance rights.) The stories rarely critique these assumptions, as they rarely critique other dubious acts on the part of Israel's ancestors; they leave readers to draw their own conclusions.

How Genesis Portrays Family

Genesis takes for granted assumptions about family so different from assumptions in Western culture that it may be wise for Western readers not to use the word "family" in connection with Genesis (perhaps the same is true of "marriage"). The OT's related words are "kin group" and "household." For the sake of clarity, I schematize a little the way the arrangement works.

A kin group comprises three or four generations of people living in some proximity. Jacob's kin group is a spectacular example, comprising as it does Jacob, his two primary wives, his two secondary wives, his twelve sons, their wives (who come from other kin groups), their children, his unmarried daughters (only Dinah is mentioned), and possibly other people such as male and female servants, orphans and widows. One implication of this last feature of a kin group is that it is a structure for the exercise of hospitality, not merely in the sense of offering visitors a meal (though that happens in Gen 18) but in the sense of being the arrangement that ensures that no one is homeless.

When Jacob's sons marry and especially when they have children, each of them with his wife starts a separate household within the kin group. In the context of Genesis this might mean that they have their own tent, and in Canaan it might mean they have their own house, but in either case the dwelling will be in proximity to those of the other households in the kin group. (In Canaan, most people likely lived in a village that might number between one hundred and two hundred people from two or three kin groups, and young people usually found their spouses from other kin groups within the village.) As children grow to adulthood, marry and have children, these continue to form a household within the kin group, so that the kin group can comprise four generations (note, e.g., the "third and fourth generation" of the commandment in Ex 20:5; Deut 5:9) until the head of the kin group dies. Whether they then stay as a kin group or divide its resources and become separate kin groups might be a question that the sons negotiate. The negotiation between Abraham and Lot is an example, though Lot is Abraham's orphaned nephew and adopted son.

Family is a whole-life arrangement. There is no division between the world of work and the world of home. The family is the basis for work in the sense of the keeping of flocks and herds or the growing of crops. In Genesis, women as well as men are involved in the work of caring for the flocks. There is no suggestion that what Westerners might see as the work and activity of the home such as cooking and caring for small children has less value than the work and activity that takes place outside the home such as caring for the flocks and herds or growing crops, and perhaps people recognized that much of the work of the home such as making food required more skill than much of the work in the fields such as caring for the flocks, though the latter might require more physical strength.

The kin group is the unit that relates to God. It is through the kin group that God is working out a purpose in the world, and God does so by taking initiatives in relation to the father of the kin group, who builds altars where the kin group's worship of God can be offered. Later parts of the Torah make more explicit that the kin group or household is the context in which its members learn the story of God's involvement with them and God's expectations of them. It is the teaching and learning unit.

Perhaps it follows from the way family is a whole-life arrangement that it is also a place of conflict. Yet many of the conflicts find resolution; family is also a place of reconciliation. Jacob (in his relationship with Esau) and Joseph's brothers (in relation to Joseph) fear that conflict will issue in ongoing resentment and rancor, but Esau and Joseph model the way it need not be so.

What sort of thing are we supposed to learn from these stories about marriages and families, with their dysfunction? Are they designed to provide us with moral examples? Or theological truths? Or insight on what it means to be a man or a woman? Or political or missiological insight? The assumptions that we make about such questions have a decisive effect on what we find in the stories. Different readers get different answers to some of these questions, which can be one clue when we are asking the wrong question. For material illustrating how this principle works, see 245.

GENESIS 12–50

How Historical Is It?

The question of the historical nature of Genesis 12–50 is again an important issue for many Western readers. And some features of Genesis 12–50 reflect later conditions than the time of the ancestors.

1. We have noted that Ur is described as "Ur of the Chaldeans" (Gen 11:31), a term that belongs to a period many centuries after the ancestors' time.

2. Rebekah rides a camel (Gen 24); it is usually thought that camels were not domesticated in the ancestors' time.

3. The Isaac story refers to the Philistines (Gen 26:14-18); they are usually thought not to have arrived in Canaan until after Joshua's day.

4. Genesis refers to the fact that Edom had kings before Israel did (Gen 36:31), which implies a time when Israel had kings.

5. Genesis has the ancestors addressing God as "Yahweh," but Exodus 3 and Exodus 6 relate how this name was not revealed until the time of Moses.

It would be foolish to call these "mistakes," any more than we would call it a mistake if a preacher speaks of Jesus driving a Ford Mustang. The things noted in the list above help people listening to the story recognize links with their own time. These stories are not about a past that was unbridgeably different from the readers' own day. Yet they do indicate that Genesis as we know it came into being centuries after the events to which it refers.

At the same time, Genesis also gives indications that it preserves memories of a way of life and a religion that were different from those of later Israel; it portrays the ancestors as a people who were indeed living centuries earlier and living a different kind of life.

1. The ancestors worship at sacred trees (Gen 12:6-7; 13:18); this is disapproved in later times (Hos 4:13).

2. They erect sacred posts and pillars in connection with worship (Gen 28:18-22); this is forbidden in later times (Deut 16:21-22).

3. Their worship is family based; there are no priests or prophets.

4. There is no reference to observance of the Sabbath or to food laws.

5. In worship God is frequently addressed by the Hebrew word "El," often in combinations such as "El Elyon" or "El Shadday" (translations usually translate "El" by the word "God"), or as the patron God of the kin group ("the God of Abraham" or "the Reverence of Isaac" or "the Mighty One of Jacob"). In any case, it's the same God.

6. Relationship with this God is based on trust in God's promises and on following where God directs; there is no list of detailed rules to obey.

7. Relationships with other peoples are characterized by openness; the kin groups are not expected to manifest holiness in the sense of separateness.

8. The kin groups practice customs that are known from other contexts in the Middle East, such as a wife providing her husband with a substitute wife if she cannot have children.

In the early decades of the third millennium A.D., much of the scholarly world is skeptical about the historical value of Genesis. It asks whether it is believable that a book written so much later could have preserved an accurate account of life in the second millennium B.C. How could the information have been preserved? Perhaps the distinctive features of religion and life attributed to Israel's ancestors belong to areas where people lived in the time of the kings in the way Genesis describes. This questioning approach starts from the conviction that Genesis was written in the exilic period or later and it puts more emphasis on the details that don't fit the ancestors' time. "All respectable archaeologists have given up hope of recovering any context that would make Abraham, Isaac, or Jacob credible 'historical figures'" (Dever, *What Did the Biblical Writers Know?* 98). (It's an exaggeration!)

But the easier inference from the way Genesis speaks of differences between the life and religion of Israel's ancestors and Israel's own life is that Genesis preserves memories of how things actually were in the ancestors' time; and the obvious inference from the way Genesis has retrojected into the stories aspects of later life and religion is that Genesis has updated the stories in detail (see further Moberly, *Genesis 12–50*; Wenham, *Genesis 1–15* and *Genesis 16–50*).

GENESIS 12–50

Looking for Clues Regarding How It Came into Existence

Whereas the heading for Genesis in the KJV is "The First Book of Moses," the book itself is anonymous, and we have seen markers of a time later in Israel's history that make it hard to accept the tradition that Moses wrote Genesis. The main reason why Christians have believed that Moses did write Genesis and the four following books is that Jesus and the NT writers refer to Moses in connection with them. But our mistake then is that we are acting as if Jesus and the NT writers were making pronouncements on questions that they were not concerned with. They were telling people that the material that they were quoting came from authoritative Scripture, and telling them where in authoritative Scripture they could find it. They were not pronouncing on a question about authorship.

It's helpful to divide the question of how the Torah came into existence into two questions, one about the narrative that begins in Genesis, and one about the instructions that dominate Exodus through Deuteronomy. The process and the end results differ between the narrative and the instructions. At this point, we will consider the question of the origin of the narrative, in particular that in Genesis 12–50.

Genesis itself contains no statements about its authorship; indeed, although the Torah goes on to say that Moses wrote some laws (and the itinerary in Num 33:2), the Torah as a whole is anonymous. Yet from the Roman period until the late eighteenth century it was an accepted tradition that Moses wrote the Torah, perhaps except the last chapter (obviously, the Holy Spirit could have inspired Moses to write an account of his own death before it happened, and the rabbis discussed whether God did so). For Exodus through Deuteronomy, Moses was close to events, but if he wrote Genesis, where did he get the information? What sources might he have used? Two clues presented themselves when scholars asked that question.

Clue #1. Some events appear more than once in Genesis. There are two stories of creation (Gen 1 and Gen 2), two accounts of the reasons for the flood (Gen 6:5-8 and Gen 6:9-12), two accounts of God's covenant with Abraham (Gen 15 and Gen 17), two accounts of the expulsion of Hagar (Gen 16 and Gen 21), two accounts of the naming of Beersheba (Gen 21 and Gen 26) and of Bethel (Gen 28 and Gen 35), and then two accounts of God's appearing to Moses and revealing the name Yahweh (Ex 3 and Ex 6).

Further, we can separate these pairs of passages into parallel sets with some recurrent characteristics. The most notable is that one set of the passages uses the name "Yahweh" for God even in Genesis, whereas the other set uses the ordinary Hebrew noun *ʾĕlōhîm*, equivalent to the more general word "God." These two sets of passages can therefore be called "J" (for "Jahwist," German equivalent of "Yahwist," from "Yahweh") and "E" (for "Elohist," from *ʾĕlōhîm*). (Concerning the traditional identification of God's own name as "Jehovah," see 115.)

Clue #2. A second pointer is the further realization that the E material could be divided into two. Some is more structured and formal and concerned with more specifically religious questions such as the Sabbath, the distinction between animals that may be sacrificed or eaten and animals that may not, and circumcision. Its concern with this kind of question led to its being called the "Priestly" version of the story, thus "P." Its material could be distinguished from other E material that is more like J in its general homespun style and its concern with everyday life. This material retained the name "E" (for *ʾĕlōhîm*). So now we have three versions of the stories in Genesis: J, E and P.

There are relatively few E stories (Gen 22 is one example). Perhaps the E stories were generally similar to the J stories and were therefore omitted when Genesis was compiled, though as a result E's existence has been a disputed element in the scheme. There is another feature about a story such as Genesis 22. It puts an emphasis on Abraham's obedience, an emphasis that reappears when Yahweh appears to Isaac in Genesis 26. Within the Torah a stress on obedience as the key to blessing is a special characteristic of Deuteronomy, so this feature raises the question of whether the kind of thinking represented in Deuteronomy constitutes a fourth element in Genesis.

2 17 GENESIS 12–50

Where the Clues Take Us—JEDP in Outline

As the Genesis narrative appears to bring together several earlier versions of the story of creation and of Israel's ancestors, Exodus through Deuteronomy combines more than one collection of instructions, which also repeat each other. The J and E versions of the story link with Exodus 19–34 and are the earliest ones. The P version of the story links with the priestly concern of the instructions in Leviticus. Deuteronomy then stands mostly on its own for its distinctive covenant theology and its preaching style, though a few stories in Genesis do have links with Deuteronomy. The classic source theory assumed that Deuteronomy was older than the P material. So the source theory concerning the origin of Genesis and the rest of the Torah puts the sources in chronological order; it is the JEDP theory. The classic JEDP theory is as follows.

J (Yahwist) is a continuous story from creation in Genesis 2–3 to Israel's arrival on the edge of the promised land in Numbers. A distinctive mark is its use of the name Yahweh in Genesis. It has often been dated in the tenth century B.C., the so-called Solomonic Enlightenment, but that element in the theory has little evidence to support it. J was written in Jerusalem in Judah, both of which have names that also conveniently begin with *J*. It is fresh, vivid, concrete and anthropomorphic in its storytelling. J is the storyteller who has God taking an afternoon stroll in the garden in Genesis 3.

E (Elohist) is an alternative version of this story, distinct because it uses the ordinary word *ʾĕlōhîm* for God in Genesis. In the Torah as we know it E was used only in fragments to supplement J. It is traditionally dated a century or two after J in the northern kingdom, Ephraim, whose name conveniently also begins with *E*. Compared with J, it is less fresh and vivid, less anthropomorphic, more theologically sophisticated. E has God's heavenly aides appearing to people rather than God appearing in person.

So far we are talking about a written version of the narrative. The similarity between J and E may mean they are variants of an earlier written or oral version, behind which would be individual oral versions of individual stories that came together into collections of Abraham stories, Isaac stories and Jacob stories.

D (Deuteronomist) is not so much a story as a systematic exhortation concerning obedience to Yahweh, with a distinctive homiletic style. The core of it is identified with the Torah scroll found in the temple in 622 B.C. in the reign of Josiah (2 Kings 22); it had perhaps been written in the previous century. Its dating was the lynchpin for the dating of JEDP as a whole.

P (Priestly) has as its framework a story paralleling J but with a more religious angle—for instance, creation links with the Sabbath. Into this framework are set large collections of instructional material, also tending to have a religious angle, the kind of things that concern priests. Traditionally, P was seen as the last of the sources, written during or after the exile, but likely preserving the practices of the first temple, or what should have been the practices of the first temple.

The four separate collections of material were then put together after the exile. The description of Ezra as a theologian who is expert in Moses' Torah and who brings the Torah to Jerusalem hints that he might have been a key figure in the emergence of the Torah as we have it.

The mature JEDP theory developed in Germany in the nineteenth century. The heroes or villains of the story (according to whether or not you like the theory) were Wilhelm de Wette, who fixed the date of Deuteronomy by linking it with Josiah's reformation; Wilhelm Vatke, who proposed a developmental or dialectical approach to Israel's religion that is expressed in the developing sources; Karl Graf, who saw that P came last; Abraham Kuenen, who saw that J came first; and Julius Wellhausen, who synthesized and popularized the JEDP scheme as a whole (see Arnold, "Pentateuchal Criticism"). For theories about the origin of the Pentateuch that have arisen as rivals to JEDP, see also 245. Interestingly, they mostly involve reviving theories that were around in the nineteenth century but that lost the argument to the JEDP theory.

The transition to Exodus marks a big transition in Israel's life; indeed, the life of *Israel* now begins. What had once been the kin group of Jacob has become a people. God's promise to Abraham has been fulfilled. The trouble is that the people are in the wrong country. Worse, the government of that country comes to treat them as state serfs, requiring them to work on state building projects and then treating them harshly as they undertake this work. The Egyptian king, or "Pharaoh," tries to control their growth as a people. But one of his own daughters adopts one of their babies, a boy, and thus ensures his survival.

Identifying with his own people when he grows up, Moses kills an Egyptian who is ill-treating an Israelite, and eventually he flees east to Midian and marries a Midianite wife. There God appears to him and gives him a new revelation of who he is as God. He is not only El Shadday (a title that suggests a similarity with the gods of Canaan) and also the God of Abraham, Isaac and Jacob (a description that matches the life of the ancestors, as God related to the people by guiding the leader of the clan and being with them wherever they were on their travels); he is Yahweh, the God who is there, the God who will be what Israel needs God to be, in different contexts. On these titles, see further 245.

Against Moses' will, Yahweh sends him to confront the king to insist that the Israelites be allowed to leave Egypt to go and serve their God. Israel is Yahweh's son, and Yahweh is commandeering his son. On the way, Moses almost dies, and it emerges that he himself has never received the covenant sign of circumcision, so his wife does what is necessary (on this episode, see further 245). Moses is empowered to bring about epidemics and other disasters on Egypt so as to persuade the king to let the Israelites go, but the king will not be persuaded, which suits God because it opens up the possibility of a more compelling demonstration of who truly holds power in Egypt (on the theme of the hardening of Pharaoh's heart, see further 245). Eventually God kills all the firstborn human and animal offspring in Egypt (this would not mean they are babies—most firstborn would be adults), and the king lets the Israelites leave. Israel will henceforth commemorate this event at an annual festival, Passover and Unleavened Bread (on Passover, see further 245).

On their departure from Egypt, God leads the Israelites by a strange route that enables the king (having had another change of mind) to pursue them and corner them. God causes an extraordinary dividing of some waters at the Reed Sea, which permits the Israelites to escape. The waters then return to envelop the Egyptian army. Moses and his sister Miriam lead the Israelites in praise for Yahweh's act of power. The Israelites proceed toward the mountain where God had met with Moses, but on the way they experience shortage of water and food, which causes crises in the relationship between them and God and between them and Moses. They don't care for having been removed from the security of serfdom into the precariousness of freedom. Their responses to these occasions of testing reveal that they are the same people as they were before God rescued them.

They are then attacked by a distantly related desert people, the Amalekites, but they defeat these attackers. They meet up with Moses' Midianite family, and Moses' father-in-law acknowledges the greatness of Yahweh; he also offers Moses' advice on governing the people.

Read Exodus 1–18.

1. How does God relate to the Israelite people as a community? How do they relate to God and to events?

2. How does God relate to the women in the story? How do they relate to God and to events?

3. What is the nature of Moses' leadership in the story?

4. What sort of person does God choose as a leader? What are his strengths and weaknesses? What evaluation does Exodus offer of him?

5. What is the nature of national leadership in the story, as embodied in the Egyptian king?

6. How does God relate to the political leader of the nation?

EXODUS 1–18 AND HOW WE LEARN FROM IT

Yahweh's presence in the midst of Israel, acting. Exodus as a whole divides into two halves that offer complementary portrayals of God's involvement and presence with Israel. In Exodus 1–18 Yahweh is present with Israel, *delivering* them from serfdom in Egypt, with Moses as mediator. In Exodus 19–40 Yahweh is present with Israel, *speaking* to them at Sinai, with Moses as mediator. The book closes with Yahweh present with Israel, *being* among them in the wilderness dwelling. (I derive this way of seeing the book from Durham, *Exodus*.)

The opening and close of the exodus story place the activity of women at the center of events, even if the men play the central role in between. At the opening, everything depends on the courage and action of two midwives, a mother, a sister, a princess (did she know what she was doing?) and a servant girl. At the close, it is the sister and her friends who lead the celebration of God's deliverance. The women's action means that human power (that of Pharaoh) turns out to be powerless.

Considerable space in the text is given to the process whereby Yahweh gets the king to release the Israelites so they can serve Yahweh instead of serving the king. The aim of God's action is not so much to liberate the Israelites from oppression so they are free to live their own lives as to remove them from the service of Egypt to the service of Yahweh. This is clearer in older translations, since the word often translated "worship" in verses such as Exodus 3:12; 4:23; 7:16 is the word for "serve."

The story makes much of the hardening of Pharaoh's heart, the closing of his mind. It's Yahweh's will that Pharaoh's mind be closed; this action is Yahweh's judgment on him (compare Jesus' words in Mk 4:11-12). Yet the implication is not that Yahweh made Pharaoh do something against his will. Before the story speaks of Yahweh hardening Pharaoh's heart, it speaks of Pharaoh's heart being hard and of Pharaoh hardening his own heart. I imagine Yahweh doing the hardening not by manipulating his neurons but by encouraging Pharaoh to think about the disadvantages of releasing the Israelites, and by whispering, "I'm God, not you" (see further 245).

Starting points in understanding. In this study we are aiming to discover what Exodus would have meant to the Israelites for whose original reading the Holy Spirit inspired it. We are concerned with exegesis. However, most people do not read Exodus out of historical curiosity but because they want to learn something for their own day. Among the starting points that shape people's study have been the following (for resources on how this process of interpretation works, see 245):

- their concern for their personal relationship with God (we needed redemption as Israel did)

- their understanding of British and United States history (Britain was Pharaoh, the United States was Israel)

- liberation theology (oppressed Latin American countries are in a position like that of the Israelites)

- black theology (African Americans are in a position like that of the Israelites)

- feminist interpretation (women play a series of key roles in the exodus story)

- minjung theology (oppressed ordinary Korean people are in a position like that of the Israelites)

- postcolonial interpretation (for Canaanites, the exodus is bad news; it means that the Israelites are attacking them)

Whether we are interested in tracing historical events or in discovering other ways in which Exodus has significance for us, the questions and assumptions that we bring to the text have an effect on what we find there, providing us with lenses to read the text. A lens makes some things clear but leaves other things obscure. Thus we will benefit from being self-aware about the lenses that we use and from trying lenses other than the ones we instinctively use. In being self-aware in this way we are showing that we understand something of the relationship between exegesis and hermeneutics. Exegesis seeks to gain an objective understanding of the text's objective meaning; but exegetical study is affected by the reader's hermeneutical assumptions. Hermeneutics allows for the fact that the perspective that I bring to the text comes from my culture and my questions, but I can let my questions be a way into the text's own concerns and not merely a way in which I find in the text only what I already know.

EXODUS 1–18
Did the Exodus Happen? Some Opinions

There are varying scholarly views about the historical factuality of the exodus, as there are with questions about the stories of Israel's ancestors. In 2007, Egyptian archaeologist Zahi Hawass commented, "There is no evidence of the exodus. It's a myth." Another archaeologist, Mohammed Abdel-Maqsoud, said, "A pharaoh drowned and a whole army was killed. . . . This is a crisis for Egypt, and Egyptians do not document their crises" (Slackman, "Did the Red Sea Part?"). The evidence for considering the historicity of the exodus is limited, a situation that is unlikely to change, so there will likely always be varying opinions. One scholarly generation is commonly in reaction against the previous one. Here are some further views:

James K. Hoffmeier (*Israel in Egypt*): The story fits the background of Egypt in the thirteenth century B.C. There are many accurate details in the story that are surprising if it was made up later. Hoffmeier thus does recognize that archaeology offers only circumstantial support for the biblical story.

Willliam G. Dever (*What Did the Biblical Writers Know?* 99): "Archaeological investigation of Moses and the Exodus has . . . been discarded as a fruitless pursuit. Indeed, the overwhelming archaeological evidence today of largely indigenous origins for early Israel leaves no room for an exodus from Egypt." The second sentence makes what is a key point for Dever. The investigation of small settlements in the West Bank has encouraged the view that the Israelites did not come from outside the land. It is this consideration that leaves no room for an exodus.

Karel van der Toorn ("Exodus as Charter Myth"): He suggests that the exodus story developed to support the life of Ephraim after it had separated from Judah; Ephraim emphasizes its link with Moses, which gives it a history that goes behind Jerusalem and the temple (which were in Judah). This theory at least provides some answer to the puzzling question of why the Israelites would have invented the idea that they came from Egypt if this was not so, but it is purely speculative.

J. Philip Hyatt (*Commentary on Exodus*): "Exodus . . . undoubtedly rests upon a solid core of historical happening. . . . It is not possible, however, for us now to disentangle all the historical and legendary elements in this book. . . . The crossing of the sea was made possible by a combination of natural occurrences and some fighting between the fleeing Hebrews and the Egyptians. . . . The number who escaped was probably not more than a few thousand." Hyatt thus seeks to make the Reed Sea event something that we can imagine happening in our world. The difficulty in this attitude is summed up by the fact that Exodus says nothing about a battle and implicitly excludes the idea. Yet neither does it describe the event as a "miracle" in the manner of Western thinking, which works with a distinction between miracles and events that one can understand in a scientific way. The point about the Reed Sea event is that it was a sign, an extraordinary event by which a key aspect of God's truth was demonstrated and a key aspect of God's purpose was realized.

Graham Davies ("Was There an Exodus?"): He notes how widespread is reference to the exodus throughout the OT; the allusions to "Pithom" and "Rameses," names that would not be known at a later period; Moses' Midianite connections, which are unlikely to have been invented; the use of the term "Hebrews" rather than "Israelites"; the archaic Hebrew of the Song of Moses (Ex 15:1-18); and the report of a frontier official on admitting Bedouin-type migrants from the east. (For further such "moderate" study of the historical questions, see Finkelstein and Mazar, *Quest for the Historical Israel*; Greenspahn, *Hebrew Bible*.)

Berel Lerner (Israeli scholar, in a personal communication): "The more audacious the historical claim involved, the harder it is to account for its acceptance by large numbers of people. Thus the fact that the entire Jewish people seems to have unquestioningly accepted, from its earliest documented self-expression, Exodus' version of rather large-scale divine interventions in world history (including some material not very flattering to the Jews) is very difficult to explain on the assumption that the Exodus story is not true."

EXODUS 1–18
The Implications, the People

What makes different scholars take different positions on the factuality of the exodus? A range of considerations lies behind the differences between scholars. Reasons of personality incline some scholars to
more conservative or to more skeptical views. Presuppositions and other
personal factors contribute to the shaping of scholars' views on this question
more than happens with other historical questions because we don't have
solid evidence for fixing the date and authorship of Exodus and thus for
establishing its likely historical value. Faith convictions (e.g., the belief that
it is unlikely that the Holy Spirit inspired a fictional story because its theological value would then collapse, or the belief that things such as the Reed
Sea event don't happen) incline some scholars to more conservative or to
more skeptical views. While much of the scholarly world thinks that the
exodus-Sinai-wilderness-conquest story is more or less pure fiction, I think
it unlikely that Israel invented such a story and more likely that it is based
on some real events, at least such as happened to a group of people with
whose story other people in Canaan then identified. I am influenced by the
consideration that I know this is God-validated Scripture, and I think it
unlikely that God inspired pure fiction here; I don't think that the story
then "works."

If an exodus did happen, when did it happen? On the basis of the figures
in 1 Kings 6:1, the exodus was traditionally dated in the 1400s B.C., but archaeological considerations are usually now thought to point to the 1200s.
Rameses II (1290–1224) is then the Pharaoh at the time of the exodus. The
implication is that 1 Kings 6:1 does not offer a literal chronology. Its "480
years" looks like a symbolic number, similar to the three sets of fourteen
generations in Jesus' genealogy in Matthew 1, where Matthew has been se-
lective with the OT material in order to generate a scheme that gives expression to the purposeful way God was involved in the family line that led
up to Jesus. Analogously, 1 Kings 6:1 pictures the passing of twelve forty-year

generations between the exodus and the building of the temple as part of a chronological scheme for picturing the shape of OT history. A similar time passes between the building of the temple and its destruction in the exile, and a similar time is also expected to elapse between this destruction or the temple's rebuilding and the coming of the Messiah. In literal terms, a generation is more like twenty or twenty-five years, so that about twelve generations do pass from an exodus in the 1200s to the building of the temple in the 900s.

A date in the 1200s fits the first concrete piece of evidence outside the OT for Israel's existence. Pharaoh Merneptah (ca. 1214–1204 B.C.) campaigned in Canaan about 1210 (just after Joshua would be arriving there) and put up an inscription (a "stela") commemorating his action. Some of its lines read,

> Canaan is captive with all woe.
> Ashkelon is conquered, Gezer seized,
> Yanoam made nonexistent;
> Israel is wasted, bare of seed.

The stela is an overstatement! Significantly, for Israel it uses the hieroglyphic symbol for a people, not a place, which would fit Israel's position, not yet in settled occupation of Canaan.

The people. Exodus 12:37 ("six hundred thousand men, plus woman and children") implies two or three million, a figure that contrasts with Moses' comment in Deuteronomy 7:7 and resembles that of Egypt's entire population; Canaan's population was perhaps two hundred thousand. If the Israelites had proceeded like a wagon train, the procession would have been 2,500 miles long. Even with wagons ten abreast (not always practicable), it would have been 250 miles long. God could, of course, easily provide food and water for all these people, but nevertheless the numbers look out of proportion. Perhaps only some of the later Israelite clans were in Egypt. Joshua 24 might be significant here. Joshua urges his audience to make a commitment to Yahweh, as if it were for the first time. Are many of them people who are now joining the exodus people and making the exodus story their own? Or perhaps the word for "thousand" (*'elep*) means "clan" or "family" (as in texts such as Judg 6:15). "Six hundred families" would make more sense than "six hundred thousand men." (Concerning large numbers in the OT, see 119.)

EXODUS 19—LEVITICUS—NUMBERS 10
Israel at Sinai

This fourth "book" into which we divide the Torah is the longest and the most complex one, though the period it covers lasts less than a year, from the first day of the third month of the first year after the exodus (Ex 19:1) to the twentieth day of the second month in the second year (Num 10:11). To focus on how the story works, I will concentrate on the narrative outline and refer to the blocks of instructions by means of square brackets.

The story begins with Israel arriving at Sinai and God laying before the people a summary of how the relationship is now to work (Ex 19:1-8). It will continue to be based on God's initiative and Israel's response, but whereas it has been based on God's promise and Israel's trust, it can now be based on God's actual action and Israel's practical obedience. In this connection God wants to renew the relationship with the whole people; God's invitation is gender-inclusive, though Moses introduces a gender element into it (Ex 19:15). The invitation issues from God's grace, but in preparing to meet with God, Israel needs to take with total seriousness the solemn nature of God's holiness (Ex 19:9-25).

[Exodus 20:1–23:33 first lays down some basic principles in the Ten Commandments (that actual phrase doesn't appear in the OT; the nearest the OT comes to the phrase is the expression "ten words" in Deut 4:13), then in "the book of the covenant" it lays down some detailed expectations about how Israel is to live its life in the land.]

Moses and representative Israelites climb Mount Sinai and renew the covenant with sacrifices and a meal (Ex 24). Moses stays on the mountain and receives the instructions for building a portable sanctuary for Yahweh and for ordaining priests to lead worship there (Ex 25–31).

Meanwhile, this revelation at the top of the mountain is accompanied by disobedience at the bottom of the mountain as the Israelites make a gold calf as an aid to worship. This action exposes the fickleness of the people of God alongside their dedication. It also brings to the surface their vulnerability alongside their security, as Yahweh threatens to annihilate them and start again with Moses; Moses does act to punish the people. The making of the calf thus causes a major crisis in the people's relationship with Yahweh. But in due course the covenant is resealed (Ex 32–34, incorporating another book of the covenant).

The people then construct the sanctuary, and Yahweh takes up residence there (Ex 35–40). Yahweh is now in the midst—being.

[Leviticus 1–7 gives instructions for offerings in the sanctuary.]

Moses ordains Aaron and his sons as priests to minister in the sanctuary, but two of the sons then offer alien fire, and Yahweh strikes them down (Lev 8–10).

[Leviticus 11–27 gives instructions about cleanness and taboo, the annual Expiation Day, what it means to be holy, and other matters.]

Yahweh gives Moses instructions for the journey to Canaan (Num 1–10).

Like the story of Moses' interaction with Pharaoh, the story of Israel's time at Sinai in Exodus incorporates sequences of narrative theological reflection, this time concerning what we mean by "God's presence" and how Yahweh deals with his people's sin (hence some of the questions suggested in 223 for your reading of Exodus 19–40).

Some theological matters are too complex to be able to be explained in a straightforward systematic way. The relationship between God's sovereignty and human free will is one. An advantage of the fact that the OT includes so much narrative is that narrative makes it possible to explore theological questions without falling into the trap of thinking that you have answered them. Exodus is a great repository of such narrative theology.

READING EXODUS 19–40
AND LEVITICUS

1. First, sum up what you yourself mean by "God's presence." How do you experience that presence? What do we mean when we say that God is present with us?

2. Then read Exodus 19; 24–31; 32–34.

   a. In Exodus, is God on Mount Sinai? In what sense?

   b. In Exodus, can the people meet with God there? In what sense?

   c. In Exodus, in what sense is meeting with God an idea to be enthusiastic about, and in what sense an idea to be apprehensive about?

   d. In Exodus, in what sense can people be sure about meeting God; in what sense does it depend on whether God wants to be met?

   e. What ideas about God's presence are suggested by the meeting tent in Exodus 25–31?

   f. In Exodus, what difference does sin make to an experience of God's presence?

3. Read Exodus 20:22–23:33 and read the "Code" put out by King Hammurabi of Babylon five hundred years before Moses (for an abbreviated version, see 245, or you can readily find a complete version on the Internet).

   a. What areas of life does this section of Exodus cover? Can you see or guess why?

   b. What does it not cover? Can you guess why?

   c. What principles or values are expressed or implied in this section of Exodus?

   d. Where do the standards of the commands impress you, and where not?

   e. What areas of life does Hammurabi's Code cover? Can you see or guess why?

   f. What does it not cover? Can you guess why?

g. What principles or values are expressed or implied in Hammurabi's Code?

h. Where do its standards impress you, and where not?

i. What are the key similarities and differences between Exodus and Hammurabi?

4. What do you learn from Exodus 32–34 about intercessory prayer? What do the passages suggest about why we pray, whom we pray to, how we pray, whom we pray for, what we pray for, what results we get? Consider these questions in connection with the following:

a. Exodus 32:11-14 (in the context of Ex 32:1-14)

b. Exodus 32:30–35 (in the context of Ex 32:15-35)

c. Exodus 33:12-23

d. Go back to Genesis 18:22-33 (in the context of Gen 18–19) and ask these same questions about that passage. What does intercessory prayer imply there?

5. What do you learn from Exodus 32–34, Leviticus 8–10 and Leviticus 16 about the way God deals with the sin of the people of God?

6. Read Leviticus 1–7, on how to offer sacrifices. Is there anything you can discern about the significance of the different sacrifices?

7. Read Leviticus 11–15, on cleanness and taboo. Is there anything you can discern about the significance of the rules concerning these matters?

8. Read Leviticus 17–27.

a. Where are these instructions similar to Exodus 20:22–23:33?

b. Where do they treat the same subjects as Exodus 20:22–23:33 but in a different way?

c. What do they add to Exodus 20:22–23:33?

d. What do they especially emphasize? What do they reveal about God's priorities?

e. What do they suggest is the nature of holiness?

f. Jesus declares that all the Torah and the Prophets depend on Leviticus 19:18b and Deuteronomy 6:5. What are the key ways in which Leviticus 17–27 is an outworking of 19:18b?

EXODUS 19–40 AND LEVITICUS
Yahweh in the Midst—Speaking

*C*ompassionate and tough; holy one. Exodus describes God as compassionate and tough; Leviticus describes him as holy. The first description comes in Yahweh's classic self-description in Exodus 34:6-7; its words reappear a number of times in the OT. Yahweh is

- **compassionate:** the word (*rāḥam*) is related to the word for the "womb," so it suggests that God relates to Israel with a mother's compassion for her children (see Gen 43:30; Job 31:13-15).

- **gracious:** the word (*ḥānan*) is the equivalent to *charis* in Greek; it suggests the undeserved favor that God shows to Israel.

- **long-tempered:** the expression suggests that God does not lose temper very quickly with Israel; God does get angry, but not easily.

- **big in commitment:** the word (*ḥesed*) is translated in many different ways, such as "steadfast love," "constant love," "mercy" or simply "love"; "commitment" is the nearest English word (see further 408).

- **big in faithfulness:** the word (*ʾĕmet*) suggests that God is steadfast and reliable.

- **keeping commitment to a thousand generations** (about twenty-five thousand years).

- **forgiving:** the word (*nāśāʾ*) literally means "carrying"; it suggest that God bears the consequences of Israel's waywardness rather than making Israel do so.

- **not clearing the guilty:** presumably, those who do not seek forgiveness.

- **visiting the consequences of sin:** presumably, on generations that persist in it, but only for the number of generations in an extended family, which is the context in which sin works itself out.

Neither Genesis nor Exodus describes God as holy, but in Leviticus God's characteristic self-description is as the Holy One (e.g., Lev 19:2). Here, as elsewhere in the OT, "holy" denotes not a moral quality but a metaphysical quality. As the Holy One, Yahweh is quite different from human beings—transcendent, awesome, distinctive. Israel is then expected to mirror God's distinctiveness. The fact that "holy" is more a metaphysical word than a moral one, a word that denotes Yahweh's distinctiveness, links with the way the first three occurrences of "holy" in the OT refer to the Sabbath, to a woman who seems to be taken as the devotee of a god, and to the holiness of the ground at Horeb (Gen 1; 39; Ex 3).

Yahweh's presence in the midst of Israel, speaking. Whereas Exodus 1–18 tells the story of Yahweh's presence in the midst of Israel, acting, Exodus 19–40 tells the story of Yahweh's presence in the midst of Israel, speaking. He is telling Israel how to live in covenant, with Moses again being the mediator. This theme continues through Leviticus and Numbers 1–10. These books are thus dominated by what is often referred to as "the Law," though we have noted that the Hebrew word "Torah" means something more like "teaching" or "instruction." Maybe it helps us to have some other ways to think of the instructions that Exodus 19—Leviticus—Numbers 10 gives:

1. Some Christians have a "rule of life," a set of disciplines that they accept with regard to what they do with money, sex, time, work and other aspects of life. One could describe these sets of instructions in the Torah as Israel's corporate rule of life.

2. Exodus 19—Leviticus—Numbers 10 are a statement of Israel's social policy. Whereas the prophets lay the law down about the way the society is failing, they do not offer proposals regarding how the society ought to work or how social problems ought to be handled. These instructions do so, in a down-to-earth way.

3. They resemble a set of canons such as those of the Roman Catholic Church, Orthodox Churches or Anglican Churches, or the provisions of the Presbyterian Book of Order or the Book of Discipline of the United Methodist Church. Such documents set policy on matters such as the way the church is governed, how decisions get made, how worship is conducted and how sexual abuse is to be handled.

Exodus 19–40 and Leviticus

Two or Three or Five Types of "Law"

The instructions in the Torah begin in Exodus 20 with categorical or "apodictic" commands and prohibitions such as "You shall have no other gods" or "Keep in mind the Sabbath day." These declarations simply lay the law down; they do not say what will happen if people disobey. "Don't even think about it," they imply. In contrast, Exodus 21–22 begins from human circumstances such as "When you acquire a Hebrew servant . . ." or "When a man steals an ox or a sheep . . ." These do not lay the law down about what should or should not happen but instead prescribe what to do in light of things that do happen. They resemble case law (so they are sometimes described as casuistic law), and one can imagine them arising out of cases. Something happens, and the community has to work out what to do and what sanction to apply. These laws tell them.

One can then imagine the case law being used in deciding cases at the "city gate." When Israelites needed to resolve some cause of conflict in their village, the main context for doing so was a gathering of the community's senior people in the open square inside the village's gate. The problem that they would need to resolve would rarely correspond exactly to one of the situations that Exodus 21–22 covers, so perhaps the idea of this collection of case law is to give the elders examples of how some situations have been handled. Their task is then to extrapolate a solution for the case they face.

The categorical general statements in the Ten Commandments would also have a role in this connection, if the elders had to deal with matters such as a family making their servants work on the Sabbath or stealing another family's animals. But they stand further back in the process whereby people discern how to solve problems. They have traditionally been read out in church worship, and in Israel they may have had a similar place. Their proclamation would draw Israel to recommit itself to the expectations of the covenant (cf. Deut 31:10-13; Ps 50; 81). The tablets inscribed with the Ten Commandments were placed in the covenant chest in the sanctuary, where they symbolized the most basic expression of the commitment that God expected of Israel within the covenant relationship.

Where did the two types of instruction come from? The case law is comparable in form and content to that of Middle Eastern law codes such as Hammurabi's (see 245). What we have in Exodus 21–22, then, is the Israelite equivalent to such collections of material. It is a plausible view that Exodus 21–22 has a similar background in Middle Eastern culture even if it is not directly dependent on a code such as Hammurabi's. In places such as Hammurabi's Babylon, as in Israel, these codes were not merely laws that were directly implemented by courts; they were collections of material to which a ruler such as Hammurabi professed a commitment. They were the kind of law that he supported. The presence of this material in the Torah indicates that God affirms the content of such codes and bids Israel to live by them. Those laws affirmed by other peoples had a background in God's general revelation, the way God has hardwired people with an awareness of right and wrong as this applies to different areas of life.

The Ten Commandments are a more distinctive document. Its location in Exodus at the very beginning of the instructions in Exodus 19—Leviticus—Numbers 10 marks it as a collection of key points. Conservative instinct sees it as a Mosaic introduction of such key points. More liberal, evolutionary instinct is inclined to see it as a later summary of these key points.

A different way of categorizing types of "law" employs a distinction between three types: moral, civil, ceremonial. The distinction was formulated by the theologian Thomas Aquinas in the thirteenth century. On the basis of this categorization, one can (1) take a literal approach to the moral instructions, (2) feel free to leave aside the ceremonial instructions as abrogated through Christ or (3) utilize the civil law in connection with principles for state and city government. The problem is that the distinction doesn't correspond very well to the nature of the material itself. Individual commands or prohibitions may belong to more than one category. Is the Sabbath moral, civil or ceremonial, or all three?

Christopher Wright therefore suggests a fivefold division into criminal, civil, family, cultic and charitable teachings (see Wright, *Old Testament Ethics*).

Six Reasons for Having "Law"

Reading the first two chapters of the instruction material in Exodus soon establishes two things: (1) it lays down some basic responsibilities and implies some basic human rights (e.g., you should respect someone else's marriage, and no one else should attempt to compromise yours); (2) it assumes that things go wrong in human societies, and that the consequent problems need to be mitigated and conflicts resolved.

One could thus compare it with the constitution and law codes of a country such as the United States, as well as with the church canons and books of order noted in 224. Theologically, one can see a series of reasons for having in the Torah a set of such instructions, some designed to lay down principles, some to show how to work with the fact of human sinfulness.

1. The Torah makes clear that the law is not a means of gaining justification by works. Exodus 24:7-8 shows how Yahweh's instructions give Israel a means of responding to Yahweh in covenant. A covenant implies a solemnly sealed, committed relationship. Although a covenant involves two parties, the initiative and commitment may be quite one-sided. One party then does the giving, while the other party simply does the receiving; such is the case with God's covenants with Noah and Abraham, and in reverse with Josiah's covenant with God in 2 Kings 23:3. In Exodus, and even more so in Deuteronomy, the covenants are mutual, but God's action comes first. God makes a commitment to Israel; in response, Israel makes a commitment to God. God's grace is the starting point, but Israel's response of obedience is an absolute requirement if the relationship is to work.

2. Gerhard von Rad (*Old Testament Theology*) describes the Torah as a gift from God to identify Israel as Yahweh's. Far from being a burden on Israel, the Torah is the means of bringing Yahweh's election of Israel to full realization. Thus Deuteronomy 4 stresses Israel's privilege in having this revelation. One might compare God's giving it with a human being

revealing what he or she wants to someone whom he or she loves; that other person will then be glad to give what the first person wants.

3. The Ten Commandments express the significance of God's commands in another way. They simply express God's authoritative will: "I am Yahweh your God, who brought you out from Egypt, from the household of serfs: For you there shall not be any other gods. . . . You shall not make yourself an image. . . ." God brought the Israelites out of the service of Pharaoh so that they could be Yahweh's servants, and they are simply to do what Yahweh the master says.

4. Yet Yahweh the master's instructions are not random. For instance, the one who speaks is the God who brought people out of serfdom, and Yahweh's instructions reflect the fact that Yahweh is that kind of God. So their life involves imitating God's acts of deliverance. The second version of the Ten Commandments makes this point more explicit (Deut 5:12-15).

5. The Torah's instructions are statements of theological ethics in the form of commands. They are not merely a law code for implementing in court, so that, for instance, Israel usually did not execute people for offenses for which the Torah prescribes execution. The instructions about capital punishment are statements about theology and ethics, not law. They say, for instance, that respect for another person's life and marital faithfulness are decisively important on God's scale of values (see Levenson, *Death and Resurrection*).

6. The Torah's instructions are a set of boundary markers for the community. Most are not very demanding. They are a set of basically fulfillable requirements. Until they get to their tenth injunction, even the Ten Commandments are concerned with boundary markers; that is, beyond here you are in foreign territory. Hence, beyond here you risk being cut off from the community. You have behaved in a way that does not fit the definition of the community, and you run the risk of being expelled from the community by God or by the community itself.

EXODUS 19–40 AND LEVITICUS
Five More Reasons for Having "Law"

1. Much of the content of the Torah, particularly of Deuteronomy, is similar to the content of the wisdom about behavior expressed in Proverbs, and also in Ecclesiastes and Job. The Torah is a quasi-legal version of the philosophers' wisdom. What the philosophers commend on the basis of its being good sense, the Torah urges on the basis of its being Yahweh's requirement. The philosophers don't link their teaching with God's acts in Israel's history. If they have an equivalent argument, it is that their teaching is based on the way God created the world. The instructions in the Torah are also sometimes commended on the same basis (see, e.g., Ex 20:8-11). The Torah is a revelation of how to live in light of creation.

2. God's expectations as expressed in the Torah are absolute yet adaptable (see Brueggemann, *Finally Comes the Poet*, 90-95). For instance, in the Torah and elsewhere God lays down an expectation that Israel should tithe and should keep Sabbath, but the object of tithing or of keeping Sabbath keeps changing (see further 244). The unchanging expectation has different significance in different contexts. Different parts of the Torah express different expectations regarding questions such as the way debt is to be handled or the related issue of how indentured servitude is to be handled. Changing contexts require issues to be covered in new ways. In the Torah a major role of priests and Levites is to teach the people about Yahweh's expectations, which will involve working out how these expectations apply in new contexts or to new issues. One might guess that much of the material in the Torah emerged from this process.

3. The Torah's instructions thus constitute a canon or ruler, and a criterion for judgment. The Lutheran understanding of the law's significance sees its role as lying in the way it exposes humanity's guilt. The promises and warnings about blessings and curses (Lev 26; Deut 27–28), with their greater stress on warning, indicate the presence of this idea within the

Torah itself. Prophets such as Hosea and Jeremiah allude to the Torah as the basis for Yahweh's judgment on the community, and the accounts of Israel's history in Kings and Chronicles explain the downfall of Jerusalem as issuing from disobedience to the Torah.

4. Thus although there is a sense in which the requirements of the Torah are humanly within reach, Israel consistently found them too demanding, especially before the exile. In one sense, it's not so difficult to avoid worshiping other gods, making images, attaching Yahweh's name to something empty or breaking Sabbath, yet Israel failed in all these areas. Thus the Torah becomes a revelation of Israel's and of humanity's problem and its need of a new creation. So Jeremiah 31:31-34 promises that the Torah will be inscribed in people's minds, and Ezekiel 36:26-27 promises Israel a new mind and a new spirit, in order that it will live by the Torah. Yahweh fulfills this promise; after the exile Israel gives up worshiping other gods and making images and is wary of what it does with Yahweh's name and with Sabbath. The NT (especially the Letter to the Hebrews) also sees the fulfillment of this promise in what happens through Jesus, and Paul sees it as destined to happen again when God's purpose for Israel is finally complete (Rom 11:27).

5. The prophets see no need to promise that God will give Israel a new Torah. There is nothing wrong with the Torah; what was needed was something to enable Israel to live by it. Neither does the NT imply that there was anything wrong with the Torah or that it wants to replace it. Yet God had kept giving Israel new Torah through Israel's history, and God does so again in the NT, in light of the new circumstances that it needs to cover. It once more adds to the community's resources for discerning God's will and living by it. Like earlier restatements of God's expectations, there is gain and loss in this restatement. The NT puts more stress on the importance of human beings forgiving one another; on the other hand, it is more accepting of slavery than the Torah is (for material on servitude and slavery in the OT and the NT, see 245).

EXODUS 25–40
How to Build a Sanctuary

Building the portable sanctuary (often referred to as the "tabernacle") is an aspect of a transition from the one-time act of the exodus to the ongoing life of a community. God's presence succeeds God's activity; visible symbols of God's presence replace visible divine acts. God wants to live together with the people and not just tell them how to serve him, though this was the motivation for bringing them out of Egypt (Ex 25:8; 29:45-46). God's reason for taking hold of Abraham and Sarah had been missional; it was an expression of something that God was committed to in relation to the nations. What God is now doing is something ecclesial—though the context in the Torah implies that coming to dwell among Israel is to contribute to God's missional purpose. Here God is in the midst rather than on the move ahead, or perhaps God is saying, "We will move on together" rather than either "You go" or "I'll go, you follow."

The wilderness sanctuary also contrasts with the temple that David will eventually plan. The wilderness sanctuary is God's plan, not theirs; it's mobile, not fixed in one place; it's more like a house than a palace; it's on the same level as the people, not in a place exalted over them; it's a home, not a mountain. It may make Yahweh vulnerable (as is observed by Fretheim, *Exodus*, from whom I derive some of the other comments in this spread), because you get hurt, abused and taken for granted at home in a way you don't if you live on a mountain or in a palace. Some features of Yahweh's instructions for this sanctuary thus implicitly undermine David's plans for a temple, before we come to those plans. Anyone reading these chapters when people were much later planning the rebuilding of the temple (see Ezra 1–6) would also be given food for thought.

Churches are keen to do worship in the proper way, though the focus of that concern varies in different traditions. In some churches it's important to get the detail of the liturgy right; in other churches the music group may practice for hours to get the music right. Leviticus is concerned for worship to be done right, though it likely has a further motivation in doing so. Worship easily assimilates to the surrounding culture, and Israel needed to safeguard against this possibility, as do churches. In Western churches worship may seem to be offered for our sake, so that we go home encouraged. The Torah's rules about worship are concerned with worship offered for God's sake. Whereas Christian worship costs us nothing, Israelite worship was costly; worshipers did not offer God worship that cost them nothing (1 Chron 21:24). These regulations raise the question how Christian worship might be more outward, concrete, physical, costly and corporate, and not just involve mind, emotions and voice.

Whereas it seems obvious to Christian thinking that the object of offerings in the OT is to put things right between God and us, this concern has hardly any focus in the OT. The OT recognizes that offerings can't put things right with God, as the Letter to the Hebrews also emphasizes (perhaps it had in mind Christians who thought they could). Christian thinking comes to make that assumption about the object of offerings because Hebrews uses the OT rules about sacrifice to help understand the significance of Christ's death; but as is often the case, the NT's use of the OT issues from its own agenda rather than from that of the OT. OT sacrifices did not focus on gaining forgiveness for sin (see 229).

The sanctuary is Israel's holy place, the place where Israel recognizes its holy God. And Israel is urged to be holy as Yahweh is holy (Lev 19:2). What would it be like to resemble God?

Gen 1–2	be creative be life-giving bring order	Ex 1–18	hear people's pain be open and self-revealing fight against oppression give people freedom
Gen 3–11	be easily hurt be realistic don't give up	Ex 19–40	be categorical be concrete and practical be there be flexible be more merciful than judgmental
Gen 12–50	give people hope give people land give people space and scope	Lev 1–18	be available be frightening

How to Worship, and How to Keep Pure

As part of Israel's worship, sacrificial offerings were to have a key place. Leviticus 1–7 outlines the procedure for making five types of offering and hints at the significance of some of them.

1. **The burnt offering or whole offering** (Lev 1; 6). The words for this sacrifice (*ʿōlâ* and *kālîl*) indicate that the entire animal goes up in smoke; God has all of it. When you make such an offering, you are giving something wholly up to God as an act of total commitment. The image of its smelling nice to God adds to the Godward significance of the sacrifice; Israel would not have taken the image too literally. It also underlines the reality of God's being a living, personal being.

2. **The grain offering** (Lev 2; 6:7-16). The word for this sacrifice (*minḥâ*) means "gift," and it can apply to any offering. Here it refers not to an offering made on its own but rather to one accompanying other offerings, such as bread to go with the meat of the sacrifice. It is shared by the offerers and God.

3. **The sacrifice of well-being or fellowship offering** (Lev 3; 7:11-34). These are alternative translations of the term for the third type of offering (*zebaḥ šĕlāmîm*). It is shared between the offerers and God; some is burnt, some is cooked so that the offerers can eat it in God's presence. Since it is a shared offering, "fellowship offering" likely gives us the right idea. It expresses peace (*šālôm*) or fellowship between offerers and God and between offerers and one another. Leviticus indicates three different reasons for offering it, which would apply on different occasions:

   a. It can be a thanksgiving offering, which expresses gratitude to God for something.

   b. It can be a votive offering, which fulfills a promise that a person made in praying for something that God has now granted.

   c. It can be a freewill offering, whereby the offerers simply want to express their love for God.

4. **The purification offering** (Lev 4:1–5:13; 6:17-23). Traditionally it has been referred to as the "sin offering" (the term is *ḥaṭṭāʾāt*, which is related to words for "sin"). But its function is to enable someone to gain purification with regard to some stain. This impurity might come from a moral stain (e.g., through failing to testify in a legal case), but it might equally come from a ceremonial stain (e.g., through being in contact with a corpse and then going into the sanctuary without undergoing the proper cleansing rite).

5. **The reparation offering** (Lev 5:14-19; 7:1-10; also Num 5:5-8). Traditionally it has been referred to as the "guilt offering," though KJV calls it the "trespass offering," and its particular significance is to offer compensation (*ʾāšam*) for some way in which one has trespassed on God's rights.

Following on the instructions for the sacrifices, Leviticus tells of the ordination of the priests but of how their work immediately goes wrong. We don't know exactly what went wrong, but the result is to show how priests must be able to distinguish between the holy or sacred and the common or everyday, and between the taboo and the pure (Lev 10:10). In this connection, Leviticus then offers five chapters of teaching that constitute the kind of information and instruction that priests must be aware of, so to take account of it in their own lives and ministries and to offer teaching and advice to the rest of Israel.

The distinctions that Leviticus makes are not in principle between things that are right and things that are wrong; rather, there are, for instance, activities that are fine in certain contexts but not in others. So work is permissible for six days but not on the Sabbath because the Sabbath is holy; people are not to trespass on this time that is sacred to God. Such distinctions help people stay aware of God's claim on all time (and all space, all action, all people) by directly claiming a proportion of each. The second categorization system involves distinguishing between the pure (*ṭāhôr*) and the taboo (*ṭāmēʾ*). English translations have "unclean" or "impure" for the second word, which sounds logical over against "clean" or "pure." However, the Hebrew words do not work that way. "Taboo" is not the mere absence of purity or cleanness; it is the presence of something mysterious and/or worrying and/or off-limits (see 230).

2 30 | LEVITICUS 11–15
How to Keep Pure

Leviticus 11–15 gives a list of creatures that are permissible or forbidden for eating, and of events and conditions that convey taboo and therefore require action in order for people to regain their pure status—hence the rules about purification offerings in Leviticus 4–6. These events and conditions include menstruation, childbirth, emission of semen, contact with a corpse and certain skin conditions. What is the significance of these requirements?

Might they relate to hygiene? But many disease carriers are unmentioned, and why then would the NT abandon these rules? This abandonment of the purity system in the NT points to a more significant approach: the purity system is missional in significance. Its purpose is to keep Israel distinctive. This point is explicit within Leviticus itself (see Lev 11:44-45; 20:24-26). Sometimes the aim was to ensure that Israel did not come to behave like other peoples in ways that were religiously or morally reprehensible, or to get Israel to avoid practices associated with other religions, but such considerations do not explain many of the practices, and the idea that the forbidden practices were associated with other religions often seems to be a theory with little evidence. Sometimes the point was simply for Israel to be different in ways that were not significant in themselves. Not mixing cotton and wool symbolized the need to keep separate people or things that are different. God intended these practices to give expression to Israel's vocation to be separate from other peoples, because God's missional purpose required Israel to be a separate people. It is for this same reason that the system is abolished in the NT (Acts 10), because God's missional strategy changes. God now wants Jews who believe in Jesus to be able to share hospitality with Gentiles rather than to be wary of doing so.

An anthropological approach helps further explain some of the rules. Things that are taboo are mysterious and/or worrying and/or off-limits. There may be several symbolisms involved in the taboos.

1. They can be a sign of the distance of Yahweh from death. Yahweh is "the living God," and the purity system may be aware of a contrast over against Canaanite gods who could die or were closely involved with death. So in Israel, corpses are taboo, and so a person in contact with a corpse is prohibited from immediately coming into the sanctuary.

2. The system can be a sign of the difference between life and death, which are in theory total opposites yet easily get confused (hence debates over abortion and about life-support machines; it is difficult to be sure when life starts and when it ends, and people may look dead but still be alive). Menstruation involves blood and thus looks like a sign of death, but it is actually a sign that a woman could conceive new life. There is something mysterious about it. The related taboo about the emission of semen recognizes that something designed to be a means of new life simply gets wasted. The prohibition on cooking a baby goat in its mother's milk suggests the same symbolism; the means of life becomes the means of death. The skin disorder covered by Leviticus 11 (it is not leprosy but rather something like psoriasis) makes it look as if people are falling apart; it looks as if their bodies are dying (cf. Num 12:12), so they are taboo.

3. The system affirms the distance between Yahweh and sex. The OT sees nothing wrong with sex, but we must dissociate sex from God, which was important in a context where the gods were also involved in sex (so it is important in a Western context, where sex is a god). So a person who has just had sex is taboo and thus is prohibited from immediately coming into the sanctuary.

4. The system affirms a proper structuring of life in God's world. It reflects and upholds the order of creation itself (Lev 11 has language in common with Gen 1). The forbidden creatures are ones that don't fit into regular categories—for example, animals that chew the cud and split the hoof, or fish that have both scales and fins. A parallel consideration may underlie the ban on mixing things that are created separate, such as wool and linen.

READING NUMBERS
Israel's Journey to the Land of Promise

Numbers 1–10 closes the account of Israel's stay at Sinai and also opens the account of Israel's journey to Canaan (my outline of Numbers is partly based on Olson, "Negotiating Boundaries"). The forward linkage of Numbers 1–10 is indicated by the way it begins with a census of the people, insofar as another census will follow in Numbers 26. The double census gives the book its name (though its Hebrew title, "In the Wilderness," is equally appropriate). The opening ten chapters give a series of instructions to Israel, which Israel willingly obeys. Yet we have heard this story before, and it perhaps leaves us a little uneasy.

Any unease is more than justified by the account of the journey, in Numbers 10–26, which is characterized by a series of crises in the people's relationship with Yahweh. These crises come to a horrific climax with Yahweh's decision not to let the exodus generation enter Canaan (Num 13–14). The account goes on to describe the people's consequent sojourn in the wilderness, which continues to Numbers 26. Yahweh there commissions the second census; it produces a similar total to the first, which is a form of good news because it shows that Israel has maintained its numbers even as one whole generation has died off and another has been born.

The last third of the book, Numbers 27–36, balances the first; as the opening chapters were an account of preparation for the people's journey from Sinai, these closing chapters are an account of preparations for the people's entry into Canaan. As is the case throughout Numbers, the chapters include a number of miscellaneous pieces of instruction; often one cannot see the logic of their being placed where they are.

Later in the OT, the final part of Psalm 95 summarizes the crises that Numbers relates, which deprived the exodus generation of their place in the land. At that later stage in Israel's life, Psalm 95 speaks as if Israel is not in the promised land yet, or as if it could lose its place there. In the NT, the church is reminded is 1 Corinthians 10 that it could experience the same disaster. The reminder recurs in Hebrews 3–4. There one gets the impression that Hebrews is about to infer that Israel did not enter God's rest but Christians have been able to do so. Actually it argues that Christians are in danger of being in the same position as Israel. We too could fail to enter God's rest.

Numbers is a story of rebellions and punishments, and it manifests a preoccupation with death. Yet it ends with notes of hope. An extended note of hope is the account of Balaam's blessing of the people, one of whose ironies is that Israel doesn't know about the act of blessing. That story also conveys an invitation to hopefulness by its use of humor, which appears also in some other stories (such as the people's longing for garlic).

Read Numbers.

1. In what ways does Numbers 1–10 prepare Israel for its journey?

2. What are the recurrent issues in the stories in Numbers 10–21?

3. When you look at the stories one by one, how are individual stories distinctive over against others?

4. What is the point of the Balaam story in Numbers 22–24 (or what are its points)?

5. Is Balaam a good guy or a bad guy or what? What does Numbers 25 then add to that?

6. How does Balaam's story fit into the plot or themes of the Torah as a whole?

7. In what ways does Numbers 27–36 prepare Israel for entering Canaan?

8. Think back over the story in Exodus through Numbers and read Deuteronomy 34. In light of the reading, can you compose a letter that Moses might have written to Miriam as she comes to the end of her life or a letter Miriam might have written to him as he comes to the end of his life?

I like this student comment on Balaam: "The donkey provides a graphic image of what Israel had been doing to God. He'd been faithfully carrying Balaam all these years, and yet the first time he behaves strangely, he is beaten by Balaam. Why wouldn't Balaam continue to trust the donkey that had always been faithful to him? He lashes out at the very faithful servant who was trying to spare his life, just because he didn't understand what was happening at the moment. It's what Israel and we do to God."

NUMBERS 11–25

How Not to Get to the Promised Land

Like Genesis to Kings as a whole, and Genesis to Joshua as a whole, the stories in Numbers about the people's rebellions on the journey through the wilderness can be seen as having the shape of a sideways pyramid or stepped structure or chiasm:

(A) 11:1-3: Resisting the toughness of the journey

  (B) 11:4-34: Wishing they had more (Moses gets away with anger)

    (C) 12:1-16: Miriam and Aaron complaining about Moses

      (D) 13:1–14:45: Not believing in the possibility of overcoming

    (C') 16:1–17:27: The Levites complaining about Moses and Aaron

  (B') 20:1-13: Complaining about water (Moses doesn't get away with it)

(A') 21:4-9: Complaining about water and food

Three kinds of problem recur in these stories.

1. The people wish that they hadn't been brought out of Egypt. In other words, they radically reject their place in Yahweh's purpose and their position as Yahweh's son and servant.

2. They don't believe that they can reach their destiny. The peoples that they need to displace will be too much for them (Num 13–14). A number of the peoples mentioned continued for a couple of centuries to be in control of much of Canaan. Even later the story would challenge subsequent generations hearing the story about their own trust that God's promises could be fulfilled. As at Sinai, Moses is the people's intercessor; when God talks about abandoning the people and starting afresh with Moses, Moses again urges God to have a change of mind, appealing to God's reputation and God's compassion, and a compromise is reached. The story reaffirms Israel's long-term security but recognizes its short-term vulnerability; no individual generation can take its position for granted.

3. The object of the people's complaint is their leadership, which is responsible for their leaving Egypt and for their being unable to enter the land. Whereas the Psalms assume that it is acceptable to complain to God, here the people rather complain to their leaders and put huge pressure on them. At one point the leaders become divided among themselves (Num 12). For later Israel listening to this story, the leaders might stand not so much for individuals as for three forms of leadership: Moses for Torah, Aaron for priesthood, Miriam for prophecy. Priests and prophets often led Israel astray; it was vital that priesthood and prophecy stay subordinate to Torah. In the end, none of the three individuals set foot in the promised land. Moses' reaction to the complaint in Numbers 20:1-13 is the reason he will not do so. He strikes the rock (rather than merely speaking to it) and asks whether "we" are to get water from the rock: he has taken over God's position in his own eyes.

Numbers 22–24 brings the entire story that began in Genesis 12 to a magnificent interim end. God is fulfilling the promise to give Abraham's people their own land. The second census will shortly confirm that the people have become a great nation. God had promised that they would be blessed, and that anyone who cursed them would be cursed, to ensure that the curse would be ineffective. Balaam brings about God's blessing, precisely when someone wants to curse Israel. Yahweh is Lord over nations other than Israel and can work even through a non-Israelite prophet such as Balaam (let alone his donkey).

The OT recognizes that prophecy, like priesthood, was known among other Middle Eastern peoples. Indeed, an inscription from OT times from Deir Alla, in the Jordan Valley, refers to a prophet called Balaam. Even if you're a foreign prophet, however, you're expected to do just what Yahweh says, and Balaam gets into mild trouble for failing to accept God's original "no" about Balak's inquiry. It's nothing like the trouble he and Israel get into later (see Num 25). A new generation has arisen, but there's been no progress in what sort of people the Israelites are.

NUMBERS

Four Reasons Why Israel Fought Wars

Numbers include several accounts of Israel's involvement in war, so it provides a convenient point to consider this issue in the Torah as a whole. It illustrates how war is not one thing. When ordinary Christians discuss war and pacifism, we easily speak as if war were simply one thing, and either you fight wars or you don't. One value of the OT war stories is that they provide us with a variety of accounts of different kinds of war that broaden our horizons and enlarge our resources in thinking about the question. In the OT, as in the modern world, people fight wars of different kinds for different reasons (for more on the significance of war in the OT, see 507).

1. The Torah's first war was a liberative one; Abraham made war in order to rescue Lot when he had been caught in the crossfire of a battle involving peoples from Mesopotamia and people from the Jordan area (Gen 14). The story's implicit assumption is that when members of your broader family (your kin group) get taken captive, you don't abandon them; you take action to gain freedom for them.

2. In Israel's own story, in its first war Israel had a passive role. It had no war-making responsibility in the battle between Yahweh and Pharaoh in Exodus 14; it simply watched Yahweh take violent action in showing Pharaoh who is sovereign in the world. Yahweh looks after the violence in that context, as is the case in the Latter Prophets and most of the Writings (where there is much talk of violence, but very little talk of Israel exercising it). The similarity between books such as Exodus and Isaiah does not point to there being any change in thinking in OT times over the question of whether violence is ever appropriate; the question in Isaiah, for instance, concerns whether Israel trusts God to look after its destiny rather than trying to look after itself.

3. The first war in which Israel takes an active part involves it in a self-

defensive but punitive role. Not long after the Reed Sea deliverance the Israelites are attacked by the Amalekites, a Bedouin tribe who are relatives of the Israelites (they are descended from Jacob's brother, Esau). Deuteronomy 25:17-18 refers to the Amalekites having attacked when the traveling Israelites were weary, and to the Amalekites specifically attacking the stragglers at the back of the company. It is Moses who takes the initiative in doing battle with them in Exodus 17. The portrait of his role implies that while Joshua is directing the earthly forces, Moses is directing the forces in the heavens, with the implication that an equivalent to the earthly battle is taking place in the heavens; the two battles somehow mirror each other. Yahweh declares the intention to blot out the Amalekites for their wrongdoing and later commissions Israel to undertake this responsibility (Deut 25:19). Failure to do so is one reason for Yahweh's later rejection of Saul.

4. In Numbers itself, the first war is the one that Yahweh commissions as a means of giving Israel the land of Canaan (Num 13–14). In general, the OT does not think in terms of there being moral issues involved in the process whereby one nation dispossesses another nation and takes over its territory, though there may be moral issues involved in the manner in which it does so. Amos 9:7 illustrates the first point; Amos 1:3–2:3 illustrates the second point. One nation's taking over the country of another is simply an aspect of the way things work in the world. Nations usually have held this assumption through history, as is implied by the history of the United States or Great Britain. Numbers 13–14 presupposes that God will give the Canaanites' country to Israel through Israel's making war, and that the size of the opposing forces is irrelevant to how this works out. Deuteronomy 28:7 will make the same affirmation with regard to defensive wars; when Israel is attacked, Yahweh will see that its attackers simply end up fleeing. The issue about war that surfaces in Numbers 13–14 is whether Israel believes that Yahweh is capable of doing the impossible in this respect, given the numbers and strength of the country's inhabitants. In a piece of poetic justice, when God has declared that their disbelief means that they will not enter the country, and when they then decide that they will try, they fail because Yahweh does not make it possible.

Five More Reasons Why Israel Fought Wars

1. The next war story (Num 20:14-21) concerns the avoidance of war. Israel nears the territory of Edom, the descendants of that brother of Jacob who are thus Israel's own close family. Later parts of the OT refer to ongoing hostility in this relationship. Here Israel simply asks for permission to pass through the Edomites' territory, promising not to take from their crops or water. "Put one foot on our territory, and we'll kill you" is the response of the Edomites. "So Israel turned away from them." Apparently, "There is a time for war and a time for peace" (Eccles 3:8).

2. Numbers 21:1-3 then tells of an attack by the Canaanite king of Arad, who takes some Israelites captive. What is Israel supposed to do? The attack is unprovoked, but Israel does have designs on the king's territory. The story is the first to refer to the "devoting" of people and cities. The word (*hāram*, with the related noun *herem*) is often translated "annihilate" or "utterly destroy," but this misses the word's religious significance; it refers to something like a sacrifice. (Previous references to *herem* in the Torah have involved dedicating things to God without killing them.) Of course, the OT prohibits human sacrifice, but the killing of a whole people in war is understood as a sort of execution that involves giving them over to God. The practice of *herem* is known from elsewhere in the Middle East, so here Israel is taking up this known practice and taking the initiative with God in promising to devote the people of Arad in this way. It's not explicit that Yahweh approves of the idea, but Yahweh does go along with the Israelites' appeal, delivering up the people to Israel knowing that they will then devote them in this way.

3. Israel's war against Sihon king of the Amorites (Num 21:21-35) is another defensive one, but one through which Israel happily acquires territory. Like "Canaanites" (and "Americans"), "Amorites" can have a broader or a more specific meaning. Like "Canaanites," it can denote the various peoples of Canaan, and it can also be used much more generally to denote

a wider collection of people who lived in Mesopotamia as well as Canaan. Here it refers to a particular group east of the Jordan. As happened on the border of Edom, Israel asks to pass through Sihon's territory, but Sihon says, "No way!" and attacks the Israelites. This time instead of turning the other cheek, they fight back, kill the Amorites, and take over their country. Moses' war against Og king of Bashan (Num 21:33-35) has a similar dynamic. It is as an "accidental" but happy result of the unwise hostility of these peoples east of the Jordan that some of the Israelite clans end up settling east of the Jordan. The promised land gets expanded, as it were.

4. Beyond Numbers, in Deuteronomy 7:1-26 Yahweh commissions Israel to make war on and "devote" the Canaanites. The logic of the commission is that the Canaanites are guilty of wicked actions such as sacrificing children, and they are due for punishment, which Israel is Yahweh's means of exacting. Genesis 15:16 has already made the same point. In Genesis and Deuteronomy, then, the OT does imply that invading another people's land involves moral questions and in anticipation responds to moral objections to Israel's treatment of the Canaanites. They are perhaps no more guilty than other peoples, but Yahweh decides it is time for them to take their punishment because it will facilitate fulfilling the purpose that Yahweh has for Israel, which is ultimately intended to benefit the nations in general. One aspect of this action is that it will mean that the Canaanites can't lead Israel astray into their own ways. In connection with questions about the modern Middle East, one can hardly say that the Palestinians are deserving of punishment in the way the Canaanites are said to be; but in any case, the OT treats Israel's attack on the Canaanites as a once-off event, not one that it views as ever repeatable.

5. The final form of war in Deuteronomy is what might be called "competitive war" (Deut 20), more the kind of war of which one reads in the conflict between Israel and the Philistines for possession of Canaan and the kind that European powers have often fought. Those later OT stories raise the question of what one thinks Saul or David should have done when the Philistines were seeking to take over Israelite land. In the modern world too they raise the question how one is to live one's life in the world and whether it is possible to be a pacifist monarch, president or prime minister.

Deuteronomy occupies a central and pivotal place in the gargantuan work extending from Genesis to Kings. It's both the end of the Torah and the beginning of a history of Israel told in light of Deuteronomy. We have read of God's creating the world, making promises to Israel's ancestors, bringing Israel out of Egypt, meeting with Israel at Sinai and leading Israel through the wilderness to the edge of the promised land. Here the story stands still for a whole "book" as Deuteronomy looks back to where we've been and looks forward to where we're going and to the kind of life that Israel is to live in the land. In the books that follow it, we're going to read of Israel's occupation of the land, the vagaries of its life there, God's granting its request for a king and a temple, and then the way everything falls apart until Israel is back where Abraham started. Deuteronomy is the introduction to that story in that it lays down the principles in light of which we can understand something of why the story unfolds the way it does. (On Deuteronomy, see further 245.)

Deuteronomy follows the shape of a Middle Eastern treaty agreement in OT times, though this shape is modified in light of the nature of a Middle Eastern code of law. Relationships between one of the big powers and one of the little powers were often formulated as a treaty with fixed components. Israel took such formulations as a way of understanding God's covenant relationship with them. The form of these treaties is best exemplified by Deuteronomy:

- the relationship between the two parties in the past (Deut 1–3)

- the big power's basic expectations, especially of loyalty (Deut 4–11)

- the big power's detailed expectations (Deut 12–26)

- regulations for the formalizing of the relationship (Deut 27)

- the blessings of cooperation, and the opposite (Deut 28–30)

The way the treaty form is modified by the law code form appears in the extensive material giving the big power's detailed expectations, which is out of all proportion to the specific expectations that regularly appear in a treaty but can be compared with a law code such as Hammurabi's.

1. Read Deuteronomy 5. Of these ten injunctions, which do you think is most important theologically? Which is most important behaviorally? What do the ten not cover that you might have expected them to cover or that they might have needed to cover if God were issuing them to us today? Compare the Deuteronomy version of the ten injunctions with the version in Exodus 20. What do you think is interesting or significant about what they have in common and about where they differ?

2. Read Deuteronomy 1–4; 6–11, which describe basic attitudes that God looks for in Israel. What are these basic attitudes? Which of them seem most important in Deuteronomy's eyes, and in yours? Why does Deuteronomy think that these things are important? What are the reasons behind what you think is important?

3. Read Deuteronomy 15. Compare it with the treatment of this topic in Exodus 21. What is the significance of the similarities and the differences? Remember that what many translations call "slavery" is more like indentured labor or even employment. Slavery in the OT does not usually refer to a relationship whereby one person can own another person and do what they like with them. In passages such as this one, it is a relationship whereby someone who has got into trouble is able to work their way back to regular life. It's more like the system of indentured service that enabled ordinary Englishmen to get to the Americas by working for some years after they arrived to pay for their passage. What are the dynamics of the chapter's understanding of work, unemployment and poverty? Does it suggest any insights for us?

4. Read through the rest of Deuteronomy 12–26. Make a list of the topics that the chapters cover. Why do you think they cover them? How does the list compare with the list that you made for Exodus 20–23 (see 223 above)? What might explain the differences? What differences are there in the way Deuteronomy handles topics that also appeared in Exodus? What might explain these differences?

5. Look through Deuteronomy 27–34 and then read Deuteronomy 27 more closely. Why do you think these particular things are prohibited?

Deuteronomy has a distinctive set of theological and ethical emphases. Its theological emphases link with its covenantal framework of thinking. It constitutes a systematic exposition of the fact that Israel is Yahweh's people and Yahweh is Israel's God. This forms important background to the frightening declaration in Hosea 1:9, "You are not my people and I will not be your God," which arises out of Israel's failure to keep its side of the covenant by treating Yahweh as its God. In due course this declaration is to be reversed: "I will say to Not-my-people, 'You are my people,' and it will say, 'You are my God'" (Hos 2:23). That reversal comes about in Isaiah 40:1: "'Comfort, comfort my people,' says your God."

Deuteronomy's distinctive ethical concerns are as follows:

1. **Justice.** One aspect of this concern is the general focus on what is right, which characterizes Israel's laws as a whole (e.g., Deut 4:8). Another is the particular concern for a judicial system that works in a fair way. It is embodied in, for instance, the provision of the asylum cities (places where people may take refuge from lynching), in the insistence on rigorous standards of evidence, and in the safeguards against perjury (Deut 19:1-21).

2. **Concern for the needy.** Israel is to take care about the needs of groups of people who might have no sure means of livelihood, such as Levites, widows, orphans, immigrants and people who become impoverished. One object of tithing is now to see that people who have no land on which they can grow crops have something to eat (Deut 14:22-29). The rules concerning indentured service provide a safety net for families that get into debt in circumstances such as the failure of their harvest, and they are also a safeguard against such people being abused (Deut 15:1-18).

3. **Brotherhood.** The instructions concerning indentured service keep emphasizing that the poor person is a member of your family (this is not clear in gender-inclusive translations, where "brothers" has been replaced by words such as "members of your community"). You are ex-

pected to regard and treat other people in your village the way you would treat someone in your family (Deut 15:1-18). The same emphasis on brotherhood appears in the instructions about the position of judges, prophets, Levites and especially kings (Deut 17:14-20): Israel may appoint a king, but he is always to remember that the people as a whole are fellow members of his family, not people to take advantage of.

4. **Womanhood.** The instructions about indentured service make explicit also that they apply to women as well as men; women have the same rights (Deut 15:12, 17). They refer to mothers, wives and daughters alongside fathers, husbands and sons. The laws are also concerned to protect the rights and status of women in connection with marriage, divorce and parenthood (Deut 21:10-21; 24:1-4). These instructions make especially clear the realistic starting point of the instructions in Deuteronomy. They do not simply say that divorce should not happen, that girls should not be captured in war and that adult sons should not rebel against their parents; they recognize that these things do happen, and provide structures for dealing with them. Deuteronomy also makes explicit that women have the same responsibilities as men. They too are in trouble if they turn to other gods.

5. **Family order.** The family is central to Israel's life. It is the means whereby Yahweh goes about the fulfillment of his purpose for the world through Israel. It is also the context in which Israelites learn the story of God's involvement with them as a people, which suggests one reason why parents are to be honored. It is the context in which people pay the price when things go wrong in a relationship with God (Deut 4:9; 5:9, 16). The structures whereby family life, marriage and parenthood are arranged therefore need to be safeguarded (Deut 22:13-30).

6. **Happiness.** Deuteronomy's vision of Israel's life is a celebratory one, and its instructions are designed to encourage festivity. Worship involves feasting, celebration and indulgence, and servants as well as the family in a narrow sense share in this festivity (Deut 12:1-21; 26:11-12). A newly married man is allowed to stay home for a year to make his wife happy; he does not have to go to war in that period (Deut 24:5).

Another way of analyzing Deuteronomy's wide-ranging theology is to note how it holds together two sets of emphases that might seem to be alternatives. Deuteronomy will not have oversimplification.

There is one God, but there are other heavenly powers. "Yahweh our God Yahweh one," Moses says (Deut 6:4). This sentence works in Hebrew but not in English, where we have to decide where to insert an "is" or two (the NRSV and TNIV and their margins suggest four ways we may do so). That uncertainty doesn't compromise the clear assertion that Yahweh alone is God and/or that Yahweh is one. There is just one Yahweh over against the many deities worshiped by other peoples. Deuteronomy's point is not one about monotheism, the fact that only one God exists. That abstract concern belongs in a much later, post-NT context. The OT is concerned not with how many gods there are but rather with who is God. It does assume that there is only one being who really deserves to be described as God with an uppercase G, though it doesn't mind referring to other supernatural entities as gods with a lowercase g (Hebrew can't make the distinction in that way, but the OT implies the distinction). But it is at least as interested in the fact that Yahweh not Baal, Yahweh not Marduk, is God. It is interested in mono-Yahwism, not monotheism.

Alongside that commitment, however, it does not deny the existence of the many other heavenly beings in whom people such as the Canaanites believed. It simply demotes them to the position of Yahweh's underlings. They are entities that Yahweh puts in charge of other peoples, while Yahweh takes Israel as a special possession whom he will look after directly (see Deut 32:8-9). Deuteronomy is less explicit than Genesis about the relationship of God's election of Israel to God's purpose for the nations.

Yahweh is transcendent, and Yahweh is near. Deuteronomy 4 reminds Israel of the overwhelming nature of God's appearing at Sinai and warns Israel about trying to represent Yahweh by means of an image. Its God is a consuming fire, a jealous or passionate or impassioned God.

Yet it also refers repeatedly to the way Yahweh's name will dwell in the place that Yahweh chooses (e.g., Deut 12:3, 5, 11, 21). The name stands for the person. The name "Yahweh" encapsulates who Yahweh is, as any name does, but this name also conveys something of the name of the person to whom it refers (see Ex 3). When Christians mutter the name of Jesus in their prayer, they remind themselves that Jesus is present. Uttering the name affirms the reality and the presence of the person. So talk in terms of the name makes it possible to affirm that Yahweh is near as well as transcendent.

Israel is about to settle in its land, yet is on a continuing journey. From its position on the edge of the land, Deuteronomy looks back on Israel's entire story so far and looks forward to the declaring of blessings and curses from the two mountains either side of Shechem (Deut 11:29).

Yet it looks far beyond this event to the trouble that will issue from failure to obey Yahweh's words, to the exile that this disobedience will mean, but also to the restoration from exile and renewal that will follow (Deut 30:1-10). It sees Israel as on a journey, and it has the whole of that journey within its purview.

Deuteronomy holds together ethics and worship, the inner and the outward, the ideal and the realistic. In the modern West, ethics and worship are two separate areas, but Deuteronomy mixes them as interwoven aspects of a commitment to God. The two main central sections of the book (Deut 4–11; 12–26) hold together principles of attitude such as justice, love and trust with practices that give concrete expression to those stances. God is not interested in attitude of heart rather than action, or the opposite. The book combines ideals and realism, most clearly in its comments about indentured service (Deut 15:1-11). There need be no needy in Israel, such will be God's blessing (Deut 15:4); on the other hand, there will always be needy people among you (Deut 15:11), so there are instructions about how to handle that fact.

Blessing and loss. This is the choice that lies before the people (Deut 27:1–28:68). Deuteronomy combines God's grace with the expectation of obedience, God's compassion with God's willingness to discipline and punish, and a commitment to hope with a further realism about how things are likely to turn out. God's grace is key to the relationship of God and people (Deut 7:6-8; 9:1-6; 30:6); obedience is possible, but the people are stiff-necked.

DEUTERONOMY
Who Wrote It?

Deuteronomy presents itself as Moses' last sermon. Is it? The best statements I know of the arguments for believing that Deuteronomy came from Moses are by J. A. Thompson (*Deuteronomy*) and Peter Craigie (*Book of Deuteronomy*). They argue not that Moses actually wrote Deuteronomy, but that he has a substantial link with its contents. I summarize their arguments and then add my comments in square brackets.

1. That Moses lies directly behind Deuteronomy is the universal tradition of early Judaism and early Christianity. [But that's a thousand years after Moses.]

2. It's implied by the attitude of Jesus (e.g., Mt 19:8). [Is that so? In the passage from Matthew, for instance, Jesus is having a discussion with the Pharisees concerning the significance of Deut 24:1-4, which they have introduced as Mosaic. It's not a discussion of who wrote Deuteronomy; the reference to Moses is a way of saying, "It's in the Torah."]

3. The book itself speaks of Moses as author of its main contents (see especially Deut 31:9, 24). If he is not, it's fraudulent. [This is to import modern Western attitudes to the question. In the ancient world people commonly honored the people whom they see as their inspiration by attributing their work to them.]

4. It envisages the state of society of the late second millennium. For instance, there is no reference to a possible capital and temple at Jerusalem. [True, but it's also the case that it envisages a settled society in the land and raises all sorts of questions that will not arise for centuries, such as the appointment of a king and the problem of false prophecy.]

5. It follows the form of a treaty between a Middle Eastern king and his vassals that is best known in the second millennium. [Perhaps, though that is disputed.]

6. Some of its laws' requirements appear in the prophets. [This doesn't prove much.]

7. Its themes match those of early OT material such as Exodus 15. [This also doesn't prove much.]

8. Its mature systematic exposition of Israel's faith matches the OT's general picture of the significance of the Mosaic period. [Again, this doesn't prove much.]

I conclude that the arguments for Moses standing behind Deuteronomy are unconvincing.

If not Moses, who? Key elements in Deuteronomy's teaching became a living force in Israel's life through the reform of Josiah in 622 B.C. (see 2 Kings 22–23). That reform overlaps with the emphases of Deuteronomy more closely than with other parts of the Torah, especially with Josiah's closing down of places of worship other than the temple in Jerusalem. So was Deuteronomy written not long before this reform rather than having been mysteriously lost for six hundred years, and if so, who wrote it?

Maybe the book's authors were members of the royal court, the king's staff (but the book downplays kingship's significance: see Deut 17:14-20); or priests (but it also shrinks their unique position); or Levites, who gained from its doing so (but in other ways it holds the Levites back and brackets them with underclass people such as aliens and orphans); or people from prophetic circles (but it almost ignores prophecy except to warn of its dangers); or the kind of wise teachers whose work appears in Proverbs (but it also fails to mention them at all). We are left with the idea that the authors of Deuteronomy were, well, the Deuteronomists, shadowy figures who feature prominently in books about the OT. Maybe they were the authors of Genesis to Kings and the theologians who put the Prophets' books in the form in which we have them. But we don't know who they were, beyond attaching this label to them.

This unhelpful conclusion suggests once more that looking for the authorship of a book is not a helpful way into trying to understand it. Rather, the OT itself suggests three contexts for reading Deuteronomy: (1) its place in the story in which it comes, Israel's position of being on the edge of the promised land; here are instructions that Israel is supposed to put into effect there; (2) Josiah's reformation; here is a context in which its instructions have particular bite; (3) the exile; this material explains why the exile happened but offers hope if Israel will now start taking Deuteronomy seriously.

EXODUS THROUGH DEUTERONOMY
Looking Back

Look back over Exodus through Deuteronomy as a whole and sum up its teaching in two hundred words. Then you can compare with my version (see 245); if you wonder about preaching on the Torah, there is also a file of sermons in the web resources (see 245).

When you have read through these four books, you may wonder how they relate and compare with each other. Here is some attempt to characterize the similarities and differences between them.

EXODUS

The framework of Exodus is a narrative that tells us the following:

- how Yahweh got Israel out of being serfs in Egypt (Ex 1–18)
- how Yahweh got Israel into being servants at Sinai (Ex 19–24)
- how Yahweh renegotiated the covenant after Israel rebelled (Ex 32–34)
- how Israel built the portable sanctuary (Ex 35–40)

Within the narrative framework are sets of instructions:

- the Ten Commandments: the basics of how to respond to Yahweh's grace (Ex 20:1-17)
- detailed instructions: how life in the village ought to be (Ex 20:22–23:33)
- detailed instructions: how to build a portable sanctuary (Ex 25–32)

LEVITICUS

In contrast, the framework of Leviticus is instructions about how to worship and live for God in a context such as that of Jerusalem and the temple—the kind of things that a priestly theologian might want to stress:

- how to offer sacrifices (Lev 1–7)
- how to stay pure, avoid taboo, and deal with taboo (Lev 11–16)
- how to be holy (Lev 17–27)

Within the framework of instructions is a narrative:

- how the first priests were ordained, but how things went wrong, and how God put them right (Lev 8–10)

NUMBERS

Here the framework is once more a narrative, concerning how Yahweh got Israel from Sinai to the edge of the promised land, the situation of many Judahites once again later, in the exile:

- how they made preparations to set off from Sinai (Num 1–10)
- how they traveled toward Canaan, taking forty years rather than a few days (Num 10–25)
- how they made preparations for finally entering Canaan (Num 26–36)

As in Exodus, within the framework are instructions:

- miscellaneous directives spread through the book, many concerned with death and its implications

DEUTERONOMY

The framework is now again a narrative, though rather nominally so:

- how Israel was marking time on the edge of the land (Deut 1:1-4)
- how Yahweh and Israel reaffirmed the covenant and Moses died (Deut 29–34)

But the heart of the book is Moses' last sermon, focusing on the kind of concerns a lay theologian might want to emphasize:

- how to live for God in an urban context like that of Jerusalem as well as that of a village
- how to work out a covenant relationship, making Yahweh Lord

Reviewing the way Exodus to Deuteronomy has unfolded helps to underscore the essential twofold nature of the Torah. On one hand, its framework is that of a narrative (recalling how it begins with Genesis makes that fact clearer). It is the story of something that God did. On the other hand, it is dominated by rules for behavior. It's not a story without rules that work out its implications, but neither is it rules without a story that backs them up.

Exodus, Leviticus and Deuteronomy often deal with the same issues, but they do so in different ways. And why does one of the books cover some area that does not appear in the others? What circumstances or needs might have brought this about? The following chart lists some parallel passages between these three collections of teaching, with Deuteronomy as the starting point. What strikes you when you look at the differences between the versions? What are the characteristic and distinctive features, and what might be the explanation and significance of the differences? Look for the key points; don't get lost in the detail. I have filled in the first few to give you the idea; see if you can do the rest.

Deuteronomy 12:1-8 *They must demolish the existent worship places and worship only at the place that Yahweh chooses.*	Exodus 20:24 *They can make an earth altar wherever Yahweh designates. Did this give them too much scope? Was it too dangerous?*	
Deuteronomy 12:16, 23 *They must drain the blood from animals before eating the meat.*		Leviticus 17:10-14; 19:26 *There's more rationale for the rule. To help people understand the rule? To make sure they obey it?*
Deuteronomy 12:29-32 *They are not to worship in the way the previous inhabitants did; but it presupposes that all those people are gone.*	Exodus 23:23-24; 34:12-14 *Assumes that these previous inhabitants are still there, so they have to be wary of relationships with them. Perhaps they were in fact still there.*	
Deuteronomy 13 *Warnings about false prophets and other enticers*	*No equivalent— Why not? Does this subject appear only in Deuteronomy because it is a problem in Israel in the context to which Deuteronomy speaks?*	

Deuteronomy 14:1-20		Leviticus 19:28; 11:2-23
Deuteronomy 14:21	Exodus 23:19; 34:26	Leviticus 11:39-40; 17:15
Deuteronomy 14:22-29		Leviticus 27:30-33
Deuteronomy 15:1-11		
Deuteronomy 15:12-18	Exodus 21:2-11	Leviticus 25:39-46
Deuteronomy 15:19-23	Exodus 22:30; 34:19	
Deuteronomy 16:1-17	Exodus 23:14-17	Leviticus 23
Deuteronomy 16:18-20	Exodus 23:6-9	Leviticus 19:15
Deuteronomy 16:21-22		Leviticus 26:1

Exodus Through Deuteronomy
The Way It Has Unfolded

Here is an outline of the blocks of teaching material in the Torah.

Exodus 20:1-17: A set of ten basic principles, which include the Sabbath

Exodus 20–23: A set of instructions for worship and everyday life, which include
> debt and servitude (21:2-11)
> Sabbath and the three annual festivals (23:12-17)
> not boiling a kid goat in its mother's milk (23:19)
> the fruit of obedience/disobedience (23:20-33)

Exodus 25–31: Directions for portable sanctuary and priesthood

Exodus 34:11-26: Another set of (ten?) basic principles, which include
> Sabbath and the three annual festivals (34:21-23)
> not boiling a kid goat in its mother's milk (34:26)

Leviticus 1–7; 11–16: Directions regarding sacrifice, cleanness and taboo, and the annual Expiation Day

Leviticus 17–26: A set of instructions for worship and everyday life, which include
> debt and servitude (25:1-55)
> Sabbath and the three annual festivals (23:1-44)
> the fruit of obedience/disobedience (26:3-45)

Numbers 15–19; 27–36: Miscellaneous instructions

Deuteronomy 4–11: Basic principles for a relationship with Yahweh, including the ten basic principles, and thus including Sabbath

Deuteronomy 12–26: A set of instructions for worship and everyday life, including instructions concerning the one sanctuary, kingship and prophecy; and also debt and servitude (15:1-18)

the three annual festivals (16:1-17)

not boiling a kid goat in its mother's milk (14:21)

the fruit of obedience/disobedience (27:1–28:68)

Exodus through Deuteronomy thus comprises a series of separate, more or less systematic accounts and individual rules that keep covering the same issues, though often in slightly different ways. Further, many of the rules will not need to be implemented even once before Israel enters Canaan, the time in which the Torah is set. Indeed, centuries will pass before some of the rules will be needed (such as the instructions for appointing a king or for distinguishing between true and false prophets).

It would have been perfectly possible for the Holy Spirit to inspire Moses to give all this teaching in this way in the same period, but that idea makes poor sense. There are other possibilities that make more sense. For example:

1. they came from different periods of Israel's history; and/or

2. they came from different groups, such as priests and prophets, in different periods; and/or

3. they came from different places, such as Ephraim and Judah, or Babylon and Judah. We have noted that the NT refers to the Torah as the Torah of Moses, but that this hardly implies that it is seeking to answer the question of the authorship of the Torah (see 238).

It makes better sense to infer that the Torah came to include different versions of the teaching, in which God addressed different historical contexts and social contexts, which required Israel's life to be shaped in different ways. My working hypothesis is that Exodus 21–23 comes from the period before there were kings; Deuteronomy reflects the period when there were kings in Jerusalem, specifically the period before Josiah's reform; Leviticus reflects the same context but was put into writing during the exile; and the Torah as we have it came into being with Ezra's mission to Jerusalem in 458 B.C. The whole was dubbed Mosaic as a way of acknowledging that it had Moses' kind of authority. It was inspired by the Holy Spirit, but in a sense also inspired by Moses. It declared the significance of his work for later ages.

T*he tension between the top of the mountain and the bottom of the mountain.* Why is the Torah sexist? Why does it accept the idea that some people have to be servants (if not slaves) to other people? One clue that Jesus suggests is the tension between how things were at the beginning (by God's design at creation) and how the Torah's God-given rules reflect human stubbornness that issues in, for instance, men throwing out their wives and the wives needing protection (Mt 19:8). Another clue is the statement that the entire Torah is the outworking of love for God and for one's neighbor (Mt 22:40).

Putting these clues together, we can ask of any command, "How does this express love for God or love for neighbor" and "Does this command reflect how things were designed to be at creation, or does it reflect condescension to human stubbornness?" One could replace the image of creation and the garden of Eden with the image of the top of Mount Sinai or the Mount of the Beatitudes or the Mount of the Transfiguration, which then contrasts with how things are at the bottom of the mountain (Ex 32:1-10; Mt 17:14-17). God's instructions allow for both realities. The top of the mountain is characterized by commitment to Yahweh alone and by fairness, generosity, joy, egalitarianism, beauty, community and families being able to work their own farms. The bottom of the mountain is characterized by the inclination to make images, employment instead of sharing in the work of the family, marriage breakdown, poverty, patriarchy and conflict. The Torah mediates between these.

Exodus 20–23 provides a first embodiment of this mediation. It divides into a set of general norms (Ex 20:1-17) and a set of realistic compromises, sample rules for dealing with sample situations. Many are situations that should not arise, but they will arise, so Exodus deals with them. These two parts of Exodus 20–23 reflect two classic functions of law. One is to reflect truth and build values; the other is to provide order in society, to prevent or restrain conflict. The command about an eye for eye constrains the instinct to behave as Lamech did (Gen 4:23-24) and requires that the punishment fit the crime, not exceed it. While creation ideals would rule out divorce, the oppression of women and the servitude of one human being to another, the Torah's rules recognize those realities and constrain them or seek to soften their impact on people. As a covenant scroll Exodus 20–23 is integral to Yahweh's relationship with Israel, but as a kind of law code it covers not merely what is right but what will work.

Contextual vehicles and contextual givens. Another pair of factors that the Holy Spirit takes into account in inspiring the instructions in the Torah are features of the culture. Describing them as features of the culture is not to slight them or imply that there is anything wrong with them. Today's Western culture is different from what it was a century ago. The differences do not make the culture morally better or worse; they just make it different. God's expectations of people relate to how the culture is. The Torah's culture is one where most houses have flat roofs, and the roof is where someone might go for privacy. The Torah's culture is based on barter or on weighing out silver or gold. Western culture is a monetary economy. The Torah's culture is one where most people live in villages of one or two hundred people from two or three kin groups, and live the whole of their lives there. Western culture is mostly urban; people live far away from their families and live among strangers. None of these features are inherently right or wrong; they are just what the culture is, and God's expectations are geared to it.

By "contextual vehicles," I mean features of the culture God uses in order to embody both the mountaintop principles and the necessary concessions to the way things are at the bottom of the mountain. In the Middle East, for instance, sacrifice, tithes and a sabbath principle (not a weekly Sabbath) are known in other cultures. They are not in themselves special revelations to Israel. The special revelation to Israel lies in the way God makes use of these features of the culture; they are contextual vehicles for expressing his priorities. In Western culture, the importance of music, movies and theater might be features of the cultural context that God could use in embodying the mountaintop principles and the necessary concessions.

Exodus Through Deuteronomy

Two Approaches to Interpreting the Torah for Today

Nome of the instructions in Exodus through Deuteronomy apply directly to people outside Israel, and none of them apply directly to people who have come to faith in Christ. Theologians have wrestled with the question of the status and role and significance of the Torah through church history and have come to varying conclusions. In the context of the Reformation, Martin Luther was wary of letting the Torah have an authority that would compromise the importance of justification by faith, while John Calvin sought to see what guidance the Torah might offer and Menno Simons was wary of settling for standards in the Torah that were not radical enough (for more detailed study, see 245).

I'm with Calvin! The Torah's instructions are expressions of what constitutes right and of proper devotion to God. So people outside Israel could expect to learn from them. Here I note two ways; there are two more on 244.

Be exegetical. The straightforward answer is this: simply work out the meaning of the words and live by them. This exegetical approach is characteristic of Orthodox Judaism and of the form of theonomy known as Christian Reconstructionism, the view propounded by Rousas Rushdoony (*Institutes of Biblical Law*) and Greg Bahnsen (*No Other Standard*), who apply this approach specifically to the way society should work.

Admittedly, it may be difficult to decide the answer to questions about the detailed working out of the Torah's requirements. Does starting the car engine count as starting a fire, so that it infringes the Sabbath prohibition against fires? Do I tithe net or gross? How far must I go to avoid any chance of cooking a kid goat in its mother's milk (the command that underlies the Jewish practice of avoiding mixing milk and meat)? Further, we have noted (see 226) that Israel did not implement many of the rules in the Torah (e.g., about capital punishment), and this does not always seem to mean that they were simply being disobedient. They knew that these points that are made in the form of rules were statements about things of importance; they were not rules for implementing. So they are designed to make us think and to shape our lives by, but not in the immediately obvious sense. But it's also possible to exaggerate the problem involved in seeing the implications of the Torah. It's not so difficult in principle to see what tithing or resting on the Sabbath means. Just do it.

Look for principles behind rules and seek to reembody them. Christopher Wright suggests two sorts of questions we might ask of any rule. The first is questions such as the following (Wright, *Ways of the Lord*, 114-16):

- Is this criminal, civil, family, cultic or compassionate law?

- What is its function in the society? How does it relate to the social system (e.g., in relation to the West now being a monetary society, to the existence of Medicare and to the existence of a taxation system)?

- What is the objective of the law?

- How can we implement the objective in our new context?

The second is questions such as the following (Wright, *Old Testament Ethics*, 323):

- What kind of situation was this law trying to promote or to prevent?

- Whose interests was this law aiming to protect?

- Who would have benefited from this law, and why?

- Whose power was this law trying to restrict, and how did it do so?

- What rights and responsibilities were embodied in this law?

- What kind of behavior did this law encourage or discourage?

- What vision of society motivated this law?

- What moral principles, values or priorities did this law embody or give concrete expression to?

- What motivation did this law appeal to?

- What sanction or penalty (if any) was attached to this law, and what does that show regarding its relative seriousness or moral priority?

Having asked questions such as these, it's important to go on to ask how we can implement the principles and considerations in our own context.

EXODUS THROUGH DEUTERONOMY

*Two More Approaches to Interpreting
the Torah for Today*

Take *the Torah as a given and apply it imaginatively in a new way.*
Whereas the first two approaches (see 243) are left-brain ones, the third
is a right-brain approach, one that may be open to insights that the Holy
Spirit gives in a more intuitive or direct way.

There is no doubt through the OT and into the NT that the people of God
should tithe, but the significance of doing so and the way it makes a demand
on people change.

1. In Genesis 14 tithing is a recognition of achievement, a common Middle
   Eastern practice, a natural human instinct.

2. In Genesis 28:22 tithing is a response to God's promise, but perhaps also
   a way of looking generous.

3. In Leviticus 27:30-33 tithing is simply an acknowledgment of God; you
   can't claim credit for tithing, and you must beware of evading its demand.

4. In Numbers 18:21-32 tithing is a means of supporting the ministry.

5. In Deuteronomy 14:22-29, in contrast, tithes are to benefit the needy.

6. In 1 Samuel 8:15-17 tithes are claimed by the king; they become a means
   of oppression.

7. In Amos 4:4 tithes are accompanied by self-indulgence; tithing is a
   means of evading real commitment (cf. Mt 23:23).

8. In Malachi 3 tithing has a promise of blessing attached, and this becomes
   the favorite text of many pastors. But there is no basis for saying that
   tithes should be paid via one's congregation.

The right-brain idea about the significance of tithes in the West is that we
should tithe to provide nourishment, education, basic health care and health
education in the Two-Thirds World; then maybe God would bless us.

Likewise, there is no doubt in the OT that Israel must observe the Sabbath, but the significance of doing so and the way it makes a demand on people varies in different contexts (see Brueggemann, *Finally Comes the Poet*, 90-95).

1. In Exodus 20:11 Sabbath-keeping participates in God's rest.

2. In Deuteronomy 5:15 Sabbath-keeping is an act of remembering God's act of liberation.

3. In Exodus 16 Sabbath-keeping expresses trust that God will provide.

4. In Amos 8:4-6 Sabbath-keeping guards the weak against the strong, the exploiters and the acquisitive.

5. In Isaiah 56:7 Sabbath-keeping becomes the crucial act of obedience that defines covenant faithfulness.

6. In Mark 2:23-27 and Matthew 12:9-14 Sabbath-keeping justifies healing and eating.

The different perspectives on tithing and Sabbath show that keeping Sabbath or tithing is not a "law" in the OT. The church would need to test whether an alleged insight on the implications for today of a rule such as Sabbath or tithing came from the Holy Spirit; the more left-brain approaches that just do exegesis or look for principles would have a further role in this testing.

Set the instructions in the Torah in light of the Old Testament as a whole. It could be easy to assume that the instructions in the Torah are *the* resource for OT ethics, but a moment's consideration establishes that this is not so. The narratives in the OT, the wisdom teaching, the Psalms and the prophets all have ethical implications. The instructions in the Torah do not stand alone. The OT's treatment of issues takes a variety of forms: telling stories, formulating policies, proclaiming God's will and warning God's people, and praying. Indeed, all have a place within the Torah itself. So we can try that pattern. With regard to a question such as the way we deal with and relate to migrant workers, we might do the following:

• tell their story in order to help the people of God see its implications

• formulate policies to protect them and implement these policies in our lives

• remind God's people what they are doing to these workers and warn of God's judgment

• pray for these workers

2 | 45 | WEB RESOURCES

See the note on web materials at the beginning of this book.

246 THE TORAH: INTRODUCTION RESOURCES

a. Genesis to Joshua as a Stepped Structure or Sideways Pyramid or Chiasm

b. Genesis to Kings as a Stepped Structure or Sideways Pyramid or Chiasm

c. What the Torah Is Not

d. The Torah: A Story in Six Acts

e. The Torah: Premodern, Modern and Postmodern Attitudes to Its Origin

f. The Pentateuch After JEDP

247 GENESIS 1–11: RESOURCES

a. *Enuma Elish* ("When on High"): A Babylonian Creation Story

b. A Possible Historical Context for Genesis 2–4

c. Genesis and Science: Some Current Views

d. Genesis and Science: Approaches to the Problem

e. Some Reflections on Genesis 1–11

248 GENESIS 1–11: RESPONSES TO QUESTIONS

249 GENESIS 12–50: RESOURCES AND RESPONSES TO QUESTIONS

a. Genesis 12–50: What Sort of Information?

b. Responses to Questions About Genesis 12–50

250 EXODUS 1–18: RESOURCES AND RESPONSES TO QUESTIONS

a. Exodus 3 and 6: The Names of God

e. Moses the Mediator (Exodus–Deuteronomy)

f. Five Amazing Things You Can Tell God Not to Do (Exodus 32)

g. Jubilee 2000 (Leviticus 25)

h. You Shall Not Covet (Deuteronomy 5:21)

i. Remembering (Deuteronomy 7:6-11)

256 THE TORAH: LOOKING BACK

a. Taking Stock: The Teaching of the Torah as a Whole

b. Attitudes to the Torah: Insights from Church History

c. Responses to Questions I Have Been Asked About the Torah

257 (Anything else I dream up after this book is published)

Part Three THE PROPHETS

3 | 01 | THE PROPHETS
Who and What Are They?

The Prophets. In the Christian order of the OT the "Prophets" means the books that close the OT, from Isaiah to Malachi. In the Jewish order the "Prophets" covers (1) Joshua, Judges, Samuel, Kings—the "Former Prophets" (in the Jewish order Ruth comes in the Writings, not between Judges and 1 Samuel); (2) Isaiah, Jeremiah, Ezekiel, the Twelve Shorter Prophets—the "Latter Prophets" (in the Jewish order Lamentations and Daniel come in the Writings, not with the Prophets.)

So when Jesus or NT writers refer to "the Torah and the Prophets" or "Moses and the Prophets" (e.g., Mt 5:17; 7:12; 22:40; Lk 16:16, 29, 31; 24:27, 44), by "the Prophets" they mean both of these sequences of books. The phrase "the Torah and the Prophets" first appears in the prologue to the book of Ecclesiasticus in the Apocrypha (see 507), which dates from the early second century B.C.

When I speak of "the Prophets" with an uppercase *P*, then, I refer to these two sequences of books or to the figures whose stories and words they bring to us. On the other hand, when I refer to "prophets" with lowercase *p*, I may be including many other figures who appear in the OT—both good guys and bad guys. In other words, not all prophets are in the Prophets. In addition, in the Torah Abraham and Miriam are called "prophets" because they take a lead in prayer and praise, which draws further attention to the fact that "prophet" in the OT can have broader meaning than what it may suggest to us. They are people who are granted admission to the meetings of God's heavenly cabinet. That means they are people who can speak on Israel's behalf to God in those meetings, as well as people who discover what God says in those meetings and can speak on God's behalf to Israel.

When Jewish terminology thus sees Joshua–Judges–Samuel–Kings as the "Former Prophets" and Isaiah through Malachi as the "Latter Prophets," these expressions do not imply a point about chronology. The Former Prophets are not the earlier prophets, and the Latter Prophets did not all come later. The terms refer to books not people, and they refer to the order of the books; the two sequences are part one and part two of the prophetic books.

The Former Prophets. We don't know why or when the title "Former Prophets" came to be attached to part one of the Prophets, and the title probably seems odd. The nature of Joshua–Judges–Samuel–Kings is quite different from the nature of Isaiah through Malachi, and it talks more about kings and other leaders than about prophets. But here are some implications that the title might have:

- Traditionally, these books were thought to have been written by the prophets Samuel, Gad, Nathan and Jeremiah.

- They provide us with background to the work of the Latter Prophets. The Latter Prophets must be seen in the context of the story of Ephraim and Judah, as they themselves imply in their characteristic opening references to the kings of the two nations.

- They include many stories about prophets such as Deborah, Samuel, Nathan, Gad, Elijah, Elisha, Micaiah, Jonah, Isaiah and Huldah.

- They thus provide many instances of how God's word functions in history, which is a key idea for prophets. That motif begins with Joshua, who, though not called a prophet, is rather like one: he receives God's promises and instructions and passes them on, and he himself usually follows the instructions and sees the promises fulfilled.

- They give us a prophetic view on Israel's history as the sphere of God's acts. Whereas they came to be described as "histories" in the context of the Greek and Christian order of the OT books, they are much more than history.

- They share the characteristics of God's prophetic words. As stories, they are powerfully effective in achieving God's purpose of drawing his people into a deeper understanding of God, a deeper trust in God and a more serious repentance—like the words of prophets. And like God's prophetic words, they speak beyond their original context. They are not just tales from the past; they are stories that continue to instruct the people of God.

Joshua Through Kings

Two More Ways of Seeing the Books

Joshua through Kings as the second half of a much longer story. We have noted that Genesis through Kings forms a continuous sequence, of which Joshua through Kings is thus the second half: (1) the Torah takes Israel's ancestors and Israel itself from Babylon to the edge of the promised land; (2) Joshua through Kings takes them from the promised land back to Babylon.

The whole of Genesis through Kings is a story of divine initiative and human response, of human obedience and divine success, of human sin and divine failure, and of human failure and divine persistence. The continuous nature of the story from Genesis through Kings means that dividing it after Deuteronomy is somewhat artificial. Admittedly, the sequence of books as a whole does not give the impression of having been written by one person or in one go. You do not need to read it in Hebrew to sense that many styles and types of material appear within it (short stories, longer sequences, lists, poems and so on). More likely the narrative accumulated gradually, like a television series that continues over a number of seasons in a way that the author may not have planned from the beginning, and that combines the ongoing work of a number of contributing writers. It might even be the case that the second half (Joshua through Kings) was written first and the first half (Genesis through Deuteronomy) was written as a prequel. Whatever the process was, after the complete sequence had come into being, Genesis through Deuteronomy was separated from Joshua through Kings, presumably because the first five books were seen as supremely important in the way they convey God's promises, tell the beginning of Israel's story and offer the community teaching on how its life needed to be lived.

Joshua through Kings as a Deuteronomistic History. We can describe the perspective of Joshua through Kings as prophetic, but we could also say that it is theological. We have noted that the work looks at history from the angle of God's involvement and incorporates a theological interpretation into the telling of its story. Much of this theological interpretation resembles the perspective of Deuteronomy, which precedes it. Deuteronomy is a systematic account of how Israel must live in the country that they are entering and of the results that will follow according to their response. The story is written in light of Deuteronomy, which provides clues for understanding how things work out, especially in key chapters expressing Deuteronomy's perspective. Thus in scholarly parlance, Joshua through Kings is the Deuteronomistic History.

Joshua 1	the challenge to obey "all the teaching that Moses my servant commanded"
Joshua 23–24	another challenge to obey this teaching of Moses; a covenant made by the people to do so
Judges	a pattern of disobedience, chastisement and deliverance
1 Samuel 8–12	the story's ambivalence about kings (cf. Deut 17:14-20)
2 Samuel 7	Yahweh's promise and challenge to David (the center of the whole story)
1 Kings 8	Solomon's prayer about the temple, a place for Yahweh's name (cf. Deut 12–16)
1–2 Kings	a second pattern of disobedience, chastisement and deliverance
2 Kings 17	the reason for Ephraim's downfall: rebellion against Yahweh's commands and covenant
2 Kings 22–23	the reforms of Josiah in Judah: trying to apply Deuteronomy's expectations

We don't know who wrote the books. A typical critical view of the origin of this Deuteronomistic History is as follows:

1. A first edition was produced in the time of King Josiah, about 620 B.C. This theory builds on the way the books can speak as if Josiah's reform might succeed in averting Judah's downfall.

2. In the event, the reform failed, and Judah's downfall followed in 587 B.C. A second edition of the work was completed in the aftermath of that downfall, so it explains why it happened.

3. The last paragraph (2 Kings 25:27-30), relating King Jehoiakin's release from prison in Babylon in 562 B.C., is then a later addition, recording a sign of hope God thereby provided.

3 | 03 | JOSHUA THROUGH KINGS
An Outline of the Books and of the History

Joshua 1–12	Israel defeats many cities and kings of Canaan (though much remains to be taken over)
Joshua 13–22	The land is allocated to the clans
Joshua 23–24	The people make a covenant
Judges 1–2	The task that remains and the discouraging/encouraging pattern that will obtain
Judges 3–16	Examples: Othniel, Ehud, Shamgar, Deborah, Gideon, Abimelech, Jephthah, Samson
Judges 17–21	The degeneracy of the time when everyone does what is right in their own eyes
1 Samuel 1–7	Samuel, the last judge, the new priest, and the prophet who will anoint kings
1 Samuel 8–31	Saul, the first king, the man unfitted for a job that God doesn't really want done
2 Samuel 1–10	David, the king who receives God's spectacular commitment
2 Samuel 11–24	David, the king who then spectacularly fails
1 Kings 1–11	Solomon, the king who triumphs but then makes things unravel
1 Kings 12–2 Kings 17	The interwoven story of Ephraim and Judah and the downfall of Ephraim, and the rise of prophecy to confront the monarchy
2 Kings 18–25	The last years of Judah

The traditional historical outline of the time from Joshua through the Prophets is then as follows (all dates are B.C.):

1220	Joshua: the Israelites who had been in Egypt gain a foothold in the land
1220–1050	The Judges period: the clans are scattered through the land without central government
1050–930	Israel as one nation under one king in the context of pressure from the Philistines 1050–1010 Saul, 1010–970 David, 970–930 Solomon Victory over the Philistines and a wider power vacuum lead to a peak of achievement
930–722	Israel splits into two nations: Ephraim in the north, Judah in the south Middle of this period: Elijah and Elisha in Ephraim End of this period: Amos, Hosea, Jonah in Ephraim; Isaiah and Micah in Judah; Assyrian pressure; the downfall of Ephraim
722–587	Judah controlled by Assyria, then by Babylon Middle of this period: Manasseh allows Assyrian practices in Jerusalem Later in this period: Josiah's reform; Jeremiah, Nahum, Habakkuk, Zephaniah End of this period: rebellion against Babylon leads to Judah's downfall
587–539	Many Judahites forced to live in Babylon for the last decades of Babylon's power Early in this period: Ezekiel, Obadiah (also Lamentations; see the Writings) Later in this period: Isaiah 40–55 (also Daniel; see the Writings)
539–333	Judah under Persia Early in this period: Haggai, Zechariah; Isaiah 56–66 (Ezra 1–6) Middle of this period: Malachi, Joel (Ezra, Nehemiah)

Joshua Through Kings

Approaches to the Stories

H ow do we go about gaining an understanding of these books?
Looking for the historical content. They record many historical events, so it's natural to try to trace the history that they refer to. But we have noted that they are "the Former *Prophets*," and that they tell the second half of a long story, related to Deuteronomy. If we focus on turning them into a modern-style historical narrative, we risk missing much of their point. In Joshua, for instance, there are facts, but there is also an arranging of the facts into a structure. The whole is put together as a sequence: the introductory challenge, the taking of the land, the allocation of the land and the closing challenges. The book gives much weight to certain stories (notably Rahab, Jericho, Ai) and skips over the detail of many other events. In order to get its message, we have to take note of the way it works as a narrative. When we are chiefly interested in tracing the history of Israel, we will properly ignore that dynamic (or rather, treat it as another form of historical evidence, for the interests and priorities of its author). If we are chiefly interested in the message of the book of Joshua, we will attend to how it works as a narrative.

Looking for the historical context. Another form of historical approach asks about the historical origin of a book, about why it was written and about the author's intention in writing. It's possible to ask these questions about Joshua through Kings as a whole and thus to think about the significance of the narrative in the context of Josiah or of the downfall of Judah or of Jehoiakin's release (see 302). But there is much material in the books whose significance will not appear through asking that question. Likewise, there have been several theories about the aim of the stories of David's rise to power and of Solomon's accession, but it is hard to be sure of the right answer to those questions. In the Latter Prophets, the book of Jonah is unusual in being more a story about the prophet and his ministry than an account of his teaching, so what was the author's intention in writing the story? It is possible to link Jonah with Ruth and see both as intending to urge Judah to be open to other peoples. But there are several other themes in both books, so that this theme of openness isn't the whole story about Jonah or about Ruth. Asking about the author's intention doesn't help an understanding of the book.

Looking for what we would expect in a story. We need to treat these stories as stories. They are not simply fictional ones, but basically factual stories that use the techniques of storytelling in order to communicate. But they use the techniques of their culture, which are different from those of, say, conventional modern Western storytelling. There are things that Western readers may expect in a story (especially a Bible story) that the Former Prophets do not provide.

- They give little description of landscape or of people's appearance or of the climate. Thus we don't know what Joshua or Rahab looked like or what the country was like. When we do get that sort of information, it is significant (e.g., when we are told what Saul and David looked like).

- They give little description of people's character as individuals. We don't know what sort of person Deborah or Josiah was. Again, exceptions such as Saul and David are thereby significant. Otherwise, we have to rein in our instinct to think that such questions are important.

- They give little information on people's feelings or thoughts, unless they contrast with their acts. They tell of people's acts and words and let these be the means of showing their feelings and thoughts. They thus work more like movies than novels. Once more, the stories of Saul and David provide examples.

- They incorporate little reflection or comment on the part of the storyteller. The story is again left to speak for itself, like a movie, not like a novel. Judges makes hardly any comment on the horrifying events that it relates, except in the brief phrase that recurs near its end and notes how people were doing what was right in their own eyes. This characteristic troubles Christians who expect a story to comment on the right and wrong of what people do (like a Sunday school teacher, as if that will do the trick for us) rather than assuming that readers must and can figure things out. In this connection an exception is the narrative in Kings, which notes how each king did or did not do what was right in Yahweh's eyes.

JOSHUA THROUGH KINGS
What to Look for in the Stories

So what should we look for in interpreting these books, if we are to get their message?

Look for scheme(s) and phrase(s). For instance, the bulk of Judges is organized as a cycle of stories about how people did what was wrong, got into trouble, eventually cried out to Yahweh and Yahweh raised up a deliverer for them, and then they had peace. The books of Kings are likewise organized as the stories of the reigns of a series of kings on whom summary judgments are explicitly made.

Look for the plot(s) in the story. Stories often have an opening that introduces some of the main characters and sets up something that needs to happen; they may then introduce some complication that threatens its happening but takes the story to a turning point, then leads it to a resolution that may or may not tie up the loose ends. One can look at the book of Jonah in light of this outline, which may be illuminating in the way a book does illustrate it and in the ways in which it is different.

Look for a recurrent theme in the narrative. In the book of Judges, the interwoven double theme is sex and violence, and in particular gendered violence. Jacques Ellul (*Politics of God*) has noted that the recurrent theme in 2 Kings is the interaction of human political will and God's political will.

Look for the way characterization is effected. We have noted that can happen just by means of showing or by telling. Joshua, Elijah, Elisha and Hezekiah are simply shown. With regard to most of the kings, we are told how to evaluate them.

Look for the different types of character portrayal. For instance, in 2 Samuel there are complex characters such as Saul and David, and simple characters such as Ishbaal and Sheba. As persons, Ishbaal and Sheba no doubt were just as complex, but the story does not seek to portray them in such a rounded way. There are also characters who simply play a role (e.g., Jesse) and people who come across as personalities (e.g., Eli). And there are characters who are central to the drama (e.g., Samuel) and people who have cameo roles (e.g., Hannah).

Look for the Israelite audience(s) that the narrative addresses. For instance, we have noted that one can ask how 1-2 Kings communicates in its three editions to an audience in the time of Josiah, in the time after the fall of Jerusalem, and in the time when there is a hint that restoration may come. It can suggest the possibility that repentance may forestall calamity, and invite people to face facts and repent after calamity, and point to seeds of hope after calamity.

Look for underlying tension(s) in the way the story is told. Sometimes a narrative emphasizes some truth in a way that gives you the impression that it's the whole truth, but when you read between the lines, you can see things are more complicated. You are then involved in "deconstructing" the construction that the narrative puts on the story. It's not a negative deconstruction, but rather a positive spotting of two sides to truths. So Joshua emphasizes how complete was Israel's conquest of Canaan; however, between the lines the book shows how it wasn't really so. The tension in 1 Samuel over whether it was a good idea to have kings provides another sort of example.

Look for the underlying structures in a story and in the roles people play. This is one of the meanings of "structuralist" interpretation. Vladimir Propp (*Morphology of the Folktale*) suggested that there are seven roles fulfilled in all stories: the hero, the rival, the sender, the helper, the princess, the donor, the false hero. In the latter part of 1 Samuel the hero is David, but a tension about Jonathan's position is that he is both rival and helper.

Look for the way stories read to later audiences. This may help us notice features of the story that we might otherwise miss. For instance, Joshua reads differently and painfully to Native Americans and Palestinians (who have been put into the position of Canaanites in the story) from the way it reads to Anglo-Americans and Israelis. Judges reads differently to men and to women, and women reading Judges as women help readers see features of the stories that they might otherwise miss.

Joshua 1–12: The Occupation of the Land

1:1-9	Yahweh's sermon to Joshua: promise and challenge
1:10-18	Joshua's bidding to the officers to get ready, and to the eastern clans to join in taking the land before settling east of the Jordan
2:1-24	Joshua's surprising stratagem to prepare for entering the land: a comic interlude that issues in recognition of Yahweh by a Canaanite and in great encouragement
3:1–4:24	Joshua's surprising way of entering the land: immigration as a religious procession
5:1-15	Joshua's religious acts on entering the land: circumcision, Passover, submission to the real commander
6:1-27	Joshua's surprising way of taking the first town: conquest as a religious procession
7:1-26	Joshua's first failure and how he handles it: defeat as God's punishment
8:1-29	Joshua's new experience of Yahweh's guidance
8:30-35	Joshua's celebration and act of dedication
9:1-27	Joshua's second failure and how he handles it: deception and its consequences
10:1-39	Joshua's victories over people who attack Israel's ally
10:40-43	A summary of Joshua's victories over the whole land
11:1-15	Joshua's victory when attacked by Hazor and its allies
11:16–12:24	A summary of Joshua's victories over the whole land

Joshua 13–24: The Allocation of the Land

13:1-7	Introduction to the allocation of the land, and the land that remains to be conquered
13:8-33	The allocations of Reuben, Gad, half of Manasseh (east of the Jordan) and a note about Levi's nonallocation
14:1-5	Introduction to the allocation of the land
14:6-15	Caleb, and the people who remain to be conquered
15	Judah, and the people who remain to be conquered
16–17	Ephraim and the other half of Manasseh, and the people who remain to be conquered
18:1-10	Setting up the meeting tent at Shiloh; preparation for allocating the rest of the land
18:11–19:51	Benjamin, Simeon, Zebulun, Issachar, Asher, Naphtali, Dan
20:1-9	Asylum cities
21:1-42	Cities for Levi
21:43-45	Summary of Yahweh's gift of the whole land
22:1-34	Relationships between the western and eastern clans
23:1–24:28	Joshua's final challenge to the people and their response
24:29-33	Joshua's death

JOSHUA

The Book's Origin

1. Traditionally, Joshua was assumed to be the author of the book, but it reads more as a story *about* him (contrast, for instance, the parts of Nehemiah where Nehemiah says "I" and not just "he").

2. There are no concrete indicators of date in the book comparable to the ones that appear when Genesis and Judges refer to the time when Israel had kings and thus indicate that these notes at least come from that period. The book of Joshua periodically refers to things that can be seen "until this day" (e.g., Josh 4:9; 6:25; 7:26; 8:28, 29; 9:27), which points to a time some while after the events, but it does not tell us when "this day" is.

3. In terms of theme, Joshua completes Genesis through Deuteronomy and tells of the last stage in the fulfillment of God's promise to Abraham. Thus Genesis through Joshua can be seen as a "Hexateuch" (a six-volume work). The natural implication is that the origin of Joshua belongs with the origin of the Pentateuch. But when people have tried to find JEDP (the traditional sources in the Torah) in Joshua, they have failed; and in any case, no one knows when the Torah was written.

4. Since the work of Martin Noth (*The Deuteronomistic History*), first published in 1943, Joshua has been treated as part of a Deuteronomistic History extending on into Judges, Samuel and Kings. Joshua thus begins the story of how Israel did (or did not) live by the challenges and promises in Deuteronomy. Joshua as we know it therefore belongs after the last events narrated in Kings, the fall of Jerusalem in 587 B.C. and the release of Jehoiakin in 562 B.C.

5. But we have also noted that a common scholarly view about the origin of Joshua through Kings as a whole is that the first edition of this Deuteronomistic History was produced a bit earlier, in the time of King Josiah, about 620 B.C., because the work sometimes speaks as if there is a possibility that Josiah's reform might be successful in averting the fall

of Judah (which was a possibility then, but not later when the final version of the work was completed). In the context of Josiah's time, Joshua himself might then provide a model for the king. Josiah faces challenges similar to those that Joshua faced and is encouraged to believe in similar promises.

6. The usual scholarly view is further that the Deuteronomistic committee would not be writing from scratch but would be utilizing existent material. It would include sources such as oral stories ([a] and [b] below) and written records ([c] and [d] below):

   a. Stories of the kind that appear in Joshua 2–6. There was an Israelite sanctuary at Gilgal near Jericho and thus near the location of the events narrated in these chapters. It was a key sanctuary before the building of the temple at Jerusalem. Festivals at Gilgal would be a natural context for celebrating the crossing of the Jordan and the entry into the land, and thus for telling these stories and keeping them alive. The authors of Joshua would have as a resource the way the stories were told in their day.

   b. Stories told among the Benjaminites in the hill country (see Josh 7–10). One can imagine these stories also being available to the authors of Joshua in nearby Jerusalem.

   c. Lists of towns conquered by Israel (Josh 10–11).

   d. Lists of clan areas, kept for administrative purposes such as taxation (Josh 13–21). The lists for the northern clans are sketchier than those for the south, which may suggest that they come from the time after the fall of Ephraim in 722 B.C., when the northern clans had been transported to Assyria and the data were not available.

7. The Deuteronomistic committee will then have assembled this material, reworked it, and turned into a whole. They will also have written the chapters with the overt "lessons," especially Joshua 1 and Joshua 22–24, which urge the same concerns as the framework of Deuteronomy. It will be evident that this way of approaching the question of the book's origin involves a lot of guesswork and inference, but it is the best we can do.

(On the Joshua and Rahab story, see 363.)

1. What are the key elements in Yahweh's biddings to Joshua (Josh 1) and Joshua's biddings to his people (Josh 23–24)? If we work with the idea that the Deuteronomistic History went through three editions, what might be the message of these biddings to people in Josiah's day, or after Judah's downfall in 587 B.C., or after the release of Jehoiakin in 562 B.C.?

2. Trace the movements and acts of Joshua and the Israelites in Joshua 2–12 on the map at 111, or on a more detailed map.

3. What do you think is the significance of each of the stories in Joshua 2–6? What do these stories suggest about the life of leaders in the people of God, about the people as a whole and about relations with other peoples? Again, what might be their message to people in Josiah's day, or after Judah's downfall, or after the release of Jehoiakin?

4. In the stories of Ai, Achan, Gibeon and the various kings (Josh 7–12), what mistakes do people make? What do the stories suggest about the life of the people of God or of the nations?

5. "Joshua took the entire country" (Josh 11:23). How far has the story indicated this to be so? What impression does Joshua 13:1-7 give regarding that question? What might be the message of this aspect of the book to the generation of Israelites after Joshua?

6. See how far you can trace on the map at 111 or on a more detailed map the allocations of the clans in Joshua 13–22.

7. What would be the significance of the information in Joshua 13–22 for Israelites in the time of David or Solomon, or after the downfall of Ephraim and the downfall of Judah?

Reflections on this study. Joshua divides into two halves. The first half closes, "Joshua took the entire country, just as Yahweh spoke to Moses, and Joshua gave it to Israel as its own, as shares for the clans; so the country had rest from war" (Josh 11:16-23; compare the summary in Josh 10:40-42). Thus is fulfilled the promise with which the book opens: "Every place on which you direct the sole of your foot I have given you" (Josh 1:3). The allocation of the country to the clans (Josh 13–21) then presupposes that the entire country indeed now belongs to Israel. Toward the end of the book the point is made again (Josh 21:41-43).

But another strand of material relates how Israel is unable to take the key towns in the country. It leaves the population of Canaan alive and in possession of the country. Israel couldn't dispossess the inhabitants of Jerusalem, Gezer, Beth-shean, Ibleam, Dor, Endor, Taanach, Megiddo or their surrounding settlements (Josh 15:63; 16:10; 17:11-12). This list comprises nearly all the significant towns in Canaan. It's as if someone said they had conquered the United States except for Washington, New York, Los Angeles and Chicago. The admission fits the picture that emerges from archaeological investigations. Even if Joshua won spectacular victories over those cities and their kings, the Israelites did not take them over. It was the sparsely populated mountain areas where the Israelites settled. This in fact fits with the spectacular archaeological evidence of new settlements in the mountain areas in the relevant period.

Near the end of the book, it's thus not surprising that the aged Joshua issues a promise that is almost the same as the one Yahweh gave to him at the beginning of the book, a promise that Yahweh will "push back" the nations in Canaan on Israel's account "so that you may take possession of their country, as Yahweh your God declared to you" (Josh 23:5).

The book of Joshua provides another illustration of the way the Bible does much of its theology by telling stories, and of how one of the advantages of doing theology in that way is that stories are good at doing justice to complex truths. One of these complicated truths is the fact that God has promised to bring complete deliverance and blessing to his people, and God does fulfill his promises. But he does so in a way that is always (so far) partial. So the NT affirms that we have been crucified with Christ, that we have been glorified, that people who are born of God don't commit sin, but it also makes clear that the church is not very crucified, glorified or obedient to God. Part of the genius of the book of Joshua is to expound the truth concerning the ambiguous nature of God's people. God has fulfilled his promises to his people and will definitely complete their fulfillment, and that fact deserves shouting from the housetops. But the fulfillment is not yet complete, and that fact needs acknowledgment too.

3 09 JOSHUA

The Book's Spirituality

There is another tension in Joshua. At the beginning of the book, alongside Yahweh's promise of complete success, is Israel's promise of complete obedience. The people respond to Joshua's promises and challenges by saying, "All you have commanded us we will do, and everywhere you send us, we will go" (Josh 1:16). At the end of Joshua's life they repeat the commitment (Josh 24:16-18, 21). In the stories they fulfill their commitment in the way they cross the Jordan, accept circumcision, celebrate Passover and watch Yahweh make Jericho collapse (Josh 3:1–6:27). But in another strand of material they fail to obey Yahweh.

The ambiguity is summed up alongside one of those statements about Yahweh completely fulfilling his promises:

> All these royal cities and their kings Joshua took. He struck them down with the edge of the sword, and devoted them as Moses, Yahweh's servant, had commanded. Yet all the cities that are standing on their mounds Israel did not burn, except that Joshua burned Hazor alone. All the plunder in these cities, and the cattle, the Israelites took as spoil for themselves. Yet all the people they struck down with the edge of the sword until they had annihilated them. They did not leave anything that breathed. As Yahweh had commanded his servant Moses, so Moses had commanded Joshua, and so Joshua did. He did not omit anything of all that Yahweh had commanded Moses. (Josh 11:12-15)

The book stutters in contradiction in its statements about the way in which the people did obey Yahweh and the way in which any declaration of their obedience has to be qualified.

The question of how complete Israel's obedience is already surfaces in the humorous story about the spies and Rahab (Josh 2:1-24). Yahweh has told Joshua that he is giving Israel the country; they will not have to fight to take Jericho. So why does Joshua send spies to reconnoiter the Jericho area? And are no issues raised by the spies' need to lodge in the whorehouse and by their almost getting captured by the king of Jericho? Yet all ends very well, as Rahab acknowledges Yahweh; she gets converted, you could say, and the spies are able to bring back encouraging news of the way the Canaanites know that their days are numbered.

Then there is the other side of the Jericho triumph. Israel experiences the initial debacle at Ai, when thirty-six Israelites lose their lives, and it turns out that Yahweh has pulled back from Israel because an Israelite family has broken faith with Yahweh in appropriating some of the spoil from the capture of Jericho, all of which belonged to Yahweh (Josh 7:1-26). So much for complete obedience.

Dan Hawk (*Every Promise Fulfilled*), to whom I owe the insight about the tensions in theology and spirituality in Joshua, comments that Rahab and Achan muddle the distinction between Canaanites and Israelites. Rahab is a Canaanite but behaves like an Israelite (indeed, behaves better than an Israelite) in being willing to acknowledge what Yahweh has done and how Yahweh's promises are bound to find fulfillment. Achan is an Israelite but behaves like a Canaanite in failing to recognize that the spoils of war belong not to Israel (which did not even fight to acquire them) but to Yahweh.

As is the case with the theological tension, the tension over spirituality expresses something about the nature of God's people, as the NT also portrays it after Jesus' death and resurrection. The church is by definition a body that acknowledges Jesus as Lord, except that it doesn't always do so. Sometimes it is like the world, and sometimes the world behaves more the way the church is supposed to behave. An understanding of church and world has to embrace both realities. The world is lost, but sometimes it sees and does things right; the church is redeemed, but sometimes it looks more like the world.

The last three chapters of Joshua systematically rework both the theological theme and the spirituality theme, still leaving us with no closure: (1) Joshua 22 takes up the motif of obedience and disobedience; (2) Joshua 23 repeats the promises of Joshua 1, reflecting how the situation has not moved on; (3) Joshua 24 constitutes a closing challenge to maintain covenant obedience.

JOSHUA
The Book's Ethics

When modern Western people read Joshua, they may be less preoccupied by the book's own agenda (its concern with the fulfillment and nonfulfillment of God's promises and with Israel's obedience and nonobedience) and more preoccupied with an issue that does not bother the book: the ethics of Joshua's taking the country of the Canaanites in an act of aggression, and the killing of many of the Canaanites. Joshua says that God told Israel to kill Canaan's inhabitants; when Israel is obedient, it does so. This fact now troubles Western Christians, though it did not do so in the past. The Canaanites were, after all, God's enemies. We are told to love our enemies, not to love God's enemies (see Augustine's comments on Ps 139:18 in his *Expositions of the Psalms*).

Western Christians assume that the idea of God commissioning Israel to slaughter the Canaanites is out of keeping with the NT. In what sense might it be out of keeping? Two issues need to be distinguished. One is whether God would punish people by slaughtering them. But in the NT too God acts to punish untold numbers of people (e.g., by sending them to hell). The second issue is whether God uses human agents as the executors of his punishment. But God's using human agents as the executors of his purpose is a motif that runs through both Testaments, and Romans 13 pictures God doing so with regard to punishment. There is thus no biblical objection to this idea in principle.

Were the Israelites simply rationalizing their warlike instincts or justifying possession of the land in claiming that God had given them this commission? Yet there is no trace of unease in the NT about Joshua, and there is enthusiasm about his work in Acts 7:45 and Hebrews 11:30-34. The NT apparently didn't think that Joshua's action clashed with the NT call to be peacemakers. Actually, being against violence is an aspect of Western liberal values. Our unease with Joshua issues not from our reading the NT but rather from our being the children of the Enlightenment, of modernity and/or of postmodernity, and of our using Jesus selectively to justify our views.

Could Joshua's action justify genocide today? Genocide is indeed at least as common now as ever, and often it is Christians (e.g., in Rwanda) who undertake it. Christian settlers in America and South Africa justified their actions by Joshua. Some Israelis have done so, allocating the role of Canaanites to Palestinians, but the substantial involvement of Israelis in anti-genocide activism is at least as significant. There is no basis for, say, Great Britain or the United States or modern Israel using Joshua as an excuse for what they do. Indeed, Israel itself did not assume that the events in Joshua's day were a pattern to be repeated, and that they could annihilate other peoples on the basis of the earlier events. They behaved as if there was something unique about what God did in Joshua's day in giving Israel the land. The Bible implies that Joshua's action is an aspect of the "once for all" nature of much of the biblical story (e.g., Rom 6:10; Heb 9:26-28). An important aspect of the message expressed in the story of Israel's conquest of the land is that God gave the land to Israel in a miraculous way in fulfillment of the promises to Israel's ancestors, which links with the "once for all" nature of this event. Canaanites as such did not exist when the Israelites were writing these stories; there was no danger of Israel going out to annihilate them now.

While the OT makes a point of the fact that the Canaanites' punishment was deserved, other peoples who are just as degenerate (such as the United Kingdom and the United States) often get away with their wrongdoing. Canaan did not get away with it, because it was in the way of God's plans. At least we can note that God's plans were ultimately designed to benefit the whole world. And the Canaanites could always escape their fate by acknowledging Yahweh, as the prostitute Rahab knew. The OT also notes that eliminating the Canaanites was designed to remove a bad influence on Israel. Actually, Israel did not slaughter the Canaanites and did adopt Canaanite ways, which fits with this note. But another aspect of the story's message is that God could bring trouble to people who disobeyed God's word and/or trespassed on God's rights and/or made a personal profit out of war making.

See further 233-34, 507.

How historical is the story in Joshua? The first two cities whose conquest Joshua narrates are Jericho and Ai. It might seem that we should read these stories in the way we read the newspaper, taking them as accounts of things that happened just as they say. But archaeological evidence suggests that these two cities about which Joshua says most were unoccupied in Joshua's day. There had been no one living in Ai for a thousand years. There had been no one living in Jericho for three or four hundred years. How do we approach the questions that this raises?

The Illustrated Bible Dictionary article on Jericho suggests an understanding that avoids the conclusions that issue from the standard archaeological approach: "It is possible that in Joshua's day . . . there was a small town on the east part of the mound, later wholly eroded away." The fact that the city was unoccupied for centuries after Joshua's day would explain the erosion; the evidence for Joshua's Jericho would have disappeared. "It seems highly likely" that the eroded remains are buried under nearby roads and fields.

One problem with this approach is that the Jericho destroyed by Joshua was then a tiny settlement, maybe thirty meters square—not exactly the size of city that Joshua implies. The approach also seems to involve accepting the findings of archaeology when they suit us but rejecting them when they do not.

Instead of assuming that we should interpret the stories as being like newspaper reports, and that the standard interpretation of the archaeological evidence is wrong, we can try the opposite assumptions and not take the stories as being like newspaper reports. Rather, Joshua is partly historical parable not direct fact (see 108-9). One reason why this understanding is reasonable is its incorporation of scatological humor (Josh 2) and liturgical portrayal (Josh 6), which don't suggest literal history. The stories are parabolic, concrete expressions of facts that we have noted in connection with the theology and ethics of Joshua. They portray the fact that God gave Israel the land, in extraordinary fashion (Israel didn't take it for itself), and the danger of trespassing on what belongs to God or of profiteering out of war.

To say that Jericho is a parable is not to question whether God gave Israel the land or to imply that Israel never conquered cities in a miraculous way or never slaughtered people. The destruction of Hazor (Josh 11) is archaeologically verified and can be attributed to Israel. It was a greater miracle than the fall of Jericho would have been. Significantly, however, it was a defensive not an offensive act; it involved standing up to people who had superior weaponry, and God's explicit command related only to the destruction of their weapons, not to killing people. So if we want to know what a story about the straightforward conquest of a Canaanite city (a newspaper report) looks like, the story of Hazor tells us. This bigger miracle is described in a straightforward way, unlike the Jericho story. Here, God enabled Israel to win a stupendous victory. In contrast, Joshua 6 does not read like a matter-of-fact conquest story; it is an account of a religious procession.

So perhaps the story in Joshua 1–6 developed out of these three ingredients: (1) Israelites knew God had given them the land; (2) they celebrated that fact in a worship drama each year at Gilgal in the Jordan Valley, near Jericho and near where Joshua had first entered the land (see 307); (3) the abandoned sites of Jericho and Ai provided them with a way of giving concrete expression to the dramatic story. There is no direct evidence for this theory; it's just a way of seeking to imagine how the Holy Spirit could have inspired the text that we have, against the background of the facts that we have.

It's easy for modern Western readers to assume that the story needs to be completely historical in order to be valid, and if it seems to combine history and parable, we are inclined to assume that we need to be able to tell where history ends and parable begins. But it seems that in inspiring the book of Joshua, the Holy Spirit did not see it that way, and God invites us to relax in reading the book as it is.

Models for How Israel Came to Be Israel in Canaan

Archaeological investigation's failure to support a literal historical understanding of Joshua is one consideration that has led to the spawning of a number of theories regarding how Israel became a people in Canaan. Here I outline four sorts of theory that have been prominent over the past century. I wouldn't be surprised if the actual process involved elements from all these pictures.

Conquest/occupation. For this approach (mid-twentieth century United States and United Kingdom), see Bright, *History of Israel*; Bimson, *Redating Exodus*.

Their picture is the one you could form on the basis of a face-value reading of the main drift of Joshua and of its account of the spectacular victories Joshua and the Israelites won, reading it the way you would read a newspaper report. Such an understanding infers a three-stage occupation of the country, beginning with the center (Jericho, Ai, Shechem), then moving south (the five kings of Josh 10), and finally north (e.g., Hazor). The archaeological investigation of Hazor provides the best evidence for this understanding.

Migration/infiltration. For this approach (mid-twentieth century Germany), see Alt, *Essays on Old Testament History*; Noth, *History of Israel*; Weippert, *Settlement of the Israelite Tribes*.

Their picture is the impression you might form from the notes between the lines in Joshua, where we have noted that the book recognizes the partial nature of Israel's initial occupation of the land. These notes can be compared with Judges 1 and the ongoing situation in Canaan, where the Canaanites continue to be dominant. In addition, this approach takes the Genesis account of how the Israelites' ancestors settled in the land as a clue to how the Israelites themselves would have settled there. Such an approach infers that the Israelites migrated into the country in a gradual way, without there being battles. On this theory, Joshua 1–6 is more like the Hollywood version of how the West was won (there is actually an old movie with that title). This approach fits the lack of archaeological evidence for a conquest of Jericho and Ai.

Liberation/conversion. For this approach (1970s United States), see Mendenhall, "Biblical Conquest of Palestine"; Gottwald, *Tribes of Yahweh.*

Their picture is the impression you might get from Joshua 24, where Joshua challenges his audience to commit themselves to Yahweh as if they had not done so before. His attitude might give us a clue to the idea that this occasion was the time when groups that had not been in Egypt and had not experienced the exodus came to commit themselves to Yahweh and to make the exodus story and the Sinai covenant their own. In this connection, Gottwald especially emphasizes early Israel's distinctiveness as a democratic rather than a monarchic society, egalitarian rather than hierarchical or stratified. Israel is a society that determined to be different from the monarchical Canaanite city-states.

Gradual differentiation. For this approach (1990s United States, United Kingdom, Denmark), see Gnuse, "Israelite Settlement of Canaan"; Gottwald, "Origins of Ancient Israel."

Their picture is the impression you might get from Israel's positive relationship with the other peoples in Canaan in a story such as Genesis 14, where the priest of God Most High from Salem blesses Abraham, or from the place of Zadok the priest, who looks like a native Jerusalemite who becomes a member of Israel, and from the understanding of Zion (e.g., Ps 48), which was once a Canaanite sanctuary and becomes an Israelite one. Israel is committed to Yahweh, but its culture (e.g., forms of pottery) and the forms of its religion (e.g., the temple and its sacrifices) are broadly similar to those of the Canaanites. There are some differences: there are virtually no pig bones in the Israelite settlements, which suggests that the Israelites did not eat pork. But the life and situation of the Israelites in the stories in Judges and the archaeology of the settlements in the hill country (see further 316) suggest that there was no such thing as an Israelite arrival from outside.

Judges

An Outline of the Book and Its Origins

An outline of Judges

1:1a	A heading, "After Joshua's death," is a kind of caption for the book as a whole; the rest of 1:1–2:10 recalls aspects of events that happened in Joshua's own day that are background to what follows.
1:1–2:5	First introduction: The Israelites' initial achievements, the task still to be finished and a rationale for Yahweh's not driving out the Canaanites
2:6–3:6	Second introduction: The recurrent plot of the stories to follow
3:7–16:31	The individual stories:

	3:7-11	Othniel
	3:12-30	Ehud
	3:31	Shamgar
	4:1–5:31	Deborah
	6:1–8:35	Gideon
	9:1-57	Abimelech
	10:1-5	Tola, Jair
	10:6–12:7	Jephthah
	12:8-15	Ibzan, Elon, Abdon
	13:1–16:31	Samson

17:1–18:31	First worrying postscript: The Danites still seeking a home
19:1–21:24	Second worrying postscript: The fate of a wife and the women of Shiloh
21:25	Conclusion: The recurrent problem behind the narrative that precedes

The origins of Judges

1. The only tradition about the origin of Judges is the statement in the Talmud that Samuel wrote the book.

2. Judges looks back to Joshua and forward to the story of the monarchy. It is thus part of the work that extends from Joshua through Kings, and

presumably it has an analogous origin to theirs. Once again, then, the Deuteronomistic committee in the time of Josiah (about 620 B.C.) perhaps produced its first edition, though the book as we have it comes from after the downfall of Judah in 587 B.C. and the release of Jehoiakin in 562 B.C.

3. The heart of the book is a series of stories about events involving individual Israelite leaders and clans (or groups of clans) in the period before Israel had central leadership or organization. These stories presumably were originally told in the areas to which these individuals and clans belonged. They might have existed as a collection of stories before the Deuteronomists' time.

4. The Song of Deborah (Judg 5) looks like a very old piece of Israelite poetry.

5. The book opens as if it were an account of the occupation of Canaan, but it becomes something with more the character of a list of places not conquered at the first stages of Israel's life in Canaan.

6. The reference to Jebusites and Jerusalem in Judges 1:21 suggests that these notes come from before David's capture of the city.

7. The lists of "judges" in Judges 10:1-5; 12:8-15 may have come from official annals.

8. It was presumably the Deuteronomistic committee that turned the separate stories in Judges 3:7–16:31 into an entity that teaches a Deuteronomy-like lesson about Israel as a whole. It did so by formulating the introduction in Judges 2:6–3:6 and by providing a preamble and a conclusion to each story (compare the evaluative summaries of the reigns of kings in the books of Kings).

1. Read the stories that occupy the bulk of the book (Judg 3:7–21:24). Think about what you learn about the following:

   a. the way God acted

   b. Israel's strengths and weaknesses (e.g., religious, moral, political, social)

   c. the kind of people God used—their strengths and weaknesses

   d. the way God used people

   e. the position, experience and attitudes of women in Israel in these times

   f. the position, experience and attitudes of men in Israel in these times

   g. the relationships between women and men

2. Of the people in these stories,

   a. whom do you admire most?

   b. who appalls you most?

   c. who gives you most food for thought?

   d. who gladdens you most?

   e. who saddens you most?

   f. who surprises you most?

3. If they came to you for counseling, think of what would you say to

   a. Deborah

   b. Barak

   c. Gideon

   d. Abimelek

   e. Jephthah

   f. Jephthah's daughter

   g. Manoah

      h. Manoah's wife

      i. Samson

      j. Samson's wife

      k. Delilah

      l. the Levite

      m. his wife? [Note: Translations commonly refer to her as a "concubine," but see 213 above. The fact that the woman was a "secondary wife" need not imply that the Levite had another wife, though it might be so.]

4. Read the beginning and end of the book (Judg 1:1–3:6; 21:25). What do they add to an understanding of it?

5. Judges includes a number of appalling stories, and reading it can be a horrifying experience. It is natural and proper to be offended by these stories, in the same way it is natural and proper to be offended by some items on the news. Yet the offensiveness of the stories does not mean they should not be told. The fact that the Bible or the news is telling them does not mean that the Bible or the news is implying approval of what happened, even though neither the Bible nor the news may explicitly say, "This is wicked, isn't it?" In Judges, however, those notes at the beginning and end of the book (especially Judg 21:25) do indicate what the stories illustrate. The fact that the news and the Bible tell such stories suggests that they think we ought to know about these events even if we would prefer not to. So what do you think we are supposed to gain from the book? Why is it in the Bible?

6. Look also at the approach to Judges in Hebrews 11 (note especially Heb 11:1-2, 29-40). I see Hebrews 11 as an example of the way the Holy Spirit often inspired the NT writers to use the OT to illustrate a point that the NT itself wants to make, without worrying too much about the OT passage's inherent meaning. Within Judges, Barak, Samson and Jephthah are hardly people of faith; the book's focus lies on their failures. But there are elements in their stories that can provide illustrations of faith, and Hebrews 11 wants to focus on those. (For material on Deborah, Jephthah and his daughter, and Samson, see 363.)

1. At the macrolevel, Judges is an episode from a longer story. Thus the preamble (Judg 1:1–2:5), though somewhat surprising after the book of Joshua's emphasis on Israel's occupying the whole land, tells you the necessary other side to that story, which was present between the lines in Joshua itself. And the ending of Judges (Judg 21:25) shows how the book provides a lead-in to 1 Samuel (remember, Ruth is a separate story). See Judges 17:6; 18:1; 19:1. So one important purpose of the book is to show why central government was needed.

2. Broadly, the story is thus one of ongoing degeneration. The greatest of the "judges" is Deborah, near the beginning; the closing chapters become more and more horrifying. The book is arranged to show this process working out.

3. Its second preamble (Judg 2:6–3:6) suggests Yahweh's religious purpose in letting Judges happen. The comments at the end of the book (Judg 17:6; 21:25) also hint at the moral significance in what was going on: people were doing what was right in their own eyes. The stories may suggest that the traditional gendered translation of the comments at the end is correct: men were doing what was right in their own eyes (see also Judg 21:1).

4. In theory, having no kings is good; Israel's only king is Yahweh. Recognizing this fact is Gideon's best feature (Judg 8:23). When my sons were young, we used to read a children's version of the Gideon story that turned it into bad poetry but kept its profound theology. Refusing the kingship, Gideon affirms, "For though it seems odd, I'm not the hero, the hero is GOD." My sons knew to join in on that last word. The achievers in this book are not kings but "judges." But this translation of the Hebrew word *šōpĕṭîm* is misleading. The word and the verb from which it comes denote the exercise of authority, but they do not suggest

either a legal function or a negative "judging." The word "leaders," used in some translations, is better. They are people who do not have an official position like kings but who act decisively in doing something that makes God's reign into a reality in some way. "Judging" people thus brings them freedom. It is not so different from "delivering" them, so that these heroes can as easily be called "deliverers" as "judges" (see Judg 3:9, 15).

5. By definition, the judges were thus people who had no place in an institutional or constitutional structure. They were Israelite equivalents to Martin Luther King Jr. and Mother Teresa. The stories of little brother Othniel, handicapped Ehud and Canaanite Shamgar put question marks by eldest-ism, able-ism and racism; there follows the story of arguably the greatest judge, who turns out to be—a woman. Deborah's story thus in turn undermines sexism.

6. Judges indicates how Israel tried and failed to exist as a "theocracy" or pure covenant community with no human kings. To put it another way, Judges is about Israel's safeguarding its identity, fighting for its identity and having its identity disintegrate (see Kim, "Postcolonial Criticism").

7. Many books on Israelite history and many commentaries on Judges focus on what the book reveals about Israel's political development on the way toward being ruled by kings; and because such books have a major interest in history (as history has been understood by modernity), they show a special interest in getting a handle on the chronological coherence of the period as whole.

8. But this focus sidesteps key features of the book. "The Book of Judges is about death . . . in all forms, each violent. . . . And murder, in this text, is related to gender. Men kill men [in war], and women kill men [heroes, generals]. . . . Men, mighty men, kill innocent daughters [i.e., women]" (Bal, *Death and Dissymmetry*, 1). The running theme of gendered violence is central to the book (see Brenner, *Feminist Companion to Judges*; Yoo, "Han-Laden Women"; see also 363). "Insecure men are the most dangerous men in the world" (Hudson, "Come, Bring Your Story").

This section is based especially on Dever, *What Did the Biblical Writers Know?* 108-24; Stager, "Archaeology of the Family"; Mazar, *Archaeology of the Iron Age.*

Judges begins by confirming the picture that we have gained from Joshua, that the Israelites won spectacular victories in Canaan but were not necessarily able to hold onto cities that they defeated or to occupy the plains, where the big Canaanite cities were, where the Philistines settled and where the big modern Israeli cities such as Tel Aviv are. The Israelites settled more in the frontier area, the hill country, which is now mostly within the Palestinians' area. After the Israeli occupation of the West Bank in 1967, Israeli archaeologists undertook much work in that area and confirmed and clarified the picture one gets from the OT.

This archaeological work discovered remains of about three hundred small agricultural villages of a hundred to three hundred people that were founded in the late thirteenth and twelfth centuries B.C., the period of Joshua and the beginning of the Judges period. They are mostly in areas where there was a water supply and where crops could be grown and animals pastured, but areas also some distance from the major Canaanite cities and areas that seem to have been little occupied previously. They are villages without fortifications rather than being walled cities. The evidence suggests that the population of these hill areas grew from perhaps 12,000 in the thirteenth century (Joshua's time) to 55,000 in the twelfth century (the Judges period), to 75,000 in the eleventh century (Saul's time), and to 100,000 in the tenth century (Solomon's time). This "population explosion" cannot be explained by natural growth. It implies people coming from elsewhere to this underpopulated fringe area of Canaan, in large numbers by the standards of the area and time. In addition to the villages, many individual farms from the period have been discovered.

The villages characteristically comprise a number of "farmhouses" in clusters. One house might have served a nuclear family (the "father's household" in the OT), while a cluster might have served an extended family (the *mišpāḥâ*, "family" or "kin-group," in the OT). On the ground floor, these houses have living areas, a courtyard kitchen area and space for sheltering the animals. People might have slept on an upper floor. The villages have no "posh" houses; everyone lives the same way. There are no indications of anyone exercising governmental authority and virtually no sanctuaries or temples or religious artifacts. Any religious observances therefore did not involve images or institutionalized practice. These discoveries remind us that Israel was always a predominantly country and village society. The subsequent importance of Jerusalem and the temple in the OT can make one assume that most Israelites lived in Jerusalem and worshiped in the temple. In reality, they would hardly be there more than once a year at most. Further, an awareness of the way the vast majority of Israelites lived in villages or on farmsteads forms illuminating background to the way much of the material in the Torah works when it gives instruction on matters such as regulating bond-service (which comes about when a family's farm fails) or resolving conflict in the community.

The pottery found in these houses is similar to that of preceding centuries, but there are new or newly developed technologies that appear in connection with the settlements. These include terracing (i.e., shaping the sides of hills so as to grow vines, olives, etc.) and storage cisterns for water or wine and storage silos for grain. There are a few fragments of pottery with writing on them, indicating that was some basic literacy. Whereas pig bones are often found in earlier (Bronze Age) sites, we have noted that virtually no pig bones have been found in these settlements.

Dever implies that many of these settlers might have come from the Canaanite urban lowlands but grants that a number may have indeed come from Egypt. Their story related in Exodus through Joshua then became everybody's story, in something like the way everyone in the United States behaves on Thanksgiving as if their forebears came with the Pilgrims to the Plymouth Colony, or on July 4 as if their forebears were here by the time of the War of Independence. Judges then also tells us stories about people who had never been in Egypt.

An outline of 1-2 Samuel

1 Samuel 1–7	The story of Samuel
1 Samuel 8–12	The request for a king
1 Samuel 13–15	The reign and rejection of Saul
1 Samuel 16–31	The designation of David and the unraveling of Saul's reign
2 Samuel 1–10	David's early triumphs
2 Samuel 11–12	David's great wrongdoing
2 Samuel 13–20	The unraveling of David's reign and family
2 Samuel 21–24	Some ambiguous footnotes to David's story

The origins of 1-2 Samuel

1. The books of 1-2 Samuel form one book in Hebrew manuscripts; they were divided into two by the Septuagint (see 104). The division is a bit artificial: while 1 Samuel ends with Saul's death, 2 Samuel begins with the news reaching David. The division between 2 Samuel and 1 Kings is also a bit artificial: the latter part of 2 Samuel is preoccupied by the question of who will succeed David, but the answer comes only in 1 Kings 1–2. Similarly, 1 Samuel itself follows seamlessly on Judges: Eli and Samuel are the last of the "judges." Thus 1-2 Samuel form another part of that continuous whole from Joshua to Kings known as the Former Prophets or the Deuteronomistic History.

2. The Talmud sees Samuel as the books' main author, but he dies in 1 Samuel 25, and the Talmud attributes the books' completion to the later prophets Gad and Nathan. The reference to the kings of Judah in 1 Samuel 27:6 indicates that the book was not written until at least a century after the events it refers to. As part of the Deuteronomistic

History, it could not have been completed until the time of Josiah (about 620 B.C.) or the downfall of Judah during the next century.

3. The books lack one of the features of Judges and Kings that is often attributed to the Deuteronomists: the narrative is not structured by means of formulae that divide it into sections concerning each judge or each king. The books do contain a number of comments on sin and disobedience such as the Deuteronomists provide. The exchange between David and Yahweh in 2 Samuel 7 also expresses the Deuteronomists' kind of convictions.

4. The books' distinctive contrasting feature is that they string together a series of longer units that are more or less self-contained. These longer units may have existed earlier than the books' final production; if so, they are here made into a new whole. They comprise

a. the story of Samuel

b. the story of the adventures of the covenant chest

c. a story of the origins of the monarchy that supports the idea of having kings

d. a story of the origins of the monarchy that attacks the idea of having kings

e. the story of how David came to be king

f. the story of how Solomon came to be king

5. Within some of these narratives are some "doublets"; that is, there are several versions of the same event, such as the first meeting of Saul and David and the identity of Goliath's killer (1 Sam 17; 2 Sam 21:19). This also suggests that the narratives were compiled from varied earlier materials.

6. The notes in the margin of modern translations show how there are many problems involved in establishing the correct Hebrew text, especially in 1 Samuel. This is partly because the text is obscure and partly because the Septuagint presupposes a more distinctive Hebrew text than it usually does. The Septuagint's text as a whole is also shorter than the Hebrew text, apparently an indication that it was translated from a different edition of the book.

3 18 | READING 1 SAMUEL
Hannah, Eli, Samuel, Saul

1 Samuel 1–7: Hannah, Eli, Samuel

1. How would you describe Hannah—her experience, her prayer, her praise?

2. How would you describe Eli—his experience, his ministry, his character, his strength, his weaknesses?

3. What is your initial impression of Samuel from these chapters?

4. What is wrong with the Israelites and the Philistines?

1 Samuel 8–12: Israel wants a king

1. Why does Israel want to have kings? Are they good reasons?

2. Why does Samuel not want them to have kings? Are they good reasons?

3. What indications are there regarding why Yahweh chooses Saul?

1 Samuel 9–31: Saul

1. What do the different chapters suggest is the character of Saul? Does it develop?

2. What are Saul's strengths? What are his weaknesses?

3. How far is Saul someone who makes decisions, and how far is he a victim?

4. Why does God prefer David to Saul? (When we come to 2 Samuel, we will be looking at David's life and character there. As you read these chapters, you might like to look at the questions for study there and make notes that will help you then.)

5. What do you think of the way Samuel relates to Saul?

6. What do you think of the way God relates to Saul?

7. Does Saul die a good death? How or why?

8. In inspiring Saul's story, what do you think the Holy Spirit meant people to gain?

9. Stories in the Bible are sometimes there for us to find ourselves in them. Are there any ways in which that happens for you in the Saul story?

A note on Saul and his "evil spirit." When Yahweh gave up on Saul, the narrative comments in 1 Samuel 16:13-14 on the fact that Yahweh's spirit came on David and left Saul. Most translations then speak of an "evil spirit from Yahweh" tormenting him. This translation gives a misleading impression. It's natural for us to understand the comment in light of the way the Gospels talk about evil spirits, but the OT virtually never speaks of evil spirits in this way, as supernatural entities operating semi-independently of God and afflicting people. Further, the Hebrew word for "evil" means "bad" in the sense of "nasty," as well as "bad" in the sense of "wicked." What seems to happen is that Saul is afflicted from now on by a nasty spirit, what we might call a bad temper, which contrasts with the steadfast, generous, holy spirit of which Psalm 51 speaks. We might compare Judges 9:23, the other text where the phrase occurs. It is part of Yahweh's chastisement of Saul. But the replacement of the spirit that enables him to serve Yahweh by this mean spirit is not a way of saying that he no longer belongs to the people of God (in Christian terms, that he loses his salvation). In 1 Samuel it is not being said that God withdraws his holy spirit in this sense.

Was God's treatment of Saul fair? Saul seems not to get away with rather trivial offenses, whereas David seems to get away with horrific ones. Actually, I'm not sure that David really gets away with his horrifying deeds, but it is true that he doesn't get replaced as king in the way that Saul was. So is God arbitrary? Is God's favor unrelated to what human beings deserve? It looks as if vocation is indeed unrelated to what people deserve. No one deserved to be called as apostle to the Gentiles less than the other Saul, Saul of Tarsus. Yet God decided to use him. It was God's purpose that counted, not Saul of Tarsus's deserve. Once again, though, being king or not being king has nothing to do with salvation or with personal happiness or fulfillment. David doesn't look happier or more saved than Saul.

FIRST SAMUEL (AND ELSEWHERE)
Attitudes Toward Monarchy

There is an ambivalence about kings in 1 Samuel 8–12: the narrative critiques the idea of having kings, yet it also portrays Yahweh as involved in the appointment of a king. That ambivalence reflects a broader ambivalence in the OT as a whole.

1. Exodus 15:18 declares that Yahweh will be king forever. Does this leave room for human kings?

2. Exodus 19:6 describes Israel as a priestly kingdom. The whole people shares in the sovereignty and responsibility of ruling. Again, does this leave room for human kings?

3. Deuteronomy 17:14-20 allows Israel to appoint kings if it wants to but places firm safeguards around them: kings must read the Torah and must not exalt themselves over the people.

4. Gideon refuses to be made king; Yahweh is king (Judg 8:22-23). We have noted that a children's retelling of the story has him saying, "For though it seems odd, I'm not the hero, the hero is GOD."

5. But Judges 18:1; 19:1; 21:25 urge, in effect, "Look what happened when Israel had no kings!" People simply did what was right in their own eyes, and the results were appalling.

6. 1 Samuel 8 sees kingship as constituting a rejection of Yahweh as king and as an institution that will mean abuse.

7. 1 Samuel 9–11 tells of how Yahweh takes the initiative in choosing someone to rule, and the result is a great deliverance.

8. 1 Samuel 12 reaffirms that asking for a king means a rejection of Yahweh but promises that this rebellion need not be the end.

9. 2 Samuel 7 tells of how Yahweh makes a far-reaching commitment to the king. He will make the king's name great and he will relate to him as father to son. He will discipline him but never cast him off.

10. Psalm 72 shows Israel how to pray for the king and shows what expectations to have if Yahweh answers the prayers. Many other psalms speak of Yahweh working through kings and responding to their prayers.

11. 1-2 Kings shows how most kings, from Solomon onward, justify the warnings in 1 Samuel 8. They bring "the paganization of Israel" (Mendenhall, "Monarchy").

12. Zephaniah 3:15 reaffirms that Israel's hope lies in the fact that the real king, Yahweh, is among them (cf. Is 6:1, 5; 33:22; 41:21; 43:15; 44:6).

13. Jeremiah 23:5 and other texts nevertheless promise that one day Israel will have a king who lives up to a positive vision of kingship such as that in Psalm 72—what will later be called a "messiah." (While the Hebrew equivalent of the word "messiah" does come in the OT, it means "anointed" and is used only to describe a present king or priest. It is not used to describe a future king. So the OT does talk about a future king in passages such as Jeremiah 23:5-6, but it does not use the word "messiah" to describe him. That usage came later, when there were no present kings.)

14. Isaiah 55:3-5 takes up the vision of a kingly people and promises that the entire people will have the kind of covenant relationship with Yahweh and the kind of vocation that applied to David.

The material as a whole suggests how human kingship is theologically inappropriate but practically necessary. It is an act of rebellion that God works with and turns into a central category with which people will understand Jesus.

The principle is one that applies not only to hereditary monarchies. It applies to presidencies and to pastors—to any system that puts one person in supreme power. Christian history, as usual, repeats the trajectory of Israel's history. The gospel seeks to reintroduce the kingdom of priests (1 Pet 2:9), and the early church has no place for the heading up of churches by one person. But that arrangement ends in chaos, so the church has to invent the "monarchical episcopate," churches headed up by a senior pastor. This system has shown the capacity to control error and also to encourage abuse. Therefore the system has to have safeguards that circumscribe power in one way or another.

David in 1-2 Samuel. It has been suggested that the key to understanding David is the tension between what he was in public and what he was in private: he was a great leader, but he was clueless as a human being. Read 1 Samuel 16–1 Kings 2 with this suggestion as a grid for understanding his character and his life.

1. How was David a great leader, a person who knew how to be a public person?

2. Are there exceptions to that generalization? Are there ways in which he blundered in his public life, in his leadership?

3. What were David's weaknesses as a human being, in his personal life?

4. What were David's strengths as a human being, in his personal life?

5. What are your reflections on the material that you have collected under these four headings and their interrelationship?

A man after God's heart? In light of what you read in his story, you may wonder how David can be called "a man after God's heart" (1 Sam 13:14). That phrase is easy to misinterpret. In itself it doesn't imply that he is a man whose heart matches God's heart. The same phrase comes in 2 Samuel 7:21, where it simply means "in accordance with your desire" (cf. Ps 20:4). So "a man according to God's heart" simply means "a man God chose." It doesn't indicate that God recognized David as someone whose heart was in the right place (though there is a key sense in which you could say it about him; see the comments at 321).

One might again compare Saul of Tarsus (see 318). One could describe Saul of Tarsus as "a man after God's heart" in the sense that God chose him, but not in the sense that we usually attribute to that phrase; at least, he was not yet such a man. Someone once asked me, "Why did God love David so much when he was such a jerk?" Both David and Saul of Tarsus were rogues whom God could use, and God's "love" related to his intention to use them. In a way, they illustrate the consistent truth that God's love is not something we earn. (And would you really want God to "love" and choose and use you the way God did David or Saul of Tarsus?)

Some implications of David's story are that leaders tend not to be holy; that God doesn't choose holy people to be leaders, though he no doubt wants them to become holy; and that leaders tend to become sinners. If you are a leader, you will quite likely make a mess of your family life and your relationships. If you are not a leader, you need to keep an eye on your leaders because they will quite likely do so.

What was wrong with taking the census (2 Sam 24)? In a traditional society such counting suggests reliance on human resources rather than on God (Githuku, "Taboos on Counting").

The women in the story. Read the stories about women in 1-2 Samuel: (1) 1 Samuel 1–2; (2) 1 Samuel 4; (3) 1 Samuel 25; (4) 2 Samuel 2:1-4; 3:1-16; 6:12-23; (5) 2 Samuel 11:1–12:31; (6) 2 Samuel 13:1-39; (7) 2 Samuel 14:1-24; (8) 2 Samuel 21:1-14.

1. What is the perception of women, their place in society, their role, their experience?

2. What is their wisdom, their courage?

3. What are their strengths, their challenges, their achievements?

4. What are their temptations, their vulnerability, their griefs?

5. In what ways are their stories encouraging?

6. In what ways are their stories worrying, in what ways troubling, in what ways do they provoke to anger?

David and Bathsheba. Their story raises a series of questions. Bathsheba is a complex character like David. Did David have any reason for staying home as commander-in-chief when the army was out at war? There is an irony about the portrait of him on the roof looking down on the city because in a sense that is what a king was supposed to do, with a view to taking action about the wrongdoing that he saw. Why was Bathsheba bathing on the roof? It could seem that she was flaunting herself. Yet the roof was the most private place in the house, the place where you would go to think and pray, and nobody would be able to see you there—except someone in the palace at the highest point in the spur on which Jerusalem sat. The story does seem to portray Bathsheba as David's victim in the story (note how she is the object of many verbs). But when it comes to fixing things in connection with her son succeeding David, note her skill in 1 Kings 1–2.

3 · 21 | FIRST AND SECOND SAMUEL (AND ELSEWHERE)
Who Was David?

The OT includes a series of treatments of David. They reflect his importance as Israel's first king after the unfortunate Saul. David is the person who sets the bar for kingship. In the study suggested in 320, we have looked at the David of 1-2 Samuel. But there is also the following:

1. *The David of Psalms (version 1).* Many psalms are ascribed as being "of David," which of course has led people to assume that he composed them and that they tell us of his relationship with God. So David becomes a model for spirituality, for praise, prayer and thanksgiving. This understanding is hard to fit with the historical David as 1-2 Samuel describes him. We will see when we come to look at Psalms that there is little reason to think that "of David" means that David wrote these psalms. But this edifying and illuminating "David" is prominent in Jewish and Christian thinking.

2. *The David of Psalms (version 2).* Thirteen psalms make links with specific incidents in David's life that are related in 1-2 Samuel. They are characteristically incidents where David is under pressure or in trouble or in need. They suggest the prayers of *David in Distress* (the title of a book by Vivian L. Johnson). This David too is thus edifying and illuminating.

3. *The David of 2 Kings.* Here David sets the standard of a good king (2 Kings 14:3; 22:2). How could the David whom we know from 2 Samuel have done so? The answer may be that the thing that David was good at was loyalty to Yahweh or commitment to Yahweh. For all his weaknesses, he showed that characteristic from the beginning and all through. In this sense, he was "a man after God's heart."

4. *The David of Chronicles.* Here David becomes the patron and benefactor of Israel's worship. Chronicles omits the stories about his private life and his exploits in battle in order to focus on this aspect of his significance,

which is so important for the age for which Chronicles is written.

5. *The David of modern Israel.* In the 1990s the British press reported a storm in Jerusalem over David's good name. A political crisis had arisen over allegations that in a debate in the Israeli parliament, the Knesset, the Israeli foreign minister, Shimon Peres, had slandered King David. This had led to motions of no confidence in the Labour Government, which did not have a majority in the Knesset but was dependent on the support of minority parties in order to get its policies agreed. The party's officials were also anxious that the controversy could have a serious effect on an upcoming general election. It was reported that the chairman of the Labour coalition had called on Mr. Peres to give a public apology for his remarks, given that the matter was "a national issue of great importance to a great many religious Jews," but Mr. Peres had refused, saying that he had not intended to denigrate King David by his remarks about the king's relationship with Bathsheba.

The words that Mr. Peres is said to have used in speaking about the king's action were, "Not everything that King David did on the ground, on the rooftops, is acceptable to a Jew or is something I like." Some members of the Knesset had been infuriated by Mr. Peres's implied criticism of King David for sending Bathsheba's husband to the battlefront with orders that he be placed in a position where he was sure to be killed.

This story along with the exalting of David in Christian thinking illustrates how we love to have heroes—both national heroes and spiritual heroes. And the Bible does not wholly discourage that (see Heb 11 and the comments on 314). Yet it seems to make a point of describing its heroes as the ambiguous characters they are (Abraham, Sarah, Isaac, Jacob, Joseph, Moses, Miriam, Joshua, Saul, David, Solomon, Peter, etc.). It directs our attention away from them to God for our inspiration. In addition, it hints at the fact that while glorious heroes may be an inspiration, the same applies to flawed heroes. They can be an encouragement in a different way, and they may enable us to see things about ourselves.

First and Second Samuel
Again, Who Was David?

Some of this analysis follows Clines, "David the Man."

1. 1 Samuel 16:16-18: He's an able guitarist (in the OT men play guitar, women sing and dance).

2. 1 Samuel 16:18: He's a courageous warrior.

   1 Samuel 17:31-54: He's a killer (his subsequent body count has been estimated at 140,000).

   These aspects of David's character fit the common assumption that toughness is important to understandings of masculinity, an understanding that finds expression in the stress on aggressiveness, fighting and sports in modern Western culture.

3. 1 Samuel 17:36-37: He's committed to Yahweh, and he stays so committed throughout his life.

4. 1 Samuel 16:18: He's handsome. The point is made despite the comment in 1 Samuel 16:7 that Yahweh doesn't look at outward appearances. Yahweh doesn't look merely at outward appearances. But you would expect God to make his chosen leader someone who looks the part. So David is ruddy-cheeked, bright-eyed, handsome (1 Sam 16:12; 17:42). It is the natural expectation that a leader would look the part that explains the significance of the fact that the servant in Isaiah 53 has nothing handsome or attractive about him.

5. 1 Samuel 16:13: He's anointed and gripped by Yahweh's spirit.

   1 Samuel 16:18: Yahweh is with him. The idea of God being with you doesn't merely mean that you have a sense of God's presence, but rather that God is active through you in a distinctive way that does not apply to everyone all the time. So as a result of God being with him, David gets things done. He's thus the designated replacement for Saul, even though he is just the kid brother (1 Sam 17).

6. 1 Samuel 16:18: He's a good speaker. The point is illustrated in 1 Samuel 17:34-37; 26:18-21.

7. 2 Samuel 14:20: He's a man of insight.

8. 2 Samuel 1: Only when Jonathan dies does David get emotional. Otherwise his friendship with Jonathan lacks the warmth that Jonathan shows. David can cope on his own; he is the lone male. Jonathan is his buddy in the sense that together they are two guys who are committed to a cause, and he values this friendship.

9. Compare his (non-)relationships with women. David has eight wives and ten secondary wives, so he has sex with at least this number of women, but did he love any of them? In 2 Samuel 15:16 we read of how he leaves his secondary wives behind; it doesn't take much insight to guess what will happen to them (2 Sam 16:21-23).

10. Compare his (non-)relationships with his family. In 2 Samuel 12:15-23 he grieves, and then he gives up grieving to pull himself together and act as a proper man. Second Samuel 13 speaks of his neglect of Tamar, Amnon and Absalom, and 1 Kings 1–2 of the pathetic nature of his last days.

We noted in 305 that stories in the Former Prophets (and elsewhere in the Bible) portray simple characters and complex characters. David is the great, rounded character portrayal in the story. He is no flat cartoon character, nor a simple model of spirituality, nor a simple cautionary example. He is a rich, complicated person, a man of contradictory qualities, of great strengths and great weaknesses, of absorbing interest. It is no wonder that he has stimulated such varying portrayals.

A particularly enigmatic element in his story is Nathan's statement that Yahweh has forgiven David's sin (2 Sam 12:13). Why, then, is David still punished? But more literally Nathan says, "Yahweh has caused your sin to pass over." It's a strange expression; it doesn't come anywhere else in this connection. God goes on to say, "You will not die," which indicates that the sin being passed over means that Yahweh doesn't exact a death penalty for it. But David does experience other consequences.

3 | 23 | First and Second Kings
Outline, Origin, Aim, Resources

An outline of 1-2 Kings

1 Kings 1–11	Solomon
1 Kings 12–2 Kings 17	The interwoven story of Ephraim and Judah
2 Kings 18–25	The last years of Judah

The origins and aim of 1-2 Kings. Once more we can begin from the hypothesis that as part of the Deuteronomistic History the books went through two or three editions.

1. If we start from the books' coda (2 Kings 25:27-30): the time is during the exile (just after 562 B.C.), when the king in exile has been released by the Babylonians. The end of the books thus offers a hint of hope for the future, based on little evidences that Yahweh is not finished with Israel and, specifically, is not finished with the line of David. The book's challenge then is "Will you hope?"

2. If we start from 2 Kings 24–25 as a whole: it is the time of Judah's downfall, just after 587 B.C. (the same time and situation as Lamentations). The books are an act of praise at the justice of God's judgment (von Rad, *Old Testament Theology*). Hope is based on God's mercy, on which the people casts itself in owning its wrongdoing and hopelessness. The book's challenge then is "Will you own this way of looking at your story and accept responsibility?" "The judgment of 587 did not mean the end of the people of God; nothing but refusal to turn would be the end" (von Rad, *Old Testament Theology*, 1:346).

3. If we start from 2 Kings 22–23: the time is the reign of Josiah, about 620 B.C. The books are a reassurance that taking God's word seriously opens up a future. The hope is based on the possibility that God's promises still stand; this applies specifically to the promise of compassion for those who turn and obey (Deut 30). There is a promise of

forgiveness for those who turn and pray (1 Kings 8:46-53). Its challenge then is "Will you turn and take seriously the word of the Torah and the word of the prophet, and start committing yourselves to obeying it?"

The vision of the community's resources in 1-2 Kings

1. *The words of the prophets.* The fact that these words have been fulfilled (e.g., 2 Kings 20:16-17 in 2 Kings 24:13) makes it possible to listen to them again—for example, Nathan, Isaiah, Huldah and prophets outside Kings such as Jeremiah. The books of Kings portray "a course of history which was shaped and led to a fulfilment by a word of judgement and salvation continually injected into it"; prophets "change the gears of history with a word from God" (von Rad, *Old Testament Theology*, 1:342).

2. *The Torah.* It is "the fundamental test of Israel's obedience and the vehicle of the divine promise" (Ackroyd, *Exile and Restoration*, 75). It provides the principles for understanding success and failure. But the books of Kings don't ignore the way stories such as those of Manasseh and of Josiah don't fit the theory. Manasseh served other gods, but he had a very long reign. Josiah was the great reformer, but he died young. Kings does not veil the fact that these things happen that show how its theology cannot be absolutized.

3. *The promise to David (1 Kings 6:12; 11:12-13, 36; 2 Kings 8:19; 19:34).* The well-being of the people has been tied up with the kings. But kingship is not an absolute: the Deuteronomist "sees the main problem of the history of Israel as lying in the question of the correct correlation of Moses and David" (von Rad, *Old Testament Theology*, 1:339). If you expect to claim the promise to David, you need to make sure you are taking note of the teaching of Moses.

4. *The temple.* One can pray in it or toward it (1 Kings 8). It is the dwelling place of God's name—a way of speaking of God's presence without seeming to talk nonsense, as if God's entire being could be there (Eichrodt, *Theology of the Old Testament*; see 237).

(For a longer introduction to 1-2 Kings, see 363.)

Solomon: Read 1 Kings 1–11.

1. How does Solomon end up on the throne, and what is your comment on that process?

2. What is the positive vision of kingship in the Solomon story?

3. Where does Solomon go right, and where does he go wrong?

4. Psalm 72 is ascribed as being "of Solomon," which need not mean he wrote it. What would be its message to him?

The stories about prophets. Summarize the significance of the prophets and the issues raised by the stories listed below. As you are doing so, note also the accounts of kings in order to study the questions about kings that come next.

Mostly anonymous prophets	Elijah	Elisha
1 Kings 1	1 Kings 18	2 Kings 2
1 Kings 11:26-40	1 Kings 19	2 Kings 3
1 Kings 13–14	1 Kings 20	2 Kings 4
1 Kings 16:1-14	1 Kings 21	2 Kings 5
1 Kings 22	2 Kings 1	2 Kings 6–7
2 Kings 14		2 Kings 8
2 Kings 22		2 Kings 9
		2 Kings 13

The stories about kings

1. As you read through the stories of the kings, decide what counts as (a) wisdom; (b) stupidity; (c) faithfulness to God; (d) unfaithfulness to God.

2. Who are the good guys in the stories, and why? Who are the bad guys, and why?

3. What is most shocking about these stories?

4. What gives the most food for thought?

5. In his book *The Politics of God and the Politics of Man*, Jacques Ellul suggests that the distinctive importance of 2 Kings lies in the way it portrays the interwovenness of divine and human responsibility and sovereignty. How does it portray this interwovenness?

The strange stories of misleading prophets. First Kings 13 is one of those scary stories in Scripture that make one glad not to have been around in scriptural times. If you falsified your pledge, you might die (Acts 5); the stakes were high in the early church, as they were in 1 Kings. First Kings 13 presupposes that it was important for a prophet not to be waylaid into disobeying what he knew God had said to him, Why did the second prophet do as he did? The story doesn't say; it's not relevant to the story. But it might be that he was identified with Bethel, the place that the first prophet was sent to condemn. Why wasn't the second prophet punished? Again, it's not a story about him. But most false prophets don't get punished, as is the case with most other kinds of sinner (in the short term or in that spectacular way).

The starting point of the strange story in 1 Kings 22 is the standard OT awareness that Yahweh is like a president with his corps of aides. It portrays a meeting of this cabinet into which Micaiah as a prophet is admitted so that he can tell people in Israel what is being decided, so that they can act accordingly. In the account of one of the aides being sent to deceive Ahab, I'm not sure whether Yahweh is fooling Ahab or whether Micaiah is fooling Ahab on Yahweh's behalf, but it makes little difference. Like Jesus saying that he tells parables so that people won't understand him (Mk 4:10-12), Yahweh or Micaiah is using any means available to get through Ahab's thick skull. Either Ahab will respond to Micaiah's story by having a change of heart, and the warning will not need to be fulfilled, or he will respond to it by persisting in his plans, and its warning will be fulfilled. The story is designed to give him the chance to make the sensible response.

FIRST AND SECOND KINGS
Prophets and Their God

Prophets are people who speak in the name of a deity on the basis of a claim that their message comes directly from God, not from wisdom that has been passed down or from scriptures or from divination. Both men and women can be prophets. The OT does not see prophecy as distinctive to Israel's relationship with Yahweh; there are prophets who serve Baal (1 Kings 18). We have examples of prophecy from Mari on the Euphrates, from Assyria and from Transjordan. In connection with Numbers 22–24 we have noted that the last of these mention someone called Balaam, who appears as a seer in those chapters (see Nissinen, *Prophets and Prophecy*).

These documents and the OT recognize that there is prophecy that supports the state and prophecy that confronts the state. The prophecies the OT approves are usually critical, whereas the prophecies preserved in those foreign state archives are usually supportive (though perhaps critical prophecies would not have been preserved in state archives). Likewise, there are prophets who work in the context of the sanctuary and get their material support there, so that they are like pastors, and there are prophets who are independent of the sanctuary as they are independent of the state. In the OT, prophets may bring good news or bad news, but if it's good news, they probably are not telling the truth. When King Josiah tells Judahite leaders to go ask a prophet what to do about what they have read in the Torah scroll that has been discovered, it's interesting that they go to a woman prophet called Huldah and not to someone like Jeremiah. Huldah is in some way a temple employee. But she certainly gives them the same straight and tough response they would have got from Jeremiah.

In 1-2 Kings three terms are used to refer to a prophet:

Man of God. Whereas in modern parlance a "man of God" is someone of deep spirituality, the OT expression denotes a somewhat austere and frightening figure with mysterious powers, one who utters words of fearful significance and who is followed by signs that can be destructive as well as constructive. See the stories in 1 Kings 13; 2 Kings 1; and especially the Elisha stories: note 2 Kings 4:9, 16, 21, 22; 5:8, 14, 15; 6:6, 9-10; 7:2; 8:2, 7-8, 11 (see also 1 Kings 17:18; 2 Kings 13:14-19).

The OT knows that God can be mysterious, unpredictable and frightening, as well as consistent, reassuring and encouraging. Compare, for instance, 2 Samuel 6 and 2 Samuel 24 for the frightening, over against 2 Samuel 7 for the encouraging (and in the NT see Acts 5, noted in 324). So "man of God" suggests someone who mediates the presence, words and actions of such a God.

Prophet (nābî'). We don't know the etymological meaning of the word *nābî'*, but it can have various implications. "Prophesying" (acting as a *nābî'*) implies behaving in an extraordinary way (see 1 Sam 10:1-13; 19:18-24). This characteristic suggests a comparison with "man of God." One might compare the behavior of the Baal prophets in 1 Kings 18. Thus such prophesying resembles speaking in tongues; like speaking in tongues, it need not imply "ecstasy" in the sense of losing control of oneself. Likewise, as one can learn to speak in tongues, so one can apparently learn to prophesy. See the stories about the prophetic community in 2 Kings 2; 4; 6; 9.

More than the other words, in 1-2 Kings the word "prophet" suggests someone who speaks words that (allegedly) come from God. They are commonly words that are anything but straightforward (e.g., 1 Kings 13; 22). You have to think about them.

Nathan, the first prophet in 1-2 Kings, is someone who works for the king. Compare 1 Kings 22 and the prophets among other peoples noted above. This characteristic links with the fact that Amos does not want to be treated as a prophet (Amos 7:12-17). It is thus ironic that "prophet" later becomes *the* word to describe such a person.

Seer (hōzeh *and* rō'eh). For the first word, see 2 Kings 17:13. Both words come from verbs that mean "to see." They thus suggest someone who can see things that other people cannot: the present but unseen world (cf. 1 Kings 22:15-23; 2 Kings 2:9-14; 6:15-23) and the visible but still future world (cf. the man of God in 1 Kings 13:1-3). Seers too are often in the service of the king; Gad is "David's seer" (2 Sam 24:11). It is the word that Amaziah applies to Amos (Amos 7:12; see also Mic 3:7), on the assumption that he can be ordered around by another royal employee.

THE PROPHETS AND THE HISTORY OF EPHRAIM AND JUDAH

The numbers given below for individual kings (and the one queen) indicate how many years they reigned, but there is argument about many dates. All the numbers are B.C. and are approximate, and they include the period when a king coreigned with his father or son.

Dates and Foreign Power	Ephraim's Kings	Prophets	Judah's Kings
1050	Saul	Samuel	Saul
1010	David	Gad, Nathan	David
970	Solomon	Ahijah	Solomon
Egypt (Shishak)	Jeroboam (22)	Unnamed men of God	Rehoboam (17) Abijam/Abijah (3)
	Nadab (2)		Asa (41)
Syria	Baasha (12), Elah (2)		
	Zimri (1 week)		
	Omri (12)		
	Ahab (22)	Elijah	Jehoshaphat (25)
	Ahaziah (2)		
	Jehoram/Joram (12)	Elisha	Jehoram/Joram (8)
			Ahaziah (1), Athaliah (7)
	Jehu (28)		Jehoash/Joash (16)
	Jehoahaz (17)	Jonah	
Assyria	Jehoash/Joash	Hosea	
	Jeroboam II (41)	Amos	Amaziah (29)

Dates and Foreign Power	Ephraim's Kings	Prophets	Judah's Kings
744 Tiglath-Pileser III	Zechariah (6 months)		Uzziah/Azariah (52)
	Shallum (1 month)		
	Menahem (10)		
	Pekahiah (2)		
726 Shalmanezer V	Pekah (20)		Jotham (16)
721 Sargon II	Hoshea (9)	Isaiah	Ahaz (16)
704 Sennacherib		Micah	Hezekiah (29)
680 Esarhaddon			Manasseh (55), Amon (2)
668 Ashurbanipal		Zephaniah	Josiah (31)
		Nahum	Jehoahaz/Shallum (3 months)
		Jeremiah	Jehoiakim/Eliakim (11)
Babylon		Habakkuk	Jehoiakin/Coniah/ Jeconiah (3 months)
587		Ezekiel (in Babylon) Obadiah Isaiah 40–55	Zedekiah/Mattaniah (11)
Persia		Haggai	(Sheshbazzar)
539		Zechariah	(Zerubbabel)
		Isaiah 56–66	
		Malachi, Joel	(Ezra, Nehemiah)
		Jonah (book)	
		Zechariah 9–14	
Greece 336			

First and Second Kings
The Books' Message

1. The books cover the last three hundred years of the story begun in Genesis, leading down to the fall of Jerusalem in 587 B.C., when Israel's history might seem to have led to a dead end (but they add the release of Jehoiakin in 562 B.C.). They thus provide an answer to the question "What went wrong?" The books illustrate lessons that the people of God continue to need to learn if our story is not to go the same way, or they explain why our story has gone the same way if we fail to learn these lessons.

2. The narrative deals with the history reign by reign; 2 Kings 21:19-26 illustrates the pattern. Usually it consists in opening and closing summaries forming a framework that incorporates detailed material about the reign (e.g., 2 Kings 18–20). In 1 Kings 13–2 Kings 17 the narrative interweaves the story of Ephraim and Judah, dating their various kings by each other, but after Ephraim's disappearance, it has to deal only with Judah.

3. That substantial middle part concentrates on Ephraim, where the major issue is whether it is prepared to make Yahweh its God or whether it is going to continue to rely on other divinities, the Baals. Behind this question is a further one: "Who really is God anyway?" Is Yahweh all-powerful? Many of the stories show how Yahweh proves to be all-powerful, but how the people are not inclined to take the point. In 2 Kings 17 the narrative closes off Ephraim's story and identifies clearly the thread that the narrative sees running through Ephraim's whole history.

4. This middle section gives great prominence to Elijah and Elisha as the representatives of Yahweh. They are almost Yahweh's embodiments, exercising Yahweh's power, executing Yahweh's judgment, manifesting Yahweh's insight and revealing Yahweh's plans. Thus people's attitude toward them *is* their attitude toward God.

5. In 2 Kings 18–25 are covered the last 150 years of Judah's life up to the fall of Jerusalem. Failing to worship Yahweh was also sometimes an issue here, especially and fatally in the reign of Manasseh. But worshiping Yahweh in the wrong way is more commonly the problem. The issue that emerges here is the need of a right relationship between king, temple and Torah (we might see an equivalent as leadership, worship and Scripture). The wrong relationship (king running temple in a way that ignores Torah) brings disaster to the whole people of God.

6. Throughout the books a center of concern is God's involvement in the people's political affairs. We have noted that this theme is the focus of Jacques Ellul's treatment of 2 Kings in *The Politics of God and the Politics of Man*. He suggests that the book makes a twofold distinctive contribution to the Scriptures. First, it pictures God's involvement in political life and thus warns both against undervaluing the importance of politics and against absolutizing this realm (since it shows how God brings judgment on politics). Second, it displays the interplay of the free determination of human beings (who in various political situations make their decisions and put their policies into effect) and the free decision of God (who gets things done through or despite these deliberate human acts). Examples are provided in 2 Kings 6–10; 18–19, though King Jehu's story needs also to be seen in the context of Hosea's later condemnation of his bloodbath (Hos 1:4). The books of Kings thus show God getting things done in history, and we may use the marks of God's footsteps here to see what God may be doing in our day. At the same time, the books challenge us as to whether we are willing to live by the conviction that Yahweh is actually Lord.

7. Although the books of Kings are gloomy ones because of the story they have to tell, they offer glimmers of hope for the people of God under judgment. God made a commitment to the ancestors (2 Kings 13:23) and to David (2 Kings 8:19; 19:34), and surely judgment will not be God's last word to the people. But we can pray along those lines only if we acknowledge that judgment was appropriate and commit ourselves to getting our attitudes to politics and worship right, in accordance with the lordship of Yahweh and the teaching of Scripture.

Canaanite Theology and Canaanite Religion

Who were the Baals that they so attracted Israel? We know most about them from discoveries at Ugarit, north of Beirut. These discoveries thus come from north of Canaan proper, and from the second millennium B.C., but they are consistent with information about Canaanite theology and Canaanite religion from Israel's own time and area, so they are assumed to be able to fill out that picture.

Canaanite theology. Like most peoples, the Canaanites assumed the existence of a number of gods. The head of the pantheon is El, the king of the gods, who presides over the divine cabinet. He is thus bull-like and powerful, yet also a gentle and merciful figure, the creator of humanity, and as such he is its father. He is called "father of years"; that is, he is a revered, bearded, senior figure. Melchizedek in Genesis 14 is a priest of "El Elyon" ("God on High"), who thus seems to be Melchizedek's version of El, and as the senior god, with this profile, he was sufficiently like Yahweh for Abraham to risk seeing Melchizedek as worshiping the same god that he worshiped. El's consort is Athirat, the creator/mother of the gods. Between them, El and Athirat are thus the father and mother of the younger gods.

In 1 Samuel 5–6, however, the name of the key foreign god is Dagon or Dagan, who is also referred to in other Middle Eastern sources. His name is elsewhere a word for "grain," which suggests that he was trusted as the god who made sure that crops grew. It looks as if Dagan is thus an equivalent to El among other peoples.

Baal is often described as a son of Dagan. "Baal" is an ordinary Hebrew word for "master," equivalent to a word for "lord," and Hebrew uses "baals" as a generic term to refer to gods. The use of the plural may reflect the assumption that the one Baal appeared in different places (the "high places"). In the Ugaritic stories Baal gets drawn into a fight with El's son Yam ("Sea"). He wins this fight and is thus declared king of the gods. He is challenged by Mot ("Death"), submits to him and thus dies, but then he comes back to life and resumes his kingly position. Baal is thus the great warrior and victor among the gods. So El seems to be the presidential figure among the gods, whereas Baal is the god who undertakes most of the action.

In the Canaanite texts, Baal has a warlike sister, Anat, but in the OT her place is taken by a goddess or goddesses variously entitled "Asherah" or "Ashtoret/Astarte" or the "Queen of Heaven," who may variously be the consort of El or of Baal. Both the OT and archaeological discoveries suggest that Israelites sometimes assumed that Yahweh also had a consort, but of course the OT never countenances this belief.

Canaanite religion. The Canaanites worshiped in sanctuaries of which there might be several in any one city, corresponding to there being a number of deities. A sanctuary comprised a walled area, a stepped stone altar in the courtyard where sacrifices of different types were offered, and a two part building consisting of an outer room and an inner one where the god's image was placed. The temple in Jerusalem thus followed the same pattern, except that it was strangely empty in the sense that it contained no image, only the covenant chest over which the invisible Yahweh sat enthroned.

Canaanite religion put an emphasis on divination, the seeking of guidance by examining organs from sacrificial animals and fetuses. Such divination could thus be associated with offering sacrifices, but it could also be sought by other means. Middle Eastern peoples kept records of events that seem to link with things that they found when they performed such examinations, to aid the process of divination. They also had ways of keeping in touch with dead family members, who could be buried near a family's home, by making offerings and by seeking their guidance and help. The OT links such offerings with human sacrifice, which would be the most costly offering a family could make in seeking guidance and help in a crisis. For Israel, seeking guidance from the Torah, interpreted by priests and Levites and from prophets, was to take the place of using the techniques of divination, but the latter were often a temptation.

The faith of the Canaanites has been described as a fertility religion involving sacred prostitution, but nothing in their texts refers to such things, and the theory may issue from overly literal interpretation of OT passages that see Israel as being unfaithful to Yahweh and as having "affairs" with Canaanite gods.

Whereas the books from Genesis through Kings lead straight into one another, when we turn over the page at the end of 2 Kings (whether in the Hebrew or the Greek/English order), it becomes clear that we are coming to something new. In the Greek/English order Chronicles comes next, and it takes us back to Adam. In the Hebrew order there come the Latter Prophets, the collection of books that focuses on preserving messages from God to Israel rather than on stories about God and Israel. The books appear as four scrolls: one each for Isaiah, for Jeremiah, for Ezekiel and for the Twelve Shorter Prophets (Lamentations and Daniel come in the Writings).

The first three come in approximate chronological order: Isaiah himself lived in the 700s, Jeremiah began his work at the end of the 600s, Ezekiel in the 500s. The books of the Twelve Shorter Prophets then come in their own approximate historical order. Hosea, Amos, Jonah and Micah lived in the 700s, Nahum, Habakkuk and Zephaniah in the 600s, Haggai and Zechariah in the 500s, Malachi in the 400s (Obadiah and Joel seem to be exceptions to the rule about historical order, for reasons we will consider when we come to them). We will study the Latter Prophets in groups, approximately in accordance with the century to which they belonged.

When we start reading them, we soon sense that, contrary to what we might expect, most of these prophetic scrolls weren't written as books with a logical order. They jump about from one subject to another in a way that can be confusing. The reason is that prophets were not writers but preachers, and their books are collections of their sermon notes.

Occasionally we discover something about how they went about their ministry. The book of Isaiah gives us some vignettes (see Is 7:1-17; 20:1-6; 36:1–39:8); we get a fuller picture in stories in the book of Jeremiah. These stories make it possible to picture prophets going up to the temple courtyard where people gathered to bring sacrifices and maybe just to hang about, as they do in stories in the Gospels and in Jerusalem today. The prophets would then deliver their prophecies to people whom they found there. Reading a book such as Isaiah or Jeremiah, it becomes clear that the actual prophecies comprise units of a few verses; each will have been a prophetic message delivered on some such occasion in the temple precincts. The prophet or someone else will then subsequently have written down the prophecies and perhaps put them into an order of sorts, in the way described in Isaiah 8 and Jeremiah 36. But it is a mistake to have too high expectations about logical links from one prophecy to another.

A series of problems lie at the background of the ministry of most of the prophets.

1. The first prophets who had books named after them were working at the time when the first big Middle Eastern empire, Assyria, started taking an interest in Judah, and even more in Ephraim, which was more powerful and sat on trade routes in which Assyria was interested. So one question that the prophets deal with is how to handle relations with the big power and with neighboring peoples. Assyria invaded both Ephraim and Judah and caused devastation. Later, the power of Babylon and that of Persia are key factors in the contexts that the prophets address.

2. The traditional religion of the country ("Canaanite religion") continued to attract people, especially in Ephraim. That temptation continued in Judah into the Babylonian and Persian periods. We have noted that it was a down-to-earth, everyday faith that gave people ways of doing something about everyday questions that concerned them such as encouraging the crops to grow and the animals to breed, being able to have a baby, staying in contact with your relatives who had passed and discovering things about the future.

3. Economic and political developments in the two nations, and an increase in urbanization, had generated a situation in which some people were able to acquire increasing amounts of land. Instead of each extended family having its own land, many families became dependent on a smaller number of landowners and on the landowners' mercy when life was tough. People such as widows and orphans were especially vulnerable.

4. In the cities people in power made use of dishonest methods and manipulation of the legal system to add to their wealth, and they were thus able to live even more self-indulgent lives.

The Scroll with a Message from Israel's Holy One

As a book, Isaiah speaks to many different periods and takes up many different themes, but a feature running through it is its frequent description of Yahweh as "Israel's Holy One." That title for God comes only about thirty times in the Bible; twenty-five are in Isaiah (one of them reappears in 2 Kings 19:22), spread throughout the whole book. Isaiah is the book of the Holy One of Israel. Three of the other five occurrences of the title are in Psalms 71:22; 78:41; 89:18 (the remaining two are in Jer 50:29; 51:5), and it may have its origin in the worship of the temple, but it was the description that naturally came to the prophet Isaiah's lips. It looks as if the background lies in the vision that gave Isaiah his commission, when the seraphs proclaimed, "Holy, holy, holy is Yahweh Armies" (the more literal translation of the title "LORD of Hosts," the phrase that usually appears in the English Bible). So Isaiah's vision of the Holy One lies behind the book as a whole:

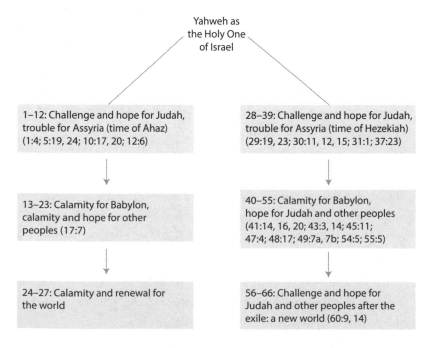

Yahweh as
the Holy One
of Israel

1–12: Challenge and hope for Judah, trouble for Assyria (time of Ahaz) (1:4; 5:19, 24; 10:17, 20; 12:6)

28–39: Challenge and hope for Judah, trouble for Assyria (time of Hezekiah) (29:19, 23; 30:11, 12, 15; 31:1; 37:23)

13–23: Calamity for Babylon, calamity and hope for other peoples (17:7)

40–55: Calamity for Babylon, hope for Judah and other peoples (41:14, 16, 20; 43:3, 14; 45:11; 47:4; 48:17; 49:7a, 7b; 54:5; 55:5)

24–27: Calamity and renewal for the world

56–66: Challenge and hope for Judah and other peoples after the exile: a new world (60:9, 14)

The Isaiah scroll can be seen as comprising two parts, in several ways (see 358). The one implied above starts from the parallel between Isaiah 1–12 and Isaiah 28–39. Both sections issue challenges to Judah about its life but also make promises about Yahweh's fulfilling his purpose, and promise that the Assyrian superpower will be put down. The difference between them is that the concrete historical references in Isaiah 1–12 relate to the time of Ahaz, while those in Isaiah 28–39 relate to the time of his son Hezekiah. In both sections the fact that Yahweh is Israel's Holy One is a key factor underlying the challenges and the warnings, and also the encouragements. Yahweh Armies is exalted in exercising authority and the holy God shows himself holy in doing the right thing; the trouble is that people scorn the Holy One (Is 5:16-19). But people will rejoice that "great in our midst is Israel's Holy One" (Is 12:6).

Both sections lead into chapters that promise the downfall of the subsequent superpower, Babylon, which means hope for Judah and for other peoples. In Isaiah 40–55 there appear the densest concentration of references to Israel's Holy One. Here the phrase's emphasis lies on its positive relational aspect: Yahweh is *Israel's* Holy One, and he will therefore act as Judah's restorer, deliverer, king and creator. The Holy One will transform things for the needy community. He will surrender his claim on other people if he can have Israel. He will take his people to their destiny (Is 41:14, 20; 43:3, 14; 48:17).

This focus on Babylon is followed by further sections that broaden out the reference, with no further allusions to figures in Judah or to specific superpowers. Isaiah 24–27 issues warnings and promises about the destiny of the world as a whole. Isaiah 56–66 envisions the glorious fulfillment of the Holy One's purpose for Jerusalem, with the nations of the world also benefiting from that action. The Holy One will transform Jerusalem and the nations will see it and acknowledge him (Is 60:9).

ISAIAH 1–12
Why It Comes in the Order It Does

We have noted that a prophet such as Isaiah proclaimed his messages in short units that are then secondarily written down and assembled in a scroll. This process explains why the book doesn't unfold like the chapters of a modern book. Yet the nature of the process doesn't mean that the arrangement of the book is random.

Isaiah's vision of the Holy One makes a good starting point for understanding the collection of prophecies in Isaiah 1–12 as a whole. This vision opens an account of Isaiah's ministry in the time of Ahaz, describing its origin (Is 6), its outworking (Is 7:1–8:10), and the consequences for prophet and people (Is 8:11–9:7). The sequence declares that Israel's Holy One must act to punish Israel's turning away but must also keep the undertaking to stand by Israel and never abandon it. Isaiah challenges Ahaz to make Yahweh his security, but he will not do so. Isaiah himself is called to wait until his word is fulfilled, even if he is convinced that it must mean punishment, because he is also convinced that on the other side of calamity there will be restoration.

This account of Isaiah's ministry is set in the context of shouts and warnings about Yahweh's anger:

> 5:8-24 Isaiah's shout ("Hey!") to Jerusalem
>
> 5:25-30 God's anger is still not satisfied
>
> 6:1-13 Isaiah's commission
>
> 7:1–8:10 How it works out
>
> 8:11–9:7 The consequences for Isaiah and for Israel
>
> 9:8-21 God's anger is still not satisfied
>
> 10:1-4 Isaiah's shout ("Hey!") to Jerusalem

We would have expected Isaiah's account of his commission to come at the beginning of the book (like the accounts by Jeremiah and Ezekiel), but the arrangement of the book puts some examples of his prophecies on either side of this account. So the effect is first of all to tell us something of what he said, and thus perhaps to raise the question of what authority he had to say it and how he delivered his message, which this account answers. These prophecies on either side of the story about Isaiah form matching pairs relating Isaiah's shout and describing Yahweh's anger.

In turn, the tension between judgment and comfort in Isaiah 6:1–9:7 also appears in the opening and closing chapters of Isaiah 1–12. In the opening part (Is 1:1–5:7) Isaiah paints long descriptions of Israel, Judah and especially Jerusalem, and of the disaster that must come, but he alternates these with lyrical pictures of how things will be when Jerusalem is restored. If the more somber picture dominates the opening part, the closing part (Is 10:5–12:6) becomes increasingly encouraging. After the last "Hey!" to Jerusalem, Isaiah shouts "Hey!" to Assyria, the one who is the means of Jerusalem's punishment, but who deserves his own comeuppance. More pictures of Yahweh's restoration of Israel follow this "Hey!" It closes with a song to sing in the day Yahweh fulfills these promises. So Isaiah 1–12 as a whole unfolds as follows:

1:2-31: Jerusalem as it is, and its punishment

  2:1-5 Jerusalem as it will be

2:6–4:1 Jerusalem as it is, and its punishment

  4:2-7 Jerusalem as it will be

5:1-7 Jerusalem as it is, and its punishment

    5:8-24 Isaiah's "Hey!" to Jerusalem

      5:25-30 God's anger is still not satisfied

        6:1-13 Isaiah's commission

        7:1–8:10 How it works out

        8:11–9:7 The consequences for Isaiah and for Israel

      9:8-21 God's anger is still not satisfied

    10:1-4 Isaiah's "Hey!" to Jerusalem

10:5-19 Isaiah's "Hey!" to Assyria

10:20–11:16 Israel as it will be

12:1-6 A song to sing on that day

In light of 330-31, read Isaiah 1–12.

1. What is Yahweh's vision for Jerusalem, Judah and Israel, and for their kings?

2. What should be the characteristics of their life?

3. What is the present reality of their life?

4. What does Yahweh intend to do about it, and how: (a) negatively, (b) positively?

5. What kind of person is Yahweh?

6. What is involved in being a prophet?

7. What other subjects appear in the chapters that are not covered by the questions above?

8. What do you think is the most important thing you have read in these chapters, and why?

9. Read through Matthew 1:18–4:16, noting the seven prophecies that are referred to. Look up at least the Isaiah ones in their OT context, work out what they mean there, and comment on what Matthew does with them.

   a. Matthew 1:23 (Is 7:14)

   b. Matthew 2:6 (Mic 5:2)

   c. Matthew 2:15 (Hos 11:1)

   d. Matthew 2:18 (Jer 31:15)

   e. Matthew 2:23 (Possibly Is 11:1; the link would lie in the fact that "branch" in Hebrew is *neṣer*, so that the Nazarene Jesus is the "branch-man"; but another possible link is that the verse refers to Judg 13:5, utilizing the similarity of "Nazarene" and "Nazirite.")

f. Matthew 3:3 (Is 40:3)

g. Matthew 4:15-16 (Is 9:1-2).

What are your reflections on this study? (For my comments, see 363.)

How Isaiah's prophecies interrelated with political events in his day

We have noted that the political background to Isaiah's prophecy is Assyria's interest in Ephraim and Judah because of their strategic position. Ephraim is more vulnerable.

1. In 736–733 Ahaz's policy was to accept Assyrian authority and resist pressure from Ephraim and Syria to join in rebellion against Assyria. Isaiah 7 relates to that situation. Isaiah affirms Ahaz's policy not to join with Ephraim and Syria, but he fears that Ahaz will seek a defensive alliance with Assyria to get help in resisting pressure from Ephraim and Syria. The Assyrians did invade Ephraim and Syria in 733 and 732.

2. In 722 Ephraim rebelled again, Assyria again invaded, and ended Ephraim's formally independent status. See Isaiah 28.

3. In 713 the Philistine city of Ashdod rebelled against Assyrian authority and was invaded. See Isaiah 20. Judah, fortunately, did not join in.

4. In 705, allying with Egypt, Judah did rebel against Assyrian authority, and in 701 Assyria invaded and all but destroyed Judah. See Isaiah 36–37 and Sennacherib's account noted in 337.

5. Isaiah 10:24-27 says that Assyria's destruction is imminent (cf. Is 29:5-8; 30:27-33; 31:5, 8-9); it wasn't. Did the Judahites keep Isaiah's prophecies, assuming that Yahweh had had a change of mind and would fulfill them one day? Another possibility is that such passages reflect later preacher-prophets expounding Isaiah's message nearly a century later, when Assyria's downfall was indeed imminent; the Babylonians and Medes destroyed the Assyrian capital, Nineveh, in 612. Ronald Clements's commentary on Isaiah 1–39 argues for this idea, following the work of Hermann Barth. Scholars who accept this view commonly also see other passages in Isaiah 29–31 as evidencing the same process of preaching on Isaiah's texts in the exile and afterward. The Holy Spirit who inspired Isaiah thus also inspires the people who re-preach his messages.

3 | 33 | Isaiah 13–27
Yahweh's Intentions for the Nations

Isaiah 13 marks a new start in the Isaiah scroll. The attracting of the nations and the fate of Assyria were referred to in Isaiah 2:2-5; 10:5-19, but the nations' destiny now comes into focus.

Isaiah 13–23: Yahweh's intentions regarding individual nations. First, Isaiah 13–23 speaks of the fate of a series of individual nations or imperial powers, with a comment at the center on the destiny of all superpowers that arise:

Babylon (13:1–14:23; 21:1-10)		Cush (18:1-7; 20:1-6)
Assyria (14:24-27; 19:23-25)		Egypt (19:1-25; 20:1-6)
Philistia (14:28-32)		Edom (21:11-12)
	The nations (17:12-14)	
Moab (15:1–16:14)		Arabia (21:13-17)
Damascus (17:1-11)		Jerusalem (22:1-25)
		Tyre (23:1-17)

The prophecies are introduced by the word *maśśā'*. A *maśśā'* can be, among other things, an imaginative picture, a lament or a poem—in other words, any kind of composition. It's the same as a word for "burden," and Jeremiah takes advantage of that fact (see Jer 23:33-38). The TNIV translates it as "prophecy *against* Babylon" (etc.), and these prophecies do speak of calamity for the nations. But they also incorporate good news for them, including the promise of a time when Egypt, Assyria and Israel can worship together as the people of God (Is 19:23-25), and the translation "against" is too specific. They are simply "the Babylon Prophecy" and so forth.

The prophets give little indication that they delivered these messages to the nations themselves. Like the rest of their messages, they are meant for Judah to hear. They are part of a ministry to the people of God, though they would also be effective in implementing God's will for these nations, as they were the word of Yahweh by which Yahweh's purpose was put into effect.

They are not particularly about nations that are simply Judah's enemies. While most are about nations that might be Judah's allies or might be threats, or might be both, at different times, some are about nations that are irrelevant to Judah. The prophecies are designed to get Judah to take the right attitude toward other nations.

It is often easy to see why specific nations appear. There are the big powers standing on either side of Judah that often seemed to determine its destiny (Babylon's coming first reflects its later position as a superpower). Others are the neighbors that might be a more local threat or temptation. Why does Jerusalem itself feature? Perhaps its appearance hints that Judah is just one among the nations and is no better than any of them, so that any talk of their being put down also implies that Judah will be put down. There is no room for Judah to presume on being the people of God and thinking that it will escape.

So there might be a series of reasons why prophets speak of the fate of other peoples:

1. Declaring Yahweh's words of blessing and trouble puts Yahweh's will into effect.

2. The destiny of other peoples is relevant to God's people.

3. Knowing God's intentions gives people chance to align their will with Yahweh's.

4. Giving the reasons for the judgment (mainly the nations' power and majesty) is instructive for God's people regarding their own destiny.

5. Talking about the nations helps God's people raise their eyes and see that God has a big purpose in the world.

6. It encourages God's people not to be overawed by other peoples or afraid of them.

7. It encourages God's people not to set out to emulate them.

8. It encourages God's people not to rely on other powers.

9. The notes of hope for the nations encourage God's people not to take too negative an attitude toward other nations.

*I*saiah 24–27: Yahweh's intentions for the world. With Isaiah 24–27 the canvas broadens still further to picture the destiny of the world as a whole. It can be seen as a series of visions of the whole world's judgment and renewal, which alternate with a sequence of songs of praise to sing "in that day."

world devastation	24:1-13	response	24:14-16
cosmic devastation	24:17-23	response	25:1-5
world renewal and judgment	25:6-12	response	26:1-18
world renewal and judgment	26:19–27:13		

The words "eschatological" and "apocalyptic" are often applied to Isaiah 24–27. These words can be used with a number of meanings. We could call the chapters "eschatological" in the sense that they refer to the final and ultimate future fulfillment of God's purpose for the world, involving a dramatic transformation brought about by God and not by any human initiative or involving any human contribution. They don't imply an end after which there will be nothing or after which there will be life in heaven rather than life on earth. Rather, God's original creation purpose will be fulfilled, and the world will be able to enjoy a full human life. The chapters don't imply that the final fulfillment will come only in the distant future, neither that it is imminent, nor that it becomes actual and real in the now. Indeed, they speak especially to a context where it is impossible to see God at work in fulfilling his purpose. They thus contrast with Isaiah 13 and Isaiah 14, which speak of the Day of the Lord happening now and of the downfall of the power of evil now. They continue to give people a prospect to look forward to, which Jesus' coming makes more certain.

The word "apocalyptic" can underline the radical, decisive and dramatic nature of God's action and the way human action makes no contribution to the achievement of God's purpose, and also the vivid imagery and symbolism in the prophecy, which makes it impossible to picture the literal reality.

Reading Isaiah 13–27

1. What does Isaiah 13–23 tell us about Yahweh's relationship with the superpowers Assyria and Babylon?

   a. What is the reason for Yahweh's interest in them?

   b. What is the bad news for them, and why?

   c. What is the good news for them, and why?

2. What does Isaiah 13–23 tell us about Yahweh's relationship with the other peoples mentioned in those chapters, smaller powers that were Judah's neighbors and/or potential allies?

   a. What is the reason for Yahweh's interest in them?

   b. What is the bad news for them, and why?

   c. What is the good news for them, and why?

3. What does Isaiah 24–27 tell us about Yahweh's relationship with the world as a whole?

   a. What is the reason for Yahweh's interest in it?

   b. What is the bad news for it, and why?

   c. What is the good news for it, and why?

4. What is the significance of Isaiah 13–27 for Christian faith? How might they apply to our nations? What is the church supposed to learn from them?

Isaiah 13 speaks of Yahweh's Day being near: when Yahweh's judgment happens, it will be Yahweh's Day arriving. Thus when that judgment has happened, it can be spoken of as Yahweh's Day having arrived (see, e.g., Lam 1:12; 2:1). Yahweh's Day is when God's ultimate purpose is fulfilled, and interim fulfillments of that purpose count as embodiments of Yahweh's Day.

Isaiah 14:12-15 has been taken as an account of the fall of Satan, but the context suggests that it pictures the coming fall of the king of Babylon. Ironically, it uses a Canaanite and Babylonian myth about the fall of a god who tried to make himself top god, but uses it to portray the king's fall. Maybe the reason for seeing Satan here is that Christians were keen for an answer to the question of Satan's fall.

See 363 on Yahweh's Day, on Isaiah 14 and on the picture of the earth laid waste in Isaiah 24.

W e return to the kind of material that occupied Isaiah 1–12, prophecies and stories directly concerning Judah and Jerusalem. The difference is that the concrete historical references in these chapters relate to a later period, the reign of Hezekiah (725-697 B.C.), though the basic issues in Judah's life have not changed. The central question is how they can live with the political pressures that assail them. Will they live by trust in the promises of God regarding king and city, treating these promises as the key to their security and freedom, or will they will insist on seeking freedom and security in alliances with stronger nations? Thus only the external politics are different. As Isaiah had warned would happen, Assyria is now oppressive overlord, not savior. In Isaiah 28–33 the references to Egypt as potential savior tell us that the period is now that of Hezekiah. The king himself is not named until we come to the stories in Isaiah 36–39. Most of these prophecies come from 711–700 B.C.

Isaiah 28, 29, 30, 31 and 33 begin with the exclamation "Hey!" (various translations have "Oh," "Ah," "Alas," "Woe"). It introduces a series of shouts to the people of God (all of similar length) and eventually to their would-be destroyer:

Hey, drunken leaders	28:1-29
Hey, city of David	29:1-24
Hey, obstinate nation	30:1-33
Hey, people who rely on Egypt	31:1–32:20
Hey, would-be destroyer	33:1-24

Following on these "Heys," threat dominates at the beginning, but reassurance becomes more and more prominent:

28:1-22	threat	28:23-29	reassurance
29:1-16	threat	29:17-24	reassurance
30:1-17	threat	30:18-33	reassurance

31:1-6	threat	31:7–32:20	reassurance
33:1-24	reassurance from the beginning		

Isaiah 33 also closes off Isaiah 1–33 as a whole. Its sequence of thought is jumpy as a result of the fact that it picks up many phrases from earlier chapters and strings them together.

In Isaiah 34–39 the "Hey" openings are first followed by two promises of reversal:

34:1-17	punishment for the nations
35:1-10	joy for the redeemed

They are then followed by two stories about Hezekiah:

36:1–37:38	Hezekiah and Assyria: his scornful challenge from Sennacherib, his prayer, Isaiah's prophecy, Sennacherib's downfall.
38:1–39:8	Hezekiah and Babylon: his illness and healing; his reception of envoys from Babylon and Isaiah's prophecy issuing from that event. Whereas the stories thus record the fulfillment of the prophecies in Isaiah 36–38 in Hezekiah's lifetime, they do not record the fulfillment of the prophecy in Isaiah 39, but the significance of this prophecy lies in the fact that its fulfillment provides background to Isaiah 40–55. It thus neatly closes off Isaiah 1–39.

God's planning is an important theme in Isaiah. It is wonderful (Is 28:29). Isaiah isn't referring to world history as a whole being an outworking of God's plan, though he would certainly assume that God has a purpose or goal that he intends to fulfill. He is more interested in the way God makes plans and executes them in connection with particular events, and he contrasts God's plans with human planning and policy making, which will never be effective if it leaves God out (e.g., Is 29:15; 30:1). Ironically, Sennacherib (Is 36:5) is right. See also Isaiah 5:19; 8:10; 9:2; 11:2; 14:26; 19:3, 11, 17; 23:8-9.

The theme of planning is related to the theme of wisdom. Judah's leaders are concerned to conduct the nation's political affairs in a smart way, but they are indeed leaving God out in formulating their political policies, which means their smartness is not smart at all (Is 5:21; 19:11-12; 29:14; 31:1-2).

Much prophecy comes in the form of poetry, so we need to understand how its poetry works if we are to understand it fully. There are classic books on Hebrew poetry by Robert Lowth (*Sacred Poetry of the Hebrews*), James Kugel (*Idea of Biblical Poetry*) and Robert Alter (*Art of Biblical Poetry*), and there is an introduction by David Petersen and Kent Richards (*Interpreting Hebrew Poetry*).

One line is commonly the unit of thought (though English verse divisions obscure this point). The poems may divide into strophes (paragraphs), but they don't have a set number of lines.

Lines generally divide into two parts that complement each other: the second part may complete or restate or intensify or contrast with or clarify the first. The name for this feature is "parallelism," but it's a misleading term, as the second half doesn't just repeat the first. A half-line is a colon, and a regular two-part line is a bicolon (there can also be three-part lines, tricola).

Lines tend to have a regular number of words, though little words may not count, and the lines are also shorter than they look in translations because Hebrew commonly combines words that come separately in English.

Here is the beginning of Isaiah 31, which is mostly expressed in the common 3-3 rhythm (for another example with the Hebrew, from Isaiah 1, see 363). I have placed a // symbol between the expressions in the Hebrew to show how the rhythm works (e.g., "you who go down" is one word in Hebrew).

¹Hey,//you who go down//to Egypt	for help,//who rely//on horses,
And trust//in chariots//because they're many	in cavalry//because they're strong,//very strong.
But haven't turned//to the holy one of//Israel	and haven't//sought//Yahweh!
²He's wise too//and has brought//disaster	his words//he hasn't//cancelled.
He'll arise//against the household of//wrongdoers	against the help of//the doers of//iniquity.
³The Egyptians//are human//not God,	their horses//are flesh//not spirit.
When Yahweh//stretches out//his hand,	helper//will trip up.
Helped one//will fall,	and all of them//will perish//together.

The rhythm is thus vital to the way the poetry works, but there can be variety about how many words come in each half-line. So Hebrew poetry works like rap; prophets were rap artists. They could use varying numbers of words as long as they keep the rhythm going.

While the use of parallelism may suggest intentional composition, it may suggest something more like the way the blues and rap work; it gives the prophet thinking time.

Why does a prophet speak in poetry?

1. Poetry is denser than prose; it uses fewer words and it omits the little words. It can also vary the word order from the order in prose (e.g., a b c c' b' a'), and some words in one colon may also apply in the other (e.g., "trust" in the second line, "arise" in the fourth). It's thus harder to grasp. People have to do more work and get involved in order to understand it. While prose is useful because it's clear, poetry is useful because it puts more challenge before people.

2. Poetry uses imagery. Images tell you what ideas feel like. But they also extend your knowledge. They make it possible to see and say new things.

3. Poetry uses ambiguity. It teases people. The next two verses in Isaiah 31 (Is 31:4-5) are an example. They describe Yahweh as a lion growling over its prey, not scared by the shepherds who are trying to rescue their sheep. They then describe Yahweh coming down on Jerusalem, and hovering like a hawk over the city. So are the people Yahweh's victim? But then Isaiah interprets the two images positively. Yahweh the lion/hawk will make sure that no one else (such as the Assyrians) can capture his "prey." He will protect it and "pass over it" as at the exodus.

Another aspect of Isaiah's technique as he seeks to get through to people is the way he puts outrageous statements on their lips: see, for example, Isaiah 28:14-15; 30:10-11. They didn't literally say these things, but they need to face up to the fact that these are the implications of their attitudes.

Isaiah 30 begins with a different example. It describes the people as treating Egypt as their protection, help, shadow and refuge. But those are words that belong to God; see Psalm 91. It is a scandalous accusation to say that they are viewing Egypt that way.

Reading Isaiah 28–39; and
How to Think About the Nations

Reading Isaiah 28–39

Read Isaiah 28–33.

1. What is the threat in each section, and what is the reason for it?

2. What does it tell you about Israel? Are there analogies in your church's life?

3. What is the reassurance in each section?

4. What does it tell you about God? Does it have good news for your church?

Read Isaiah 34–39.

1. What is the effect of using poetry again for Isaiah 34–35, 37 and 38?

2. What should the portrait of judgment in Isaiah 34 do to us?

3. What should the portrait of restoration in Isaiah 35 do to us?

4. What is the Assyrian's argument in Isaiah 36:1-20? Is he right?

5. What is the reaction of the Judahites in Isaiah 36:21–37:7? Are they right?

6. What are the dynamics of Hezekiah's prayer in Isaiah 37:7-20?

7. What is the logic of Yahweh's response in Isaiah 37:21-38?

8. What is the logic of the way Hezekiah behaves in Isaiah 38?

9. What is the logic of the way Hezekiah behaves in Isaiah 39?

10. Does Hezekiah finally come across as a good guy or a bad guy?

The Assyrian king Sennacherib included in his own records his account of the events of which Isaiah 36–37 gives us a Judahite version (see Pritchard, *Ancient Near Eastern Texts*, 287-88):

> As for the king of Judah, Hezekiah, who had not submitted to my authority, I
> besieged and captured forty-six of his fortified cities, along with many smaller
> towns, taken in battle with my battering rams. . . . I took as plunder 150 people,

both small and great, male and female, along with a great number of animals including horses, mules, donkeys, camels, oxen, and sheep. As for Hezekiah, I shut him up like a caged bird in his royal city of Jerusalem. I then constructed a series of fortresses around him, and I did not allow anyone to come out of the city gates. His towns which I captured I gave to the kings of Ashdod, Ekron, and Gaza.

Sennacherib thus emphasizes the extent of his achievement and makes no mention of any reversal (we have no record outside the Bible of the events related in Is 37:36-38). Hezekiah includes reference to the disaster that overcame Judahite cities such as Lachish, but he emphasizes the extraordinary nature of Jerusalem's deliverance, which built up Judahite trust in Yahweh's commitment to the city.

What Isaiah 1–39 implies about how to think about the nations

1. The great power is Assyria. Modern equivalents might presumably be Great Britain and the United States. The great power is destined to be put down, to make clear that it is not of ultimate significance. Of course, if it managed to stay in submission to God, it might be able to stay in power. So there is a vision here for the church to share with the nation, and a basis for prayer.

2. There is also good news for the smaller nations that are the victims of the great nation: they can be sure that it will not stay in power forever.

3. The smaller powers are peoples such as Babylon, Moab, Edom and Philistia, who would like to attain independence from Assyria and topple it. The trouble is that they are inclined to think that they will be able to achieve that victory for themselves by working together. In effect, they want to make the same mistake that Assyria makes.

4. Faced with all this, Judah is challenged not to fall into the other smaller nations' way of thinking. They must not think that their own destiny lies in planning for their safety. The church has to see itself as Judah and ask what it trusts in for its destiny in the world.

(We will pick up reading Isaiah at Isaiah 40 in 354 below.)

Read Micah.

1. He is preaching in Jerusalem at the same time as Isaiah. In what ways is his message similar?

2. In what ways is it different?

3. So if they ever met, what might Micah want to tell Isaiah he should say more about? And what would Isaiah want to tell Micah he should say more about?

4. What does Micah say about (a) prophets and (b) rulers?

Three well-known passages from Micah

1. *Micah 4:1-3.* This is the same as Isaiah 2:2-4. Maybe God gave it to Isaiah and it also got included in Micah, or vice versa, or maybe most likely it was a message given to an anonymous prophet and it got preserved in both places.

2. *Micah 5:2.* This is applied to Jesus in Matthew 2:6. One can see that in general it applies to Jesus, but that in the original context it speaks of someone in Micah's day who will deliver Judah. There is also a difference in the text as Matthew quotes it. Matthew has been inspired by the Holy Spirit to reword it in light of the way it applies to Jesus.

3. *Micah 6:8.* Traditionally translations use the words "justice," "mercy" or "kindness," and "humility." The first word (*mišpāṭ*) denotes the proper exercise of authority or power or leadership (it's related to the word for "judge" in the book of Judges). The second word (*ḥesed*) refers to an extraordinary commitment to people that you show even when they have forfeited any right to it. The third word (*ṣānaʿ*) comes only once more in the OT (Prov 11:2), but in later Hebrew it suggests modesty or reserve, an inclination to hold back. The Message translation conveys the idea of the verse: "Do what is fair and just to your neighbor, be compassionate and loyal in your love, and don't take yourself too seriously—take God seriously."

Micah 7. This passage is not as well-known, but it suggests valuable insight on how to hold the city before God. Much of the metropolitan area in which I live is characterized by poverty, deprivation, decay, family breakdown, neglect, violence and other troubles and waywardness. Micah suggests five reactions and awarenesses before God with which one might respond to a situation of that kind.

1. Micah expresses *lament* (Mic 7:1-6). Micah speaks as if he were a poor person allowed to collect the gleanings after harvest. But when he looks, there is nothing to collect. What he is looking for is signs of hope in his society, but all he can see is gloom—in the nation, in the local community, in the family.

2. Despite that fact, Micah's reaction is *expectancy* (Mic 7:7-10). There are no grounds for expectancy in the situation, yet he faces the facts rather than hiding from them. His realism includes a facing of sin: in these verses he speaks for Israel, acknowledging the sin of the people of God that has brought them into humiliation before oppressors such as Assyria. He can face all manner of facts because the basis of his hope is that God is a deliverer and will vindicate God's own honor.

3. In response to expectancy, there is *God's promise* (Mic 7:11-13). Micah speaks of a future that will restore the blessing lost and even add blessing never before experienced.

4. In return, the response to God's promise is *prayer* (Mic 7:14-17). Prayer lays hold on the promises of God. It is a prayer for the blessing of the people (Bashan and Gilead, areas east of the Jordan, were places of rich pasturage) and for the honoring of their God.

5. The whole book closes with the reaction of *worship* (Mic 7:18-20). "Who is a God like you?"—powerful to deal with the waywardness of the people of God, compassionate with its failures, faithful to the promises to it that stand forever. Micah's affirmations correspond to Yahweh's declarations about his character at Sinai, though they emphasize Yahweh's forgiveness and mercy, and they are expressed in Micah's own way, with a couple of distinctive images (Mic 7:19).

Like Isaiah and Micah, Joel preached in Jerusalem. The placing of his book suggests that he worked in the 700s, as they did. But the book contains no reference to a date, which makes it more like Malachi, who preached when there were no kings to give dates by. Maybe the book of Joel is put here because it makes for a good link between Hosea (who urges people to turn to Yahweh) and Amos (who has Yahweh calling from Zion, which is where Joel ends). Fortunately, the date question makes little difference to the message.

Apparently, there has been a locust plague. Such an event has devastating implications. Imagine going to the supermarket and finding nothing on the shelves because the delivery truck has not arrived or someone has pillaged the store. You would have nothing for yourself and your family to eat. Such is Judah's situation. A locust plague has the same effect as an enemy invasion; an enemy army also scoops up all the crops or burns them. Indeed, Joel might be speaking about either a locust army or a human army, or he might be using one as an image for the other. Either way, he sees the disaster that has happened as a pointer toward something else.

Read Joel.

1. What is the appropriate reaction to what has happened?

2. What is Joel's warning?

3. What is his exhortation?

4. What are his promises?

The best-known passage in Joel is his promise about God's spirit being poured out on everyone. In English Bibles this is Joel 2:28-32. In printed Hebrew Bibles these five verses are a chapter of their own (so that chapter 3 in English Bibles becomes chapter 4). From the beginning of their life as a people, God's spirit had been alive in Israel's midst (see, e.g., Is 63:10, 11, 14; Hag 2:5). A person's "spirit" is his or her personal dynamic, expressing itself in powerful actions that fulfill the person's will. So God's spirit is God's personal dynamic, expressing itself in powerful actions that fulfill God's will. Although Israel knew that God's spirit had come to dwell in their midst, at the same time they knew that it was possible to grieve God's spirit and for God's spirit to be withdrawn (see Ps 51:11; Is 63:10). The failure that had led to the locust plague and/or the military invasion would be bound also to involve the withdrawing of that spirit.

Renewing nature (Joel 2:23-27) is crucially important to the survival and future of the people. But this renewal would not resolve the problems that the disaster had exposed. Something else was needed. Joel 2:28-29 promises a further gift. In the past women and men had prophesied, had revelatory dreams and seen visions. In Joel's day that activity perhaps seemed to belong to the distant past. God promises that it will again become reality. Indeed, Joel may be promising that God will do something more spectacular than the people have previously known. Prophecy, dreams and visions will be more prevalent than they have been before. Whether it is something new or not, age, sex or class will not constrain the pouring out of God's spirit.

Acts 2 sees this promise being fulfilled at the first Pentecost, but it is not now fulfilled in the life of most of the church in the way Joel promised or the way Acts described. So the promise provides a basis for praying, expecting and acting so that it may be so. Acts 2 also sees Joel 2:30-32a as fulfilled at Pentecost. This part of the promise looks more like a description of cataclysmic events at the End, of the kind that are also described in a passage such as Luke 21. And Pentecost was itself indeed a partial realization of the End. Joel promises that when disaster threatens the world, it is an invitation to turn to God for protection.

The closing prophecies in Joel speak of a final judgment with an ironic reversal of the vision that appears in Isaiah and Micah, where plowshares will be turned into swords. To speak of it as a reversal is not to imply that the Isaiah/Micah version is necessarily older. It may be more likely that "turn your plowshares into swords" is a traditional call to take up arms when Israel is under attack. The version in Micah and Isaiah is then a creative reversal of that familiar idea, while Joel is reaffirming the traditional cry. Either way, there is evidently a time for one transformation and a time for the other.

Isaiah, Micah, Hosea and Amos were approximately contemporaries, all working in 700s, but Isaiah and Micah preached in Judah (as did Joel and Obadiah), but Hosea and Amos (and also Jonah) preached in Ephraim.

In a variety of ways the situation in Ephraim was more parlous and perilous than in Judah. Two centuries previously Ephraim had split off from Judah and thus from Jerusalem (Yahweh's chosen city) and from the Davidic kings (Yahweh's chosen line). So even if in its own thinking Ephraim stayed committed to Yahweh, its commitment was compromised. Geography then made Ephraim more open to outside pressures and influences. It came under pressure from Assyria before Judah did, because of the trade routes that ran through its territory. Amos's critique of Ephraim emphasizes how disorderly was its internal community life. The story of Naboth from the previous century (1 Kings 21) gives a concrete example. Hosea puts more emphasis on the disorder of its religious life than the disorder of its community life. Ephraim was deeply involved in religious observances that Hosea saw as deeply unfaithful to Yahweh. Ephraimites either were consciously praying to other deities or took such a perverted approach to Yahweh that it was as if they were praying to other deities.

In this connection, Hosea is bidden by God to work out his theology and his message in light of his relationship with his wife, Gomer, and their family. Hosea 1–3 relates how he marries someone who either is already known for her promiscuity or who soon becomes unfaithful. Translations refer to her as a prostitute, but the Hebrew word need not mean that she was involved in the sex trade. It simply implies that she was known to be promiscuous or that she was the sort of person who might become promiscuous. In this sense, she was a whore. Hosea thus begins by working out his message in terms of Yahweh as a cuckolded husband. But when he comes to reexpress his message in Hosea 11, he talks in terms of being a father or mother, and about the impossibility of throwing out your children even if they do fail to respond to your love and care.

Read Hosea in the light of this dynamic. Be aware of how your reading is influenced by whether you are a man or a woman. Remember that the prophet himself was a man, so we get a man's angle on it all. Then answer questions 1-4, or questions 5-8, or all eight questions:

1. In what way do Hosea and Yahweh think, behave, feel and speak like men?

2. What is the image of masculinity in the book?

3. Are there any positive or negative insights that emerge from the male perspective in the book?

4. How do you as a woman or a man relate or react to all that?

5. In what way do Gomer and Yahweh think, behave, feel and speak like women?

6. What is the image of womanhood in the book?

7. Are there any positive or negative insights that emerge from the female perspective in the book?

8. How do you as a woman or a man relate to or react to all that?

If you are curious or worried about the names in Hosea 1, compare some Zimbabwean personal names: Godknows, Lovemore, Tellmore, Trymore, Oblivious, Funeral, Anywhere, Enough (he was the thirteenth child), Hatred (because there was trouble in the family), Question (because the mother was not married), Nevertrustawoman (because the father didn't think that the child was his) (Wines, "Land of Homemade Names"). Maybe they have something in common with the kind of names that come in Isaiah, when names such as "Leftovers will return" and "Plunder-hurries-loot-rushes" don't look like the names whereby Isaiah's sons were known every day. So perhaps was the case with Hosea's children's names.

If you wonder whether God would really ask Hosea to marry someone who would be unfaithful, I fear that the answer is that God is prepared to ask the most outrageous things of people. Of course, they can always try to run in the opposite direction. Jonah failed, but maybe other people succeeded.

Reading Amos.

1. Who was Amos, where did he come from, and where did he work? See Amos 1:1; 7:12-15.

2. What was the situation to be addressed, as the book reflects it? See (a) Amos 1:3, 6, 9, 11, 13; 2:1; (b) 2:4, 12; 7:10-17; (c) 2:6-8; 3:10; 5:10-12; 8:4-6; (d) 4:4-5; 5:18-25; (e) 5:26; 8:14; (f) 6:1-6; 9:10; (g) 4:6-11.

3. What is the news that Amos brings?

   a. What does God plan to do about the situation? See Amos 1:3–2:8; 2:13-16; 3:12; 6:7; 8:11-12; 9:1-4.

   b. Is that all? What about Israel's special relationship with Yahweh? See Amos 2:9-12; 3:1-2; 9:7-8.

   c. Who says? See Amos 4:12-13; 5:8-9; 9:5-6.

   d. Is the end really the end? See Amos 9:11-15.

   e. Is there no way out? See Amos 5:14-15; 7:1–8:3.

   f. Why is God sending a prophet to Israel? See Amos 3:3-8.

Amos comes to Samaria, the capital of Ephraim, as a man from the south preaching in the capital in the north, like a country bumpkin from the hills of eastern Tennessee preaching on the steps of the White House. He knows that you can't keep religion out of politics. There he is confronted by the White House chaplain, Amaziah, who tells him that his preaching is not in his own interests or anyone else's; he would be wise to catch the first plane back to Chattanooga. Amaziah doesn't realize that it's always wise to listen to your enemies and to voices from strange quarters. Amos has two things to say in reply. One is that Amaziah doesn't understand what is going on. Amaziah thinks that a prophet is someone who works for the king, as maybe most prophets did (see 1 Kings 22). Amos's response is a bit ambiguous: either Amaziah's assumption makes him deny being a prophet or he says that he indeed became a prophet, yet not because he chose to be but because Yahweh turned him into one.

Amos also knows that you can't keep politics out of religion. He couldn't be faithful to God without raising the kind of questions that he is raising. It's impossible to be interested in spirituality without political involvement or to be politically involved without being in close touch with God.

The other thing that he says in reply is that Amaziah (and the whole country) is in danger of paying a terrible price for thinking that you can send a prophet back home. It is dangerous to ignore gloomy prophets. What happens to people who seek to get Europe to own the state of the church there, or to get the church in the United States to see how it is headed in the same direction?

Reading Obadiah. Obadiah focuses on Yahweh's Day coming for Edom, the people whose own land lay south and southeast of Israel. The book's placement between Amos and Jonah would suggest that Obadiah prophesied in the 700s, but the prophecy itself seems to refer to Edom allying itself with the Babylonians when they invaded Judah and took Jerusalem in 587 B.C. We know that later, in the Persian period, the Edomites took over much Judahite land. More likely, Obadiah lived in one of these two contexts, and the book comes where it does because of the link with the promises at the end of Amos.

Read Obadiah.

1. What will Yahweh's Day be like for Edom, and why?

2. Can you see situations in our own history that we can look at in the light of Obadiah's insights?

Nicely, Edom was never destroyed in the way the prophecy warns; the Edomites became part of Judea. You could even say that God delayed their judgment (as God often does), and they evaded it through being converted. That closing promise in Amos had declared that God would restore Jerusalem and make it possible for Judah to take possession of what was left of Edom, and it is in this way that the promise is fulfilled. (It would be odd for Amos himself to make promises of this kind, when he makes no other reference to the destruction of Jerusalem, which happened over a century after his day. So maybe the close of the book of Amos is a prophecy God gave to a later prophet which was then appended to Amos.)

Amos

*How Amos Believes Things Should
Be or Should Have Been*

Amos's opening chapters express Yahweh's convictions about war.

- War should be fought in a way that avoids what we might call war crimes (Amos 1:3, 13).

- It should not involve transporting a whole people (Amos 1:6).

- It should not ignore treaty obligations (?) (Amos 1:9)

- It should be tempered by brotherhood (Amos 1:11; cf. 1:9?).

- It should be tempered by compassion (Amos 1:11).

- It should respect people who lose their lives (Amos 2:1).

Amos goes on to confront Israel about its community life. The OT assumes that the local community and the extended family are key to how work operates; very few people are "employed" in the sense that they sell their labor. The extended family is expected to incorporate people who might be without resources: servants ("slaves" in many translations) and immigrants ("sojourners/aliens"). Families whose farm is doing well enough are expected to make loans to people whose farm gets into difficulty and to exercise charity toward people who fall out of this network. But the development of the state and urbanization has undermined the system, as Samuel warned it would (see 1 Sam 8:10-18). People who are doing well can take over the land of families whose farm fails, using lending as a means of making money rather than helping other people recover from a reversal. So people end up in poverty or servitude. In keeping with these assumptions, Amos's vision is of

1. Community life shaped by *mišpāṭ* and *ṣədāqâ*. The usual English translation of these words is "justice" and "righteousness," but more precisely they denote the making of decisions and the exercise of leadership and authority in accordance with faithfulness and doing right in relation to the people in one's community (Amos 5:6-7; 6:12) (see further 346).

They are equivalent to our phrase "social justice" (Weinfeld, *Social Justice*), but they give that idea more precise meaning.

2. Community life that thus reflects the way Yahweh has treated Israel (Amos 2:9-11).

3. The vision shaping the way the community makes decisions about land and debt and thus its attitude to the poor (Amos 2:6-8; 4:1; 5:10-15).

4. A community marked by moderation rather than indulgence or consumerism (Amos 4:1; 6:1-6; 8:4-6).

5. People in power not using their power to make themselves considerably more comfortable than others (Amos 3:15).

6. Worship that is simple; there is no need for big sound systems and media presentations (Amos 4:4-5; 5:21-27).

Can the vision be realized?

1. Amos condemns the way things do not follow that pattern, but he does not see it as his job to be very specific about what action needs to be taken. He is not a social reformer.

2. He believes that Yahweh will fulfill the vision (Amos 9:11-15).

3. It is the Torah that does propose concrete moves to this end, though mostly to offset the grim results of the kind of ills that Amos protests.

4. For most Galileans in Jesus' day, the structure of life was not so different from what Amos presupposes. They lived in villages and life was family based. It is easy to imagine Jesus liking the idea of our forming communities today that realized Amos's vision, maybe doing the following:

   a. Little communities fulfilling something of the function of the extended family and village.

   b. Lending without interest in these communities to give chance to recover from reversals.

   c. Spending less on education, transport, clothes, computers and so on.

   d. De-professionalization of legal processes.

   e. Communities meeting in houses rather than (costly) churches.

On the relation of all this to modern concern for social justice, see 363.

Reading Jonah. Read Jonah, and decide which of these suggestions about the aim of the book are more or less plausible:

- to show people how not to be a prophet
- to bring out the problem of running away from responsibility, challenges, pain and loneliness
- to encourage Israel to a more open attitude to other nations (Jon 4:2 applies Ex 34 to them!)
- to encourage us to care about the animal world
- to encourage Israel to repent ("If Nineveh can, you can.")
- to provide a figure who is a type of Christ
- to assure us that God can have a change of mind
- to show us how to recognize God's rescue (e.g., a large fish swallowing you) and respond to it

Systematic theology in Jonah (and Hosea and Isaiah): The shape of prophetic theology and ethics

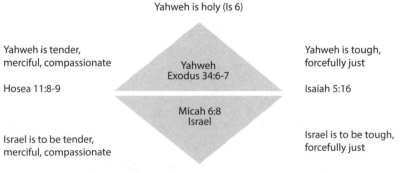

Yahweh is holy (Is 6)

Yahweh is tender, merciful, compassionate

Hosea 11:8-9

Yahweh
Exodus 34:6-7

Yahweh is tough, forcefully just

Isaiah 5:16

Micah 6:8
Israel

Israel is to be tender, merciful, compassionate

Israel is to be tough, forcefully just

Israel is to be modest
Israel is / is to be holy (Exodus 19:6; Lev 19:2)

"I knew you were a God gracious, compassionate, long-tempered, vast in commitment, and relenting about evil," says Jonah, resentfully (Jon 4:2). How does he know? It goes back to Exodus 34:6-7 (see 224), which is also picked up elsewhere (see Num 14:18; Ps 86:15; 103:8; 145:8; Joel 2:13; Neh 9:17). The diagram suggests how it's presupposed in different words by other prophets. The basic thing about Yahweh is that he is holy (Is 6)—majestic, extraordinary, august, supernatural. Hosea 11 and Isaiah 5 then spell out Yahweh's holiness: Yahweh can be tender and compassionate, and also tough and forcefully just, the two sides to Yahweh that come in that basic revelation in Exodus 34.

Then, as Yahweh is holy, so Israel is holy and is expected to be holy (Ex 19:6; Lev 19:2). The modesty to which Micah refers (see 338) expresses in another way what Israel must be toward the Holy One. As Yahweh's holiness is spelled out in being tender and tough, so is Israel's vocation in Micah 6:8.

The diagram might imply that compassion and toughness are equally central aspects to who Yahweh is. But the balance in Exodus 34:6-7 shows that compassion is more central and toughness more marginal to Yahweh. Isaiah 28:21 makes that point by saying that it's strange to Yahweh to get angry; Yahweh can do it, but it's alien to his central nature of compassion, grace and commitment. But God can summon up the capacity for anger when this is needed. Compare also the confession in Lamentations 3:33 that afflicting people doesn't come from God's heart. It's the point in Jonah too.

Is Jonah a historical story or a parable? How would you try to decide?

It's worth noting two considerations that should not exercise too much influence. One is the question of whether or not it's possible for someone to survive for two or three days inside a fish. Humanly speaking it may be impossible, but if God decides to make it happen, God can make it happen. The other is the fact that Jesus refers to Jonah being in the fish for two or three days. That doesn't mean Jesus is making a pronouncement about the story being historical, any more than I imply that Hamlet existed if I refer to Hamlet saying something. With Jonah, the question is rather whether the story has the features of fact or fiction, and the considerations outlined in 109 suggest fiction.

JEREMIAH

The History and the Book

Jeremiah's ministry spans nearly fifty years, and the book of Jeremiah is the longest in the Bible apart from Psalms (Isaiah has more chapters, but it's shorter in length). Jeremiah was called to prophesy in 626 B.C. (Jer 1:1-2) and was still prophesying after the fall of Jerusalem in 587 B.C., after which he was taken off to Egypt. Thus his ministry covered the monumental series of events that took place over the last decades of Judah's independent existence. You can read the story in 2 Kings 22–25.

621	The discovery of a Torah scroll in the temple gives new impetus to reform in Judah designed to throw off Canaanite- and Assyrian-style theology and worship.
612	Nineveh, the Assyrian capital, falls to the Babylonians.
609	King Josiah is killed in a military action designed to support the Babylonians against Assyria.
609	Jehoahaz (aka Shallum) is made king; the Babylonians replace him with Jehoiakim (aka Eliakim).
605	The Babylonians defeat the Egyptians (Assyria's ally) at Carchemish in Syria, which means that Syria and Palestine pass to Babylonian control.
601	Jehoiakim rebels; the Babylonians invade Judah.
597	Jehoiakim again rebels, and the Babylonians again invade. Jehoiakim dies; Jehoiakin (aka Coniah or Jeconiah) becomes king, as a teenager. The Babylonians invade Judah, deport the king and replace him by Zedekiah (aka Mattaniah).
587	Zedekiah rebels, and the Babylonians again invade, capture Jerusalem, and destroy the temple. Judahites again rebel, kill the Babylonian governor and flee to Egypt, taking Jeremiah with them.

Forms of speech in the prophets. Claus Westermann (*Prophetic Speech*) distinguishes three basic forms of speech: (1) words from the prophet or from

God to people; (2) words from the prophet to God; (3) stories about the prophet. The first is what we would especially expect to find in a prophetic book. In Jeremiah they take the form of warnings of disaster to come, confrontations that indicate the reasons and promises of deliverance and restoration. Jeremiah often dramatizes these messages. But much space is also given to his address to God (prayers and protests) and to stories about Jeremiah. Both reflect the way in which the prophet is part of the prophecy.

The book divides almost equally into poetry and prose (whereas Isaiah is mostly poetry, and Ezekiel is mostly prose). There is a lot of prose narrative and also a lot of prose sermons. The material divides as follows:

Form of Prophetic Speech	Poetry	Prose
Words from the prophet or from God to people	Yes	Yes
Words from the prophet to God	Yes	Yes
Stories about the prophet	No	Yes

If prophets mostly preached in verse, as Isaiah did, then we might infer that the prose sermons came from later preachers who were preaching sermons on texts from Jeremiah. But that's a big "if," and it seems just as likely that Jeremiah himself sometimes preached in verse and sometimes in prose. But the stories about Jeremiah presumably were written by other people, the sort of people who brought the book itself into existence. They have told the stories so as to bring home Jeremiah's significance for people living in the decades after Jeremiah, and it wouldn't be surprising if they have adapted the messages too to this end (see Holladay, *Jeremiah*; Nicholson, *Preaching to the Exiles*).

Reading Jeremiah thus involves two different sorts of exercise. One is to imagine Jeremiah engaged in his ministry in Jerusalem (and on the way to Egypt, at the end) so as to be able to hear his words as people would have heard them. The other begins from the fact that the actual book of Jeremiah was put together to be read to the next generation, people living in the exile. For them it functioned like the books of Kings as an explanation of why the exile had happened and as something from which they must learn lessons. In the last decades before the fall of Jerusalem, Jeremiah did not succeed in getting Judah to come to its senses. The question is whether the next generation will learn the lesson, start taking Yahweh's challenges seriously and claim the hopes the book offers.

Like Isaiah, Jeremiah is a confusing book to read, though it can be divided approximately as follows:

Jeremiah 1–25	Mostly poetry	Jeremiah's messages about Israel and his prayers
Jeremiah 26–45	Mostly prose	Stories about Jeremiah
Jeremiah 46–52	Mostly poetry	Jeremiah's messages about other nations, with a historical coda

The first two main blocks mostly seem to be simply one thing after another, so readers just have to deal with it. But although the book is not arranged by topic, a number of topics recur, so as you read through the book, it's possible to keep in mind the following four subjects.

Jeremiah's life and the course of events. Although a few of Jeremiah's messages have dates (e.g., Jer 25) and we can guess at the dates of some of the others, the book shows little interest in chronology. Thus, trying to put it into chronological order involves a lot of guesswork. But we could collect the sermons and stories that specifically refer to the different kings' reigns (Josiah, Jehoahaz/Shallum, Jehoiakim/Eliakim, Jehoiakin/Coniah/Jeconiah, Zedekiah/Mattaniah) and to the aftermath of the fall of Jerusalem, to see what profile emerges.

Being a prophet. We can ask a series of questions under this topic:

- What does a prophet do?
- What is life like for Jeremiah?
- How as a prophet does Jeremiah relate to God?
- How does God relate to him as a prophet?
- How does he pray as a prophet?
- How does he relate to other prophets?
- How does he relate to priests and other leaders?
- How do they relate to him?

- What does he have to handle in life?

- How as a prophet does he handle it?

- How you can tell whether or when a person is a genuine/faithful prophet or a deceived/deceiving one?

Yahweh's critique of Ephraim and Judah and his promises to them. Again, we can pose a series of questions under this topic:

- What are the faults that Yahweh finds in the community life of Ephraim and Judah?

- What are the faults he finds in their religious life?

- What are the faults he finds in their political life?

- What are his promises for their future?

Yahweh's view of other peoples. Under this topic we can ask these two questions:

- What does Jeremiah say about the superpower and Yahweh's relationship to it?

- What does Jeremiah say about the other nations around Judah?

A distinctive feature of Jeremiah is that there are two versions of the book, a longer one in the Hebrew Bible and a version one-eighth shorter in the Greek Bible, the Septuagint. But there are fragments of a Hebrew original of this version among the Dead Sea Scrolls, and while it's possible that some of the elements that the Greek version lacks had dropped out by accident, it's usually assumed that the edition in the Greek Bible is older. Apart from length, the big difference between the two is that the prophecies about other nations come in the middle of the Greek edition but come near the end of the Hebrew Bible's version and express more hope for these nations; the Hebrew Bible's version also expresses more hope for Israel itself. So the Hebrew Bible's version is a bit more distanced from the gloomy and threatened context of Jeremiah's own ministry and a bit more distanced in its capacity to be hopeful for Israel and for the world. The data prompt the reflection that the oldest version of something isn't necessarily the "best" or the most inspired or the most illuminating.

Social Justice (aka Faithful Judgment)

We've noted that *mišpāṭ* and *ṣədāqâ* are important to the prophets of the 700s. They're also important to Jeremiah. The word *mišpāṭ* is commonly translated as "justice," but it has a more concrete meaning than that word implies. It denotes the proper exercise of authority or leadership or government, or proper decision-making (e.g., Jer 17:11). The KJV uses "judgment," which is nearer to the meaning than "justice," though it has the disadvantage that "judgment" commonly denotes something unpleasant, whereas *mišpāṭ* is commonly a positive word. The word *ṣədāqâ* is commonly translated as "righteousness," but the disadvantage of that translation is that it suggests individual holiness. The NIV often uses "what is right," which is better. Since *ṣədāqâ* means doing the right thing in relation to other people and God, it's nearer to faithfulness. To complicate things a bit more, there is also a word *ṣedeq*, which has more or less the same meaning as *ṣədāqâ*.

Jeremiah 22:3 spells out the implications of *mišpāṭ* and *ṣədāqâ*. Jeremiah 22:13-17 indicates the nature of its opposite. Jeremiah 23:5-6 suggests a wicked subversive use of the expression. The point there is that the name of Judah's king for its last decade is Zedekiah (*ṣidqî-yāhû*). The word *ṣedeq* lies behind that name, which means "Yahweh is my faithfulness/righteousness." If Zedekiah lived up to his name, he would be pursuing *ṣedeq/ṣədāqâ*, but he is not doing so at all, any more than his predecessors who have been censured in the previous chapter. So Jeremiah affirms that Yahweh is going to raise up a branch from David's tree—the person who would later be called the "messiah"—who will be "a faithful/righteous branch." His name will be "Yahweh is our righteousness/faithfulness" (*Yahweh ṣidqēnû*). In other words, Zedekiah will be replaced by someone who lives up to his name in a way that Zedekiah himself does not.

Mišpāṭ and *ṣədāqâ* come together in Jeremiah 4:2 in association with *ʾĕmet* ("truthfulness"). There they refer to making commitments and/or giving testimony in court. They come together in Jeremiah 9:24 in association with *ḥesed* ("commitment") to describe Yahweh's own way of working in the world.

That occurrence in Jeremiah 9:24 draws attention to the way these words are used of Yahweh. Jeremiah 51:10 declares that Yahweh has brought forth our *ṣadāqâ*. The idea is that God has set about the process whereby his righteous, faithful purpose is going to be realized in Judah. This usage is frequent in Isaiah 40–66 (e.g. Is 45:24; 46:12, 13; 51:6, 8; 56:1). The word *ṣedeq* is also used with this meaning in Jeremiah 11:20 to describe the faithfulness Jeremiah looks for from Yahweh. Jeremiah describes Yahweh as one who shows faithfulness in the way he exercises authority: the verb is *šāpaṭ*, from which the noun *mišpāṭ* comes. And when Yahweh acts to restore Judah, people will be able to greet the land as an "abode of *ṣedeq*," or "faithful abode" (Jer 31:23; 50:7), a country that is an embodiment of God's faithfulness and/ or of Judah's faithfulness. This use of *ṣedeq* is also frequent in Isaiah 40–66 (e.g., Is 41:2; 42:6, 21; 45:13; 58:8).

Jeremiah has a hard time finding anyone in Jerusalem who is "doing *mišpāṭ*" (Jer 5:1). No one is exercising government or authority in the proper way (cf. Jer 21:12; 22:3). The wealthy take no notice of God's *mišpāṭ* (Jer 5:5). But it is not just the powerful or wealthy who have the responsibility to do so. None of the ordinary people are taking any notice of God's *mišpāṭ* either—for example, by running their family life and family business in a rightful way (Jer 5:4). Whereas birds acknowledge nature's framework for living their lives, the people as a whole do not acknowledge Yahweh's *mišpāṭ* (Jer 8:7). A good example comes in Jeremiah 5:28: scoundrels "do not *šāpaṭ* the *mišpāṭ* of the poor" (KJV: "the right of the needy do they not judge"). While *mišpāṭ* denotes judgment and thus can have the negative associations attaching to that English word (e.g., Jer 1:16; 4:12; 12:1), the example in Jeremiah 5:28 shows that God's judgment can have positive implications. It means taking action *for* the needy *against* the people who are ignoring them or taking advantage of them (cf. Jer 7:5). This word is also used in Isaiah 40–66 to refer to Yahweh's exercising his governmental authority in implementing his purpose in Israel's life (e.g., Is 40:27; 42:1, 3, 4; 59:9).

S*in.* The OT has a series of ways of picturing sin's nature, and all but one of the major ones come in Jeremiah. It helps us understand them if we look at when the image is used in ordinary life.

1. Sin is like rebelling against a superior authority (*pāšaʿ*; see Jer 2:8, 29; 3:13; 5:6; 33:8; translations often have "transgression"). For the everyday usage, see 2 Kings 1:1.

2. It leads to God paying you a visit (*pāqad*: see Jer 5:9, 29; 6:15; 30:20; translations often have "punish," but "visit" is the literal meaning). The image thus suggests a mafia-like experience.

3. It's like infidelity to a wife or husband (*šûb*; see Jer 3:6, 7, 8, 10, 11, 12, 22). Literally, it suggests turning away and turning to someone else.

4. It's like betraying a friendship (*bāgad*; see Jer 5:11; 9:2). See also Jeremiah 12:1, 6; Job 6:15.

5. It's like getting dirty (*ṭāmēʾ*; see Jer 2:23).

6. It's like wandering off the road (*ʿāōn*; see Jer 3:21; 5:25; 9:5; 11:10). Waywardness is thus the idea (translations often have "iniquity").

7. It's like transgressing the law, going over or beyond it (*ʿābar*; see Jer 34:18). For the everyday usage, see Jeremiah 5:22.

8. It's like failing to achieve a standard (*ḥaṭṭāʾāt*; see Jer 3:25; 8:14; 14:7, 20; the word commonly translated as "sin").

9. It's like something bad that happens to you (*raʿ*; see Jer 1:16; 18:8; 36:3). As in English, the same word is used of bad things that you do and bad things that you experience.

10. It's like trespassing on someone's rights or property or honor (*māʿal*, the image that doesn't come in Jeremiah; see, e.g., Ezek 14:13; 20:27). For the everyday usage, see Numbers 5:27.

Hope. Christians sometimes think that in the OT God has a hard time forgiving people, and that certainly you can't gain forgiveness unless you offer a sacrifice. In 343 we have noted that actually God loves to have the excuse to forgive people (this is what Jonah objects to), and in 228 we have noted that the OT doesn't make much of a link between sacrifice and forgiveness. In effect, it recognizes the point made in Hebrews 10:4, that the blood of sacrifices can't take away sin (though Heb 9:13 notes that it can deal with impurity). God is merciful and compassionate and forgives freely when people turn to him.

Jeremiah thus speaks of God forgetting the people's sin (i.e., putting it out of mind) (Jer 31:34). He doesn't use the OT's most common word for "forgive," *nāśāʾ* (literally, "carry"). He does use its less common word *sālaḥ* ("pardon"), and in that connection he also pictures God cleansing them from the impurity that attaches to them because of sin (Jer 33:8). God needs to clean them up if they are to be allowed in his presence. Jeremiah promises this cleansing and pardon in the context of mentioning waywardness, failure and rebellion, but he does not refer to any conditions for such pardon. On the other hand, Jeremiah 36:3 envisages them turning from their bad ways and then finding pardon, and Jeremiah 13:27 implies that they need to clean themselves up. So there is the usual OT tension between God's action and our action (as there is in the relationship between two human beings); the first move may come from the one party or it may come from the other. The trouble is that either way there is a problem about getting Judah to turn (see Jer 14:10).

Jeremiah 31:31-34 perhaps suggests the solution. There's no use God waiting for the people to turn back before restoring them; he will wait forever. He has to restore them anyway, in the conviction that this action will bring about a change in them. It will be this pardoning and declining to keep their sins in mind that bring the transformation whereby they start obeying the Torah and no longer need to urge one another to acknowledge Yahweh. To a fair extent it happened: after Yahweh restored them from exile, they did obey the commandments (e.g., not worshiping other gods, not making images, keeping the Sabbath) in a way they had not before. He pardoned them, and that changed them.

Jeremiah
What Makes a False Prophet?

James Crenshaw's study of false prophecy in the OT is titled *Prophetic Conflict: Its Effect upon Israelite Religion*. The title reflects the fact that that the line between true and false is usually difficult to draw when you are in the situation. Further, a true prophet may become a false one, and a false prophet may speak an authentic word. Perhaps all prophets have the capacity for either. So what factors influence a prophet to speak false rather than true? We'll look at four.

A longing to succeed. A prophet wants to be right, wants to be listened to and wants both of these for God's sake. But both may not be possible. The truth may not be acceptable to people, and falsehood may be preferred. Jeremiah came near to downfall through being unable to cope with the rejection of his word (see Jer 15). Surely God's own purpose demands that God's servant gain a hearing? Surely God has an interest in the prophet's success? But no. God's servant may contribute by accepting failure and affliction, as Isaiah 40–55 makes clear. The desire to succeed, to succeed for God's sake, is the desire of the false prophet as well as of the true one.

The pressure of the institution. In Israel this usually meant the king. Amaziah's attempt to silence Amos provides a good example (Amos 7). There is a paradox here. The kings were a main reason why prophecy existed. The institution always threatens to supplant God, so it requires a voice of God that stands up to it. A prophet's job is to confront it. But the institution also makes prophecy almost impossible, except at the risk of one's life, or at least of one's ministry. So whether we see the state or the church as the institution, we need to note that prophecy's job is in part to rescue the institution from divinizing itself. And we must remember that our "in-groups" can function as institutions and inhibit the word of God, even when they officially reject anything institutional.

Popular religion. Sometimes popular religion too easily assumes that God is with us. God is committed to us. We are alright. That was the message of Hananiah, not Jeremiah (see Jer 28). If our message is that God is with us, we may be only a hair's breadth, if that, away from false prophecy. At other times, however, popular religion may be convinced that God has abandoned us, as it was convinced in the exile (see Is 40). Expending energy on the church is like rearranging the deck chairs on the *Titanic*. The church's demise is inevitable. The prophets who join in this chorus may also be false. We must beware of both the optimism and the pessimism of popular religion. The prophet is characteristically called to confront the attitudes that are widely held among the people of God, not to confirm them or assimilate to people's beliefs as to what God's attitude to us is bound to be.

The power of tradition. Hananiah's assumption that God is with us had its basis in tradition, in the Psalms, in the prophecies of Isaiah, in Deuteronomy—in Scripture, you could say. It was sound and biblical. The trouble was that his word was out of due time. He was preaching a biblical message, his theology was orthodox, but it belonged to the previous century. It was not what God was saying now, in a different situation. A prophet turns into a noisy gong or a clanging cymbal by simply repeating truths as they applied yesterday.

The OT does offer two words of comfort about when gifts go wrong. One is that this can be part of God's plan. It can have a place in God's purpose. It can be God's means of bringing out into the open judgments that people are bringing on themselves by their inner attitudes. One can see this both in the story of Jehoshaphat and the four hundred prophets (1 Kings 22) and in Paul's assertion that there has to be untruth so that those who are untrue have a flag to rally to (1 Cor 11:18-19).

The other word of comfort is that as a true prophet can fall away, so a false prophet can return and be restored. A prophet is not necessarily lost, even though making radical mistakes. Elijah and Jonah show that, as does Jeremiah: "If you return, I will restore you, and you shall stand before me. If you utter what is precious, and not what is worthless, you shall be as my mouth" (Jer 15:19).

Through most of OT Israel's history, one superpower or another dominated the political, economic, cultural and religious life of Israel's world.
The sequence of superpowers continues in much of subsequent history over
much of the world. Like the other Latter Prophets and some other books,
Jeremiah pays considerable attention to the theological significance of the
superpower of its day. Part of the background is the role and history of the
superpowers in his day. At the beginning of his life, Assyria was the great
power, to which Judah had been subordinate in the time of King Manasseh.
But Assyria was in decline, and the political situation made it easier for King
Josiah to introduce reforms in Judah. You could even see them as an assertion of independence. But Assyria's decline did not mean that little nations like Judah simply gained their autonomy. In the middle of Jeremiah's
life, Babylon took over from Assyria as the superpower, which meant that
one superpower was simply replaced by another, for Judah; hence the importance of the great event of 605 B.C. (see 344), referred to in Jeremiah 25:1;
36:1; 45:1; 46:2. Relations with Babylon were then the key political reality of
Judah's life until Judah's downfall in 587 B.C.

Jeremiah makes four key points about the superpower (for a fuller version
of this section, see 363).

The superpower is subordinate to Yahweh. "I am sending and taking all
the northern clans . . . , yes, Nebuchadrezzar king of Babylon my servant,
and bringing them against this country . . . and against all these nations
around" (Jer 25:9). As destroyer, Nebuchadrezzar is Yahweh's servant. "I am
the one who made the earth . . . , and I give it to whomever I please. Now I
myself am giving all these countries [Edom, Moab, Ammon, Tyre, Sidon]
into the control of Nebuchadnezzar, the king of Babylon, my servant. . . . All
the nations are to serve him . . . until his country's time comes too, and many
nations and great kings make him a servant" (Jer 27:5-7). Judah needs to
settle down under Babylonian authority. The exile will not last forever, but
it will last a long time.

So Yahweh can be tough by means of the superpower, but can also be compassionate by means of the superpower. Yahweh had once withheld compassion (Jer 13:14; 16:5) and used the superpower's refusal to have compassion to that end (Jer 6:23; 21:7). But Yahweh always intended to have compassion again (Jer 12:15; 30:18; 33:26), and superpowers are capable of being merciful toward subordinate peoples. Under Yahweh's control, a superpower can have a positive theological role as a means of fulfilling promises and furthering a positive purpose. In both respects, its acts bring a partial realization of Yahweh's ultimate purpose in the world. It brings Yahweh's Day. But all this is unwitting. It is not trying to serve Yahweh but rather is doing its own thing.

As a result, every superpower gets its turn. All the nations were to serve Nebuchadnezzar, his son and his grandson, but only until his country's time also comes. Then many nations and great kings would make him a servant (Jer 27:6-7). "Toward Yahweh it has been insolent, toward Israel's Holy One" (Jer 50:29; cf. Jer 51:11). Whereas it was supposed to be acting as Yahweh's servant in its involvement with Israel, Babylon has been pursuing its own agenda in its preoccupation with carving out its own empire. The one who has shown no compassion will receive none (Jer 50:42). Yahweh is also punishing the Babylonians for what they did to Yahweh's palace in Jerusalem (Jer 50:25-28; cf. Jer 51:11). The plunderer thus becomes the plundered, and the rest of the world is rescued from the superpower (Jer 30:10-17). Other peoples are therefore unwise to identify too closely with the superpower, or at least are wise to be able to tell the time and to know when to abandon it. The way Yahweh puts a superpower down is by raising up another. After Babylon, the Medo-Persian Empire was to be next, its first act as superpower being the putting down of its predecessor. And it is Yahweh who stirs the Medes against Babylon (Jer 50:45).

Is there any good news for the superpower? A paradoxical form of good news is the declaration that the powerlessness of its religious resources will be exposed (Jer 50:2). The correlative positive confession is that the nations will acknowledge Yahweh's power and might. But in the meantime, it's never too late, even for a superpower (Jer 18:7-8).

READING NAHUM, HABAKKUK
AND ZEPHANIAH

These three prophets worked in the late 600s; Zephaniah gives a date in Josiah's reign and may have been the first of the three. The time is the early part of Jeremiah's working life, when Assyria is in decline and Babylon is in the midst of taking over (the Assyrian capital, Nineveh, fell to Babylon in 612 B.C.).

Nahum

1:1-15   The book begins with some principles. What does it say Yahweh is like?

2:1–3:19   The principles are applied to Nineveh, under attack by the Medes and Babylonians. What is to be the nature of Nineveh's experiences, what pictures are used to describe it, and what are the reasons for it?

In Nahum, Yahweh takes a similar attitude toward Nineveh as that of the prophet Jonah, and thus a different attitude from Yahweh's own attitude in the book of Jonah. The temptation for Judah in Nahum's day would be to believe that its situation is hopeless, and that the great Assyrian oppressor is going to rule the Middle Eastern world forever. It helps to appreciate Nahum if we can look at it from the perspective of a colonial people who need to be encouraged to believe that God can deliver them. The book was an encouragement to the oppressed in South Africa in the 1980s. The fall of Nineveh in 612 B.C. will have helped to establish that Nahum's promises about its fall really came from Yahweh. Nahum had been a true prophet. But it's worth noting that there are only two specific references to Nineveh after Nahum 1:1 (English translations add some more), which suggests that readers are invited to see that the prophecy relates not merely to Nineveh but to any wicked city (such as Jerusalem).

Habakkuk. Habakkuk takes the form of an argument between the prophet and God, which leads into proclamation and worship. (Regarding the prophet's name: in English pronunciation some people put the stress on "Hab" and some on "akk," while the Masoretes put the stress on "kuk." So do what you like, and do it with confidence.)

Trace the nature of the discussion in Habakkuk:

1:2-4	Habakkuk to God	What does Habakkuk see in Judah?
1:5-11	God to Habakkuk	What does God intend to do?
1:12–2:1	Habakkuk to God	Why does Habakkuk object to God's plan?
2:2-5	God to Habakkuk	How does God intend to answer Habakkuk's objection?
2:6-20	Habakkuk to Babylon	What does Habakkuk proclaim in light of God's answer?
3:1-19	Habakkuk to God	How does Habakkuk pray and worship in light of God's answer?

In the context of oppression by Babylon and oppression in Judah, Habakkuk declares that "the righteous will live by his faithfulness"; in other words, people who live in the right way will live and not die. Yahweh will see to it. It doesn't look that way, but people have to hold on to Yahweh's faithfulness. Paul is inspired by the Holy Spirit to use the words with a different meaning (Rom 1:17; Gal 3:11); Hebrews 10:38 is closer to Habakkuk's own meaning.

Zephaniah. Josiah (Zeph 1:1) came to the throne of Judah in 640 B.C. Zephaniah apparently prophesied early in his reign before his religious and social reforms and just before Jeremiah. Zephaniah's great emphasis is on Yahweh's Day. Read through Zephaniah and summarize his warnings and promises.

1:2-3	What is Yahweh's intention regarding the whole world?
1:4–2:3	Does this apply to the people of God? What will Yahweh's Day mean for the people of God? Why? What then must they do?
2:4-15	What will Yahweh's Day mean for Judah's neighbors and for the great Assyrian power?
3:1-8	What will Yahweh's Day mean for Jerusalem, given its failure to respond?
3:9-20	What will Yahweh's Day of restoration look like?

One of Zephaniah's key phrases is "in your/its midst" (see Zeph 3:3, 5, 11, 12, 15, 17).

E zekiel was a younger contemporary of Jeremiah, but he was a Jerusalem priest deported to Babylon in 597 B.C. with other priests, ten years before the city's final fall. So during the years just before and after that final fall he was preaching at the same time as Jeremiah, but he was in Babylon, while Jeremiah was in Jerusalem. Like other prophetic books, the book of Ezekiel is a collection of messages given in many different occasions, but in contrast to Jeremiah, his book is neatly arranged.

1. Read Ezekiel 1–3, the book's introduction. What are the features of Ezekiel's account of his call, especially as you compare it with other prophets' account of their call? Why do you think we are told about it? How does it relate to his context and his ministry?

2. Read Ezekiel 4–24, messages about calamity coming to Judah. What is Ezekiel commissioned to communicate, and how he is commissioned to communicate it? What is the problem with Jerusalem, and what does Yahweh intend to do about it?

3. Read Ezekiel 25–32, messages about calamity coming to other peoples. What is the point of these messages to the Judahite exiles to whom they are given?

4. Read Ezekiel 33–48. What are Yahweh's promises for Israel's renewal? Why do you think Yahweh makes these particular promises? What is new here?

Did Ezekiel really do those weird things? Did he lie on his side for 390 days (Ezek 4:4-5)? I assume that he did do weird things, but we don't have to be overly literal about them. For instance, maybe he lay there with the equivalent of a flip-over calendar to symbolize the time that passed. Was he really transported to Jerusalem (Ezek 8:1-4)? I don't see any reason to question that he had this experience in a vision (as someone from a priestly family, he was familiar with the temple from when he lived in Jerusalem, so he knew the sort of place it was and the sort of thing that was going on there).

How are we to take the pornographic chapters (Ezek 16; 23)? Ezekiel here offers five male ways of looking at a woman, all of which may be objectionable to a woman. The risk the Holy Spirit takes is that Ezekiel may seem to validate these ways of looking at a woman, but there's no evidence that the chapters have actually encouraged abuse of women. Ezekiel takes that risk in the hope that it may jolt his (male) hearers into seeing something about themselves. "You know you look at women in a way that suggests contempt? Well, that's the way Yahweh looks at you."

Individual responsibility? "The individual who sins—that is the one who will die" (Ezek 18:4). People won't die because of their parents' sins (Ezek 18). Is Ezekiel contradicting the commandment that sees the sins of the parents bringing trouble to their children and grandchildren? As is often the case, different parts of Scripture are emphasizing complementary points; sometimes one point needs emphasizing, sometimes the other. The sins of one generation do bring trouble to the next generation, just as their faithfulness brings blessing to them. Yet the implication is not that one generation can blame its parents for the mess it is in, as if it has no way out. It has to accept responsibility for itself. In Ezekiel's day Judah was in a mess because of the faithlessness of previous generations. But it must not make that an excuse for taking no action. If it turns back to Yahweh, Yahweh will restore it.

Gog and Magog. When you reach the end of Ezekiel 37, you could think that the book is coming to an conclusion. In Ezekiel 38–39 it's surprising to find the prophecy talking about another crisis to come some years after Judah's restoration. This fact may support the idea that Ezekiel 38–39 is a later addition to the book and represent a later preacher's development of Ezekiel's message in light of events after Ezekiel's day. Ezekiel 40–48 may comprise a further expansion of Ezekiel's own message.

Most of the places that are mentioned would have been known to the audience one way or another, some would be more mysterious, but they look as if they are places and peoples from the north of Judah (mostly Turkey), which suggests that they are further embodiments of the "enemy from the north" in Jeremiah—the north being the direction from which danger usually came.

Like Other Prophets, Only More So

1. *Other prophets had visionary experiences*, but Ezekiel's are Technicolor, IMAX, 3D. Other prophets speak of Yahweh's glory, his dazzling splendor; Ezekiel speaks of it nineteen times. Some of Ezekiel's visions started from things that anyone could have seen. Others, such as the events that were happening hundreds of miles away in Jerusalem, or the scroll he ate (Ezek 3), were things that he alone saw. In the extraordinary nature of his experiences Ezekiel especially resembles Elijah and Elisha.

2. *Other prophets were seized by Yahweh's hand*, but it happened to Ezekiel seven times (e.g., Ezek 3:14, 22). God grabs him, whisks him off somewhere, knocks him over, jerks him to his feet.

3. *Other prophets could be propelled by Yahweh's spirit*, but this experience is characteristic of Ezekiel. The word for "spirit," *rūaḥ*, also means "breath" and "wind," which encourages the stress on that experience; sometimes it's hard to tell which meaning the word has (e.g., Ezek 8:3; 11:1).

4. *Other prophets speak as Yahweh's messengers and heralds*, but Ezekiel speaks nearly fifty times about Yahweh's message "coming" to him (literally, it "became/was/happened") from the heavenly king to pass on to his subjects.

5. *Other prophets use pictures and parables*, but Ezekiel can turn a folktale into a four-page allegory (Ezek 16) or turn a metaphor into an allegory (Ezek 34).

6. *Other prophets act in mimes and act out parables*; Ezekiel does so on a vaster scale. His mimes do more than illustrate his message; they embody Yahweh's will and put that will into effect (e.g., Ezek 4–5). He himself is a sign for the people (Ezek 12:6; 24:24).

7. *Other prophets are concerned for the whole people's destiny*; Ezekiel often speaks to "the household of Israel," even though addressing a mere Ju-

dahite group in exile. But he also promises the restoration of an Israel comprising both Judah and Ephraim (Ezek 36–37).

8. *Other prophets look for Yahweh to be recognized*; this theme is central to Ezekiel. There are over seventy occurrences of phrases such as "they/you shall acknowledge that Yahweh is God," which implies submitting to Yahweh as Lord.

9. *Other prophets are aware of the community's hostility to Yahweh.* Ezekiel knows from the beginning that Israel is "a rebellious household," strangely resistant and stubborn.

10. *Other prophets are ignored by people.* It happens to Ezekiel when he is bringing bad news (Ezek 4–24) and then when he is bringing good news (Ezek 33–37).

11. *Other prophets declare judgment on the people.* Ezekiel's judgment message is so extensive that it occupies both sides of a scroll (Ezek 2:10).

12. *Other prophets promise a glorious future the other side of disaster.* Some of Ezekiel's most elaborate visions picture Israel's wonderful future, and they have a big influence on Revelation.

13. *Other prophets affirm Yahweh's lordship*, but "sovereign Yahweh" is Ezekiel's characteristic title for God. Anything that happens can be attributed to his sovereignty (e.g., Ezek 3:20; 14:9). Yahweh's correlative term for Ezekiel is "son of man," mere "human being."

14. *Other prophets give us dates*; Ezekiel is the most chronologically specific, giving us a series of dates for all his messages. One significance may be that they make it possible to check his message against its fulfillment.

15. *Other prophets are appalled at religious wrongdoing;* it's the focus for Ezekiel. Thus the focus of judgment is the temple, but the focus of restoration lies there as well.

16. *Other prophets are thus aware of Yahweh's holiness.* "The key to Ezekiel's proclamation of God is this: God will not be mocked. God will not be presumed upon, trivialized, taken for granted, or drawn too close. God takes being God with utmost seriousness" (Brueggemann, *Hopeful Imagination*, 53).

Ezekiel

What Do His Promises Refer To?
Promise and Fulfillment

1. In understanding the significance of prophecies, a place to start is that prophecies are not isolated individual declarations about events to come. They relate to God's overarching promises and purpose. The main aspects of that purpose go back to two points in the OT: (a) Genesis 12, the promise of having a land, becoming a nation and being a blessing; (b) 2 Samuel and 1 Kings, the promise about David's line and about the temple. It's instructive to look at the promises in Ezekiel 33–48 in light of these promises because they underlie every element in Ezekiel 33–48. In other words, the thing that Yahweh is saying through Ezekiel is, "You know those promises I made to Abraham and David? Well, here is an updated version in light of how things are now."

2. In many centuries Jews and Christians have thought they have seen prophecies being fulfilled in their own day. Events involving Israel in the twentieth century are examples (e.g., it was suggested that "Gog" and "Magog" refer to Russia). But the prophets' account of their call suggests that their calling was to minister God's word to the people among whom they lived. Ezekiel is specific that he is not speaking about far future events (Ezek 12:21-28).

3. This is not to say that prophets such as Ezekiel did not talk about future events. These might be events that were imminent and therefore directly relevant to their hearers; the fall of Jerusalem and the restoration of Judah are notable examples. Or they might be events that turned out to be far distant (e.g., the final "Day of the Lord"). Prophets talk about them because they relate to their hearers, even though it may transpire that they are far off. It compares with Paul talking about Jesus' final coming to people of his day. They were to live in light of that event, even though they would not see it.

4. The NT finds significance in OT prophecies of a kind that would have been unknown to the prophets themselves. But it does so by starting from what it knows is God's great act of salvation, what God is doing in Jesus. Finding new meaning in prophecies in light of the newspaper is different from finding new meaning in light of Jesus' coming.

5. When Paul talks about the coming of Jesus, he uses language that will be appropriate if it happens in his day (e.g., "the trumpet will sound"). In the same way, the prophets talk about a coming deliverance and a coming deliverer, using the terms that will apply if it happens in their day. They are reaffirming a promise, not predicting an isolated event. When Jesus came the first time and when he comes at the End, he fulfills the underlying promise, not the literal prediction. And/or he fulfills the promise, but in a reinterpreted sense in light of the context being different.

6. Likewise, when God fulfills promises for the Jewish people today, it is a matter of fulfilling the underlying commitment (the promises listed above in #1), not fulfilling a mere literal prediction.

7. Whether prophecies get fulfilled depends on the response they receive (see Jer 18 and Jonah). There is no assumption that prophecies that do not get fulfilled in the prophet's day will be fulfilled at some future date. They are not like a schedule of football games that may get postponed but must be played sometime. But those underlying promises will be fulfilled.

8. The broader principle is that God's promises are not fulfilled in a way that ignores moral questions. Abraham's family have to wait centuries before they possess the land, because God cannot be unfair to the Amorites/Canaanites (Gen 15:16). God's dealings with Israel and Palestine likewise have to take into account both God's promises to the Jewish people about the land and the rights of the Palestinians as people for whom it has long been their land (and also his promises to Ishmael, to whom Muslims look as their ancestor). God keeps working via political processes to square this circle in the least unsatisfactory way possible.

(For more on these questions, see 363.)

Wₑ left off reading Isaiah after Isaiah 39, where the historical context changes (see 335). Isaiah 1–39 ends with the prospect of Judah's fall to Babylon, which happened in the time of Jeremiah and Ezekiel. Isaiah 40–55 begins with that event in the past. Judah's downfall has happened between Isaiah 39 and Isaiah 40; Isaiah 40 promises that Yahweh is about to come back to Jerusalem (and so are its people). Babylon is about to fall by the hand of the Medo-Persian king Cyrus (Is 44:24–45:7).

The Medes had been around as a power for some time, living north and west of Persia (including eastern Turkey), and Isaiah 13 had promised that they would be the means of putting Babylon down. Cyrus the Great created the Persian Empire in 550 B.C. by conquering the Medes and reversing the power relations between Media and Persia (rather as Babylon had taken over the Assyrian empire in the 600s). In the 540s Cyrus then conquered Lydia in western Turkey, to the west of his empire. This empire then stretched from India to Greece—but north of Mesopotamia, where the Babylonian Empire lay. Then he moved on Babylon. It is these events that are the background to the prophecies in Isaiah 40–55 (see, e.g., Is 41). Cyrus took Babylon in 539 B.C. That event happens in between Isaiah 55 and Isaiah 56 as the fall of Jerusalem happens between Isaiah 39 and Isaiah 40. Like Isaiah 1–39, Isaiah 40–55 and Isaiah 56–66 comprise collections of shorter prophecies each of which originally stood on its own.

Isaiah 40–55: How the prophecies got home to people. Communication happens not only through the content of our words but also through the forms we use. We communicate against the background of things that speaker and audience take for granted, and much of the communication happens through the relationship of what is said and what is taken for granted. Form criticism looks at the way things are said (the genres or forms) against the background of the social context speaker and audience share (the *Sitz im Leben*). With regard to Isaiah 40–55, what follows is based on Westermann, *Isaiah 40–66.*

1. *The way people speak in sorting out legal disputes in a gathering at the city gate* (see Jer 26). In Isaiah 41:1-7, 21-29 Yahweh challenges the nations; in Isaiah 43:8-15; 44:6-8 Yahweh challenges the gods, appealing for witnesses in connection with the case; in Isaiah 42:18-25; 43:22-28 Yahweh issues a countercharge when Israel has made an accusation against him (Is 43:28). "Do you see? You're trying to put Yahweh on trial, but you are bound to lose."

2. *The street-corner accusation that might lead to a legal case,* along the lines of #1 above (see Ruth 4). Here, Isaiah 40:27 leads to Isaiah 40:12-31. Compare Isaiah 45:9-13 (note the idea of going to law; cf. Is 45:12-13, the kind of claims that Yahweh makes in court). "Do you see? You are accusing Yahweh of being inept or uncaring, but it won't get you anywhere."

3. *The way a prophet or priest speaks at the coronation of a king* (see 2 Sam 7). In Isaiah 41:8-9 Yahweh speaks as if addressing a king, when he is addressing Israel. Isaiah 42:1-4, 5-9 describe a king's role. Isaiah 44:24-28; 45:1-7 describe God as installing a strange person as king. Isaiah 52:13–53:12 then describes a strange coronation. "Do you see? Yahweh is speaking to you as if you were a king being crowned; Yahweh is speaking to Cyrus as if he were a Davidic king; the servant is being crowned, but he has a strange experience on the way to that crowning."

4. *The way a prophet or priest speaks in exercising a counseling ministry* (e.g., in the temple; see Ps 12; 28; 56). Isaiah 41:10-16 has God speaking that way to Israel (cf. Is 43:1-7; 44:1-5). "Do you see? Yahweh is speaking to you with words of comfort like someone ministering to one in need."

5. *The way the community prayed and lamented their fate* (see Lamentations; also 1 Kings 8:46-53; Zech 7). Isaiah 41:17-20; 42:14-17 are then Yahweh's responses to the community's prayer, picking up their lament. "Do you see? Yahweh is responding to your prayer."

The prophets (like Jesus) were brilliant at communicating; nevertheless, in their lifetime they were failures (see Buber, *On the Bible*, 142-44, 147-48, 166-71). Success in communicating depends on more than your brilliance.

The Message and the People That It Addresses

In Isaiah 40–55 individual prophecies have been arranged into longer sequences, so that the prophecies on different topics come together, or so that pairs of themes are interwoven:

40:1-31	The prophet's call and challenge
41:1–44:23	Israel as God's servant: status, calling, indictment, promise
44:24–48:22	Cyrus as God's anointed: the fall of Babylon
49:1–52:12	The servant's certainties and Zion's uncertainties
52:13–55:13	The servant's suffering and the people's joy

The chapters begin with an account of a call (Is 40:1-11). The prophet hears God commissioning comforters or encouragers. The situation of being under God's punishment is now to be reversed. Not long after Jerusalem's fall, Lamentations 1:1-5 spoke of Jerusalem as being without comfort and experiencing harsh labor because of its sins. Isaiah 40 takes up these same words to declare that the moment of Jerusalem's comfort has come, the harsh labor is over, the sins have been duly punished. Further, the words "Comfort my people, says your God" take up Hosea's declaration of judgment on Israel (Hos 1:8-9) and promise that it is now reversed.

God's commission receives three responses. The voices apparently belong to angelic servants who are to see to the fulfillment of Yahweh's will. The first requires the preparing of a road through the desert. While it will be a road for the exiles' own return, it is first a road for Yahweh's own return in glory to the city abandoned to destruction in 587 B.C. Another voice declares, "Preach." But what is someone to preach when people are withered by the hot wind of God's wrath and cannot believe that God is speaking to them? The angel's answer comes in Isaiah 40:8: "The grass withers, the flower fades." The people are like that, but there is another factor that needs taking into account. The third voice speaks good news for Jerusalem itself: the sovereign Yahweh is indeed returning to it, in divine power (Is 40:10) and divine gentleness (Is 40:11).

The prophet's problem will be that the Judahites find this message incredible. Isaiah 40:12-31 comprises a first attempt at breaking through their incredulity. Isaiah 40:27 sums up their feelings before God. The prophet's task is to convince people that their God has the power and the will to care about them and act as their Lord, and to counter the impressiveness of apparent rivals to Yahweh.

1. One obstacle that they are aware of is the Babylonians' own power. If Yahweh had not been able to defend Jerusalem against them, could he defeat them on their own territory? The prophet reminds the Judahites of their own faith that Yahweh is the world's Creator; no nation keeps its impressiveness when compared with this God (Is 40:12-17).

2. How easy it is to be impressed by Babylon's idols, splendid figures carried in processions through the city. How pathetic, in comparison, is Judah's temple—destroyed by the people who worshiped those idols, and who brought its sacred vessels from that temple to their idols' sanctuaries. Yet how silly it is to compare the world's Creator with an idol made by human beings (Is 40:18-20).

3. How easy it is to be impressed by the kings and princes of Babylon. They had deported the last two kings of Judah, who had languished in prison in Babylon. How could Judahite leadership reassert itself against that? But how foolish it is to compare the power of foreign leaders with the power of Israel's Creator God, of whose praise Israel's psalms still reminded the exiles (Is 40:21-24).

4. And how easy it is to be impressed by the actual gods of Babylon, the powers of the heavens that (as the Babylonians believed) determined how events worked out on earth. Yet, who created the sun, the moon and the stars, and parades them obediently each day (Is 40:25-26)?

It is that vision of God as Creator that is the prophet's answer to the question whether God has the will or the ability to be involved with Israel any more (Is 40:27-31). Those who believe in Yahweh as this kind of God believe that this Yahweh will act to redeem, and this conviction begins to bring them renewed strength even when they are still living in hope.

Read Isaiah 40–55.

1. Can you see a "plot" in the chapters? Are they going somewhere? What themes appear earlier but not later, and vice versa? What is the message of the whole?

2. How does the prophecy talk about creation? What is creation's theological significance?

3. How does the prophecy speak of Yahweh's sovereignty in history?

4. The chapters say much about Yahweh's servant: see Isaiah 41:8-10; 42:1-4; 42:18-25; 43:8-13; 44:1-5; 44:21-22; 44:24–45:7; 48:20-22; 49:1-6; 50:4-9; 52:13–53:12. What is his role or nature in each passage?

5. When you read these passages about Yahweh's servant in their context in Isaiah 40–55, who do you think the servant is? Might it be someone different in different passages? If so, who in each one, in its context?

6. What is the message of Isaiah 40–55 for the church?

Who is this prophet? Turning on from Isaiah 39 to Isaiah 40, one would assume that we continue to read the words of Isaiah. But the address in Isaiah 40 doesn't look forward to the deportation of the Jewish leadership to Babylon (as Isaiah did); it refers to this deportation as something that has happened, and happened a long time ago. It speaks from the context of Babylon's rule over the Judahites in Babylon and in Judah. This prophet is someone who lives during this period. So it is a different person from Isaiah, but one who walks in his footsteps, takes up his calling, shares emphases of his ministry and brings the message that he might bring if he were alive in this very different situation.

The foundation of this message is a strong and multisided faith in Yahweh. Yahweh is the God of gods, the God of creation, the God of Israel's history (e.g., the story of Abraham and the exodus), the God of present history (the power behind Cyrus the Persian), the God of deliverance (Zion's husband

and Israel's *gô'ēl*, the next-of-kin and restorer or redeemer, the one who is committed to looking after her), the God whose word will be fulfilled, and the Holy One of Israel. Because this God is the true God, he can and will act now, bringing the downfall of the people's oppressors, the restoration of deported Judahites to Palestine and the rebuilding of Jerusalem, through the up-and-coming Persian king Cyrus.

But the Judahites also have a deeper need, of the restoration of their inner self and their relationship with God, and through special servant(s) whom God will send to them God will also achieve these ends. Israel itself will then be able to function again as Yahweh's witness and Yahweh's servant, so that Yahweh may be acknowledged, vindicated and praised through the world (see further 363).

Who is this servant? The first passage that refers to the servant explicitly identifies him as Israel (Is 41:8-10). But Acts 8 tells a story involving Philip the evangelist and an Ethiopian state minister who was reading Isaiah 53 and asked Philip whether the servant is the prophet or someone else. Philip uses the passage to tell him about Jesus. Isaiah 41 and Acts 8 thus point us to a range of possibilities.

1. The servant is Israel, as is stated in Isaiah 41:8-10; 44:1 and elsewhere. It is the usual Jewish view of the servant. The vivid description of the servant as an individual does not argue against this idea; Israel is often described as one man (see Is 1:5-6). A variant on this view is that the servant stands for faithful Jews (Is 50:10 calls them to follow the servant).

2. The servant is the prophet. Isaiah describes himself as the servant of Yahweh in Isaiah 20:3, and where the servant speaks as "I" (Is 49:1-6; 50:4-9) the natural view is that the prophet is speaking.

3. The servant is some contemporary of the prophet such as Jehoiakin the Judahite king in exile or Cyrus the Persian king who is about to defeat Babylon and allow the Judahites to go home; Cyrus is described as Yahweh's shepherd and Yahweh's anointed in Isaiah 44:28; 45:1.

4. The servant is the Messiah. The NT often sees Jesus as the fulfillment of the passages about Yahweh's servant, but it also sees the church as called to be their fulfillment.

What makes best sense, in light of your reading of the chapters (see further 363)?

Isaiah 40–55 comprises glorious proclamation and visionary promise. The atmosphere of Isaiah 56–66 is different again; it reflects yet another historical context. When Isaiah 1–39 refers to historical events, they belong to the 700s B.C. When Isaiah 40–55 refers to historical events, they belong to the 540s B.C. The context addressed by Isaiah 56–66 is a few decades later. It belongs to the same time as the story told in Ezra and Nehemiah and as Haggai, Zechariah and Malachi, and it brings a similar message to these prophets.

The wondrous vision of Second Isaiah (Is 40–55) has seen a partial fulfillment in the restoration of Judah, but it fell short of the glory promised, as Ezra and Nehemiah and those other prophetic books show. So these are prophecies for people who still need encouragement and challenge. Maybe they are disappointed, puzzled and hurt by the gap between hope and experience. The prophecies bring such people warnings about where sin leads, prayers that embody how the people may talk to God about their experience, responses to such prayers that reveal how God looks at those who pray and at their needs, and promises about how God's word will still be fulfilled.

The prophecies unfold chiastically as follows:

56:1-8: Preface

  56:9–59:8: Challenges about Israel's life

    59:9-15a: Prayer for forgiveness and restoration

      59:15b-21: Vision of Yahweh in judgment

        60:1-22: Visions of Jerusalem restored

          61:1-9: The prophet's commission

        61:10–62:12: Visions of Jerusalem restored

      63:1-6: Vision of Yahweh in judgment

    63:7–64:12: Prayer for forgiveness and restoration

  65:1–66:16: Challenges about Israel's life

66:17-24: Postscript

The prophecies presuppose life back in Canaan and more likely come from a later prophet or prophets than from the figure whose work is preserved in Isaiah 40–55, a prophet or prophets called by God to take up in yet another context the ministry that the earlier prophets whose work appears in the book of Isaiah had exercised (see further 363).

The opening verse of Isaiah 56–66 indicates its relationship with what proceeds and sets its agenda. "Exercise authority and do what is right": that sums up much of Isaiah 1–39. "Because my deliverance is near to coming, my doing right is near to revealing itself": that summarizes much of Isaiah 40–55. The closing chapters of the book urge the people of God to keep on living with that obligation and that promise.

Reading Isaiah 56–66.

1. What is Yahweh's vision for or promise to Jerusalem, according to Isaiah 60–62? What would count as fulfillment of these promises?

2. What is the significance of the vision of warrior Yahweh acting to punish in Isaiah 59:15b-20; 63:1-6?

3. What is the nature of the prayers in Isaiah 59:9-15a; 63:7–64:12? Are they theologically surprising? What do they teach us about God and about prayer?

4. What are the main points in the opening and closing sections, Isaiah 56:1–59:8; 65:1–66:24? How do they link to the material in between?

Isaiah 65: The Isaiah agenda.

(The following is based on Fung, *Isaiah Vision*.) Isaiah 65 speaks of a new heavens and a new earth, but it soon makes clear that it is not a new cosmos. It is a way of talking about a renewed Jerusalem, a renewed city. The "Isaiah agenda" is that children don't die, old people live in dignity, people who build houses live in them and people who plant vineyards eat their fruit. It is not a description of paradise; people do die. It is a vision of God's intention for the human community here and now. It is realistic not idealistic. It is modest; it makes no reference to education, leisure, democracy or culture. It represents a minimum that God might be satisfied with. If this is God's agenda, we will wish to act accordingly toward it. It is not difficult to do so.

The Three (or Four) Voices in the Book

The book of Isaiah addresses widely separate times. So how did it come into existence? I have implied that God did not speak out of context to people through a single Isaiah who lived centuries before most of his audience. God spoke pastorally and directly to people where they were, through a number of agents. God does speak about the future, but it is the future as it brings encouragement or challenge to people in the present, as when Paul talks about the second coming of Christ to people who themselves will not see it in this life. In Isaiah God's revelation comes through four human voices (or pens).

The ambassador, the actual prophet called Isaiah ben Amoz. He speaks autobiographically in Isaiah 6; 8, but his voice is much more pervasive. Because he volunteers to be the person whom Yahweh "sends" and he often speaks as one "sent," he is like the ambassador of a human sovereign. It is especially through his voice that we hear Yahweh's voice in Isaiah 1–39.

The poet, the voice that we hear in Isaiah 40–55. He hears a command to "cry out." This voice speaks more poetically or more lyrically than the other voices. He speaks to a time 150 years after Isaiah ben Amoz's day. He wonders what to cry out in the circumstances of his day, but he becomes the one who now acts as Yahweh's representative like Isaiah. He too meets with little success and is tempted to be gloomy, but he remains convinced of Yahweh's support and vindication (Is 49:4; 50:7).

The preacher, the voice that we hear in Isaiah 56–66. He is one anointed to be a bringer of good news, a binder up of the broken-hearted (Is 61:1). It had already been the task of the poet, but this further preacher's ministry (he is also a poet, though) addresses a different community with different needs and different temptations from the one a few decades previously, people that may have been in Babylon. So a new preacher takes up the task of being Yahweh's ambassador.

The disciple. The ambassador, the poet and the preacher are known as

First, Second and Third Isaiah. But their work is arranged and orchestrated by one or more disciples. The book actually begins with someone speaking about Isaiah in the third person to introduce him (Is 1:1). The one who speaks about "Isaiah the prophet" (Is 37:2; 38:1) is evidently someone other than the ambassador himself. Now Isaiah commissions his "disciples" to preserve his teaching (Is 8:16), so we may infer that it is such a disciple or disciples who tell us stories about Isaiah such as those in Isaiah 7; 26; 36–39. It is they who structure the book with other introductions such as the one in Isaiah 13:1. They presumably put the book together. By doing so, recognizing in the words of Isaiah the words of Yahweh, they sought to make them available to future generations so that these words of Yahweh addressed them too.

It would be natural for them to seek to show how these words addressed later generations. We have seen that a currently popular scholarly theory is that some parts of Isaiah 1–39 represent the way Isaiah's own words were expounded to this end, a century after his day in the time of King Josiah, and we may think of this exposition as the work of one of Isaiah's later disciples. Within Isaiah 1–39, as a very rough guide the passages in poetry may be thought of as Isaiah's actual oracles, while the prose may be thought of as the disciples' sermons on texts from Isaiah.

The poet was in part a disciple of the ambassador; that is, Second Isaiah sometimes preached on texts from First Isaiah and perhaps produced the first edition of the material that now appears in Isaiah 1–55. The preacher was also in effect a disciple of the poet; that is, Third Isaiah sometimes preached on texts from Second Isaiah and perhaps produced a new edition of Second Isaiah's words. Theories of this kind regarding the origin of the book are popular in the scholarly world, but they change with fashion.

At some time in the Persian period (or possibly in the Greek period) there came an end to the process whereby the book called "Isaiah" developed, but the evidence is insufficient for us to be confident about the process. At least these four voices speak from the book; it as mediated by them. The book called "Isaiah" is a multivoiced one, throughout which the voice of Yahweh comes to us.

If Isaiah 40–55 and Isaiah 56–66, which directly address much later periods than that of Isaiah ben Amoz, do come from later prophets, why are they part of the book called "Isaiah"? Wherein lies the book's unity?

In his commentary *Das Buch Jesaiah*, Bernhard Duhm suggested that the three main parts of the book were of quite separate origin and were artificially joined. That idea can't be right. There is too much that holds them together. If readers ask what theology emerges from the book as a whole, what do they discover?

1. The book has some unity of themes. The fact that Yahweh is the Holy One of Israel runs through it. So does the importance of Zion. So does the relationship between Yahweh and the nations. So does a concern with doing right/faithfulness (*ṣədāqâ/ṣedeq*).

2. Other themes develop through the book. The exhortation "Fear not" comes to king and people, then king and people again (Is 7; 10; 37; 41), thus across the divide between Isaiah 1–39 and Isaiah 40–55 (Conrad, *Reading Isaiah*). It is possible to trace the developing negative and positive significance of images such as trees and water (Quinn-Miscall, *Reading Isaiah*).

   The three parts of the book are in conversation. Isaiah 1–39 says, "You must do *mišpāṭ* and *ṣədāqâ*"; Isaiah 40–55 says, "Yahweh will do *mišpāṭ* and *ṣədāqâ*"; Isaiah 56:1 sets up the relation between these statements as the agenda for Isaiah 56–66 (Rendtorff, *Canon and Theology*).

3. The three parts reflect a continuing ministry or inspiration. The prophet who speaks in Isaiah 40–55 is taking up the ministry of the one who speaks in Isaiah 6 and is inspired by him, or is inspired by the Holy Spirit to take up his ministry; the prophet who speaks in Isaiah 61 is inspired by the Holy Spirit to take up the ministry of both his predecessors or mentors.

4. The insights in the three parts move on from each other; the book has a kind of plot. The first part speaks about a new David; the second part

divides the David role between Cyrus and the people as a whole. Isaiah 39:8 raises a question that Isaiah 55:3-5 answers.

5. The first part makes prophecies (notably Is 13) whose fulfillment the second part can look back on or affirm (Is 41). The first part speaks of first events, the second of new events (see Childs, *Old Testament as Scripture*, 328).

6. The first part declares God's word, the second and third expound it further. See (a) Isaiah 2:2-4 taken up in Isaiah 42:1-4; (b) Isaiah 6:9-10 taken up in Isaiah 42:18-25; (c) Isaiah 29:16 taken up in Isaiah 45:9-13; (d) Isaiah 35 taken up in Isaiah 40–66; (e) Isaiah 1–39 taken up in Isaiah 56–66 (Beuken, "Unity of the Book of Isaiah").

7. The whole is structured as one work. Isaiah 1–27 and Isaiah 28–66 form concentric circles. Isaiah 1–39 and Isaiah 35–66 form hooked complexes. Isaiah 1–33 and Isaiah 34–66 are the two halves. Isaiah 1 and Isaiah 65–66 bracket the whole of the book.

8. The two main parts exhibit a binary theology: punishment and deliverance; ethics and promise; Jerusalem and exodus; David and the servant.

9. A theology emerges from the book (for an expanded version, see 363):

    a. Revelation: it's a vision from God and it's God's word.

    b. Yahweh as the God of Israel is the Holy One.

    c. Holiness implies uprightness and mercy.

    d. Ephraim and Judah both matter to God; Jerusalem/Zion is the city that he will judge and restore.

    e. The leftovers (the remnant): Yahweh will reduce to a remnant but will preserve the remnant.

    f. The nations, the empires and their kings: Yahweh is lord of and concerned for the whole.

    g. Divine sovereignty/planning and human responsibility/planning interweave.

    h. Yahweh will be faithful to David; Yahweh's Day will come in the short term and the long term.

READING HAGGAI, ZECHARIAH
AND MALACHI

The background of the work of the three prophets is the same as that of
Isaiah 56–66. The story is told in Ezra–Nehemiah. In 539 B.C. Cyrus took
control of the Babylonian Empire and encouraged exiles to go back to Judah.
The Judahite community did some reordering of things in the still-devastated
temple but soon gave up the work (see Ezra 1–4). In 520 B.C. Haggai and
Zechariah set about urging them to take it up again, and they rebuilt the
temple (see Ezra 5–6). The Second Temple period thus begins.

Zechariah 9–14 is particularly complicated, but at least we can see the sort
of situation it addresses from the two distinctive features of its prophecies:
(1) they look for a future decisive act of God to sort out the people's destiny,
which implies pessimism about the present and any immediately or humanly imaginable future; (2) they are disillusioned with the leadership of
the community, which they often attack. They promise that one day God will
sort things out and fulfill the destiny of the people and the world.

The relationship between Zechariah 1–8 and Zechariah 9–14 looks similar
to that between First Isaiah and Second Isaiah (for more on Zech 9–14,
see 363).

Malachi refers to a number of the same problems as Ezra and Nehemiah
and belongs in their period, sometime in the fifth century.

Reading Haggai, Zechariah and Malachi

1. What issues regarding the people's religious life are these three prophets
   concerned about?

2. What do the people therefore have to do?

3. What are the theological issues—the facts about God that they need to
   take account of?

4. What are issues in their community life? What does God promise, and
   what do they have to do?

5. What other issues do these three prophets raise?

6. How do they compare and contrast with Isaiah 56–66?

7. How do they compare and contrast with earlier prophets?

8. Where do you think their importance lies?

God's encouragements and exhortations to the Second Temple community

Haggai 1	Build God's house, not your own.
Haggai 2	Don't be discouraged because of how things are—get on with the job.
Zecharlah 1	Say to God, "How long?"
Zechariah 2	Don't try to measure Jerusalem.
Zechariah 3	Don't think that God can't reestablish someone.
Zechariah 4	Don't think that God can't do it (cf. Hag 2).
Zechariah 5	Keep believing in God's cleansing and renewal.
Zechariah 6	Keep believing in the fulfillment of God's promise.
Zechariah 7	Get your community life right.
Zechariah 8	Keep believing that God will attract the world.
Zechariah 9	Believe that God is committed to Zion and will defend and restore it.
Zechariah 10	Believe that God will remove bad shepherds and care for the flock.
Zechariah 11	Be realistic about the way things have been over the centuries.
Zechariah 12	Believe that Yahweh will pour out a spirit of grace and prayer.
Zechariah 13	Believe that God will cleanse Zion and terminate (false) prophecy.
Zechariah 14	Believe that Zion will become a source of living water, a place of worship for all peoples.
Malachi 1	Bring God the best.
Malachi 2	Beware of laments.
Malachi 3	Bring the tithes.
Malachi 4	The future is always open.

What Is a Prophet—Then and Now?

Prophets are different from kings, priests, judges and experts, different from pastors, teachers, apostles and evangelists, different from worship ministers, youth pastors, counselors and spiritual directors, and different from social activists. I assume that we shouldn't be surprised if God sends prophets to the church, though neither should we be surprised if it is a rare thing. Not all the ten points that follow will then be true of every prophet, but to judge from the OT, in general a prophet is someone who

1. Shares God's nightmares and dreams. Prophets are not social reformers or political commentators. They see calamity hanging over God's people and they tell them about it, and about why it is so. They also know what is God's dream for his people and they tell them that dream. They know the dream because they know the story of God's involvement with Israel and know God's promises and God's expectations, and they want to get Israel to live in light of the story, the promises and the expectations.

2. Speaks like a poet and behaves like an actor. Prophets describe things not prosaically and literally but poetically and figuratively, partly because of the depth and mystery of which they speak. Prophets use pictures. They also picture what God intends by acting it out.

3. Is not afraid to be offensive. Prophets have the capacity to be outrageous. People thought that they were offensive and crazy.

4. Confronts the confident with rebuke and the downcast with hope. The calling of prophets is to get their own people to live in light of the reality of what God is going to do. God's people do not need prophets to confirm what they already think. They need prophets to disagree with them.

5. Mostly brings this rebuke and encouragement to the people of God. Prophets speak *about* other nations, so that God's people understand what God is doing and so that they shape their lives and attitudes ac-

cordingly, but they do not speak *to* other nations. Within their own nation, they are not social reformers. They do not give concrete practical directives to the people. They minister to the broader world indirectly by encouraging the people of God to become something more like an alternative community that will then commend itself to the broader society.

6. Is independent of the institutional pressures of church and state. It's virtually impossible to be a prophet if you are on the nation's payroll or the church's payroll. People such as pastors who are on the church's payroll have to encourage other people to be prophets. But they will have to remember that the OT prophets tended to be people who did not expect to be prophets (e.g., a foreigner or a priest or a kid) and whom other people did not expect to be prophets

7. Is a scary person who mediates the activity of a scary God. Like the OT, the NT makes clear that God is both loving and capable of doing frightening things. Prophets bring home to us the fact that you can't mess with God.

8. Intercedes with boldness and praises with freedom. As well as mediating God's word to us on the basis of knowing what God intends for us, prophets pray for us and tell us how to pray. They also articulate praise for what God does in fulfillment of their words.

9. Ministers in a way that reflects his or her personality and time. Paradoxically, the people who especially speak directly from God are also people whose message shows the influence of their own person, which God is using. And prophets are people who know what time it is, who know what needs to be said concretely *now*.

10. Is almost certain to fail, one way or another. Prophets make mistakes. In addition, they are usually rejected and persecuted because of the fact that their message characteristically confronts what the people of God think. Only a fool wants to be a prophet. Sensible people run away. But they may not get away.

(For a fuller version, see 363.)

Prophecy

What Does the Fulfillment of Prophecy Mean?

What counts as the fulfillment of prophecy? In what sense was prophecy fulfilled in Jesus? In what sense is it open to fulfillment in modern events—for instance, in modern Israel?

1. What do we mean by prophecy being "fulfilled"? The English word "fulfill" can have a number of meanings, and we would be unwise to assume that all of them apply to OT prophecy.

   a. We talk about a football schedule being fulfilled. If a game has to be called off, it has to be rescheduled later. Is prophecy like the football schedule, so that prophecies that don't get fulfilled at the time are rescheduled for later? Prophecy then prescribes things.

   b. Or is the fulfillment of prophecy like a weather forecast being fulfilled? A weather forecaster is then vindicated by the fulfillment of predictions. Is prophecy prediction, so that we can prove that Jesus is the Messiah by showing how prophecies were fulfilled?

   c. Or is prophecy like a promise or a warning that is due for fulfillment? It might then be like telling the children you will take them to the beach or saying that you will punish them for something: whether the promise or warning gets fulfilled depends on the response. See Jeremiah 18, of which Jonah's preaching in Nineveh provides an illustration.

   d. Or is prophecy like a commitment that must be fulfilled? When you marry, you promise to share all your worldly goods with someone, and you do so.

2. All those ideas of fulfillment may be present in Scripture, but the last two make sense of the way in which prophecies can be fulfilled more than once. Prophecies represent God making undertakings (positive or negative).

3. The meaning of the word "fulfillment" in Scripture can also vary. The most common verbs are *mālē'* (Hebrew) and *plēroō* (Greek), which are the ordinary words meaning "fill." They are not technical-sounding

words like "fulfill." They could suggest that prophecies are being "filled out" or "filled up" and not merely literally fulfilled like a weather forecast or a schedule of football games (see 353).

4. This suggestion fits with the fact that most NT "fulfillments" don't look very literal. For example, consider the following:

   a. Isaiah 1:9 is a passage that relates to Isaiah's day, but Romans 9:29 applies it to Paul's day.

   b. Isaiah 6:9-10 likewise addressed Judah in the eighth century B.C., and it was fulfilled then, but in Mark 4:12 and Acts 28:26-27 Jesus and Paul both declare it to be fulfilled in their analogous situations.

   c. Isaiah 59:20 looks like a passage that could have been applied to the coming of Jesus, but Romans 11:26 applies it to the future.

   d. Isaiah 7:14 and Isaiah 9:1-2 are further passages that relate to Isaiah's day, but the NT applies them to Jesus.

   e. Jeremiah 31:31-34 was a promise for people in Jeremiah's day, and it was fulfilled in following decades, but then Hebrews says that it was fulfilled at Jesus' first coming, and Romans 11:27 says that it will be fulfilled at the End.

5. Fulfillment may have nothing to do with the text's original meaning. John 11:49-52 is instructive. John says that Caiaphas spoke not on his own but as high priest, prophesying that Jesus would die for the Jewish nation. Of course, in a sense Caiaphas did speak on his own, but John sees a second meaning in his words. In a parallel way, one might say that Isaiah spoke on his own when he made the statement about a girl having a baby (Is 7:14), but there was a twinkle in the Holy Spirit's eye when he inspired those words to give to Ahaz. So we want to understand them in their God-given meaning in the context of Isaiah's ministry and also in the context of the further significance they have in light of Jesus' coming.

6. So when we are seeking to understand prophecy and its fulfillment, we will look for the fulfillment in the lives of the people to whom the prophecy is given. But we won't be surprised if the prophecy's words are also illuminating is some later context.

(For more resources on prophecy, see 363.)

S ee the note on web resources at the beginning of this book.

364 JOSHUA: RESOURCES AND RESPONSES TO QUESTIONS

 a. Joshua and Rahab

 b. Joshua: Responses to Questions

365 JUDGES: RESOURCES AND RESPONSES TO QUESTIONS

 a. Deborah

 b. Jephthah and His Daughter

 c. Samson

 d. Judges: Responses to Questions

366 SAMUEL–KINGS: RESOURCES AND RESPONSES TO QUESTIONS

 a. 1-2 Samuel: Responses to Questions

 b. 1-2 Kings: Outline, Origin, Characteristics, Emphases, Message, Implications

 c. 1-2 Kings: Responses to Questions

367 PROPHETS: RESOURCES

 a. Prophecy in Matthew 1:18–4:16

 b. Interpreting Prophecy: Premodern, Modern, Postmodern

 c. Lenses for Looking at the Prophets

368 ISAIAH: RESOURCES

 a. Isaiah 1:2-4 as Poetry/Rap

 b. Isaiah 6: So What Does Holiness Mean?

Part Four THE WRITINGS

THE WRITINGS
What Are They?

The "Writings" is the name of the last section of the OT in its Jewish order. A neat thing about the vague name is that it corresponds to the fact that the Writings are rather a miscellany, an assortment of different sorts of books from different backgrounds. The Greek and English Bible spreads them among the other books (see the diagram in 104), so that, for instance, the narrative books Chronicles, Ezra and Nehemiah follow the narrative books from Genesis through Kings.

The title "Writings" (Hebrew "Ketubim") more literally means "written," and the most attractive theory about why they come together with this name is that they are the written books as opposed to the read books. That is, the Torah provided the first reading for each synagogue service and the Prophets provided the second reading, but the Writings were not part of the weekly readings, though they featured in worship in other ways. Psalms were used at different times, and Song of Songs, Ruth, Lamentations, Ecclesiastes and Esther (the "Scrolls," in Hebrew "Megillot") were each the focus for one worship occasion each year.

Historically, these books belong together through their being connected with the Second Temple period (the periods of the Persian and Greek Empires) more explicitly than the Torah and the Prophets are. Chronicles, Ezra, Nehemiah, Esther and Daniel all make some reference to the Persian Empire, and Daniel also to the Greeks. The book of Psalms has been called "The Hymnbook of the Second Temple," not because all the psalms were composed then, but because the book of Psalms was put together then. One illuminating way to look at the Writings is as a resource for faith and life in those times, which in some ways were tough times.

The miscellaneous nature of the Writings is matched by the variety in the ways they have been organized. For instance, in different versions of the Hebrew Bible, Psalms, Ruth, Job and Chronicles have all come first. That variation gives me the excuse to cover them in an order of my own. In outlining it, I also note the variety of ways in which these books that close the OT link with the NT.

An outline of the Writings

1. *Story: Ezra–Nehemiah, Chronicles, Ruth, Esther.* These books tell you about the situation of people in the Second Temple period and how God related to them, and also retell Israel's earlier story to speak to that situation. They give you background you need in order to understand the NT story. Matthew 1:1-17 follows the pattern set by Chronicles. Luke 1–2 sets Jesus in the context of the kind of community that Chronicles describes.

2. *Worship: Psalms, Lamentations.* These books tell you how Israelites worshiped and prayed—or how they were supposed to do so. They give Christians the examples that they need in order to be able to worship and pray the way they are urged in Ephesians 5:18-20; 6:18-19.

3. *Wisdom: Proverbs, Song of Songs, Job, Ecclesiastes.* These books expound what it means to be smart. They give people the background to being a wise teacher like Jesus in his parables or preaching, and in a letter such as James.

4. *Bringing it all together: Daniel.* Daniel declares both that God's reign is here and that it is coming, as Jesus will in the Gospels and as Revelation will.

How the Writings are designed to transform people's lives

- They set our lives not in the context of a set of beliefs but in the context of a story, and of some smaller stories too. They also encourage us to tell our stories.

- They see us in a relationship with God—a relationship of praise, protest, trust, repentance and testimony. They encourage us to say what we feel.

- They set our thinking in the context of an argument. They encourage us to face questions. They thus rescue us from the limitations of what we believe already.

- They are there to help the people of God live concretely, worshipfully, wisely and hopefully.

The two books called "Ezra" and "Nehemiah" relate a series of episodes from the story of Judah from 539 to 445 B.C.—the first half of the time when Judah was part of the Persian Empire, and the first century of the Second Temple period. They aren't a continuous history like Samuel–Kings, but they are our main source for knowing something of what happened in this period. The books combine (1) stories about events that took place; (2) first-person memoirs by Ezra and Nehemiah; (3) official documents; (4) lists of people.

The documents and lists presumably were kept in official records in Jerusalem. The list in Ezra 2 reappears in Nehemiah 7; its reference to Nehemiah himself suggests it is a list of people who returned over the period covered by the books as a whole. Apparently, the books were assembled by someone late in Ezra and Nehemiah's time or later; we don't know who it was.

The first verses of Ezra are the same as the last verses of Chronicles, which encourages us to treat Chronicles–Ezra–Nehemiah as one work, as does the arrangement in the English Bible. It might mean that Ezra–Nehemiah was written to follow Chronicles, but it could just as easily mean that Chronicles was written as a prequel to Ezra–Nehemiah. Ezra and Nehemiah originally comprised one book; they were first divided into two in the church, and Judaism later followed. It would have been more helpful to divide them into four books, as outlined below. In considering this fourfold outline, it will help to bear in mind the sequence of the main Persian Emperors, the Achaemenids (named after Achaemenus, an earlier Persian ruler):

559 B.C. Cyrus
530 B.C. Cambyses
522 B.C. Darius I
485 B.C. Xerxes I (Ahasuerus)
465 B.C. Artaxerxes I
424 B.C. Xerxes II

1. Ezra 1–6 begins with Cyrus's takeover of Babylon in 539 B.C. He encouraged Judahites who had been taken to Babylon (or rather, their children and grandchildren) to return to Jerusalem to rebuild the temple. They did clean up its site and start the rebuilding work, but they were put off by opposition from other local peoples. In Darius's reign they resumed the work and completed it between 520 and 516 B.C. with prods from Haggai and Zechariah (for more information, see their books; see also 360). Note that the accounts of opposition in Ezra 4:6-23 relate to the later time of Xerxes I and Artaxerxes I; the book has collected together stories about opposition. (Lamentations tells of how people in Jerusalem had been praying through the period up to Cyrus's day, and the stories in Daniel tell of the situation of Judahites in Babylon.)

2. Ezra 7–10 jumps on to the reign of Artaxerxes I. In 458 B.C. he commissioned Ezra, a learned Judahite, to take a scroll of the Torah and see that its rules were implemented in Jerusalem and Judah. Note that Ezra has nothing to do with the original return from the exile; his family had stayed in Babylon. He thus has nothing to do with the rebuilding of the temple. His concern was the purification of the community. (Esther tells another story about the Judahite community in Susa, one of the key Persian cities, in the slightly earlier time of Xerxes I.)

3. Nehemiah 1–7 jumps on again to the twentieth year of Artaxerxes I, 445 B.C., when he agreed to commission one of his palace staff in Susa to go and organize the rebuilding of the Jerusalem city walls, which apparently were still in ruins as a result of the Babylonian destruction in 587 B.C. Evidently, Nehemiah's family too had not taken the chance to return to Judah. (Some of the wrongs that Malachi protests about in Jerusalem parallel the kind of thing that Ezra and Nehemiah take action about, and Malachi likely dates in this general period.)

4. Nehemiah 8–13 has Ezra and Nehemiah together in Jerusalem, evidently at some later date in Artaxerxes I's reign, working together at the rebuilding of the community on the basis of the Torah and the building up of the population of the city itself.

Read Ezra and Nehemiah.

Ezra 1–6

1. What do you learn about the way God can work through and with a superpower?

2. What were the community's reasons for joy, and what were their reasons for worry?

Ezra 7–10

1. What sort of person is Ezra? What strikes you about him?

2. What are the features of the prayer that he prays (Ezra 9)?

3. The action in Ezra 10 horrifies many Western readers. How might Ezra have justified it?

Nehemiah 1–7

1. What sort of person is Nehemiah? What strikes you about him?

2. What are the features of the prayer that he prays (Neh 1)?

3. How does he go about his wall-building project?

4. What problems does he face, and how does he deal with them?

Nehemiah 8–13

1. What are the dynamics of the gathering in Nehemiah 8–10?

2. What are the features of the prayer (Neh 9)?

3. How does Nehemiah go about the other aspects of his work in Nehemiah 11–13?

Looking back over Ezra–Nehemiah

1. Are there ways in which the situation of the church is similar to Judah's? If so, does the story have implications for the church?

2. Are there ways in which questions about the church's relationships in the world are similar? If so, does the story have implications for the church?

3. Does the story suggest insights on how to pray for the church?

4. Does it suggest insights on leadership?

5. How do you see the characters and qualities of Ezra and Nehemiah? How would you talk with them if you were their pastor?

The adversaries. The reference to the peoples of the countries (Ezra 3:3), the community's "adversaries" (Ezra 4:1), introduces a key feature of the community's situation. These groups include (1) neighbors such as the Moabites and Ammonites, (2) the Samarians (i.e., people in the north, the area of Ephraim) and (3) people in Judah who had not gone into exile. The returning exiles would have reason to be suspicious of these peoples for political reasons (they wanted to take over Judah) and/or religious reasons (they said they worshiped Yahweh, but was their worship true?).

The breaking up of marriages. One way to think about this action is to ask what would have happened if the process of intermarriage had continued. A plausible view is that it would have meant that the distinctive Jewish community would have ceased to exist. There would have been no Israel, no Messiah, no Jesus. Note that the story does not concern foreign women like Ruth who become worshipers of Yahweh; it concerns women who keep their ethnic and religious identity. Further, there is no reason to think that the women and children were simply left to fend for themselves. But what happened to them is not the story's concern; it wants to record the action that Ezra and Nehemiah took to reform the community.

Cultural revitalization. A sociological understanding of the book of Nehemiah sees it as reporting a project aiming to restore a society characterized by economic exploitation, community deterioration, cultural distortion and social disillusion. In accordance with the principles of cultural revitalization, Nehemiah applies himself to prayer, communication with the people, organization, adaptation, reform and the implementation of a new orderliness (see Tollefson and Williamson, "Nehemiah as Cultural Revitalization").

We have noted that the overlap with the beginning of Ezra indicates that Chronicles is designed to lead into Ezra–Nehemiah, either because Ezra–Nehemiah is the sequel or because Chronicles is the prequel. At the same time, Chronicles stands on its own, and many Jewish versions of the order of the books do not have Chronicles leading into Ezra-Nehemiah. In the most common order Chronicles is the last book in the Torah, the Prophets and the Writings. While Chronicles has some similar emphases to those of Ezra–Nehemiah, the books also have distinctive features. So we will consider Chronicles separately.

In 323 we noted that 1-2 Kings tells the story from Solomon to the downfall of Judah as an act of praise at the justice of God's judgment. Chronicles retells the story from Adam to the end of the exile, but 1 Chronicles 3 includes a list of descendants of David via Zerubbabel that goes down to the time of Ezra and Nehemiah. So it is a retelling of the story designed to speak to the people's situation in the late fifth century B.C. (or later, for all we know). We don't know who wrote it, but it is a more coherent composition than Ezra-Nehemiah. It does not just bring together a collection of separate pieces.

Zechariah 4:10 describes the situation at the time of this prophecy as a "day of small things," and it wouldn't be surprising if many of the Judahites for whom Chronicles was written, a bit later, identified with that description of their own time. Chronicles is a retelling of Judah's story designed to encourage them. Much of it is word for word the same as Samuel–Kings; the author started from Samuel–Kings and produced a revised version of its story, sometimes omitting things, sometimes adding things, sometimes rewriting things. It is a new version of the story because the people are in that new situation and need a new message from God, and the Holy Spirit inspires the writing of a new version of the story. The presence of two versions in Scripture compares with the presence of four versions of the Jesus story in the NT. A rich story can be told in several ways in different contexts.

1. Review your study of 2 Samuel and 1-2 Kings. Then read quickly through Chronicles. What strikes you as distinctive about Chronicles?

2. What is Chronicles' big picture compared with that of Samuel–Kings? What are the similarities and differences in what they cover?

3. What is Chronicles' big picture compared with the outline of the OT story as described in 106 above? What are the similarities and differences in what they cover?

4. What is Chronicles' big picture compared with the outline of OT Israel's history in 106? What are the similarities and differences in what they cover?

5. Now look at the following examples of Chronicles taking up sections of Samuel–Kings, look at the differences and ask what might be the point of the changes.

   a. 2 Samuel 24: Yahweh inspires David to take a census.

      1 Chronicles 21: The Adversary inspires David to take a census. (Most translations have "Satan" for "The Adversary"; see 433.)

   b. 1 Kings 8:46-53: In exile people can pray toward Jerusalem, repenting, and Yahweh may hear and forgive, because of the exodus.

      2 Chronicles 6:36-42: Yahweh dwells in this temple. Yahweh has answered this prayer of Solomon's. Yahweh is in our midst. Yahweh has not forgotten David.

   c. 2 Kings 24:18–25:30: We, the people of Jerusalem and Judah, have done wrong by God, and God has been angry with us; that's why we are in trouble (2 Kings 24:18-20). This is how it happened; it was terrible (2 Kings 25:1-26).

      2 Chronicles 36:11-21: The king did not obey the prophetic word (so we should); Yahweh had kept sending prophets. The leadership defiled the temple. So the city fell, and its people were taken into exile (but there is less detail on what happened).

   d. 2 Kings 25:27-30: But the king has been released—a hopeful event.

      2 Chronicles 36:22-23: Jeremiah's prophecy has been fulfilled; that is the hopeful event.

4 | 05 | CHRONICLES
A Narrative Contextual Theology
of Music in Worship

Chronicles thus covers the same ground as Genesis through Kings, but does it more briefly and takes it a bit further. Furthermore, its telling of the story has some distinctive characteristics (on these, see further 442).

Chronicles' emphases. *Worship* emerges as one of Chronicles' main themes when you compare it with the parallel story in Samuel–Kings. Worship is not its only theme, but it is one basis for the selection of stories from Samuel–Kings that it includes or omits, and for additions that it makes. The theme of worship is part of a stress on God being with people. God is not involved in Judah's national life as he had been before the downfall of the state, but he is with them in the present not absent, nor do they simply have to look to the future (compare and contrast Ecclesiastes and Daniel).

Music is an emphasis. Chronicles shares the worship theme with Leviticus and Psalms, but Leviticus is concerned with sacrament, and Psalms is a resource book of words. In Chronicles the Levites are key figures, and they are *music* leaders. Chronicles emphasizes prayer, joy and praise, in life as well as in the temple. Gerhard von Rad (*Old Testament Theology*) asks "whether a theology that saw Israel's existence so strongly conditioned by praise" could have been very wrong.

In its *theology*, Chronicles stresses God's might, justice, word and grace, with the expected response of purity, trust and obedience. Its concern with music in relation to God and its theological perspective on worship and music need to be set in the context of the angle on worship in books such as Amos and 1 Peter as well as Leviticus and Psalms. Chronicles is concerned to show that God honors those who honor God in order to encourage people in their commitment to God, and it provides answers to puzzling questions about how Manasseh came to reign so long even though he served other gods and how Josiah cane to die early even though he was the great reformer.

It is *contextual*. Why should God want to inspire another version of the story in Samuel–Kings? The differences from Samuel–Kings reflect Chronicles' distinctive context in the Second Temple period, when the faith is under pressure and God seems inactive. Samuel–Kings tells the story of the time of the kings in a way that shows people how they had gone wrong, which fits the context of the exile. They needed to face these facts. Chronicles tells the story in a way that encourages people, which fits the context after the exile, when they need such encouragement. In telling the story, it does not always try to be literally accurate; it dresses the figures of history in the costumes of its own day in order to make the links clear to the people's own day.

It is a *narrative*. Thus it does not (overtly) tell its own story but retells the old, old story (as in the examples suggested for study) and abbreviates it (e.g., omitting the story of Ephraim and the human interest stories) or expands it (e.g., in the information on David's plans for the temple building). It portrays David rather more positively than 2 Samuel does, something like the way Hebrews 11 talks about OT characters. The way the first Christians kept rewriting the Gospel story (Mark, then Matthew and Luke, then John, according to the traditional view) takes up the assumption that an important story needs repeated retelling and gains from repeated retelling.

Some notes on the reading

1. In 2 Samuel 24 Yahweh is punishing David (we are not told explicitly why, but we know something of his wrongdoing). In 1 Chronicles 21 the Adversary is Yahweh's means of acting. Yahweh is thus distanced from the act.

2. 2 Chronicles 6 refers to Zion and the temple rather than the exodus, because Zion and the temple are the special privileged possessions of the Judahite community. The exodus occurred a long time ago; further, it can also be claimed by the Samarians as part of their history.

3. In 2 Kings the fall of Jerusalem is the white-hot, grievous, recent event. The story is told in all its painful detail. In Chronicles the fall of Jerusalem is past history, and its theological significance is more important.

4. In 2 Kings the release of Jehoiakin is a recent sign of hope. Chronicles knows that Cyrus's arrival turned out to be the more significant sign of hope.

Esther tells of how a Judahite girl gets drafted into the Persian king's harem in Susa and is thus in a position to get the king to halt a plan by one of his senior ministers to eliminate her people. The king is called "Ahasuerus," which is an alternative transliteration of the Persian name usually rendered "Xerxes" in English (see 402). Presumably, the story was written in Persia in the Persian period (or perhaps the Greek period), but it is anonymous. It has some of the features of a fictional story (see 109). In particular, it has cartoon features (a six-story-high gallows; a twelve-month-long beauty treatment!). These features give added spice to its annual retelling in the Jewish community at the festival of Purim, an important occasion each March that may also lie behind the emphasis on feasting in the story. There have been occasions when a Jewish community has indeed been threatened with annihilation but has escaped; I assume that this story is a "based on fact" version of such an event (for a play-reading version, see 442). By the time to which it refers, Judahites have been free to return to Judah. They are no longer in exile; exile has become dispersion. But Esther parallels Daniel in reflecting the way living in a foreign country can be dangerous to faith and even to life.

Read the story and think about the characters and roles of Ahasuerus, Vashti, Haman, Esther, Mordecai and any of the other characters that you find interesting. Then answer the following questions:

1. What is the structure or shape of the story? What are its main turning points? What are its key moments or key verses?

2. What are the main points of the story? (There's no need to establish only one main point, I think.)

3. The story describes the position of Jews under pressure in a pagan environment and under threat of holocaust. Precisely what encouragement does it bring them?

4. The story is humorous and entertaining. What do you think is the point

of these features? What effect do they have on the content of the book's message—its world or its view of life?

5. God is never mentioned in Esther, and neither are prayer or faith or the Torah. The version of Esther in the Greek Bible (see 507) adds many such references. What are the points or implications or effects of this aspect of the story in the Hebrew version?

6. What understandings and vision of womanhood appear in the story? How would you characterize the personalities and actions of Vashti, Esther and the other women?

7. The story portrays both Jews and Gentiles acting for the most part from equally dubious motives of pride, greed and cruelty. What do you think is the significance of this aspect of the story?

8. The story depends on a series of coincidences; as a result of them, what happens is the opposite of what people might have expected, planned or feared, and thereby justice is done. Is life actually like that? What is the significance of the book's portrayal of it in these terms?

9. Ahasuerus and Vashti, and Esther and Mordecai, appear as royal or quasi-royal figures exercising royal or quasi-royal power. How does the story portray power being exercised? What does it see as the potential of power and the temptations of power?

10. The theme of obedience or disobedience to authority is important in the stories of Vashti, Mordecai and Esther. What do they suggest are the risks and obligations of civil obedience or disobedience?

11. The characters have been seen as embodiments of wisdom and folly. How far can one see them in this way?

12. "The rampant destruction of European Jewish communities in the recent past is similar to a threat described, but not fulfilled, in Esther. Haman's spiritual descendants proved more successful in attaining their goal of genocide. . . . One message of the Book of Esther, with its emphasis upon Jewish solidarity and human responsibility and action, remained unheard by Mordecai's and Esther's descendants" (Berg, *Book of Esther*, 183-84). What do you think of this comment?

ESTHER

*Its Significance in the Context of
Scripture as a Whole*

Afamous biblical theologian once commented that he couldn't see how a Christian preacher could ever take their text from Esther. Actually Esther is worth a series of sermons.

Esther is the biblical discussion of anti-Semitism. Anti-Semitism has been encouraged by Christian talk about the Jews being Jesus' murderers. Esther is an account of an attempt at genocide that is typological of the Jewish people's experience. Michael Fox (*Character and Ideology*) describes the way the book speaks to him every year at Purim because of what happened to his family in nineteenth-century pogroms and in the Holocaust. It expresses the promise that things do not always work out in that way. Haman anticipates Adolf Hitler's comment in 1939:

> I have very often been a prophet, and have usually been ridiculed for it. During the time of my struggle for power it was in the first instance the Jewish race which only received my prophecies with laughter when I said that I would one day take over the leadership of the State, and with it that of the whole nation, and that I would then among many other things settle the Jewish problem. Their laughter was uproarious, but I think that for some time now they have been laughing on the other side of their face.

Haman is already looking for a final solution to the Jewish problem (Bauckham, *Bible in Politics*).

Esther is an expression of the way God often works in history. It makes no reference to God, Israel or prayer, yet its silence speaks loudly. It compares and contrasts with the story of Israel in the days of Joseph and Moses. In Moses' day God visibly intervened, but God's acts are not usually visible. Even in the Joseph story God's involvement eventually is explicitly mentioned, but not in Esther. It illustrates the themes of wisdom expressed in Proverbs, and the characters embody wisdom and folly (Gordis, "Religion, Wisdom and History"). Esther encourages Jewish people to take responsibility for their destiny in the conviction that God is at work behind coincidences and chance (compare the Berg quotation in 406). The whole story hangs on the king's sleepless night!

Esther reminds us of the realities of power in the world. It's not about what should happen but about what does happen (Fuerst, *Books of Ruth, Esther*). It's not what you know that counts, but who you know. The males have power—or do they? The king turns out to have no power over Vashti, and the men assume that her action will encourage rebellion among the other wives in Persia. Esther turns out to have power in another sense, by using the system rather than defying the system (though the book does close with Xerxes and Mordecai). The fact that women have usually had to survive and exercise power out of a position of structural weakness makes a woman an appropriate image for the position of the Judahite people in the Dispersion (White, "Esther").

Esther draws attention to the theological significance of the Jewish people. One can apply its principles to the church, but in itself it's about God's preserving of Israel. Wilhelm Vischer wrote on Esther in 1939, when the Holocaust was about to happen. He suggested that the most offensive truth in all revelation is the fact that God has connected himself indissolubly with Israel's history, and he pointed to Romans 11:25. He notes that it is through the Jewish people that we all receive salvation. "Jesus Christ is the fulfiller of the promise of the Book of Esther." Given current Christian sympathy with the Palestinians, it is important not to lose sight of this point.

Esther shows how if you want to survive, you'd better learn to laugh. In a typically Jewish way it encourages Jews to cope with adversity by laughing at their foes and at themselves. So humor runs through the story: Vashti and Esther as sex objects, the six-month banquet, the six-story-high gallows, the year's preparation for entering the harem, Haman's ending up honoring Mordecai, the king's assumption that Haman is raping Esther when he is actually begging her for mercy, the fact that the only people in danger are those who attack the Jews and seventy-five thousand do. And in that connection, the ultimate irony is that the Jews let themselves be drawn into the massacre that they had managed to escape (Goldman, "Narrative and Ethical Ironies"). But irony is always dangerous, and readers usually don't get it.

The Book of Ruth is anonymous, and we don't know when it was written. Its location among the Writings points to its having been written in the Second Temple period, when the question of relations with people such as the Moabites was a lively one (see Ezra–Nehemiah). Its closing with a genealogy leading up to David suggests that it is a basically historical story; it would be foolish to give David a Moabite great-grandmother if this idea was a fiction. On the other hand, the detailed story with its accounts of conversations in the bedroom is presumably "based on fact" rather than simply history.

Reading Ruth. Read the story of Ruth (for a play-reading version and an exposition, see 442).

1. What do you think is the significance of the story for Ruth herself?

2. What do you think is the significance of the story for Naomi?

3. What do you think is its significance for Boaz?

4. What do you think is its significance for David?

5. What do you think is its significance for Israelites such as the people of Bethlehem?

6. You could also imagine your way into the story from the perspective of Elimelek or Mahlon and Kilion or Orpah or Ruth's mother or the man who declined to be Ruth's restorer.

What is ḥesed? The word *ḥesed* plays a key role in the book; the story illustrates *ḥesed* at work even when it doesn't use the word. A common translation of *ḥesed* is "steadfast love," but sometimes it is translated as devotion, faithfulness, favor, kindness, love, loyalty or mercy. The word denotes an extraordinary act of self-giving. It is the nearest Hebrew word to Greek *agapē*. It is used in two chief connections.

1. It can refer to an extraordinary act of generosity, graciousness or mercy that one person shows to another when they are under no obligation to

do so; there is no prior relationship between the parties. In this sense, it overlaps with grace or favor (*ḥēn* in Hebrew, *charis* in Greek). "Grace" or "favor" maybe refers more to the attitude, *ḥesed* to the action.

2. It can also refer to an extraordinary act of self-giving, loyalty or mercy that one person shows to another when they are already in relationship with them. In this sense, it overlaps with faithfulness (*ʾĕmet* or *ʾĕmûnâ* in Hebrew). "Faithfulness" then denotes a general quality, *ḥesed* a faithfulness that goes beyond anything one might have expected.

Ḥesed is also translated "covenant love," and it does sometimes link with covenants. But it can exist outside of any covenant relationship, and it can denote a loyalty that goes beyond anything that a covenant would demand (e.g., staying faithful when the other party is not faithful). My suggestion is that "commitment" is an English word that covers both senses of the Hebrew word. (It is odd that the word "commitment" hardly comes in English translations to translate any Hebrew or Greek words.)

The word *ḥesed* occurs three times in Ruth: (1) in Ruth 1:8, Orpah and Ruth have shown *ḥesed* to their husbands and to Naomi, and she asks for God to show it to them (sense #2 above); (2) in Ruth 2:20, God has done so for her and Ruth (sense #2 above); (3) in Ruth 3:10, Ruth has done so for Boaz (sense #1 above).

Here are some examples of *ḥesed* from elsewhere in the Writings:

1. Chronicles: Yahweh will not withdraw his *ḥesed* from David's son (1 Chron 17:13); Solomon appeals to Yahweh's *ḥesed* to David (2 Chron 1:8).

2. Lamentations: Yahweh's *ḥesed* continues even when people have been unfaithful (Lam 3:22, 32).

3. Daniel: The officer shows unexpected *ḥesed* to Daniel; the officer was under no obligation (Dan 1:9).

4. Esther: Esther has the same experience of *ḥesed* as Daniel did, in her case with the king (Esther 2:17).

5. Psalms (among very many references): God's goodness and *ḥesed* chase us (Ps 23:6); the world is full of Yahweh's *ḥesed* (Ps 33:5); Yahweh's *ḥesed* extends to the heavens (Ps 36:5); Yahweh is slow to get angry and of great *ḥesed* (Ps 145:8).

RUTH

What Kind of Story?

Jewish. Ruth is about how David acquired his great-grandmother; and like Esther, it's one of the Five Scrolls used at different occasions each year in the Jewish calendar. Ruth is read at Pentecost; one reason is the motif of the barley harvest.

Nice. When Scottish missionaries translated the Bible into the Tamahaq language of the Tuaregs of the Sahara, they started with Ruth because they thought that it might be a good influence on the wild men (Knight, *Ruth and Jonah*).

Edifying. A rabbinic comment asks how Ruth is designed to be useful when it doesn't concern itself with classic Jewish themes such as cleanness and taboo, and answers that its significance lies in its exposition of the nature of *ḥesed* (see 408).

Encouraging. Ruth is about God's involvement in some ordinary people's ordinary lives: a woman whose life falls apart, a woman who finds a new family, a man who finds a wife. It reminds us that everyone has a story to tell and a genealogy to find (Peterson, *Five Smooth Stones*).

Theological. Ruth is not a Harlequin romance. Like Esther, it portrays God at work behind the scenes and through human action and chance. It illustrates what being a "redeemer" or "restorer" means, and thus what it means for God to be a redeemer or restorer: someone who has resources that he could expend to reestablish the lives of people in his extended family. For Christians, it's also background to Jesus, since Ruth appears in his genealogy (Mt 1:5).

Hopeful. Ruth begins with a reference to the period of the judges, and the book of Judges is characterized by unsavory accounts of how life works out in that time, especially for women.

Inclusivist. The book keeps emphasizing that Ruth is a Moabite, and it complements Ezra–Nehemiah in describing a proper openness to foreigners. It thus compares with Jonah (see 343).

Popular. Ruth is a folktale that starts from aspects of life and customs that the audience knows about, though this means that aspects of the story are obscure to us in a different culture (e.g., the details of the redeemer obligation and of the shoe ritual).

Underclass. Ruth might seem a rural idyll, but it discusses urban issues: it's about losing your livelihood, having to move to find work, coping as a single parent, living as an ethnic minority.

Literary. Ruth is told with a combination of economy over matters that aren't significant to the main plot (e.g., Ruth 1:1-5) and expansiveness when it comes to its main concern. In both respects the story keeps moving. Its plot raises problems and uses suspense, then solves and resolves them. It works partly through leaving gaps that you have to fill in a way that makes sense in the context (e.g., you have to work out whether to read Naomi's character sympathetically or unsympathetically).

Female. Ruth is about how to survive as women in a man's world (see Trible, *Rhetoric of Sexuality*). One facet of this aspect is the way Ruth propositions Boaz, or rather proposes to Boaz, as she surely is not just offering him a one-night stand. But it's risky plan. She is taking the initiative in the relationship in a way that contrasts with cultural norms.

Intertextual. Ruth resonates with other stories such as Tamar (Gen 38) and the Moabite women in Numbers 25, as well as Ezra–Nehemiah. We come to understand each text by comparing and contrasting them. Proverbs 31 has painted a portrait of a powerful or resourceful woman (Prov 31:11); only Ruth in Scripture is actually described in terms of that phrase from Proverbs. Her action in leaving her family and committing herself to Naomi and to Yahweh is like Abraham's. The portrait of life in Bethlehem (the care taken of some vulnerable women and a relative's willingness to marry a widow) bears comparison with the expectations of the Torah (another significance of reading it at Pentecost, when Jews celebrate the gift of the Torah).

Postcolonial. Ruth is about a woman finding security in a foreign country, about welcoming foreigners, about hybridity—creating new cultural forms (see Han, "Migrant Women," on migrant women in Korea; Lee, "Neo-Confucian Ideology," on the significance of Ruth in Korea).

4 | 10 | PSALMS

One Hundred and Fifty Examples of
How to Talk to God

The book of Psalms, or the Psalter, is a collection of praises and prayers that as such is also a book of teaching on worship and prayer. One indication that it is a book of teaching is the way it divides into five books. So before Psalms 1; 42; 73; 90; 107 are the headings "Book One," and so forth, and at the end of Psalms 41; 72; 89; 106 are some blessings, amens and hallelujahs (finally, Ps 150 is in effect one long closing hallelujah). These are not part of the psalm to which they are attached; they close off each book as a whole. In five books, the Torah told Israel about what God had done and about the way of life that should issue from what God had done; in five more books, the Psalter told people how God was involved with them now, how to respond in worship to what God had done and does, how to urge him to do it again, and what kind of life people were committed to, outside their life of praise and prayer. However, the Psalms teach not by telling but by showing. They speak *from* God by showing us how to speak *to* God.

Eugene Peterson has commented that the Psalms are where Christians in the past have always learned to pray (Peterson, *Working the Angles*, 50, 54-56). If that's so, they were learning in accordance with the Psalter's own nature and purpose. The Psalter presupposes that we shouldn't assume that we know how to pray and can do so intuitively on the basis of the Spirit's guidance. It presupposes that God wants to guide us, and it constitutes that guidance (see Bonhoeffer, *Life Together*, 53-58). There is some indication of this fact in the NT. The NT uses the Psalms to get help in understanding Jesus (Heb 1–2), the gospel (Rom 3–4), the future (Rev 2:23, 26; 3:5), the church's mission and ministry (Rom 15:9, 11), its spirituality (Mt 5; Heb 3–4), and its lifestyle (1 Pet 3:10-12) (on the Psalms in the NT, see further 442). But in addition, Ephesians 5:18-20; 6:18-20 and Colossians 3:16-17 urge people to speak to one another in psalms, hymns and songs in the Spirit, to give thanks, and to pray in the Spirit for people and for Paul himself. These prayers and praises will no doubt include new songs and prayers like those of Mary, Zechariah, Peter and John

(Lk 1; Acts 4; Revelation), but they will include the Psalms, and those new songs and prayers follow models from the Psalms.

The books within the book of Psalms. Behind the five books in the Psalter we can see many subcollections of psalms that have similar introductions or similar subject matter or similar use. Many of these introductions suggest a background in the psalms' use in worship.

- David Psalms: 3–41; 51–72 (except 10; 33)

- Korah Psalms: 42–49

- Asaph Psalms: 50; 73–83 (though it's odd that 50 is separate)

- Korah Psalms: 84–85; 87–88 (though it's odd that 86 is an isolated David psalm)

- Kingship Psalms: 93; 95–99

- Hallelujah Psalms: 105–107

- The Egyptian Hallel, used at Passover: 113–118 (113–114 before the meal, 115–118 after the meal; see Mk 14:26)

- Psalms of Ascents, used on pilgrimage or in procession: 120–134

- The Great Hallel, also used at Passover: 135–136

- David Psalms: 138–145

- Hallel Psalms: 146–150

Note also the Elohim psalms, Psalms 42–83. These are psalms that mostly use the ordinary word for "God" (*'ĕlōhîm*), not the special name "Yahweh." Some might have been written that way; many look as if they have been revised that way (e.g., compare Ps 53 with Ps 14). On the reasons for this, see 115.

The compilers of the Psalter thus usually kept earlier groups of psalms together. Beyond the division into five books, however, there isn't much structure to the Psalter as a whole. Sometimes one psalm leads into another, but psalms often follow from one another on a random basis.

Many scholars think that they can detect a careful arrangement in the Psalter as a whole, and that they can see, for instance, ways in which psalms have come to be interpreted messianically in the Second Temple period. For me, these theories involve overly speculative connecting of dots. But for such theories, see Grant, "Editorial Criticism."

READING PSALMS OF PRAISE
How to Worship Together

Read Psalms 95 and 100, and read Hebrews 3:7–4:13 for a sermon on Psalm 95.

1. Review the comments on Isaiah 31 as poetry (see 336) and look for how far these psalms work in the same way.

2. How do the two psalms work as a whole; what is their structure or logic?

3. What do they have in common, and how do they differ?

4. What do they tell us about worship?

You could then read the other psalms of praise and see how they are similar or different, and what they add to what you learn from those two: Psalms 8; 19; 29; 33; 47; 48; 65; 66; 68; 78; 87; 93; 95–100; 104; 105; 111; 113; 114; 117; 122; 134; 135; 145–150. One a day might be better than all at once!

Psalms as poetry. The Psalms might seem to be instinctive outpourings of praise and pain, but the point assumed by Robert Lowth (who "discovered" parallelism) was that they follow poetic form, so things are more complicated. Poetry reflects human experience, but it's crafted (etymologically, the word "poem" suggests something "made"). It's concerned to reach an audience not just to reveal the poet's heart. It does so by representing what the author has experienced, using meter and imagery to communicate. In the case of psalms, hymns and prayers, its aim is to get the readers to praise and pray as the author did.

After Lowth, the second great name in modern study of the Psalms is Hermann Gunkel, who more or less invented "form criticism" at the beginning of the twentieth century. Form criticism came to be applied to the Gospels in a way that was inclined to cast doubt on their historical value, but this more troublesome aspect of form criticism is not significant in relation to the Psalms.

Traditionally, readers have tried to treat the Psalms historically, as we do the Prophets, and thus tried to connect each psalm with a specific situation in the life of Israel. For example, Psalms 42–43 tell of somebody's exile; Psalm 44 tells of some military defeat; Psalm 45 tells of some royal marriage; Psalm 46 tells of some invasion and deliverance. But which exile, defeat, marriage or invasion do they relate to? Commentators try to work it out, but they differ in their conclusions because within the psalm there's no way of telling. That conclusion applies to Psalms in general (Ps 137 is the nearest to an exception, since it explicitly refers to exile).

It was Gunkel who provided the way out of this impasse (see Gunkel, *The Psalms*). He suggested (1) looking at the Psalms against their recurrent social context rather than their once-for-all historical context (the German term for "social context" is *Sitz im Leben*, but you don't need to use it); (2) analyzing and comparing the various examples of the different ways of speaking to God that appear in the Psalter (genre criticism might be a better expression than form criticism). The main genres are songs of praise or hymns, prayers or protests (corporate and individual), and thanksgivings or testimonies (corporate and individual). Most psalms fit into these main categories. In these pages I have allocated all the psalms to a category, but sometimes the designation may be forced.

Given that there isn't a structure to the Psalter itself, one way of getting a feel for the Psalter as a whole is to collect the examples of the different types of psalms. In addition, however, in the interrelationship of the ways of speaking to God, the Psalter does suggest a structure of spirituality of which these different ways of speaking to God form the parts.

Gunkel's first category was what he called the "hymn," by which he meant an expression of praise and worship for who God is and for the great things God has done and given. A hymn has two features: (1) an exhortation or commitment to praise, or a declaration of God's praiseworthiness; (2) a statement of the reasons for praise or its content: who God is, what God has done for the people, or God's creation, God's word, God's city, or God's sanctuary. Admittedly, many praise psalms have only the second feature, while Psalm 150 in effect has only the first feature.

*Psalm 95 and Psalm 100 as Examples
of How to Worship*

1. Both psalms have the two features of a hymn: an exhortation to praise (Ps 95:1-2, 6; 100:1-2, 4) and the reasons for praise (Ps 95:3-5, 7a; 100:3, 5). Three times out of four, the clue to the transition is the word "because."

2. Both psalms thus go through the sequence twice; there are other psalms that do so, or even go through it three times (see Ps 147). Saying it once isn't enough.

3. As is the case with parallelism within a line, the second sequence doesn't simply repeat the first. Psalm 95 starts off with out-loud enthusiasm and then moves on to face-down prostration.

4. The reasoning changes too. Psalm 95 starts with God's greatness as Creator and moves on to his care for his people. We might have expected enthusiasm to be based on his care, and prostration to be based on his greatness, but the psalm's order is more profound. It's when we realize that the great Creator is the one who cares for us that we bow low.

5. Psalm 95 is very physical. Literally, it urges, "Come, let's resound for Yahweh, let's shout for our crag! Let's draw near his face with confession; we will shout for him with music!" and "Come, let's bow down, let's bend low, let's bow the knee before Yahweh our maker." Translations make the verbs a bit more respectable and churchy sounding, but the psalm isn't like that.

6. In Psalm 95 the invitation addresses Israel, as a psalm can literally do. In Psalm 100 it addresses all the earth, a more metaphorical indication that all the earth is due to recognize Yahweh.

7. The standout feature of Psalm 100 is that every line has three parts instead of the usual two. Other psalms occasionally have three-part lines, which often come at the end or otherwise mark some emphasis. In Psalm 100 every line surprises us by not stopping when we expect.

8. The standout feature of Psalm 95 is the last part, with its unexpected

turn-around. It's therefore ironic that this last part is often omitted when the psalm is used in worship. In this turnaround, instead of our speaking to God, God is answering back, and his outburst is not much fun. How might we understand the movement in the psalm? Maybe it follows on naturally after the move from enthusiasm to prostration. Maybe it facilitated a move from celebrating God's acts to listening to his teaching in the Torah (traditional Christian use whereby Psalm 95 came as we move toward reading the Scriptures fits with that idea). My imaginative fancy is that Psalm 95:1-7a existed as a complete praise psalm, until on one occasion God gave a prophet this response to the people's worship (compare prophetic challenges such as Isaiah 1:10-20). It then got attached to the psalm itself.

9. The way Hebrews takes up the last part of Psalm 95 shows how it issues a challenge to churches. God gets angry with us as God did with Israel.

10. Form criticism helps us to identify what is characteristic of particular ways of praying and thus to perceive the central features of a psalm. It also enables us to identify the distinctive features of a particular psalm, features that are uncharacteristic.

11. Form criticism also helps us see that composing a psalm is not so complicated. It suggests that the Psalms could be the prayers of ordinary Israelites—"perhaps some just like me," not just "a few lustrous heroes," as a student once put it to me. Thus the praise psalms are for us to use as they are, but also for us to learn how to praise. They suggest that our worship songs might do the following:

   a. Tell people what we are going to do and/or invite them to join us.

   b. Declare why God is praiseworthy, what God always is, key things God has done, key gifts of God.

   c. Help us to express ourselves in images, which carry depth.

   d. Reflect our own experiences, but do so indirectly, so other people can identify with them.

   e. Avoid, on the other hand, being too personal; the focus isn't God's deeds for us personally or what we feel.

   f. Say things more than once, in different words or from different angles.

We noted two aspects to form criticism as Hermann Gunkel conceived it, analyzing different genres and asking about the recurrent social context in which they were used. With regard to the second of these, Gunkel had a blind spot or a dilemma:

- The Psalms look like temple songs and prayers; they refer to singing, processing, making music, coming into the temple and so on.

- They evidently reflect real spiritual life.

- Yet we "know" (Gunkel thought) that temple worship was dominated by outward rites such as offering sacrifices, and that it didn't have real spiritual life, so the Psalms can't be songs and prayers that actually come from the temple and its worship.

- Therefore (Gunkel inferred) many of them must have been imitations of temple songs and prayers, composed by individuals out of the background of their personal relationship with God.

In the 1920s Gunkel's student Sigmund Mowinckel spotted that Gunkel's prejudices had led him astray. The Psalms' setting is indeed the worship of the people of God, what Mowinckel calls the "cult" (he doesn't mean heretical cults; compare the Spanish word for worship, *culto*); and Israel's worship was spiritually alive.

> The cult is thus a general phenomenon appearing in all religions, even the most "anti-cultic" Protestant sects and groups. It is indeed an essential and constitutive feature of a religion, that in which the nature and spiritual structure of a religion is most clearly manifested. . . . Cult or ritual may be defined as the socially established and regulated holy acts and words in which the encounter and communion of the Deity with the congregation is established, developed, and brought to its ultimate goal. In other words: a relation in which a religion becomes a vitalizing function as a communion of God and congregation, and of the members of the congregation amongst themselves. (Mowickel, *Psalms in Israel's Worship*, 15)

Mowinckel emphasized the idea of Yahweh being king in, for instance, Psalms 47; 93–99. In the 1980s, in his book *Israel's Praise*, Walter Brueggemann took up this emphasis on Yahweh reigning as king over the nations. Israelites knew that life outside worship made clear that Yahweh often did not reign in the world, as Christians know that life outside worship makes clear that Jesus is not Lord in the world. But Israelites and Christians come into worship and acknowledge that actually those are the real facts: Yahweh is King, Jesus is Lord. Worship is thus world-creating. It denies that the world we experience outside worship is the ultimate world, declares that the real world is one where Yahweh reigns and sends us out into that world to live in this conviction.

Mowinckel tried to give more precision to the link between the Psalms and worship festivals; he spoke in terms of a festival of Yahweh's enthroncment. Other scholars suggested variants on this theory (e.g., that this festival celebrated the covenant or Yahweh's commitment to Jerusalem and to David). In my view, this attempt at greater precision has failed. The general idea that the psalms link with worship is secure, but we cannot be specific beyond that (for more detailed discussion of these theories, see 442).

Psalm 104 and the way the Egyptians saw things. Psalm 104 is one of the great hymns in the Psalter. One of its features is several models for understanding God's relationship with creation:

- God is the clockmaker who started it off and can then leave it to work on its own.

- God is the farmer who keeps looking after it, being personally involved in an ongoing basis.

- God is the energy or system of nature, including frightening realities such as volcanoes.

- God is the "God of the gaps," the explanation for miraculous/disastrous things that happen.

There is an Egyptian "Hymn to the Sun" that has similarities with Psalm 104 such as make it possible that the composer of the psalm knew the Egyptian hymn. You can read the hymn in the web resources (see 442) and see how Psalm 104 is similar and how it is different.

THE PSALM INTRODUCTIONS AND
THEIR LINK WITH WORSHIP

The introductions to Psalms make statements such as "The leader's. With strings. On the eighth. A composition. David's" (Ps 6) and "The leader's. On the Gittite. A composition. David's" (Ps 8). Those examples show that many of these introductions are difficult or impossible to understand. There are indications that they are of later date than the psalms themselves, but they are just as much part of the text as anything. In fact, they have verse numbers in printed Hebrew Bibles.

- Note that there is a cause of confusion here. If the Hebrew Bible gives the introduction its own verse number, the succeeding verse numbers will be different from the English verse numbers, sometimes by two. Thus Psalm 51:1 in English Bibles corresponds to Psalm 51:3 in the Hebrew Bible. Sometimes modern books will give both numbers, giving the reference as Psalm 51:1 [3] or Psalm 51:3 [1]. Sometimes they will give just one number, and you may have to "translate" it. The higher number is always the Hebrew one, the lower number the English one.

- Note also that the Greek Bible, the Septuagint, makes Psalm 9 and Psalm 10 one psalm (as it originally was), so Psalm 11 (Hebrew) then equals Psalm 10 (Greek), and so on, until Psalm 147. The Latin Bible (the Vulgate) follows the Septuagint numbering, as then do some Roman Catholic English translations. But most English Bibles follow the Hebrew for the numbers of the psalms.

- Beware of the fact that many English translations provide psalms with extra introductions. For instance, one edition of the NRSV calls Psalm 6 "Prayer for recovery from illness" and Psalm 8 "Divine majesty and human dignity." These are not part of the biblical text.

There are two main indications that the introductions are later than the content of the psalms.

- Sometimes the introductions look like adaptations. For instance, Psalms

120–134 are "Songs of Ascents"; that is, they were used for pilgrimage (as people "went up" to Jerusalem) or for procession (as they "went up" to the temple itself). But these psalms do not look as if they were written for either of these purposes. More likely these introductions reflect changing ways in which the psalms were used. Similarly, Psalm 30 has an introduction that links it with the temple "dedication" (the word is *ḥănukkâ*, which is the name of the festival that celebrates the restoration of the temple after its defilement by Antiochus Epiphanes in the 160s B.C., referred to in Daniel; or it might be the dedication in Ezra 3). Psalm 92 has an introduction that links it with the Sabbath, and Psalm 100 has one that links it with the thank offering, but none of these psalms look as if they were originally composed for those occasions.

- The Septuagint Psalter and the Qumran Psalter have extra introductions (e.g., Ps 95 is "of David"), which suggests that introductions were still developing.

The introductions that we can understand suggest that they relate to how the psalms were used in worship:

1. As just noted, some refer to liturgical occasions such as the temple dedication or the thank offering (e.g., Ps 30; 100).

2. Some refer to temple ministers/choirs/choirmasters (e.g., Ps 6; 8; 139).

3. Some seem to refer to ways of singing or tunes (e.g., Ps 6; 8; 88).

4. Some seem to refer to instruments (e.g., Ps 6).

5. Some seem to denote types of psalms (e.g., Ps 6; 8; 88; 89).

In general, they are like the introductions to hymns and songs that come in our hymnbooks, such as "common meter" or "capo on second fret." It is natural that these are difficult to understand in a different culture, but it is significant that in general they point us to worship as the psalms' context.

The word "selah" is also a puzzle, and there are many theories about it. The word means something like "rise," but we don't know what kind of "rise." The best theory is that it was what David said when he broke a string. This is the best theory because there is no logic about when you break a string, and there is no logic about the occurrence of "selah."

The most frequent introduction to psalms is the expression "David's." This sounds as it if means that David composed the psalm. But in the first examples noted in 414 above, Psalm 6 and Psalm 8 are described both as "the leader's" and as "David's." It's hardly the case that the choirmaster and David both composed the psalm. English translations disguise the problem by translating "for the leader" and "of David," but "of" and "for" are the same Hebrew expression each time, the preposition *lĕ*.

As in English, "of" or "for" could have various meanings. To open up the possibilities further, in the OT "David" doesn't always denote David ben Jesse. It can denote whoever is the current Davidic king, or denote a coming David (see Jer 30:9; Ezek 34:23-24; 37:24-25; Hos 3:5). Here are some of the meanings of *lĕ* according to the Brown, Driver and Briggs *Hebrew and English Lexicon of the Old Testament* and the way they might apply in this context:

1. "to": addressed or offered to the Davidic king, present or future?

2. "belonging to": for example, "belonging to the Qorahites" (Ps 42); compare "Sankey and Moody's hymns" (only a few of which were written by Ira Sankey or Dwight Moody)?

3. "for": for the Davidic king to use or learn from?

4. "on behalf of": to be prayed on his behalf?

5. "about": about the future Davidic king, the Messiah?

6. "by": Habakkuk 3:1 is the only passage outside Psalms where the preposition might suggest authorship; usually the OT uses the genitive.

The lexicon implies that the meaning of the phrase changed over the centuries. It might originally have suggested that a particular psalm is for the present king, then have suggested it related to the future king, then have been understood to denote authorship when people wanted to associate the psalms with someone famous, which also encouraged people to link some psalms with particular incidents in David's life. These long introductions (e.g., Ps 51) must be referring to David ben Jesse, though they could still be "to," "for" or "on behalf of" him (see further 426). I use the translation "David's," which leaves the meaning open.

One argument that makes people assume that David wrote the psalms is the notion that Jesus refers to them as David's. However, Jesus actually only refers to one psalm as David's, Psalm 110 (Mt 22:43). Other parts of the NT do describe Psalms 16; 32; 69; 109 as David's. The NT also describes Psalm 2 and Psalm 95 as David's, whereas the OT itself doesn't make the link. This fact in itself hints that the NT is often speaking conventionally (as when it speaks as if the sun goes round the earth); it is not pronouncing on the authorship question.

If we don't assume that David wrote all the psalms, it gets us out of the problem of understanding how he could have been a combination of Napoleon (great general), John F. Kennedy (great leader and womanizer) and Henri Nouwen or Eugene Peterson (great expert on spirituality). It also helps to bring out that neither accepting the Psalms as the word of God nor understanding and using them depends on knowing who wrote them, as is the case also with Christian prayers and hymns. Their power and authority come not from their being written by someone important, but rather from their having been true prayers and praises that God accepted.

Often the power and meaningfulness of our hymns derives from their having been the expression of real people's personal turning to God (e.g., Charlotte Elliott writing "Just as I am"), which our experience resonates with. But we usually don't know what that experience was, and we don't need to know it in order to sing the hymns; neither do we need to know it in order to sing the Psalms.

Admittedly this assumption goes against a contemporary Western instinct to want to know what is going on in the lives of individuals and between them and God, but the OT does not share that instinct. It's best to assume that we know nothing about who wrote the Psalms, and that this knowledge is unnecessary to using them, although you could consider this possibility: outside the Psalter many main composers of prayers are women (e.g., Ex 15:21; Judg 5:1; 1 Sam 2:1), so maybe within the Psalter as well.

4 | 16 | PSALMS OF PRAYER
How to Pray for Ourselves

Interwoven with the praise psalms in the Psalter are prayer psalms. In the praise psalms, one can't tell who is praying; the point is to put the spotlight on God. In the prayer psalms, the person or the people praying come into focus. Many of these psalms center on protesting about the way life is turning out for them. Here are features that often come in a protest psalm, illustrated from Psalm 22 and Psalm 28.

1. Invocation of God ("My God, my God")

2. Protest: "I/we": how things are for me/us ("I am a worm, not a human being")

   "They": what they are doing to us ("All who see me mock me")

   "You": how you are neglecting us ("Why have you abandoned me?")

3. Recollection of God's deeds in the past: painful but hopeful ("Our ancestors trusted in you, and you rescued them")

4. Confession of trust ("Yahweh is my strength and my shield")

5. The actual prayer: "Listen to me" ("Don't be deaf toward me")

   "Deliver me" ("Save my life from the sword")

   "Put down my oppressors" ("Render their wages to them")

   The balance of protest and prayer in psalms is thus the opposite to that typical of Christian prayers. The psalms spend a lot of time telling God what the situation is; they assume that God can work out what to do. The aim of the protest in which they tell God how things are is to press on God the fact that things are very tough for the person praying, and thus to prevail on God to act.

6. Promise to come back with praise when God has acted ("In the midst of the congregation I will praise you")

7. Transition to actual praise ("You who are in awe of Yahweh, praise him")

Every psalm is different, and some features come out strongly in particular psalms, while other features may be missing. So it's worth looking at how a particular psalm compares with this profile.

Some aspects of Psalm 22 are striking:

1. The first two-thirds keep alternating between protest (Ps 22:1-2, 6-8, 12-18) and recollection/trust (Ps 22:3-5, 9-11). The psalm insists resolutely on facing two sets of facts: the facts about God and the facts about the situation. It won't give up either. It compares with Psalms 42–43, which encourage people to keep arguing with themselves ("Why do you bow low, my spirit. . . . ? Be expectant of God").

2. Jesus quotes the opening of Psalm 22, and the NT quotes other verses, but the psalm itself is not a prophecy; it doesn't say, "One day the Messiah will pray this way." Like other psalms, it is a prayer that any Israelite might pray. Jesus took it up because he was going through the kind of experience that it refers to.

3. There is a sharp transition to praise in the last part, which makes it look as if the prayer has been answered. The OT sees answers to prayer coming by two stages: in words and then in action (see the story of Hannah in 1 Sam 1, where Hannah is transformed by the answer in words and only later sees the answer in action). The first stage of the answer has evidently come.

4. In Psalm 12 and Psalm 60 the transition comes as a result of a prophetic word of response to the prayer. God's answer to prayer came via a minister, the kind of person sometimes termed a "cultic prophet"—someone with prophetic gifts who took part in worship.

   Such a prophet might bring words of comfort or words of warning (see Ps 50; 82; 95). You couldn't assume that God's answer to your prayer would be positive, even if you yourself are a prophet (see Jer 14–15; Hos 6). A cultic prophet might also bring words of encouragement or challenge to the king in particular (e.g., Ps 2; 45; 72; 91; 110). Thus, while most psalms are addressed to God, others bring words of teaching and blessing from God to people (e.g., Ps 1; 37; 49; 112; 127; 128; 133).

More than half the Psalms are prayers, but there are several ways of dividing them up. One is to distinguish between ones that especially express urgent and anxious protest and ones that have more of an attitude of hope and trust. It's not a sharp distinction, but it's a useful one. The two sorts of psalms have different places on a spectrum. Protest psalms frequently incorporate some statement of trust or confidence, but protest is more prominent. In psalms of trust, the balance between protest and trust is reversed.

Reading psalms of protest. So these prayers don't lack trust, but their hurt and pain is more overt. Read Psalm 88 and Psalm 89.

1. What kind of experience lies in the background of each of them? How are they similar, how different?

2. What is the aim of each psalm; what are they trying to achieve?

3. Can you see a structure in each of them, as one can in Psalm 95 and Psalm 100?

4. If they are more stream of consciousness, is there a structure to the psalm's underlying thinking? What are the main points it makes to God?

5. What forms of parallelism appear in each of them?

6. What does each of them suggest about the nature of prayer?

7. According to Claus Westermann, in the Psalms, "There is no petition that did not move at least one step on the road to praise" (*Praise and Lament*, 154). Are they exceptions?

8. Is each psalm depressing or encouraging?

Here are some notes on these two psalms:

Psalm 88. On the terms in the introduction, see 414. On Sheol, see 119 for the material on death and afterlife in the OT.

Psalm 89. This psalm works by first speaking at great length about God's love expressed in creation and in God's commitment to the Davidic king.

One can imagine Psalm 89:1-37 existing on its own as a praise psalm. But if it did, it has become too scandalous for a psalmist to cope with in light of the way God has been acting toward the people, and in particular toward the current Davidic king, so the psalmist has added Psalm 89:38-51. But my hunch is that the point about Psalm 89:1-37 all along was to prepare the way for Psalm 89:38-51. Either way, the dynamic is the obverse of that in Psalm 95 (see 412).

Psalm 89:39 raises the question of how far the negative experiences described in Psalms were deserved. Psalm 89:30-37 implies that Yahweh's abandonment goes beyond anything that was deserved. Psalm 26 goes further: trouble has come even though the person praying has lived with integrity and been faithful to Yahweh. While the Psalms do not claim sinlessness, they do assume that praying in the way they do requires one to be able to claim that one has been fundamentally committed. If you are a gross sinner, you can't protest when trouble comes.

Psalm 89:52 is the "amen" to book three of the Psalter (see 410); compare Psalm 41:13; 72:18-19; 106:48. It is not strictly part of Psalm 89.

You could then read the other protest psalms, which are listed at 423. Again, try to read them one a day rather than all at once. That section also suggests another way you can divide up the protest psalms.

Reading psalms of trust. Psalms of trust are more like praise psalms. These are the prayer psalms in which trust is prominent: Psalms 4; 11; 14; 16; 23; 27; 36; 41; 46; 52; 62; 67; 75–77; 84; 101; 108; 115; 119; 121; 125; 129; 131; 132; 139. Yet again, try to read them one a day rather than all at once.

1. What are they trusting God for?

2. What basis in one's own experience do they suggest for trusting God?

3. What basis outside one's own experience do they suggest for trusting God?

PSALMS OF PRAYER
How to Keep Hoping and How to Keep Praying

S*ome comments on psalms of trust*
    The content of trust. The content of trust, as I have noticed it, is this:

- Yahweh is watching (Ps 11; 14)

- Yahweh keeps me safe (Ps 23; 27)

- Yahweh puts down the wicked (Ps 62; 75)

The bases for trust. Not all of these will work all the time, I guess. When one conviction is under pressure, we turn our minds to another.

The basis for trust within my own experience:

- Yahweh speaking to me on my own (Ps 16)

- Yahweh's presence in the temple (Ps 36; 84)

- Yahweh keeping me safe in the past (Ps 41; 129)

- Yahweh's material provision (Ps 67)

- My commitment to Yahweh (Pss 101; 119)

- My standing against wrongdoing (Ps 139)

The basis for trust outside my own experience:

- Yahweh's power and love (Ps 62; 115)

- Yahweh's creation of the world and sovereignty in it (Ps 93; 121)

- Yahweh's deliverance of the people at the Reed Sea (Ps 77)

- Yahweh's commitment to Jerusalem (Ps 46; 76; 132)

- Yahweh's commitment to David (Ps 132)

- Yahweh's specific promises (Ps 108; 119)

    In light of your study, you might write a psalm of trust taking up the elements in these prayers that are appropriate to you at the moment.

Psalms of protest. We might wonder whether it is really appropriate to pray in the way that psalms of protest do. But Jesus prays in this way. He prays Psalm 22 on the cross. And his prayer in Gethsemane takes up the language of Psalm 42. Paul also implies that he prays this way, when he quotes Psalm 44 (Rom 8:36). And the martyrs pray that way; God tells them they will have to wait for an answer, but not that their prayer is wrong (Rev 6:9-11). So presumably we too can pray this way. Theologian Jürgen Moltmann describes how it was crying "out of the depths" in this way (Ps 130) that put him in touch with God when his entire life seemed hopeless, when he was a prisoner of war at the end of World War II (Moltmann, *Experiences of God*, 6-9). The Psalms are thus a resource for evangelism; they indicate how it's possible to talk to God in a real way, and to talk about things that you may not be able to talk about anywhere else.

You can also write your own protest psalm. Examples such as Psalms 22; 88; 89 may help you to see how to do so.

- Remind yourself and God of key facts about who God is or things that God has done in the past, perhaps ones relevant to the prayer.

- Tell God straightforwardly about your need: the facts, the feelings, the fears.

- Tell God that you still trust, or tell him you can no longer trust. The variety among these psalms implies that we don't have to get ourselves into the right state of mind in order to be able to pray. There are psalms for people who are able to trust, and psalms for people who are unable to trust.

- Acknowledge the way you fail God, but don't blame yourself for your trouble unless you've got special reason.

- Tell God what you need, in one line.

- Listen for God's answer, imagine you have heard God's answer or ask someone else to listen for you and tell you what God says.

- Respond to the answer. Decide what you need to say to God in light of these possibilities that come in the Psalms. But don't just say what your instincts tell you or what you have been told by other people is the right way to pray. Learn to pray in a scriptural way.

PSALMS AS INTERCESSION
How to Pray for Other People

The Psalms include many prayers for ourselves but hardly any prayers that look to us like prayers for other people, hardly any intercessions. The prayers of the prophets and of leaders such as Ezra suggest a clue regarding this oddness. When they pray for other people, they nevertheless pray for "us" rather than for "them." Intercession involves identifying with another person and praying as "I/we," not praying for "him/her" or "them." This identification opens up the possibility of using protest psalms on behalf of other people, and to see how to use protest psalms when you don't need to protest on your own behalf. They offer a way of entering into the experience of people in need and interceding on their behalf (etymologically, "interceding" involves "intervening" on someone's behalf). We weep with people who weep and rejoice with people who rejoice. "If we are to mirror God . . . we have to be prepared to enter our individual wounds and through them the wounds of the community . . . not hide them through casuistry, not seal them up" (Ross, *Pillars of Flame*, xviii-xix).

This approach to prayer applies to praying for and with individuals. Donald Capps, in his book *Biblical Approaches to Pastoral Counseling*, thus notes the usefulness of the protest psalms in pastoral ministry. The psalms give people the means of expressing the pain that they need to express, but of expressing it to God. We help them do so; then we listen to God on their behalf, to see what God has to say in response. The story of Hannah and Eli (1 Sam 1) provides a bad example at first as Eli fails as pastor, but he then gets his pastoral act together. Conversely, when I am the one who needs to protest and pray, I can recall that I am not alone.

> We are not alone when we pray; we have more support than most of us realize. We are part of a great tradition which has formed our identity as human beings. This tradition stretches right back to the unknown beginnings of the history of mankind. (Metz, "Courage to Pray," 157)

The prophets and leaders such as Ezra show how this approach to prayer particularly applies to times when the community needs to grieve or pray or get angry (see Arbuckle, *Grieving for Change*). The stories in 2 Kings 19 and 2 Chronicles 20 illustrate the dynamics when the community needs to be at prayer.

The example of the protest psalms illustrates how individuals and communities sometimes need to get angry on other people's behalf and on their own. The psalms encourage it. They presuppose that it is appropriate to get angry with God as well as with situations, on our own behalf as well as on other people's behalf. Being free to get angry with someone presupposes that the relationship is strong enough to survive it. It is a sign of strength in God's relationship with us if we can get angry with God, and the Psalms presuppose that this is possible. Their understanding of people's relationship with God contrasts with that of the people in Exodus and Numbers, when Israel gets angry but never expresses its anger to God, and instead gets angry only with Moses.

The Psalms point us toward the idea that one significance of this expression of anger on our own behalf is that expressing it to God is better than pretending it is not there or taking it out on other people. According to one survey, 37 percent of pastors say that pornography is a current struggle for them. What makes someone vulnerable to pornography? It's said that addiction is prevalent among people with high-demand jobs who spend a lot of time at their computers, and that sexual addiction is fostered by loneliness, anger and boredom. Clergy fit this profile. Sexually addicted clergy are also likely to be addicted to work, and to be people who give the appearance of being above the crowd. People don't like their pastor to get angry. Yet everyone needs places where they can talk about the things that they can't talk about anywhere else. The Psalms encourage such talk.

As well as composing prayers for ourselves along the lines of the Psalms, then, we can do so for other people. Decide who are the people you are praying for (your church, your city, your people, some other person in need). Put yourself in the position of the person or people you are praying for. And pray *as* them. (For the Psalms used in prayer for healing and at the World Trade Center site, see 442.)

Psalms as Intercession
How to Pray for the Government

R ead Psalm 72. What does this psalm suggest about how to pray for the government? What is its vision of government? (The psalm, of course, presupposes a traditional context where the king has the power to decide what happens in the nation. In a Western context, then, it is profitable to think of it as a psalm of prayer for the government—president, prime minister, elected assemblies.) Note the key OT ideas that come together in this psalm:

mišpāṭ	*ṣədāqâ*	*yāšaʿ*	*šālôm*	*bĕrākâ*
judgment	justice	salvation	peace	blessing

How does the psalm link these ideas, and link fairness, prosperity, prayer, witness, fame, victory?

In his State of the Union speech in January 1944, Franklin Roosevelt proposed, in effect, "a second Bill of Rights." Among these proposed rights would be

- the right to a useful and remunerative job in the industries or shops or farms or mines of the nation
- the right to earn enough to provide adequate food and clothing and recreation
- the right of every farmer to raise and sell products at a return that will give the farmer and his family a decent living
- the right of every business, large and small, to trade in an atmosphere of freedom from unfair competition and domination by monopolies at home or abroad
- the right of every family to a decent home
- the right to adequate medical care and the opportunity to achieve and enjoy good health

- the right to adequate protection from the economic fears of old age, sickness, accident and unemployment

- the right to a good education

How does Roosevelt's proposal compare with Psalm 72? What elements in his proposal correspond to scriptural values? What elements simply reflect Western values? What would need to be added if one wanted to formulate a biblical proposal?

There are two Christian versions of the psalm: "Jesus Shall Reign Where'er the Sun" (Isaac Watts) and "Hail to the Lord's Anointed" (James Montgomery) (see 442). The first of these reinterprets the psalm more radically in applying it to Jesus, through whom "the weary find eternal rest." The second describes how Jesus "comes with succor speedy to those who suffer wrong" but also recognizes that this action is not complete in the present age. How far can we pray for God to be putting things right now? Is God involved in the world now or only at the End? Do we have responsibility, or can we leave things to God? Is God concerned with the political or only with the individual? Is God concerned with the material or just the spiritual? What light does the psalm throw on these questions? (For further ideas on "How to Pray for Your Nation" from the Psalms, see 442.)

The king in the Psalms. The king has a prominent place in psalms other than Psalm 72. How do we understand its way of talking about the king in a context where the people of God don't have an earthly king? The background to such psalms is the importance of the covenant with David and his successors (2 Sam 7); see especially Psalm 132. Other psalms addressed to the king or presupposing his importance are, for instance, Psalms 2; 45; 110; 118. For Israel, what was the significance of these psalms after the downfall of Judah, when there were no kings? I can think of three possibilities: (1) they become a basis for prayer that God will again fulfill the promises to and about David; (2) they become themselves implicit promises of a future king and what God will do through him (see, e.g., Jer 23:5-6); (3) they become implicit promises of what God will do through the people as a whole (see Is 55:3-5, where God turns his commitment to David into a commitment to the entire people).

PSALMS AS IMPRECATION
How to Pray Against Other People

Many psalms ask for God to put down the psalmist's enemies and/or God's enemies. Western Christians are puzzled by these psalms and may think they are pre-Christian, but the NT also includes such expressions of anger and antagonism about enemies (e.g., Mt 23:33; 24:50-51; 25:30, 46; 2 Thess 1:5-9; Rev 6:9-11). More likely the problem is that these prayers don't fit into modern Western culture. We are inclined to think, "All you need is love." Neither OT nor NT agrees. When we pray, "Come, Lord Jesus" (Rev 22:20; cf. 1 Cor 16:22), we are praying for people's punishment. That our difficulty with these psalms arises out of our culture is supported by the fact that they do not trouble African indigenous churches, which see them not as expressions of violence and hate but as a way of taking wrongdoers to God's court and as means of protection and defense when other people are using spiritual means to cause harm to them, such as curses (see Adamo, *African Indigenous Churches*).

Two of the most striking examples of praying against other people are Psalm 69 and Psalm 109, and the NT quotes both of them with appreciation (Acts 1:20; Rom 11:9-10). Another one that troubles us is Psalm 137, with its horrifying blessing on whoever smashes Babylon's babies on the rocks. The NT doesn't quote this psalm, but the psalm itself is quoting Scripture, because Isaiah 13 promises that God will put down Babylon in this way. Psalm 137 simply claims God's promise. It's possible that we shouldn't be too literalistic about the promise or the prayer; maybe the OT thinks more concretely than we do. In Western culture we may be happier to pray less concretely for God to take action against evil. But we may then not be facing the reality of what judgment looks like (Keel, *Symbolism of the Biblical World*, 7-9).

One significant feature of such psalms is that they are expressions of trust in God to act on our behalf when we are oppressed. Like the Prophets, the Psalms contain virtually no indication that people expected to take action against their enemies. You could say that the Psalter is quite a pacifist book, though that statement may treat it as if its logic worked in modern Western categories. Its principle is not nonviolence, but trust. "The capacity to leave vengeance to God may free Israel for its primary vocation, which is the tenacious hope that prevents sell-out. Indeed, one may speculate that if Israel could not leave vengeance boldly to God . . . , Israel might have had no energy or freedom to hope." Psalm 137 is thus less a childish outburst than "the voice of seasoned religion. . . . It is an act of profound faith to entrust one's most precious hatreds to God, knowing they will be taken seriously" (Brueggemann, *Message of the Psalms*, 74-77).

Psalm 137 prays the way it does because of a depth of need, of conviction about God and of trust in God. It prays the way it does because it thinks it important that God put down oppressors and aggressors. It prays the way it does because it believes that God is involved in the world and brings judgment. The Israelites knew that God cared about other nations as well as them, but they also knew that such caring did not mean that God forever let the nations off, as God did not forever let Israel off. If you turn your back on God's love and forgiveness, then God's redress falls on you. And the NT speaks of the church's joy on the day when it happens (see 1 Cor 16:22; Gal 1:8-9; Rev 18; 19; 20:11) (Bonhoeffer, *Life Together*, 174-76).

One way Western readers have coped with such psalms is by allegorical interpretation. Thus C. S. Lewis takes the smashing of babies in Psalm 137 to signify our little self-indulgences and resentments that need to be killed before they become fully grown (Lewis, *Reflections on the Psalms*, 113-15). The trouble is that this lets us off from caring about the oppressiveness of the nations, which may be our own oppressiveness. There is a reggae version of Psalm 137, "By the Rivers of Babylon," in which "Babylon" stood for the United Kingdom. When C. S. Lewis wrote his book, we British people wouldn't have liked that idea. Allegorical interpretation helped us avoid the threatening implications of taking the psalm literally.

Western devotional reading of such psalms, then, will drive us to repentance for the way we are implicated in the oppression of less powerful peoples. It will also provide us with a way of praying for people who are oppressed (see 420).

Reading Thanksgiving Psalms

How to Give Your Testimony

We have noted that many protest psalms (such as Ps 22) close with a declaration of confidence that God has answered the prayer, but that such declarations relate to stage one in the answering. God has listened and said yes, but has not yet acted. When God has acted, another declaration is appropriate. Hannah's story again illustrates the dynamic of this process. When Hannah knows that God has said yes to her prayer, her face is no longer downcast, yet she is no more pregnant than she was before. When she has had her baby, there is reason for a psalm of thanksgiving and testimony (1 Sam 2).

Like other types of psalm, this type switches between speaking to God and speaking to the other members of the congregation. So these psalms are at the same time thanksgiving to God and testimony to other people. Claus Westermann (*Praise and Lament*) likes to call them "declarative praise" rather than thanksgiving because they declare to other people what God has done. He then likes to use the term "descriptive praise" for the praise psalms that Gunkel called hymns; those praise psalms describe the things that are always true about God and the things that God has done for everyone in creating the world and redeeming it (e.g., delivering Israel from Egypt). Thanksgiving psalms focus on something that God has done just now for Israel or for the individual. You could be expected to be involved in praise every week. You might be involved in thanksgiving only occasionally.

Psalm 30. Read Psalm 30. Can you see its structure and its different elements? What does it suggest constitutes thanksgiving or testimony? Then look at the other thanksgiving/testimony psalms: Psalms 9; 18; 32; 34; 73; 92; 103; 107; 116; 118; 124; 136; 138. In what way do they compare with Psalm 30? In what way are they different?

One importance of these psalms as testimony addressed to other people lies in the way they encourage other people to expect God to act in their lives when they are in trouble. Thanksgiving relates to what God has just done for someone. It may be instinctive to give God thanks for what he has done, but such thanksgiving might be silent. Yet because it is silent, it is not enough. Silent thanksgiving has to become vocal and public testimony before the congregation. Testimony in the psalms doesn't mean telling your life story or recounting how you were converted or talking about something that happened years ago; it means talking about something that God has done recently, that shows how God is active now.

Psalm 116. This psalm illustrates the characteristic elements of a thanksgiving/testimony psalm:

1. an expression of commitment to praise or an invitation to praise

2. a recollection: (a) how things went wrong in my life; (b) how I prayed; (c) how God responded

3. the facts about God that my experience illustrates

4. a further expression of commitment to praise or invitation to praise

A testimony psalm thus essentially tells a story. The Hebrew word *tōdâ* is both the word for "thanksgiving" and "thank you" and the word for "confession," whether the confession acknowledges what I have done wrong or acknowledges what God has done; either way, it is a story. With a testimony/thanksgiving, it's a story about me, but it's even more a story about God. It is not so much about how grateful I feel as about what God has done; God is the subject of many of the verbs (he even has the glory in the grammar).

When people needed to ask God for something, to protest, they might well do so in the company of their family and friends, and they might accompany the prayer with an offering. They might also promise to come back with a thank offering when the prayer had been answered. Thanksgiving psalms would be the accompaniment of a thank offering (the word *tōdâ* also refers to this sacrifice), and a thank offering would be the natural accompaniment of a thanksgiving psalm (see Ps 116:17-19). The reference to the deliverance chalice (Ps 116:13) reflects the way this thank offering would be part of a festive celebration with family and friends in God's presence in the sanctuary; it thus would also be the occasion when you kept your promise to give testimony to people about what God had done for you.

Psalms of Protest and Thanksgiving for an Individual, a Leader, a Community

There are protests and thanksgivings prayed by an ordinary individual, by a leader and by a community:

- Protests for an individual: Psalms 6; 10; 22; 26; 31; 38–40; 42–43; 54–59; 64; 70–71; 86; 88; 109; 120; 141–142

- Protests for a leader: Psalms 3; 5; 7; 13; 17; 25; 28; 35; 61; 63; 69; 102; 140; 143

- Protests for the congregation: Psalms 12; 44; 60; 74; 79; 80; 83; 85; 89–90; 94; 106; 123; 126; 137; 144

You can map the use of these protests, and the thanksgivings that would follow, in the following way (I don't mean that Ps 30, for instance, was specifically designed to complement Ps 38; these are just possible examples).

We have noted that it wouldn't be surprising if even an individual protest were used at the sanctuary (cf. Ps 73:17; also the Hannah story), with one's family and friends, or in some other corporate context. Further, the mere use of "we" or "I" may not tell us which are for an individual, a leader or the community, and some of the listing above is thus a matter of guesswork. Consider Numbers 20:14-21 (given here in the ASV because it provides the "thy," "thee" and "thou" pronouns that indicate singular "you" in older English):

> And Moses sent messengers from Kadesh unto the king of Edom, Thus saith thy brother Israel, Thou knowest all the travail that hath befallen us. . . . And,

> behold, we are in Kadesh, a city in the uttermost of thy border. Let us pass, I
> pray thee, through thy land; we will not pass through field or through vineyard
> . . . until we have passed thy border. And Edom said unto him, Thou shalt not
> pass through me, lest I come out with the sword against thee. And the children
> of Israel said unto him, We will go up by the highway: and if we drink of thy
> water, I and my cattle, then will I give the price therof: let me only . . . pass
> through on my feet. And he said, Thou shalt not pass through. And Edom
> came out against him with much people. . . . Thus Edom refused to give Israel
> passage through his border: wherefore Israel turned away from him.

You can see that the Israelites could use "I" when it was the people as a whole
that was speaking or was speaking in the person of their leader. So it's worth-
while to try listening to psalms in all three ways: as on the lips of an individual (which may be our default assumption), or on the lips of the leader,
or on the lips of the congregation as a whole.

Psalm 51, for instance, works as a confession by an ordinary individual.
But the heading suggests a connection with Israel's leader, and its reference
to the possibility of God's taking away his holy spirit fits with the way the
OT speaks of God's endowing leaders with his spirit. But then the closing
prayer for God to build up Jerusalem makes one think of the community as
a whole (which also knew the presence of God's spirit, and the psalm would
work well in the context of the exile as an expression of penitence by Israel
as a whole). The same possibilities apply to other psalms we may instinctively take as individual, such as Psalms 91 and 139.

Psalm 118 offers another illustration of this dynamic, one that involves
leader and people. In celebrating Yahweh's acting to deliver, it suggests the
way a leader might have prayed when the protest in Psalm 89 had been answered. So it is a thanksgiving or testimony psalm, which one can compare
and contrast with Psalm 30. There is lots of switching to and fro in who is
talking in Psalm 118 (e.g., from first-person singular to first-person plural).
Maybe the psalm is a liturgy for priest, people and leader.

In Psalm 118:22 "the stone" refers to the leader as someone whom the nations thought nothing of, but the image comes to be applied to Jesus in the
NT. In Psalm 118:25 "Save us" is Hebrew "Hosanna." Much of Psalm 118:22-26
(and the psalm as a whole) underlies Mark 11:9-10.

PSALMS
How the Prayer-Testimony Process
Gets Short-Circuited

HOW IT'S SUPPOSED TO WORK

1. You pray.

2. Some servant of God brings God's yes (first stage of answer to prayer).

3. You express your response of trust.

4. God acts (second stage of answer to prayer).

5. You praise God.

SHORT-CIRCUIT (1): GENESIS 11–21

1. Sarai doesn't pray for a baby, as far as we are told.

2. God says yes anyway.

3. Sarai sometimes tries to fix things herself, sometimes laughs in disbelief.

4. God acts.

5. Sarah praises God for giving her a different laugh.

SHORT-CIRCUIT (2): 1 SAMUEL 2

1. Hannah prays.

2. (a) Eli misreads the situation; (b) Hannah puts him right; (c) Eli brings God's yes.

3. Hannah expresses her response of trust.

4. God acts.

5. Hannah praises God.

SHORT-CIRCUIT (3): LUKE 1

1. Zechariah prays.

2. Gabriel brings God's yes.

3. (a) Zechariah doesn't believe it; (b) Gabriel says that Zechariah's unbelief will result in his being unable to talk at all.

4. God acts.

5. Zechariah gets his voice back and praises God.

Short-circuit (4): Luke 17

1. Ten people with skin disease call on Jesus.

2. Jesus brings God's yes.

3. They express their response of trust.

4. God acts.

5. Only one comes back to praise God.

Short-circuit (5): Mark 7

1. The Canaanite woman calls on Jesus.

2. (a) He says no; (b) she won't accept no for an answer; (c) he says yes.

3. She expresses her response of trust.

4. God acts.

5. [Missing, but maybe implicit in the story being here?]

Short-circuit (6): Mark 14–16

1. Jesus prays.

2. No one answers.

3. Jesus expresses his response of trust.

4. (a) God abandons Jesus; (b) God acts.

5. Jesus praises God (Heb 2:12, from the anticipatory testimony at the end of Ps 22).

The Interrelationship of Praise and Prayer

Sigmund Mowinckel sees the essence of Israelite psalmody as lying in the hymn of praise. In contrast, Claus Westermann emphasizes the interrelationship of prayer and praise: "There is no petition that did not move at least one step on the road to praise. But there is no praise that is fully separated from the experience of God's wonderful intervention in time of need" (*Praise and Lament*, 154). He contrasts Egyptian psalms, which praise God only in general terms, not in relation to God's doing anything, and Babylonian psalms, which praise only as a lead-in to prayer, never for its own sake (subsequent research has qualified the contrast, but it is still illuminating). One might compare Walter Brueggemann's comment: "The praise has power to transform the pain. But conversely the present pain also keeps the act of praise honest" (*Israel's Praise*, 139). But how do praise and prayer interrelate?

Westermann sees the "vital, tension-filled polarity" of plea/praise as having its center in declarative praise:

Lament ⟶	Declarative Praise	⟶	Descriptive Praise
	(God has . . .)		(God is/does/did . . .)
	(thanksgiving)		(hymn)

Brueggemann (*Message of the Psalms*) sees a different relationship between these elements, building on the work of Paul Ricoeur. Ricoeur suggests that life regularly involves a movement from orientation through disorientation to new orientation. Orientation means you know who God is, who you are and how life works. Disorientation comes about when something happens that imperils your understanding of those basic realities. Reaching a new orientation means that something enables you to see how to integrate that first understanding and the disorienting experience. Brueggemann's point is that the Psalms reflect these three stages of experience:

Orientation ⟶	Disorientation ⟶	Renewed orientation
(hymn)	(lament)	(thanksgiving)

Elsewhere Brueggemann ("Obedience and Praise") suggests that the Psalter is a kind of journal recording a journey from obedience via questioning to praise.

My suggestion is that a spiral understanding helps to combine these understandings and also to do justice to the linear element in our lives with God. Praise feeds prayer; prayer feeds praise:

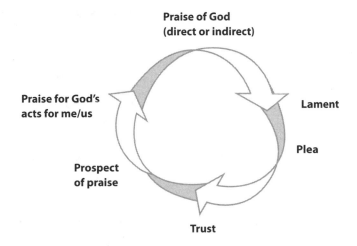

In principle, all the psalms fit on this spiral. They can join it at any point and go around it as far as they need. All the elements are in Psalm 22 (protest) or Psalm 30 (thanksgiving) and also in the story in 2 Chronicles 20.

A classic Christian understanding of the dynamics of prayer sees it in light of the acronym ACTS: adoration, confession, thanksgiving, supplication. The acronym is attractive, but it has little overlap with Scripture. Among the contrasts is that the psalms give little place to confession of sin. They acknowledge sinfulness, but they don't emphasize sin in the manner of much of Christian spirituality. Indeed, we have noted that they are inclined to emphasize the way the suppliant has lived a life of commitment, not a life of waywardness. If we are to pray, it's necessary to be able to make that claim. Cassiodorus, a Roman statesman, teacher and writer in the sixth century A.D., did identify a group of seven "penitential psalms" (Ps 6; 32; 38; 51; 102; 130; 143), and the designation has stuck. But are they penitential psalms? Read them and see how far they are such.

W e noted in 425 that there are seven so-called penitential psalms (Ps 6; 32; 38; 51; 102; 130; 143). The one that is most clearly penitential is Psalm 51.

Some questions in reading Psalm 51

1. What are its key features?

2. What does it suggest is the nature of penitence or confession?

3. When we are confessing ours sins, what does it suggest we appeal to?

4. What do the other so-called penitential psalms add to an understanding of how to say you're sorry?

5. Review the penitential psalms in Ezra 9 and Nehemiah 9. Prayers such as these outside the Psalter (see also Dan 9) tell us more than the Psalter does about confession. What do they suggest about it?

6. How does the practice of confession illustrated in those prayers and in the psalms compare with the practice of confession in your church?

7. You could read the examples of how the Babylonians prayed for forgiveness (see 442) and compare them with the penitential prayers in the OT.

8. Read 2 Samuel 11–12, the story to which the introduction to Psalm 51 refers. Can you see ways in which the psalm fits that story and/or ways in which it doesn't?

Psalm 51: Some comments. Why does the psalm say in one breath, "You don't want offerings" (Ps 51:16), and then in the next breath, "You will delight in them" (Ps 51:19)? The answer is that when you have done wrong, sacrifices or other forms of worship are no use; you can't bribe your way back to God (see 228-29). You need to repent and throw yourself on God's mercy and change your ways. But when things are right between you and God, you can start the normal life of worshiping and sacrificing again. In other words, the

OT's understanding of sacrifice is the opposite of the one that Christians often assume. You don't offer sacrifice in order to get right with God. You offer sacrifice because you are right with God (because God has accepted you), and being right with God, you can give this concrete expression of praise, prayer and thanksgiving.

Does the psalm's content match the story in 2 Samuel 11–12? There are a number of psalms with introductions that make a link with a specific incident in David's life in this way (Ps 3; 7; 18; 34; 51–52; 54; 56–57; 59; 60; 63; 142). It's typical of them that when you compare the introduction and the story, you can see points of contact that fit with the link, but also points of contrast that make it seem odd. In Psalm 51 much of the penitence and the plea fit, but "against you only have I sinned" and "build up Jerusalem's walls" don't fit.

What might explain both features? The other elements in the introductions to psalms relate to Israel's worship (see 414), so it would seem likely that these introductions also do so. Brevard Childs ("Psalm Titles") suggests that they are lectionary notes or Bible study notes, not authorship notes. They don't tell us about wrote the psalm and when. They invite us to read this psalm and this bit of David's story alongside each other in order to see one kind of situation in which this prayer might be prayed or one kind of prayer that might be prayed in this situation. Making this link helps bring psalm and story alive for the congregation, as happens when people try to link other "David psalms" with incidents in David's life, which may be a helpful exercise in imagination, but not a piece of historical study. There is no external evidence that Childs is right, but it does explain both features of the introductions: the way they fit and the way the fit is incomplete.

What happens when we follow the link? When we notice both the points of contact and the points of difference, correlating Psalm 51 and 2 Samuel 11–12 makes us reflect on the following: (1) Psalm 51:4 seems inappropriate: is David hiding from responsibility? (2) God didn't seem to answer the prayer in Psalm 51:7-12; (3) maybe there's a connection between these two facts; (4) maybe David didn't really repent, which would explain what follows in his story. Note that something similar appears when we set Psalm 72 alongside the story of Solomon.

G iven that the Psalter includes few confession psalms, Lamentations is another more feasible place to start in understanding confession in the OT, alongside Ezra 9, Nehemiah 9 and Daniel 9. One feature of Lamentations is then that it's corporate (like Ezra 9; Neh 9; Dan 9). Its background is the destruction of Jerusalem and the exile of people from Judah, presumably the destruction in 587 B.C. Lamentations is the surviving community's prayers in the years after that event. We know that the community had fast days in that connection (see, e.g., Zech 8:19), and we can imagine it using these prayers on those occasions. The Jewish community still uses them on the Ninth of Av (July–August) in this way.

Lamentations' five poems each have twenty-two verses (sixty-six in Lam 3); there are twenty-two letters in the Hebrew alphabet, and in Lamentations 1–4 each verse begins with a different letter. They thus express sorrow from A to Z (as we would put it in English). Lamentations 1–2 and Lamentations 4 are like funeral laments; only Lamentations 5 is entirely prayer. In the Greek and English Bibles Lamentations follows Jeremiah, but like the Psalms, the poems are actually anonymous; there is no concrete evidence to link them with Jeremiah, though no doubt he would approve of them.

There is parallelism within their lines, as in psalms. Whereas in praise psalms the commonest rhythm is 3-3, lines in protest psalms can have short second halves, often 3-2. The point is not so clear in translations because Hebrew combines words that are separate in English (see 336). In the following translation of the opening lines of Lamentations I have placed the symbol // between the expressions in the Hebrew to show how the rhythm works (e.g., "she who was great" is one word in Hebrew.

Oh!//The-city//sits//alone,	that-was-great//with-a-people.
She-became//like-a-widow,	she-who-was-great//among-the-nations.
She-who-was-a-queen//among-states	became//a-slave.

The second halves keep bringing you up short, in the way that life itself has. The poetry limps.

Read through the five poems

1. What are their chief characteristics?

2. How are they like psalms, and how are they unlike psalms?

3. What is their understanding of the community, of God, of confession, of prayer?

Some notes on Lamentations

Lamentations 1. The leadership has been deported; here ordinary people are mourning the city's fate. They accept responsibility for what has happened (contrast, e.g., Ps 89). The prayer keeps noting that Mt. Zion has no comforter; in due course Isaiah 40:1-2 will respond to this fact.

Lamentations 2. The motif of Yahweh's anger is prominent, reflecting the experience of being on the receiving end. It indicates that Yahweh has all the passion of a person; Yahweh is not a cold judge. Note the situation's horror (Lam 2:11-12), and also the disproving of a faith conviction (Lam 2:15; cf. Ps 48:2).

Lamentations 3. Now a man speaks; compare Psalms and Jeremiah (with first-, second- and third-person verbs). Hope has gone (Lam 3:16-18); remembering is painful (Lam 3:19-21a). Then there is an astonishing reversal (Lam 3:21b); Yahweh's other passions make hope possible (Lam 3:22-30). Yahweh is angry only unwillingly (Lam 3:33—the central line). Literally, the Hebrew says that it doesn't come from his heart. These facts make an exhortation to repentance possible (Lam 3:40-42); there is the possibility of forgiveness.

Lamentations 4. If Lamentations 3 was the highpoint, the poems now revert to pained, concrete description. Yahweh has not kept his commitment to David and to Zion (Lam 4:20; contrast Ps 132).

Lamentations 5. This is the least concrete of the poems, and the one most like a psalm. Lamentations turns out to be linear; it takes us to the end of its journey. But it is an unsatisfactory end (Lam 5:22). The story is still incomplete.

> Whenever I pick up this book and give myself over to Lamentations (which I do whenever I want through the reading to dampen excessive optimism), my voice chokes, and I dissolve in tears, and the suffering comes vividly before my eyes, as it were, and I join the lamenter in his lament. (Gregory of Nazianzus, *Select Orations*, Oration 6.18)

Job 28:12 asks rhetorically, "Where is wisdom to be found?" Within the OT, the answer is in Proverbs, Job and Ecclesiastes. Proverbs 1–9 comprises homilies on the avoidance of folly and other women; Proverbs 10:1–22:16 collects one-verse sayings on these and many other subjects; Proverbs 22:17–31:31 is five further mixed collections; Ecclesiastes offers more homilies, but with a questioning atmosphere; Job involves more questioning, in the form of the script of a play.

The wisdom books look at life itself in order to discuss directly how to see life and how to live life. Their resource for these questions is neither the story of Israel and the covenant nor the declarations that God made in the Torah or the Prophets, but rather the way life itself works. They are inductive not deductive, and experiential in the sense of empirical. They are the fruit of general revelation rather than of special revelation. They imply that God planted in the world and in our experience truths about God and life that we can discover. They link with the way people presuppose the reality of God by believing in order, play, hope, judgment and humor, which are "signals of transcendence" (Berger, *Rumor of Angels*).

The connection between wisdom, the way life works and God's general revelation links with the parallels between OT wisdom and other Middle Eastern wisdom works such as Egyptian "Instruction" documents, Akkadian proverbs, and Ludlul Bel Nimeqi ("The Babylonian Job"; see 442). It also links with the parallels between the book of Proverbs and African proverbs (e.g., Golka, *Leopard's Spots*) and Latino proverbs (e.g., Tamez, *When the Horizons Close*, 146-54). All cultures seek to understand how life works and to pass on their discoveries, whether or not they realize that they are profiting from God's general revelation.

Although Proverbs, Job and Ecclesiastes are the classic OT books that work this way, there are other works that overlap with them. The Apocrypha (see 507) includes Wisdom of Solomon and Wisdom of Jesus Ben Sira.

Within the OT itself, Song of Songs shares the focus on life itself and the link with Solomon that appear in Proverbs and Ecclesiastes. Daniel's place in the Writings in the Hebrew order of the OT reflects the way Daniel is presented in the book as a wise man rather than as a prophet. Elsewhere in the OT, the stories of Joseph and Esther portray life as it works out empirically rather than portraying God acting in an interventionist way; thus they compare with wisdom thinking.

"Solomon wrote the Song of Songs in the springtime of youth, Proverbs with the wisdom of maturity, Ecclesiastes with the disillusion of old age" (Rabbi Jonathan in *Song of Songs Rabbah*, the rabbinic commentary on Song of Songs). Did he really? Proverbs 1:1 does describe Proverbs as "the sayings of Solomon," but it later refers to "the words of Agur" and "the words of Lemuel" (we don't know who they were) as well as to the activity of King Hezekiah's men (Prov 25.1; 30:1; 31:1). Like ascriptions to Moses and David, ascriptions to Solomon are not statements about authorship in a Western sense. They suggest the authority of the works. Solomon is wisdom's patron saint as Moses is the patron saint of the instruction that appears in the Torah and David is the patron saint of psalmody. Wisdom that is Solomonic is wisdom that is the real thing. The portrait of Solomon's wisdom in 1 Kings 3–4 shows how wisdom is practical as well as theoretical, communal as well as individual, political as well as private, royal as well as egalitarian, ethical as well as empirical, and God-given as well as humanly achieved.

The background of wisdom material may lie in three social contexts. (1) Family life: many everyday sayings in Proverbs would then be older than Solomon. (2) The state educational system: in Egypt, wisdom writings were used in the court college where people were trained for service in the administration, and references to the king and other political notes in Proverbs suggest a similar context for some of this material, beginning in the period of the monarchy. (3) The development of theological schools in the Second Temple period: here the theologians who are later referred to as "the scribes" would learn to think through issues such as revelation and creation, which appear in Proverbs 1–9, and to think through the puzzling life questions that are the focus of Job and Ecclesiastes.

"Proverb" is a misleading translation of the Hebrew word *māšāl*. As well as actual proverbs, the book of Proverbs includes homilies and also sayings that make provocative rather than straightforward statements; "saying" gives a better idea. Proverbs 1:1-7 has "figures" and "riddles" as subsets of "sayings." Those verses go on to describe the book's contents as wisdom, which, we have noted earlier (see 428), is a practical not merely a theoretical business. It is instruction or discipline, which implies that it is not obtained without effort or pain; Proverbs rubs our noses in truths that we wish we did not have to face. It is insight, the capacity to be discerning and to look behind things. It involves shrewdness, the characteristic of the snake (Gen 3:1-7), but a positive quality too in helping us live wisely. It refers to knowledge, which means acknowledgment: not mere awareness of the truth but commitment to living by it. It speaks of skill, a word that suggests "knowing the ropes," being able to steer one's way through life.

The wisdom that Proverbs commends. Wisdom can't tell you the gospel, but it can tell you other things; it compares with psychology, philosophy, social sciences, insights from other faiths and other sources of knowledge. To such human insight, wisdom in the OT says, "Yes, but . . ." This stance links with the parallels between OT wisdom and other Middle Eastern wisdom literature, some of which it has utilized. It models a way of learning from the world: this learning involves setting the world's "wisdom" in the context of Yahweh's involvement with Israel and the truths that emerge from that involvement.

Thus, in the midst of the pragmatic expressions in the introduction in Proverbs 1:1-7, there is the assumption that wisdom involves making decisions in a way that is right and has integrity, and that it involves awe for Yahweh, obedience to Yahweh; indeed, this stance is wisdom's foundation. So wisdom presupposes ethics and faith. Learning from life is different from the empiricism of modernity. Right and wrong and God's involvement in the world are inherent aspects of the reality of life as wisdom examines it.

Proverbs 1:1-7 also indicates who are its targets. It speaks first of the simple or young, the unlearned, who need to let their lives be shaped by it. But it goes on to people who are already wise and discerning, who can still learn from it. Many people insist on being fools, which does not mean being intellectually feeble but rather ignoring the way actions have consequences, the way life works and the way ethics and God's involvement are integral to the way life works. Proverbs 1 is most distraught about scoffers, the people who think that they know everything and have nothing to learn.

Reading Proverbs. Read Proverbs and then undertake the following studies.

1. Collect its material on its key topics: (a) wisdom itself; (b) husbands and wives; (c) sex; (d) wealth; (e) power; (f) work; (g) the relationship between our plans and God's plans; (h) the relationship between the inward person and the outer person; (i) any other topics that you see as prominent.

2. For each topic, try to formulate an understanding that does justice to the varying insights that Proverbs offers. For material on some of these subjects, see 442.

3. Read the "Babylonian Proverbs" (see 442) and compare them with Proverbs (many of the Babylonian proverbs are hard to understand; do what you can with the intelligible ones).

4. Read the thirty chapters of the Egyptian Instruction of Amenemope (see 442). Compare it with the thirty sayings in Proverbs 22:17–24:22 (see Prov 22:20), where similar phrases recur.

5. Notice when you read something and think, "Yes, that's true." Such resonances illustrate the point about the link between Proverbs and experience or general revelation.

It can seem that Proverbs itself sees things in a black-and-white way, but from time to time it makes clear that it recognizes the complexity of what life teaches us (see especially Prov 26:4-5). Those moments remind us not to be wooden in interpreting it. It knows that its rules do not work 100 percent of the time, but it knows that they often work, and therefore that they are worth basing one's life upon. (On childrearing according to Proverbs, see 442.)

PROVERBS 1–9
How to Stay Faithful

Proverbs 1–9 is the section of Scripture that gives most sustained attention to sexual faithfulness. The next most significant stretch of Scripture in this regard is 1 Corinthians. So there are contexts in the life of the NT church as well as in Israel's life where sexual unfaithfulness becomes a particular problem. Together, the two books point to various contexts where it becomes an issue:

1. Corinth was a notoriously pagan and immoral city. Some cultural contexts put more pressure on people than others.

2. The Corinthian church knew great spiritual renewal. This can also be a context in which sex becomes a problem.

3. Proverbs 1–9 comes from a social context (after the exile) where within God's people old certainties had gone (compare Ecclesiastes) and old social structures no longer obtained.

4. Proverbs 1–9 suggests an audience involved in studying deep theological questions.

5. Proverbs 1–9 sees insight embodied as a woman, Ms. Wisdom, and 1 Corinthians assumes that women prophesy. Both thus commend openness to learning from women.

6. Proverbs 31, which pairs with Proverbs 1–9 as a bracket around the book, pictures a woman exercising responsibility, not simply following a man, and 1 Corinthians 11 also implies women exercising freedom from old constraints.

Given parallels in context, it is not surprising that sexual unfaithfulness is a problem for churches and seminaries and among pastors in the West today. The church agonizes more over same-sex relationships than over heterosexual unfaithfulness, but it may thereby be evading what is at least as big an issue.

Proverbs 1–9 discusses the problem only from a man's angle. Perhaps there were few women in theological school in its context. And/or perhaps in that context women were less inclined to unfaithfulness—less "liberated." In a Western context, at least, the sexual politics will need to be seen both ways. But here I leave the points in the gendered form in which Proverbs presents them.

Proverbs 1–9 sees the issue this way:

1. Married men within the people of God do have affairs.

2. One reason for this is that there is a thrill in falling in love with someone when your first love has grown cold, and/or an excitement in an affair (Prov 5:20; 9:17).

3. Married women also have affairs. Here they are presented as outsiders, possibly like the women from surrounding peoples who are mentioned in Ezra–Nehemiah. But the traditional idea of "the other woman" similarly presents such a person as an outsider.

4. Proverbs' key point is that having an affair is really stupid. As a wisdom book, it speaks especially in terms of what is wise or stupid, not in terms of what is right or wrong, but the end result is the same. Whether you have an affair because you have fallen in love with someone or because of the thrill, it is almost certain to end in pain and loss, and it is quite likely to ruin your life.

5. But Proverbs does also add that having an affair can't be consistent with awe for Yahweh and obedience to Yahweh. When believers have an affair, they may well tell themselves that this love is a gift from God. If it is love, it can't be wrong, can it? Yes, it can, Proverbs implies.

Positively, Proverbs points to some guidelines for safeguarding against the temptation.

1. Own it. The chapters bring the issue out in the open.

2. Keep your head (be wise). Don't be led by your emotions or by some other part of your anatomy.

3. Keep in daily touch with God over your life. See Proverbs 3:1-8.

4. Keep watch over your heart. See Proverbs 4:23.

5. Develop your enthusiasm for your wife. See Proverbs 5:15-19, which is elaborated by Song of Songs.

Read Song of Songs.

1. What kind of relationship is it describing?

   a. Is it the relationship of God and Israel?

   b. Or of Jesus and a believer?

   c. Or of a husband and a wife?

   d. Or of an engaged couple?

   e. Or of two people who are just in love?

   f. Or of Solomon and the woman he loves?

   g. Or what?

2. As a set of poems, does it seem to have a story to tell, or are they simply separate poems?

3. What does it say about the relationship that it describes?

4. What do you learn about the man, the woman and their community?

Here are five understandings of Song of Songs. In light of your reading, what are the arguments for and against each of them?

1. Is Song of Songs a parable of God's love for Israel? Jews use it this way in reading it at Passover as an allegory of God's love for Israel over the centuries, and Scripture does use human love in this way (cf. Hos 1–3; Is 5:1-7, which is particularly interesting because it is a love song about a garden; Eph 5). Books often say that it was on the basis of this interpretation that Song of Songs was included in the canon of Scripture, but I know of no evidence for this suggestion.

2. Are they songs to celebrate the marriage of two gods (Tammuz and Ishtar?) or of a priest and priestess (see Pope, *Song of Songs*)? This suggestion is based on parallels with other poems from the Semitic and Egyptian world (cf. Jer 44:17-18).

3. Are they simply songs to celebrate sexual love, like ancient Egyptian love songs (see 442)? Note their perspective on the woman's role in the relationship with the emphasis on her freedom to take the initiative in it. "There is no male dominance, no female subordination, and no stereotyping of either sex. . . . Never is this woman called a wife, nor is she required to bear children. In fact, to the issues of marriage and procreation the Song does not speak. Love for the sake of love is its message, and the portrayal of the female delineates this message best" (Trible, *Rhetoric of Sexuality*).

4. Is Song of Songs a book to bring sex into the context of wisdom and the covenant? The book starts off by describing itself as "Solomon's Song of Songs"; Solomon is the great patron of wisdom, and the beginning of Song of Songs thus parallels that of Proverbs and Ecclesiastes. The book is not merely a secular poem; it is drawn into the religious orbit of wisdom. Song of Songs excludes a profane view of sex (Childs, *Old Testament as Scripture*). "The Song of Songs is one long description of the rapture, the unquenchable yearning and the restless willingness and readiness, with which both partners in this covenant hasten towards and encounter. . . . We may well ask where the authors found the courage to treat the matter in this way, speaking so bluntly of eros and not being content merely with the restrained and in its own way central reference to marriage and posterity" (Barth, *Church Dogmatics* III.1, 313).

5. Is Song of Songs a muted celebration of love that recognizes that love can't take you back to the garden of Eden? Note the garden image in the book. But "in the Song, paradise is limited by the fallen world; Death is undefeated, society imposes shame on the lovers, time inevitably separates them. . . . The ideal harmony of 'I am my beloved's and my beloved is mine' disappears on the last appearance of the formula: 'I am my beloved's and his desire is for me'" (Landy, *Paradoxes of Paradise*) (cf. Song 7:10 with Gen 3:16).

For my take on the significance of Song of Songs, see, under 442, "What Might the Song of Songs Do for People?"

The book of Job is a piece of theological reflection in the form of a drama about a man who becomes the subject of debate in the heavenly court, and whose life then falls apart (Job 1–2). It centers on a dialogue between him and three friends discussing appropriate reactions to an experience like his, and appropriate ways of understanding it (Job 3–27). After a poem reflecting on the issues, and a final statement by Job (Job 28–31), a latecomer storms in to make his contribution (Job 32–37). Then God appears and speaks (Job 38–41). Finally, Job's life is restored (Job 42).

The story takes place in the land of Uz, in Edom (see Lam 4:21); Edom had a reputation for wisdom, and Uz is familiar from Genesis (Gen 10:23; 22:21; 36:28). Job is mentioned in Ezekiel 14:12-20 along with Noah, and Eliphaz is the name of a son of Esau/Edom (Gen 36:4-16). Elihu is the name of several people in 1 Samuel and 1 Chronicles (1 Sam 1:1; 1 Chron 12:20; 26:7; 27:18); there is no other occurrence of the names Bildad and Zophar. So several of the names would suggest a background in the period of Israel's ancestors, but among people who were not of Israel's line.

In Job people mostly talk to one another in poetry, which is one indication that the book is not a transcript of a series of actual conversations. Possibly it is pure fiction; if so, it would not undo the validity of its message. But the experience of tragedy in people's lives, of having arguments with God, of having God respond and even of restoration and renewal are not so uncommon, and it may be better to see it as a (perhaps highly) fictionalized version of actual events. The account of the scene in heaven at the beginning must come from the author's divinely inspired imagination. Maybe this account is an indication of something that has happened or could happen in heaven, though in somewhat extraordinary circumstances in connection with the life of a somewhat extraordinary person; the story is not about your average Israelite (or Christian). Or maybe the scene in heaven is a dramatic device to get the story going, and so its theological implications should not be pressed, like the details in Jesus' parables or in visions in Revelation.

The book of Job is anonymous. It is usually assumed to have been written after the exile, but there is little hard evidence on which to date it, and the question of date makes no difference to its message. There are some unevennesses in the book; notably, the third round of speeches between Job and his three friends is incomplete, and the poem in Job 28 and Elihu's address (Job 32–37) could be removed without leaving obvious holes. Possibly the book was not written in one go but rather has grown over time. But again, we have no hard evidence of this, and removing parts from the book would impoverish it; we do best to take the text as it stands.

People sometimes look to the book for an answer to the problem of theodicy or the problem of suffering. It has no one answer to those questions (nor does the rest of the Bible). It focuses on how we live with suffering, especially if we don't have an answer. But it offers a number of partial answers to the problem. It works in a postmodern way by recognizing that we have no total answer but by noting a number of partial insights, which will have to be enough for us to live with. It's not the case that some of the answers are wrong and some are right, though some are more and some less applicable to Job.

Read the book of Job. If you prefer, you can read the shorter dramatized version (see 442; there's also an account there of how Job has been used in mourning).

1. What do you think the book is about? What is its problem, and does it solve the problem?

2. What are the main points that the different participants or sections of the book make?

Then read "The Babylonian Theodicy" and/or "The Babylonian Job" (see 442).

1. What do you think this Babylonian document is about? What is its problem, and does it solve the problem?

2. In the "Babylonian Theodicy," what different contributions do the different participants in the debate make?

3. How does the Babylonian document compare with Job? Where are the similarities and the differences?

4 │ 33 │ JOB
Two Possible Insights

The book of Job is concerned with the awful things that God sometimes lets happen to people. That issue can raise the question of what the relationship between God and us is based on, and then the question of whether we can understand how God runs the world. Further, the story is concerned with how we react to suffering and how we may help other people do so.

The way it proceeds is by offering us a number of answers to its question(s), all of which have some truth to them but need to be applied with discernment to different situations. The basic problem with Job's friends is their inability to do so.

Here are two insights from the book (four more are discussed in 434).

Suffering is a test. The introduction to the book raises the question of whether the relationship between God and Job is a genuine personal one or a more contractual one. Job's troubles come to him in order to establish that God is right; the relationship is personal, not contractual. Setting up this answer involves hypothesizing Job as someone who is as near as you could get to a perfect human being. The drama also depends on the role of the being who is called "Satan" in most English translations; but this translation gives a misleading impression (see 119). The word *śātān* is an ordinary (if rather poetic) Hebrew word meaning "adversary," with legal or military connotations. The Adversary is here a member of God's cabinet whose responsibility is to make sure that people don't get away with things that they shouldn't get away with (a role that recognizes that God has a hard time being tough with people, and so needs to be persuaded to do so when it is appropriate). God is inclined to trust people; the Adversary's responsibility is to ask sharp questions. Thus there's some overlap with Satan (with a capital S) but not total identity, though a significant link is that neither have too much power; they have only as much rope as God allows them. So Job's suffering comes as a test of the genuineness of his relationship with God. The idea that suffering is a test recurs in the Bible; Jesus is tested by the devil (*diabolos* in

Greek, which etymologically also means "false accuser"). It's important to the test's reality that God doesn't know how it will turn out. So the first answer to the question of suffering is that suffering can come to vindicate our relationship with God; that relationship is not based on what we can get out of it.

Suffering is a consequence of our personal human sinfulness. Eliphaz, Bildad and Zophar affirm the biblical insight that the relationship between people and God is based on people living the right kind of life: God honors those who honor God and treats with contempt people who treat God with contempt (1 Sam 2:30). Or, as Jesus assumes, a person may become ill as a result of having done wrong, and so be in need of forgiveness and not merely healing (Mk 2:5; cf. 1 Cor 11:29-32). So the second answer to the question of suffering is that suffering can come as a result of our personal wrongdoing. This insight is the kind that appears in Proverbs, a generalization that can be mistakenly turned into a hard-edged rule. Job's three friends treat it thus, belaboring their point when they can no longer keep silent. They assume that Job's troubles show that he must have failed in his relationship with God and with life. The problem with the friends is thus not that their theological theory is wholly wrong, but rather that it is irrelevant to this particular case. Truth is more complicated than they think. Their further great contribution to the book is to embody the danger that a sufferer's friends think that they must supply answers, that the sufferer needs answers and that one needs to be able to defend God against any charge of unfairness. Ironically, people who study the book may hope then to have the answer to its problem, which they can then share with sufferers, and thereby they repeat the mistake made by Job's friends.

In the course of the debate between the friends and Job comes his declaration that he knows that his redeemer lives, and that he will in due course see God (Job 19:25). George Frideric Handel gave these words a key place in his famous choral work *The Messiah*. For Job himself, they form another declaration that, one way or another, Job will surely get the chance to confront God and have his commitment to God vindicated. Job is not looking for someone to redeem him from sin; he needs someone to vindicate him from his friend's accusations.

Four More Possible Insights

Suffering challenges us to insist on facing God with the facts. Job knows that there are none of the wrongs in his life that his friends hypothesize. He acknowledges that he sins, like everyone. But he knows that his suffering is out of proportion to his sin. He therefore wants the opportunity to meet up with God in order to argue his case, so that God will recognize his integrity. At present, and until he can do so, the relationship between God and him is an enigma. The troubles are inexplicable. Job's great contribution to the book is to model steadfastness in insisting on facing God with the facts. This third answer to the question of suffering (see also 433) is thus that we react to suffering by insisting on its painfulness and by protesting about it to God in the conviction that God is really there even if not behaving in the way that we know we have reason to expect. One way of seeing the book is as a gargantuan protest psalm (see 416-18). Related to this answer is the good response of Job's friends when they simply weep for Job and sit there with him in his pain, the best form of pastoral care they ever exercise.

Suffering is designed to encourage us to grow spiritually. Elihu urges Job to see his troubles in this way. A relationship with God is based on humble submission to God; suffering encourages that submission. There are overlaps between Elihu's address and Yahweh's eventual address, and in a way Elihu thus prepares the way for Yahweh. The first three friends are censured at the close of the book, but God does not condemn Elihu. This fourth answer to the question of suffering recurs in Christian spirituality, and it is the one often offered by Christians who are more enlightened than Job's three friends. It may prepare the way for God's answer, but it is not God's answer.

There is no answer to the question about suffering even when there is one. When Yahweh eventually appears, initially it is to confront Job, not to vindicate him. Yahweh takes Job on a tour of the created world to show how much of it does not circulate around human need. It exists in its own right. There was nothing wrong in principle with Job's protesting to Yahweh about the way he has been treated, as people do in the Psalms. His problem lies in his having come to speak as if he is the center of the world (as readers, we know that in this story there is something bigger afoot than factors involved in one individual's relationship with God). In his second address, Yahweh moves on to the question whether Job could do a better job of running the world and putting down evil than God does. God's capacity to control Behemoth and Leviathan comes into focus. These two monsters are more like equivalents of Satan than the Adversary is. They are embodiments of power asserted against God, but embodiments that God has under control. Job's task is to accept his troubles on the basis of his relationship with God and on the basis of acceptance of limits and trust in God. A feature of Yahweh's addresses is that he does not tell Job about the background to his suffering, which we the readers know about from Job 1–2. The most delicious fact about the book of Job is that there is an answer to the question of why Job suffers, but it is never given to him. So this fifth answer to the question of suffering is that there is no answer even when there is one. Job therefore has to live with the experience the same way as many others, trusting God (as one who can control the forces of chaos, Behemoth and Leviathan) and letting God be God even when he cannot understand God. It is because Job expects that the world and revelation should revolve around him that he is rebuked.

Everything will turn out happily at the end. This certainly is the case at the end of the book for Job's three daughters, who are identified by name (his seven sons are not identified) and who receive a share in Job's inheritance—both unusual features in the OT. The book's ending constitutes the vindication that Job has looked for. The troubles are over. The relationship is genuine. The ending involves an irony. In a sense, the friends are right after all. God honors the one who honors God. Of course, not every sufferer's story ends in this "they all lived happily ever after" way; but the picture in this sufferer's story embodies that promise of God's faithfulness. The sixth answer to the question of suffering, that everything will turn out happily at the end, is unrealistic in earthly terms, but it makes an important statement about the way God surely will make things turn out all right in the End. The most significant difference that Jesus makes to the book of Job is that his resurrection gives firmer grounds for this expectation.

Reading Ecclesiastes

1. What are the main aspects of life that it covers, and what does it say about each of them?

2. What themes or attitudes or phrases or convictions or questions keep recurring?

3. Why do you think the Holy Spirit inspired this book?

4. What does it say to you?

The origin and nature of Ecclesiastes. Ecclesiastes opens with a double introduction. On one hand, it is a collection of "the words of *qōhelet* the son of David, king in Jerusalem." The Hebrew word *qōhelet* comes from the word *qāhāl*, the word for "congregation," so we could take it to mean "member of the congregation" or "congregational leader"; it is often translated "preacher." Whichever is right, the author is being identified as a regular believer, an orthodox member of Israel. This is underscored by describing him as the son of David. There are many people to whom that description could apply, but there is one son of David who is especially identified as a wise teacher, and the close of the book will refer to *qōhelet* in those terms (Eccles 12:9). This description would make one think of Solomon, which would reinforce the invitation to take this book as the embodiment of wise teaching.

After that first introduction, however, the second is astonishing. *Qōhelet's* own first words are, "Total emptiness, total emptiness, everything is emptiness." To illustrate the point, he immediately goes on to expound a stance that will run through the book: as far as one can see when one looks at the world, he says, the world is going nowhere. It is only going round in circles (Eccles 1:3-11). How can this be wise congregational teaching? What is a book that expresses such views doing in the Bible? The tension between the two introductions opens up the tension that runs through the book. It comprises a repeated movement between expressions of the classic wisdom illustrated in Proverbs and declarations that face the reader with ways in which this teaching is not borne out by experience.

The book's first line would seem to invite us to see Solomon behind the book, though its not naming Solomon as its author is then odd. Solomon is semi-present again in Ecclesiastes 1:12–2:26, which begins as an apparent testimony: "I *qōhelet* was king over Israel in Jerusalem." The reason for making us think of Solomon is immediately apparent because the testimony goes on to reflect on the acquisition of riches, wisdom, enjoyment and possessions, and on other achievements, and to conclude that while there is some merit in them, they are finally empty. Solomon would be the ideal person to give this testimony because he made his mark in all these connections, but restraint in naming Solomon again hints that he is not the real author of the reflection but is rather the one who can be portrayed as reflecting on these questions.

Other indications confirm that the book is not claiming Solomon's actual authorship. The way it speaks about kings and about relating to kings (Eccles 4:13-15; 8:2-4; 10:16-20) is not what one would expect if it were the king who is speaking. The Hebrew of Ecclesiastes is like that of no other OT book and resembles Hebrew as it was spoken after OT times. It includes two words imported from Persian, which suggests the Second Temple period, during or after the time when Judah was part of the Persian Empire. Its grammar is influenced by Aramaic, a sister language that became common among Jews at the end of OT times. So the only real argument about its date concerns whether it belongs to the fourth, third or second century before Christ. One factor in that discussion is whether its questioning nature reflects an acquaintance with Greek works that raise similar questions. But the fact that there are also Mesopotamian works that discuss these questions makes it an unnecessary hypothesis that Ecclesiastes belongs in a context of acquaintance with Greek thinking.

As is the case with Job, the question of date is not very important in connection with understanding the book. Its questions are real, whatever the century in which they were articulated. This fact ironically illustrates the book's opening comment: there is no such thing as progress.

ECCLESIASTES

Its Characteristic Slant

There have been many attempts to find a structure or plot to Ecclesiastes, all of them different. There is no movement in the book. Yet it is not simply one random thing after another. It keeps juxtaposing expressions of orthodox wisdom teaching and of faith in God as the great giver (Eccles 5:18-20) (we might call it "biblical teaching") with down-to-earth gloominess concerning how things are "under the sun" or, as we might put, "in real life." Ecclesiastes insists on experience more resolutely than any other wisdom book.

So, what is the relationship between the orthodox statements and the gloomy ones?

Traditional critical scholarship saw Ecclesiastes as gloom tempered by orthodoxy. The gloomy material came first, and the positive statements were added as corrections of the gloomy ones. We might then take the former as the way the world sees things, the latter as Israel's answer to questions concerning the human predicament. The bulk of Ecclesiastes might then be seen as expressing the darkness into which the gospel would eventually shine. It has sometimes been used in evangelism in this way. Perhaps, then, the writer wrote in this gloomy way with that aim, or perhaps a book that meant every word of its gloom was included in Scripture by God's providence so that it could be used in this way.

Another tradition of critical scholarship sees the book as tempering orthodox theological commitments by realism concerning facts about life that we gloss over. It urges us not to hide from the emptiness of life "under the sun," but rather to accept the challenge to believe nevertheless. It forms a warning not to think that we have the truth all buttoned-up. It issues a protest like that in Job against the oversimplified truths of Job's comforters. It constitutes Scripture's permission to doubt. Biblical truth may sometimes seem full of holes, but we may still recognize that there are no better answers than the biblical ones. Ecclesiastes is then like Job himself. The problem is not that Ecclesiastes is depressed—or if he is depressed, it is because he is facing facts. The book is about how to live with doubt.

Possibly we should not try to decide whether the negative or the positive "wins," since they are simply set alongside each other. Some readers need to read the book one way, some the other way, and/or to read it in different ways at different times. The book's ending, a double conclusion to match the double introduction, supports this idea. A closing statement about total emptiness (Eccles 12:8) pairs with the opening statement (Eccles 1:2); they constitute one bracket around the book as a whole. That statement leads into a set of observations (Eccles 12:9-14) that affirm the first introduction (Eccles 1:1) in a way that takes account of the book's questioning nature. The sayings of the wise are like spurs, they say; spurs propel a horse forward, but these sayings make a reader say, "Ouch! I wish you hadn't said that." In what is the favorite text of many an OT student, they affirm that there is no end to the making of books, and that much study wearies the flesh (Eccles 12:12). Their point is that one Ecclesiastes is good, but a Bible full of Ecclesiastes wouldn't be. They affirm that *qōhelet* was a wise teacher, spoke the truth and gave teaching from one shepherd—a positive affirmation whether the shepherd is God or *qōhelet*. They close with a reaffirmation of the basic wisdom exhortation to be in awe of God and keep his commands, because he is the one who is judge.

Death is the key experience on which Ecclesiastes insists. You cannot understand life unless you keep in focus the fact that we are on our way to death. In understanding that fact, even the limitations of wisdom have to be emphasized. Although Jesus' resurrection provides evidence that was not available in Ecclesiastes' day for the fact that death will not be the end, this does not make a lot of difference to the facts Ecclesiastes notes about death.

Elsa Tamez (*When the Horizons Close*) suggests that Ecclesiastes points to three aspects of an attitude toward life: (1) own what you cannot do (understand the times, achieve justice, avoid dying); (2) enjoy food, wine, work and relationships (Eccles 2:24-26; 3:12-13, 22; 5:17-19; 8:15; 9:7-10; 11:9-10); (3) do so in appreciation of God's giving and in awe of God.

Daniel
Narrative, Worship and Wisdom

The Writings embrace narrative, worship and wisdom; Daniel brings together these three.

Daniel as a narrative book. More than half of Daniel comprises a series of stories. They occupy most of Daniel 2–7, which is structured as a chiasm:

(A) A vision of four empires (Dan 2)

    (B) A trial of faithfulness and a marvelous deliverance (Dan 3)

        (C) An omen interpreted and a king confronted (Dan 4)

        (C') An omen interpreted and a king confronted (Dan 5)

    (B') A trial of faithfulness and a marvelous deliverance (Dan 6)

(A') A vision of four empires (Dan 7)

Thus, there are three pairs (A and A', and so on). In each case, it's worth comparing each member of the pair with the other in order to see what the two have in common and points where they differ. Daniel 1 is then an introduction, concerning the exile and the questions that it raises, which receive a preliminary answer in this opening story that is then expanded in what follows. Daniel 8–12 in turn constitutes further treatments of the issues introduced in Daniel 1 and in Daniel 2–7.

Like other narrative books, Daniel raises the question of whether it is more history or parable; and like other books, I take it as being like a movie based on fact, an inspired mixture of fact and fiction. In terms of theme, it offers a series of takes on the same issue, a recurrent plot, the question of whether it is possible to stay faithful and survive or even do well in a foreign country. It expounds a narrative politics: it parallels Esther in its setting, but it parallels Ezra–Nehemiah in having a male hero. In discussing its question, it presupposes an underlying issue: Who is responsible for the way history works out? Is it God or human actors? The stories emphasize God's sovereignty, yet they portray events working out in a way that involves human initiative by Judahites and kings. In this sense, the story deconstructs (see

Fewell, *Circle of Sovereignty*), in a positive sense; it invites us to reflect on two truths that stand in tension.

The narrative starts with the Babylonians besieging Jerusalem and taking people off into exile, but it does not speak of this event as God's punishment for Judah's sin in the way that 2 Kings and 2 Chronicles do. No doubt it assumes that understanding, but its focus lies elsewhere. As is the case in the story of Esther, living in a foreign country is just an aspect of life for the kind of people for whom the stories are told. It is the life into which they are born. The stories are designed to resource them as they face the challenges of that life.

Daniel as a worship book. Worship is a recurrent theme, especially in the stories.

Daniel 1:1-2	The temple worship implements are taken to Babylon.
Daniel 2:20-23	Daniel prays, and worships as a response to answer to prayer.
Daniel 3	The form of worship required by the empire puts pressure on Israelites.
Daniel 4:1-3, 34-37	The foreign king is drawn into worship.
Daniel 5:1-4	The worship vessels are used blasphemously.
Daniel 6	Prayer is under pressure.
Daniel 9	Daniel offers a prayer of confession.

Daniel as a wisdom book. At the beginning of the book the young men are introduced as men of insight, and through the stories they manifest that insight in a variety of ways. The chapters also refer to God's wisdom and many times to the "wisdom" of the so-called Babylonian wise men. The kind of insight that the young men manifest is the insight of people who need to know how to function at court—the kind expounded in Proverbs 10–31. It's wisdom about how to live in history. In Daniel 7–12 the focus moves to theological wisdom, to how we are to think about history, more the kind of wisdom that Proverbs 1–9 speaks of when it refers to God and creation. Here wisdom comes in the form of divine revelation (apocalypse). Daniel 9 manifests a particular concern with understanding.

Daniel as prophecy. In the Greek Bible and English Bibles the book of Daniel appears among the Prophets, and Jesus refers to Daniel as a prophet (Mt 24:15). But not all prophets are among the Prophets (see 301). In the book of Daniel the visions given to Daniel are not seen as prophecies, even though they do announce future events. There is one point where Daniel especially acts as a prophet: see Daniel 4:27, where he confronts the king in the manner of Jeremiah.

The book of Daniel combines stories about Daniel and his friends (Dan 1–6) and visions given to Daniel (Dan 7–12). The stories show how God reigns now; the visions promise that God will reign at the End. The stories presuppose life in a foreign land as part of an ethnic minority in the sixth century B.C. and focus on how to survive in politics. The visions speak to the situation of Jerusalem in the second century B.C., where people are under pressure from a foreign ruler (e.g., Dan 8:19-25; 11:29-39; 12:1).

Daniel 1–6. Read these chapters and compare the six stories with each other.

1. Which ones are similar to each other?

2. What issues do they raise?

3. What challenges or what good news do they offer? (Don't focus on the four empires in Dan 2, as we will look at that more in connection with Dan 7–12.)

4. What are the characteristics of Daniel and the other three Judahites?

5. What are the characteristics of the kings in the stories?

6. What are the characteristics of the kings' "wise men"?

7. What are the characteristics of the other people in the stories?

8. What do you think is the importance of the stories?

Daniel 7–12. These chapters comprise four visions of the future from the exile onward. Each extends from Daniel's day to the End and thus offers the Judahites a perspective on the whole of international history from the exile to the End.

Daniel 7. Four empires are pictured as four animals, leading to an arrogant climax and a great deliverance.

Daniel 8. The kings of Media, Persia and Greece are pictured as a ram and a goat, leading to terrible destruction and a great deliverance.

Daniel 9. Jeremiah's prophecy of seventy years of exile becomes a prophecy of seven times seventy years, leading to a terrible abomination and a great deliverance.

Daniel 10–12. This vision includes three more kings to arise in Persia, battles in the Greek empire, a terrible abomination and a great deliverance.

Read Daniel 7–12 and compare the four visions with each other and with Daniel 2.

1. What were your starting assumptions about the purpose and significance of these visions?

2. In what ways are the five visions similar?

3. What is distinctive about each of the visions?

4. How might the visions offer insight on historical and political events as they are unfolding in our time?

5. What food for thought do the visions offer, and what encouragement?

So what are these four empires in Daniel? There were five Middle Eastern empires in pre-Christian times: Assyria, Babylon, Medo-Persia, Greece and Rome. Daniel and his friends were taken off into exile by the Babylonians in the 600s B.C. Medo-Persia took over from Babylon in 539 B.C. The Greeks under Alexander the Great defeated the Persians in 333 B.C. The Roman general Pompey came to Jerusalem in 63 B.C.

1. So are the four empires Assyria, Babylon, Medo-Persia and Greece? These are *the* four empires of OT times. But the vision seems to begin from the exile and thus from Babylon.

2. Are the empires Babylon, Medo-Persia, Greece and Rome? These are *the* four empires in Scripture. But introducing Rome involves adding yet another historical context for the book of Daniel (to add to the 500s and the time of Antiochus).

3. Are the empires Babylon, Media, Persia and Greece? Identifying the empires in this way fits the more specific visions in Daniel 8 and Daniel 10–12 (see 439). It means that the visions form a unity as they offer four variants on the same message. All four describe the unfolding of history from the exile to the promised deliverance from Antiochus, and thus all four bring encouragement to the people of God as they go through persecution.

In Daniel's visions things get more specific and concrete chapter by chapter, so there is something to be said for reading them backwards. At the end of the book, Daniel 10–12 is one long vision, subdivided for convenience. Within it, Daniel 11 is a portrait of the history to unfold from Daniel's day onward, focusing on the Greek period. It refers to the way Alexander the Great became ruler of Macedon in 336 and in 333 invaded the Middle East, defeating the Persians and creating an empire that stretched from Turkey to India. Alexander died less than a decade after crossing into Asia. Four major units emerged from his shattered realm. One centered on Egypt and was ruled by Alexander's general Ptolemy and his successors. Another centered on Syria and Babylonia and was ruled by another general, Seleucus, and his successors. These two realms on either side of Judah were the ones that directly concerned Judah, which constituted a bone of contention between them.

The story in Daniel 11 thus relates substantially to relationships between these "northern" and "southern" kings, giving most space to the northern kings Antiochus III and Antiochus IV Epiphanes. Engineering his way to the throne in 175, Antiochus IV won the support of the Tobiad family in Jerusalem, a group willing to cooperate with him in order to win power there, and not too concerned about detailed observance of the Torah. On two occasions in the course of campaigns against the Egyptians, Antiochus also took action against Jerusalem, both to augment his resources from those of the temple and to put down rebellion on the part of conservative Jews against the Tobiad ruling party. He then stationed a Syrian garrison in Jerusalem to guard against the possibility of further rebellion, but this action also involved introducing the worship of the garrison's Syrian gods into Jerusalem. Perhaps as a result of a further act of rebellion at this provocation, in due course he banned orthodox Jewish worship. Conservative Jews then had to choose between apostasy and resistance. Courageous active rebellion saw the temple worship restored, and Antiochus withdraw from Judah. He was assassinated at the end of 164. In this sense, the End came, as the vision said it would.

There is a horrifying but then gripping account of these events in 1 Maccabees in the Apocrypha (see 507). The vision in Daniel 11 describes them as if it is a prediction, but it is strange to imagine God giving all this information to Daniel centuries before the events would happen, and hard to see why God would do so. We do have instances of history written as if it is prophecy from elsewhere in the Middle East. The following example gives a reign-by-reign account of the history of Akkad (a city not far from Baghdad) (see Vanderkam, *From Revelation to Canon*; Collins, *Apocalyptic Imagination*).

> A ruler will arise, he will rule for thirteen years.
> There will be an attack of Elam against Akkad, and
> The booty of Akkad will be carried off.
> The temples of the great gods will be destroyed, the defeat of Akkad will be
>   decreed.
> There will be confusion, disturbance, and unhappy events in the land, and
> The reign will diminish; another man, whose name is not mentioned, will
>   arise, and
> He will seize the throne as king and will put to death his officials.

Like Daniel 11, such texts are anonymous or pseudonymous; they may be said to come from a seer or prophet; they express themselves cryptically but in a way that someone familiar with the history of the times could understand; they may segue into actual prophecy at the end; they focus on historical events more than revelations about heaven and hell, creation, and the End; they make it possible to trust the message's assessment of the present situation or the actual prophecies that come at the end, but they express themselves in a way that need not be calculated to deceive people into thinking that the message was an actual prophecy—people knew how to read it. Daniel 11, then, is (mostly) not prophecy but rather history cast into the form of prophecy, using this familiar form of speech, to declare that Yahweh is actually the one who is in control and active in Middle Eastern events.

The visions in Daniel 8 and Daniel 10–12 tell us that they refer to the Medo-Persian and Greek empires; their climax is then Antiochus's act of sacrilege in 167 (see 439). The visions in Daniel 7 and Daniel 9 do not tell us what they refer to, but if we assume that the visions fit together and if we move from the known to the unknown, we conclude that those two chapters also come to a climax in the Greek period. The four empires in Daniel 7 are the Babylonians, the Medes, the Persians and the Greeks. The 490 years of Daniel 9 stretch from the exile to the persecution by Antiochus. All the visions cover the time from Daniel to Antiochus's defilement of the temple, and then they promise that God will marvelously deliver Jerusalem.

What subsequently happens to these visions is what often happens in the interpretation of Scripture. Later readers rightly assume that the text speaks to their own day, and they interpret it accordingly. An example comes in 2 Esdras, in the Apocrypha (see 507). The book of 2 Esdras is a visionary work written in the aftermath of the fall of Jerusalem in A.D. 70, but presenting itself as coming from the time after the fall of Jerusalem in 587 B.C. Esdras (Ezra) has a dream vision somewhat like Daniel's. God tells him that it portrays the Roman Empire of the time in which the real author and his hearers are living. God introduces the explanation, "This is the interpretation of this vision that you have seen: The eagle you saw coming up from the sea is the fourth kingdom that appeared in a vision to your brother Daniel. But it was not interpreted to him as I now interpret it to you" (2 Esdras 12:10-12). In other words, Esdras is identifying the fourth empire in Daniel's vision as Rome, but also noting that this interpretation was not the original one; it is not what the vision would have meant to the author of Daniel and its hearers. Thus 2 Esdras is explicit that its understanding of Rome as the fourth empire is a reinterpretation, not the vision's original meaning.

It is in keeping with the way Daniel has been reapplied to the Roman period that Jesus speaks of a desolating sacrilege (see Dan 7; 9) as part of the

Roman Empire's treatment of Jerusalem, in a day to come soon after his time; Rome is thus the final empire in the Gospels too. Jesus is applying Daniel to his day, as 2 Esdras does. Subsequent interpreters have seen the fourth empire as Turkey, Islam, the church, the pope, Nazism, communism, capitalism, the World Council of Churches, the European Community and the United States. The text's use of symbolism enables later readers to apply the text to their own day, as similar realities keep recurring in world history. Its cryptic nature means that one can hardly establish from the text itself whether any of these is right; whether one finds them plausible depends on one's political and ecclesiastical commitments. Not naming the vision's referents makes it possible to apply it to many subsequent situations, which is what Jesus does.

The chapter achieves much of its effect by its use of symbolism. These symbols make possible a way of speaking that communicates without removing all allusiveness. Referring to historical realities by means of symbols hints that there is something mysterious about them. It points to aspects of their inner meaning without quite making these overt; so it works subliminally. The symbols come from earlier Israelite tradition, which gives them extra resonances and power. They also utilize ancient mythic motifs that identify the empires as contemporary embodiments of primordial forces. This way of speaking expresses and adds to their horrific aspect, yet it also conveys the sense that they represent nothing novel or immune from judgment. Further, the use of mythic motifs makes it possible to speak of realities that by their very nature could not be spoken of in some other, more straightforward way.

The "ancient one" in Daniel 7:9 is a revered, senior human figure. The "one like a human being" in Daniel 7:13 is a more ordinary, less senior figure. The Aramaic term is literally "a son of man," but this phrase is a fairly ordinary way of saying "human being" (as "man of importance" means "important man"). It's not a title. The vision pictures one human figure bestowing power on another humanlike figure. The first stands for God; the second stands for the people of God (see Dan 7:27). This might mean Israel or might mean the angels. In a reapplied sense, Jesus is the humanlike figure who appears in Daniel's vision.

DANIEL

Two-Stage Origin, Binary Theology

The origin of Daniel. The stories in Daniel 1–6 speak directly to the needs of people in dispersion, in a context such as that of the Persian Empire. In contrast, the visions in Daniel 7–12 speak directly to second-century B.C. Jerusalem, to the community under persecution from Antiochus Epiphanes whose leaders were being martyred. It's odd to think of God revealing the visions in the 500s to the people in dispersion; they were not really relevant to those people. Yet it's also odd to think of the stories being written from scratch in that Jerusalem context. So I suggest this hypothesis:

1. In Babylon in the Persian period (539–336 B.C.) God inspired people to tell the stories about Daniel and his friends to encourage them about the possibilities and challenges of life there.

2. These stories included Daniel 2, which originally promised God's sovereign involvement in the succession of Babylonian and Persian kings (it's much less specific than the later visions).

3. Judahites who returned to Jerusalem over the next few centuries (people like Ezra and Nehemiah) took the stories back there, and in the time of Antiochus people realized how they also spoke to the pressures of that time (cf. 1 Macc 2:59-60).

4. One or more people were inspired by the prophecy in Jeremiah 25 to gain a new understanding of what God been doing over the centuries since Daniel's day and what he would do in their day (see Dan 9). They were also inspired by Daniel's vision (Dan 2), and by other Scriptures, to gain further new understandings of what God been doing since Daniel's day and would do in their day (see Dan 7–8; 10–12). Crediting your work to the person who had "inspired" you was not unusual in the ancient world. It was an act of piety and humility, not deception.

5. The marvelous deliverance of the people from Antiochus and his downfall proved that their new visions really came from God. Thus the

book of Daniel was very quickly accepted as Scripture.

The theology of Daniel. As we noted, the two halves of the book have different backgrounds: the dispersion and the second-century crisis in Jerusalem. Arising out of that difference, they offer different perspectives on a series of key questions (see further 442).

1. *On God's relationships with people and God's involvement in the world.* Throughout, God is powerful and sovereign (titles such as "God of heaven" and "Lord of Lords" emphasize the point). God is *known* by his people in both halves, but in the first half God is active now, in the second half he is not; the visions promise that he will be active again.

2. *On the kingdom of God.* This theme is central to Daniel as to no other book in the Bible. In the stories God rules via the heathen king, who recognizes that God is the real king, though he usually needs some challenge from the leaders of God's people to make him do so. In the visions the king stops God's rule from becoming reality. There are times when God's reign is being implemented in politics, and times when it is not.

3. *On the meaningfulness of political history.* In the stories God is involved in this history, and you can see his mercy, grace, purposefulness and justice there. In the visions God is in control in the manner of the prison governor during a riot; things can't get totally out of hand. God's hand in history will be visible only in bringing it to an end. In neither half does the book see history as moving toward a goal.

4. *On the leadership of the faithful in community life.* The stories picture leaders able to be involved in the life of government; they match Romans 13. In the visions there seems to be no such possibility; they match Revelation 13. Here, the task of leaders is to help their people understand events in relation to God. In both halves a key role of leaders is prayer.

5. *On life in dispersion and life in Jerusalem.* The book has a vision for both. Dispersion life is not simply the result of sin but of God's sovereignty, and it is a place where Judahites can serve the empire. Jerusalem is nevertheless the location of God's sanctuary and temple. Both locations are places where life is precarious.

S ee the note on web resources at the beginning of this book.

443 CHRONICLES AS THEOLOGY

444 CHRONICLES: RESPONSES TO QUESTIONS

445 ESTHER: PLAY-READING VERSION

446 ESTHER: RESPONSES TO QUESTIONS

447 RUTH: PLAY-READING VERSION

448 RUTH: RESPONSES TO QUESTIONS

449 PSALMS: RESOURCES

a. Psalms in the New Testament

b. Do the Psalms Have Links with Particular Worship Festivals?

c. The Egyptian Hymn to the Sun (Hymn to Aten)

d. Using Psalms in Prayer for Healing

e. The Way Psalms Were Used at the World Trade Center Site

f. Hymn Versions of Psalm 72

g. How to Pray for Your Nation

h. How the Babylonians Prayed for Forgiveness

450 PSALMS: THE LETTER OF ATHANASIUS TO MARCELLINUS ON THE INTERPRETATION OF THE PSALMS

461 Daniel: Theology

462 Daniel: Responses to Questions

463 (Anything else I dream up after this book is published)

Part Five LOOKING BACK OVER THE WHOLE

Looking Back over the Old Testament

The Narrative

The variety in the Old Testament. The OT is an extraordinarily varied collection of books, varied in their form as well as in their content. The chief forms are narrative, instruction, prophecy, wisdom and psalmody.

1. Narrative tells of things that have happened or of the kind of thing that one can imagine happening.

2. Instruction tells people what to do.

3. Prophecy reveals God's nightmares and dreams.

4. Wisdom reflects on the implications of regular human experience.

5. Psalmody addresses God in praise, protest and thanksgiving.

It's not by chance that the OT takes these varied forms. Different ways of writing or speaking match different types of content; they also communicate in different ways. All five may be quite consistent with one another in what they speak of, but they focus on different aspects of it. Their combination tells us something significant about the nature of the OT and about a faith built on the OT.

Narrative. The OT is dominated by narrative. In a way, the point is even more obvious in the usual Jewish order because there, Ezra, Nehemiah and Chronicles come at the end of the Scriptures, so that narrative is the frame within which the rest of the scrolls are set. The OT is dominated by narrative because it focuses on what God was doing in Israel's story over the centuries. OT faith is not essentially a collection of statements about God's nature or God's expectations of Israel, but rather a story. Israel is a people defined by this story; God is a person defined by this story. Yahweh is the God who

- created the world,
- made promises to Abraham,
- brought Israel out of Egypt,
- resealed a covenant with Israel at Sinai and in the steppes of Moab,

- gave Israel its land,

- wrestled with Israel over centuries,

- agreed semi-willingly to Israel having a king and a temple,

- wrestled with Israel again over centuries,

- allowed Israel's state and land to be overrun by superpowers,

- opened up the possibility of Israel reestablishing a continuing community and rebuilding the temple,

- gave Israel the completed Torah as a foundation for its reestablished life as the covenant people,

- enabled Israel to survive and even triumph in its dispersed form elsewhere,

- delivered Israel from oppression by the Seleucids.

Throughout its history Israel lived its life in the context of that story, and after the time of Persian and Seleucid rule it lived its life in the context of that total story. Ezra and Nehemiah and the visions in Daniel imply that, in a sense, the story must be incomplete. God's purpose for Israel can hardly end with the people in Judah as a reduced entity under the control of a superpower.

When Jesus came, he proclaimed that God was about to assert sovereignty in this people's life again and to be the means of this reign of God coming about. Henceforth the people of Israel in its vastly expanded form as a Jewish-Gentile body was designed to live its life in the context of an extended version of the story, a version that goes on to tell the story of Jesus and of the consummation of God's plan. That intention was not realized. God's plan has still not reached its consummation. Among the reasons were the Jewish people's hesitation about recognizing that God's reign was becoming a reality through Jesus, and the largely Gentile church's inclination to ignore the OT part of the story.

Although the OT narrative is dominated by the story of Israel as a whole, it incorporates stories about the lives of ordinary individuals who become part of the bigger story, people such as Hagar and Hannah, and of "important" people, such as David and Hezekiah, whose lives also illumine the nature of ordinary people's relationship with God. Outside the main narrative this feature recurs in the stories of Ruth, Jonah and Esther. The nature of narrative in its concreteness gives us stories against which to think about our own lives in their concreteness.

Looking Back over the
Old Testament

Instruction and Prophecy

I *nstruction.* Within Exodus through Deuteronomy, the main OT narrative
embraces considerable material that instructs Israel about the nature of
its life. The presence of such material in this context suggests several insights.
First, the story of God's relationship with Israel is incomplete without its
incorporating some account of the life that God looks for in Israel, and any
account of the life God looks for in Israel must properly appear in the
context of that story. That rules out the possibility that Israel could see itself
as the beneficiary of Yahweh's commitment without also becoming committed to Yahweh. To put it in the terms of later theology: Israel's relationship
depends on God's grace but requires a response of obedience. It is misleading to think in terms of God's grace being conditional; Paul points out
in Romans 4 how that point is made particularly clear by the Abraham stage
in the story. But God's grace doesn't reach its designed end without a response of commitment on Israel's part.

The way God's expectations appear in the context of the story telling of
God's commitment to Israel also makes the converse point: Israel's obedience is not the way its relationship with God comes about. Although
Christians do not believe in theory that their commitment is what determines the development of their relationship with God, in practice they often
think and behave as if is the case. The OT puts us right.

The nature of this instruction material indicates that it is not enough to
say, "Love God, and do what you like." As Jesus notes, the instruction puts
flesh on the commands to love God and love one's neighbor, and the way
Jesus lays out concrete expectations of people, and the way people such as
Paul and James do so, makes the same assumption. As they also illustrate,
putting flesh on the commands is something that needs to be done in
changing ways as times change.

One other significance of the instruction material is worth mentioning.

Christians often assume that the actions of Yahweh and/or the actions of human beings in the story from Genesis through Esther are there for us to imitate. They are examples for us. However, there is little indication that this is so. God is God, and God's actions are not necessarily examples for us. The human characters in the stories are mixed-up people like us and are not in the story to show us what exemplary disciples of Yahweh are like. It is the instruction material set in the context of the narrative that shows us how to live.

Prophecy. Whereas narratives with their enfolded instruction are past focused, prophecy is future focused. It does not speak of a distant future that has no significance for the present, as if, for instance, it were speaking of political events to take place in the twenty-first century. Often its future perspective relates to a time that will soon arrive. Jeremiah, Ezekiel and Isaiah 40–55 speak of a restoration of the nation that will come about, and to some degree did come about, in the lifetime of the people to whom the prophecies spoke or in the lifetimes of their children.

Prophecy does also speak of the final consummation of God's purpose when the world will be transformed, and that event has not yet taken place, but it speaks of it because it is significant for people in its own day. We see this in the way Paul urged people to live in light of the second coming of Christ even though (we now know) that coming would not happen for centuries after his time. People need to live in light of the fact that God is going to fulfill his purpose for Israel.

The prophets share God's dreams. But before they speak of these dreams, they share God's nightmare vision of how things will turn out if the people do not change. Again, we know that insofar as they were speaking of a final implementation of God's judgment of Israel and of the world, they were not speaking of an event that happened in their people's lifetime. Yet, in another sense, they were speaking of such an event, because "Yahweh's Day" finds embodiment in events such as the fall of Samaria and the fall of Jerusalem, and also in the falls of Assyria, of Babylon, of Persia and of Seleucid power in Jerusalem in 164 B.C.

Wisdom and Psalmody

Wisdom. The wisdom books complement both the narratives relating what God has done and the instruction material relating what God has said. They speak of God's ongoing, regular involvement in the life of community and individual. They assume that one can perceive this involvement by looking at life and by listening to other people telling of their experience. Their assumption about humankind's capacity to make sense of things coheres with their kinship with writings from other Middle Eastern cultures, where other thoughtful men and women have asked questions about life and have come to sensible conclusions. As they go about their reflection on human experience, the wisdom books assume that we allow for the involvement of God in our life and for the reality of right and wrong. They also recognize the limited extent to which we can make sense of things. Ecclesiastes does so by simply affirming this limitation; Job does so by having God appear in a special way to Job that undermines any rigorous wisdom perspective that relies exclusively on regular human experience.

Human wisdom is also involved in the narrative and instruction material. The narratives themselves do not claim to offer a divinely inspired perspective on events, though the community came to recognize that they did so. To judge from the account that Luke gives of how he came to write, their authors wrote their story in the ordinary human way. They do not speak in terms of receiving divine dictation, as prophets do. They were using their human wisdom. Genesis through Esther is human wisdom (the kind that begins with reverence for God) applied to Israel's story; Proverbs, Job and Ecclesiastes are the same human wisdom applied to regular human experience.

Something similar is true about the instruction material in the Torah and its relationship with human wisdom. As the Israelites' wisdom literature is often similar to the works of other peoples, much of the teaching in the

Torah is similar to the teaching of other Middle Eastern codes, as well as to the teaching about behavior in the wisdom books. Most cultures recognize that murder, theft and adultery are wrong; humankind is hardwired to recognize that it is so. These assumptions from what one might call "general revelation" or "natural theology" (natural but God-given) are taken up into the instruction in the Torah and made into something explicitly God sanctioned. Human wisdom is involved in the entire process. God did not literally dictate to Moses, for instance, the instructions in Exodus 25–31 about how to build a sanctuary while Moses was on top of Mount Sinai. Picturing God doing so expresses parabolically the truth that when Israelites formulated these plans for a dwelling for God, using their human minds, the Holy Spirit was involved in that process and affirmed it.

Psalmody. In narrative, instruction and wisdom we have human beings speaking to human beings and God speaking to human beings. In most of the Psalms and in Lamentations we have human beings speaking to God. As is the case with those other forms of speech, this is human speech that God has accepted, and thus we can also see it as speech that God commends to us. In a sense, it is thus God's speech, inspired by the Holy Spirit. Yet it takes the form of human speech. It thus gives expression to the fact that the two-way relationship between God and Israel involves not only action (God acts and human beings act) but also words (God speaks and human beings speak). The human speech of the Psalms is sometimes a response to the kind of divine acts and divine characteristics of which the narrative books and the wisdom books tell. The human speech consists in praise for what God has done and who God is, and in thanksgiving for what God has been and done for us as a people just now or for me as an individual just now. It also consists in a response to the way God is not now behaving consistently with those acts or that character, and a challenge to God to do so and be so.

The significance of this variety. The varied forms of the OT material thus make it possible to embrace past, present and future; God's one-time acts and God's regular acts; God's acts and our acts; God's words and our words; the blessings and the trouble that may soon come; and the blessing and the trouble that will fulfill God's purpose at the End.

THE CONVERSATION WITHIN THE CANON
A Complex Reality

Given the variety in the OT, what holds it together? Does it have a consistent theology, and if not, in what sense could it be one book inspired by one Holy Spirit?

The baseline of its theology is the fact that Yahweh is "compassionate and gracious, long-tempered, big in commitment and steadfastness, preserving commitment to a thousand generations, carrying waywardness, rebellion, and offense, and in no way acquitting the guilty, visiting the waywardness of parents on children and on grandchildren to the third and fourth generation" (Ex 34:6-7). A number of OT texts refer back to that description.

We have noted that the same understanding emerges from the OT's comments about Yahweh's holiness. In Hosea 11 Yahweh meditates on having loved Israel as a child and seen this son turn away when he grew up. But it is impossible to give him up. "I will not implement my angry burning, I will not turn to destroy Ephraim, because I am God, not a man" (Hos 11:9). Hosea interestingly uses the word ʾîš, which suggests an individual male, rather than ʾādām, which suggests a human being without having gender implications. I am "the Holy One in your midst," Yahweh goes on. Being the Holy One means that he cannot act in judgment. In contrast, at the end of a declaration of judgment in Judah, Isaiah 5:15-16 first comments that "humanity bows, the individual falls, the eyes of the majestic fall," and then declares that thus "Yahweh Armies is majestic in authority, and the holy God proves holy in doing the right thing." "Yahweh Armies" and "Holy God" are two ways of describing the same God (see 330). To spell out the parallelism in prosaic terms: "Yahweh Armies, the Holy God, is majestic and proves holy in exercising authority in accordance with what is right." The context makes clear that this exercising of authority in the right way involves acting in judgment on Judah. Being the Holy One means that he *must* act in judgment.

Hosea and Isaiah spell out the two sides to God's character described in Exodus 34:6-7. Holiness implies mercy; holiness implies judgment. Like any parent, Yahweh is continually having to decide whether a particular moment is one to be long-tempered or one where it has become necessary to say, "That's it!" If Hosea and Isaiah together see Yahweh's holiness expressed in mercy and judgment, then Micah 6:8 is a summary of what God expects by way of human response to this triad of holiness, mercy and judgment. God has told us what counts as goodness, what God requires, and it involves doing the right thing in the way that God does (e.g., taking action against oppression), showing loving commitment in the way that God does, and walking humbly before God as the Holy One. In turn, we might see this mirror-image picture of God and us as spelling out another phrase that could be seen as a summary of the faith that runs through the OT: "I am your God, and you are my people."

The wisdom books are the exception to any suggestion that "you are my people" is an invariable part of OT faith. Esther makes no mention of God or of Israel, though the Esther example shows how books may presuppose truths that they do not articulate. Israelites reading the wisdom books would likewise assume the truths that the books do not articulate, in reading them as part of their Scriptures.

The tension between Hosea and Isaiah illustrates how reality is complex. Different aspects of the truth need to be affirmed in different contexts or by different people. One may see this necessity within individual books. Job offers at least six answers to the question how we look at and deal with suffering and the questions that it raises concerning how God relates to us. The book is in conversation with itself in affirming its variety of partial insights on its questions. The Psalter embodies a conversation between praise for God's acts of deliverance and consistent character, protest at God's not acting in that way in the life of the suppliants or showing that character, and thanksgiving for the experience of God's doing so again. Daniel juxtaposes chapters about God's servants knowing God's protection under pressure, ruling via the human king, and thus being at work through political history, with chapters presupposing that God's servants do not find such protection, that the human king stops God's rule from becoming reality, and that political history means nothing. In different contexts either may be the case.

THE CONVERSATION WITHIN THE CANON
Different Emphases

Sometimes different books manifest different perspectives and emphases, and one can imagine their authors as members of the same community engaging in conversation, not to mention argument. "Proverbs says, 'These are the rules for life; try them and you will find that they work.' Job and Ecclesiastes say, 'We did and they don't'" (Hubbard, "Wisdom Movement," 6).

If it is right that the books of Ruth and Jonah come from the Second Temple period, like the books of Ezra and Nehemiah, one can imagine lively conversation between their authors. Jonah and Ruth presuppose the imperative deriving from the Torah that the community must be open to other peoples who are prepared to turn to Yahweh, whether they are big imperial powers or individual marginal people, and Ruth is prepared to include intermarriage as one of the ways that principle works out. Ezra and Nehemiah presuppose the imperative deriving from the Torah that the community must keep itself pure and make sure that it does not lose its identity among the peoples around, and they are prepared to exclude intermarriage as one of the ways that principle works out. Both attitudes have the Torah on their side and have on their side a concern for the destiny of Israel and for that of the nations destined to find Yahweh through Israel. In some contexts people are instinctively sympathetic to Ruth and Jonah and horrified by Ezra and Nehemiah, in other contexts the reverse; whichever is their instinct, people have to work at seeing the importance of the opposite perspective.

If Ruth and Jonah do not come from the Second Temple period, then it is the canon of Scripture itself that puts them into conversation with Ezra and Nehemiah. Other conversations come about in this way. Leviticus, Chronicles and Psalms enthuse about worship and imply that God is concerned for sacrifices to be offered in the right way, rejoices in the worship of the temple, and wants people to express themselves in praise, protest and thanksgiving. Prophets such as Isaiah and Amos blow a fuse at such ideas (e.g., Is 1:15; Amos 5:21-22). Leviticus, Chronicles and Psalms do make clear that they also care about the society working in the right way, and Amos and Isaiah make clear that worship and prayer matter. But each book emphasizes the issue that is important in its context. Scripture as a whole then puts them in conversation. In some contexts people emphasize social action and need to see the importance of worship; in other contexts people emphasize worship and need to see the importance of making sure that what we do outside church matches what we do inside.

Genesis 37–50, Exodus 1–15 and Esther offer three different portraits of God's activity in political events as these involve the people of God. In the Joseph story everything works out through a series of human decisions and "coincidences" that finally have Jacob's family able to find provision in Egypt when famine hits Canaan, and Joseph's comment to his brothers is, "Whereas you intended trouble for me, God intended it for good, in order to act this day so that a vast people might live" (Gen 50:20). The story of Israel's escape from the Egyptians works in a different way. Human decisions do not contribute to that escape, except in that Pharaoh's resistance makes it a greater demonstration of his feebleness and God's power. Moses does not lead Israel in an act of rebellion, and Israel does not take any action against Egypt. God acts, and Pharaoh bids the Israelites go; God acts, and the Egyptian army drowns. The Esther story works differently again. Although it tells of an extraordinary escape like the exodus, the escape comes about in the same way as happens in Genesis 37–50, except that neither Mordecai nor Esther makes a statement like Joseph's. God and Israel are unmentioned. So the three stories provide their readers with three ways of looking at their story and three ways of telling it.

Here are other examples of the complementarity within the OT:

- Proverbs warns us about sex going wrong; Song of Songs enthuses about sex.

- Lamentations acknowledges guilt; Psalms puts more insistence on having shown faithfulness.

- Kings tells its story to emphasize the people's wrongdoing; Chronicles does so to emphasize God's grace.

- Ezekiel promises a new David; Isaiah 40–55 sees David's vocation fulfilled in the entire people.

The Relationship of the Old
Testament and the New Testament

For the first Christians, the Old Testament was not the Old Testament. It was not the old one, because there was no new one. It was simply the Scriptures. These Scriptures were a primary resource for the church, inspired by the Holy Spirit. The church's focus lay in the story of Jesus and in the present activity of the Holy Spirit. But the Holy Spirit used the Scriptures to help them understand Jesus. A look at the NT reveals ways the Holy Spirit did so and thus reveals the way the NT writers saw the relationship between the Scriptures and the gospel. Matthew, Romans, Hebrews and Revelation offer the most systematic NT insight on this question, but as it happens, the opening chapters of Matthew, and thus the opening chapters of the NT, do so particularly systematically.

1. Matthew 1:1-17 looks back on the OT as the story that comes to a climax with Jesus. Thus you understand the OT story best when you see it coming to this climax, and you understand Jesus only when you understand him as the end term of this story.

2. Matthew 1:18–2:23 looks back on the OT as indicating who Jesus will be when he comes. One or two of the passages that it quotes are "messianic prophecies," and Jesus is the fulfillment of such prophecies. But most of them are not messianic prophecies; what happens is that the NT looks back from Jesus to the OT and finds that passages illumine who Jesus is even though that wasn't their original intention. They get "filled out" rather than "fulfilled" in this way (see 332).

3. Matthew 3:1-17 looks back on the OT for the images, ideas and words with which to understand Jesus. John the Baptizer talks about repentance, God's reign, a tree and its fruit. Then God the Father speaks about Jesus in terms of his being God's son (like the Davidic king), God's beloved (like Isaac in relation to Abraham), and the one with whom God is pleased (like the servant in Isaiah). All these terms require to be understood in light of the OT.

4. Matthew 4:1-11 looks back to the OT for guidance about how to live one's life with God. It is Deuteronomy that provides Jesus with the basis for evaluating the suggestions made by a weird character in the wilderness.

5. Matthew 5:1-12 looks back to the OT for the raw material out of which to compose a guide to spirituality. Jesus' "beatitudes" are mostly based on phrases from Psalms and Isaiah; Jesus creates a new whole out of them.

6. Matthew 5:17-48 looks back to the OT for the raw material for ethics. Like an OT prophet, Jesus comes to "fill out" or "fill up" the Torah and the Prophets, sometimes sweeping away accretions, sometimes building on their teaching, sometimes showing how they have made allowance for human stubbornness.

In reading an OT text, then, the NT invites us to ask, "Is this a part of the story of which Jesus is the climax, so do I learn something about it and about Jesus by looking at it that way? Or is it a promise of which Jesus brings a fulfillment, whether or not it started life as a promise? Or is it an aspect of the OT's theology that needs to inform my understanding of Jesus? Or does it offer us guidance about how to live our lives with God as people who follow Jesus? Or does it contribute to the spirituality of people who have faith in the God of Jesus? Or does it contribute to shaping the ethical principles on whose basis we live our lives, particularly where they need to make allowance for human stubbornness?"

Does the NT go beyond the OT? It's hard to find the NT saying so. For the first Christians, the question wasn't whether the OT fitted in with the gospel but rather whether the gospel fitted in with the OT, with the Scriptures. For Jesus, the entire Torah and Prophets were an exposition of love for God and love for one's neighbor; that declaration would cover Joshua as well as Isaiah 53. For Hebrews 1, Jesus is the embodiment of the revelation spread through the Prophets; Jesus does not take people on from the God of wrath to the God of love. The entire OT Scriptures are God breathed, Spirit inspired and instructive for our discipleship (2 Tim 3:16-17) (see further "Do We Need the NT?" at 507).

5 | 07 | WEB RESOURCES

See the note on web resources at the beginning of this book.

509 THE APOCRYPHA

510 DO WE NEED THE NEW TESTAMENT?

511 WAR IN THE OLD TESTAMENT

512 LOOKING BACK OVER THE WHOLE: RESPONSES TO QUESTIONS

513 (Anything else I dream up after this book is published)

Under other tabs on my web page you'll also find other things I have written and lists of books. Here I will just mention two print resources: (1) the series Old Testament for Everyone (seventeen commentaries on the entire OT, published by Westminster John Knox and SPCK); (2) my *Old Testament Theology*, 3 vols. (Downers Grove, IL: InterVarsity Press; Milton Keynes: Paternoster, 2003–2009).

SOME OF MY FAVORITE BOOKS ON THE OLD TESTAMENT,
FOR TAKING YOUR STUDY FURTHER

Alexander, T. Desmond, et al., eds. *Dictionary of the Old Testament*. 4 vols. IVP Bible Dictionary Series. Downers Grove, IL: InterVarsity Press, 2003–2012.

Alter, Robert. *The Art of Biblical Narrative*. New York: Basic Books, 1981.

Alter, Robert, and Frank Kermode, eds. *The Literary Guide to the Bible*. Cambridge, MA: Belknap Press of Harvard University, 1987.

Bauckham, Richard. *The Bible in Politics: How to Read the Bible Politically*. 2nd ed. Louisville: Westminster John Knox, 2011.

Borowski, Oded. *Daily Life in Biblical Times*. Society of Biblical Literature Archaeology and Biblical Studies 5. Atlanta: Society of Biblical Literature, 2003.

Brueggemann, Walter. *The Prophetic Imagination*. Philadelphia: Fortress, 1978.

Coogan, Michael D., ed. *The Oxford History of the Biblical World*. Oxford: Oxford University Press, 1998.

Dever, William G. *What Did the Biblical Writers Know, and When Did They Know It? What Archaeology Can Tell Us About the Reality of Ancient Israel*. Grand Rapids: Eerdmans, 2001.

Ebeling, Jennie R. *Women's Lives in Biblical Times*. London: T&T Clark, 2010.

Fritz, Volkmar. *The City in Ancient Israel*. Biblical Seminar 29. Sheffield: Sheffield Academic Press, 1995.

Jenni, Ernst, and Claus Westermann, eds. *Theological Lexicon of the Old Testament*. Translated by Mark E. Biddle. 3 vols. Peabody, MA: Hendrickson, 1997.

Josipovici, Gabriel. *The Book of God: A Response to the Bible*. New Haven: Yale University Press, 1988.

MacDonald, Nathan. *What Did the Ancient Israelites Eat? Diet in Biblical Times* Grand Rapids: Eerdmans, 2008.

Martens, Elmer A. *God's Design: A Focus on Old Testament Theology*. 2nd ed. Grand Rapids: Baker Books, 1994.

Miles, Jack. *God: A Biography*. New York: Simon & Schuster, 1995.

Perdue, Leo, et al. *Families in Ancient Israel*. Louisville: Westminster John Knox, 1997.

Trible, Phyllis. *God and the Rhetoric of Sexuality*. Philadelphia: Fortress, 1978.

———. *Texts of Terror: Literary-Feminist Readings of Biblical Narratives*. Philadelphia: Fortress, 1984.

van der Toorn, Karel. "Nine Months Among the Peasants in the Palestinian Highlands: An Anthropological Perspective on Local Religion in the Early Iron Age." In *Symbiosis, Symbolism, and the Power of the Past: Canaan, Ancient Israel, and Their Neighbors from the Late Bronze Age Through Roman Palaestina*, edited by W. G. Dever and S. Gitin, pp. 393-410. Winona Lake, IN: Eisenbrauns, 2003.

von Rad, Gerhard. *Old Testament Theology.* Translated by D. M. G. Stalker. 2 vols. New York: Harper & Row, 1962.

Wolff, Hans Walter. *Anthropology of the Old Testament.* Translated by Margaret Kohl. Philadelphia: Fortress, 1974.

Wright, Christopher J. H. *Old Testament Ethics for the People of God.* Downers Grove, IL: InterVarsity Press, 2004.

Other works cited in this book

Ackroyd, Peter R. *Exile and Restoration: A Study of Hebrew Thought of the Sixth Century B.C.* Old Testament Library. Philadelphia: Westminster, 1968.

Adamo, David Tuesday. *Reading and Interpreting the Bible in African Indigenous Churches.* Eugene, OR: Wipf & Stock, 2001.

Alt, Albrecht. *Essays on Old Testament History and Religion.* Translated by R. A. Wilson. Garden City, NY: Doubleday, 1967.

Alter, Robert. *The Art of Biblical Poetry.* New York: Basic Books, 1985.

Arbuckle, Gerald A. *Grieving for Change: A Spirituality for Refounding Gospel Communities.* London: Geoffrey Chapman, 1981.

Arnold, B. T. "Pentateuchal Criticism, History of." In *Dictionary of the Old Testament: Pentateuch*, edited by T. Desmond Alexander and David W. Baker, pp. 622-32. Downers Grove, IL: InterVarsity Press, 2003.

Augustine of Hippo. *Expositions of the Psalms, 121–150.* Translated by Maria Boulding. Edited by Boniface Ramsey. The Works of Augustine 3/20. New York: New City Press, 2004.

Bahnsen, Greg L. *No Other Standard: Theonomy and Its Critics.* Tyler, TX: Institute for Christian Economics, 1991.

Bal, Mieke. *Death and Dissymmetry: The Politics of Coherence in the Book of Judges.* Chicago Studies in the History of Judaism. Chicago: University of Chicago Press, 1988.

Barth, Hermann. *Die Jesaja-Worte in der Josiazeit.* Neukirchen: Neukirchener, 1977.

Barth, Karl. *Church Dogmatics.* Edited by G. W. Bromiley and T. F. Torrance. 5 vols. in 14. Edinburgh: T&T Clark, 1956–1977.

Berg, Sandra Beth. *The Book of Esther: Motifs, Themes, and Structure.* Society of Biblical Literature Dissertation Series 44. Missoula, MT: Scholars Press, 1979.

Berger, Peter L. *A Rumor of Angels: Modern Society and the Rediscovery of the Supernatural.* Anchor Books. Garden City, NY: Doubleday, 1969.

Beuken, Willem A. M. "The Unity of the Book of Isaiah." In *Reading from Right to Left: Essays on the Hebrew Bible in Honour of David J. A. Clines,* edited by J. Cheryl Exum and H. G. M. Williamson, pp. 50-62. Journal for the Study of the Old Testament: Supplement Series 373. London: Sheffield Academic Press, 2003.

Bimson, John. *Redating Exodus and Conquest.* Journal for the Study of the Old Testament: Supplement Series 5. Sheffield: JSOT Press, 1978.

Bonhoeffer, Dietrich. *Life Together; Prayerbook of the Bible.* Translated by Daniel W. Bloesch and James H. Burtnes. Edited by Geffrey B. Kelly. Minneapolis: Fortress, 1996.

Brenner, Athalya, ed. *A Feminist Companion to Judges.* Feminist Companion to the Bible 4. Sheffield: Sheffield Academic Press, 1993.

Bright, John. *A History of Israel.* Westminster Aids to the Study of the Scriptures. Philadelphia: Westminster, 1959.

Brueggemann, Walter. "Bounded by Obedience and Praise." *Journal for the Study of the Old Testament* 50 (1991): 63-92.

———. *Finally Comes the Poet: Daring Speech for Proclamation.* Minneapolis: Fortress, 1989.

———. *Hopeful Imagination: Prophetic Voices in Exile.* Philadelphia: Fortress, 1986.

———. *Israel's Praise: Doxology Against Idolatry and Ideology.* Philadelphia: Fortress, 1988.

———. *The Message of the Psalms: A Theological Commentary.* Minneapolis: Augsburg, 1984.

Buber, Martin. *On the Bible: Eighteen Studies.* Edited by Nahum M. Glazer. New York: Schocken, 1968.

Bultmann, Rudolf. *Existence and Faith: Shorter Writings of Rudolf Bultmann.* Translated by Schubert M. Ogden. New York: Meridian, 1960.

Capps, Donald. *Biblical Approaches to Pastoral Counseling.* Philadelphia: Westminster, 1981.

Childs, Brevard S. *Introduction to the Old Testament as Scripture.* Philadelphia: Fortress, 1979.

———. "Psalm Titles and Midrashic Exegesis." *Journal of Semitic Studies* 16 (1971): 137-50.

Clements, Ronald E. *Isaiah 1–39.* New Century Bible Commentary. Grand Rapids: Eerdmans, 1980.

Clines, David J. A. "David the Man: The Construction of Masculinity in the Hebrew Bible." In *Interested Parties: The Ideology of Writers and Readers of the Hebrew Bible*, pp. 212-41. Journal for the Study of the Old Testament: Supplement Series 205. Sheffield: Sheffield Academic Press, 1995.

Collins, John J. *The Apocalyptic Imagination: An Introduction to Jewish Apocalyptic Literature*. 2nd ed. Grand Rapids: Eerdmans, 1998.

Conrad, Edgar W. *Reading Isaiah*. Overtures to Biblical Theology. Minneapolis: Fortress, 1991.

Craigie, Peter C. *The Book of Deuteronomy*. New International Commentary on the Old Testament. Grand Rapids: Eerdmans, 1976.

Crenshaw, James L. *Prophetic Conflict: Its Effect upon Israelite Religion*. Beihefte zur Zeitschrift für die alttestamentliche Wissenschaft 124. Berlin: de Gruyter, 1971.

Davies, Graham I. "Was There an Exodus?" In *In Search of Pre-exilic Israel: Proceedings of the Oxford Old Testament Seminar*, edited by John Day, pp. 23-40. Journal for the Study of the Old Testament: Supplement Series 406. London: T&T Clark, 2004.

Douglas, J. D., and N. Hillyer, eds. *The Illustrated Bible Dictionary*. 3 vols. Wheaton, IL: Tyndale, 1980.

Duhm, Bernhard. *Das Buch Jesaia*. Handkommentar zum Alten Testament 3/1. Göttingen: Vandenhoeck & Ruprecht, 1892.

Durham, John. *Exodus*. Word Biblical Commentary 3. Waco, TX: Word, 1987.

Eichrodt, Walther. *Theology of the Old Testament*. Translated by J. A. Baker. 2 vols. Old Testament Library. Philadelphia: Westminster, 1961, 1967.

Ellul, Jacques. *The Politics of God and the Politics of Man*. Translated and edited by Geoffrey W. Bromiley. Grand Rapids: Eerdmans, 1972.

Fewell, Danna Nolan. *Circle of Sovereignty: A Story of Stories in Daniel 1-6*. Journal for the Study of the Old Testament: Supplement Series 72. Sheffield: Almond Press, 1988.

Finkelstein, Israel, and Amihai Mazar. *The Quest for the Historical Israel: Debating Archaeology and the History of Early Israel*. Edited by Brian B. Schmidt. Society of Biblical Literature Archaeology and Biblical Studies 17. Atlanta: Society of Biblical Literature, 2007.

Fox, Michael V. *Character and Ideology in the Book of Esther*. 2nd ed. Grand Rapids: Eerdmans, 2001.

Fretheim, Terence E. *Exodus*. Interpretation. Louisville: John Knox, 1991.

Fuerst, Wesley J. *The Books of Ruth, Esther, Ecclesiastes, the Song of Songs, Lamentations: The Five Scrolls*. Cambridge Bible Commentary. Cambridge: Cambridge University Press, 1975.

Fung, Raymond. *The Isaiah Vision: An Ecumenical Strategy for Congregational Evangelism*. Risk Book Series 52. Geneva: World Council of Churches, 1992.

Githuku, Sammy. "Taboos on Counting." In *Interpreting the Old Testament in*

Africa: Papers from the International Symposium on Africa and the Old Testament in Nairobi, October 1999, edited by Mary Getui, Knut Holter and Victor Zinkuratire, pp. 113-18. Bible and Theology in Africa 2. New York: Peter Lang, 2011.

Gnuse, Robert. "Israelite Settlement of Canaan." *Biblical Theology Bulletin* 21 (1992): 56-66, 109-17.

Goldman, Stan. "Narrative and Ethical Ironies in Esther." *Journal for the Study of the Old Testament* 47 (1990): 15-31.

Golka, Friedemann W. *The Leopard's Spots: Biblical and African Wisdom in Proverbs.* Edinburgh: T&T Clark, 1993.

Gordis, Robert. "Religion, Wisdom and History in Esther." *Journal of Biblical Literature* 100 (1981): 359-88.

Gottwald, Norman K. "Rethinking the Origins of Ancient Israel." In *Imagining Biblical Worlds: Studies in Spatial, Social, and Historical Constructs in Honor of James W. Flanagan,* edited by David M. Gunn and Paula M. McNutt, pp. 190-201. Journal for the Study of the Old Testament: Supplement Series 359. London: Sheffield Academic Press, 2002.

———. *The Tribes of Yahweh: A Sociology of the Religion of Liberated Israel, 1250–1050 B.C.E.* Maryknoll, NY: Orbis, 1979.

Grant, J. A. "Editorial Criticism." In *Dictionary of the Old Testament: Wisdom, Poetry and Writings,* edited by Tremper Longman III and Peter Enns, pp. 149-56. IVP Bible Dictionary Series. Downers Grove, IL: InterVarsity Press, 2008.

Greenspahn, Frederick E., ed. *The Hebrew Bible: New Insights and Scholarship.* Jewish Studies in the 21st Century. New York: New York University Press, 2008.

Gregory of Nazianzus. *Select Orations.* Translated by Martha Vinson. Fathers of the Church 107. Washington, DC: Catholic University of America Press, 2003.

Gunkel, Hermann. *Introduction to the Psalms: The Genres of the Religious Lyric of Israel.* Completed by Joachim Begrich. Translated by James D. Nogalski. Mercer Library of Biblical Studies. Macon, GA: Mercer University Press, 1998.

———. *The Psalms: A Form-Critical Introduction.* Translated by Thomas M. Horner. Philadelphia: Fortress, 1967.

Han, Kuk Yom. "Migrant Women and Intermarriage in Korea." In *Korean Feminists in Conversation with the Bible, Church and Society,* edited by Kyung Sook Lee and Kyung Mi Park, pp. 90-100. Bible in the Modern World 24. Sheffield: Sheffield Phoenix Press, 2011.

Hawk, Dan. *Every Promise Fulfilled: Contesting Plots in Joshua.* Literary Currents in Biblical Interpretation. Louisville: Westminster John Knox, 1991.

Hoffmeier, James K. *Israel in Egypt: The Evidence for the Authenticity of the Exodus Tradition.* New York: Oxford University Press, 1997.

Holladay, William L. *Jeremiah: A Commentary on the Book of the Prophet Jeremiah*. Edited by Paul D. Hanson. 2 vols. Hermeneia. Philadelphia: Fortress, 1986–1989.

Hubbard, David Allan. "The Wisdom Movement and Israel's Covenant Faith." *Tyndale Bulletin* 17 (1966): 3-33.

Hudson, Don. "Come, Bring Your Story." www.leaderu.com/marshill/mhro1/story1.html.

Hyatt, J. Philip. *Commentary on Exodus*. New Century Bible. Grand Rapids: Eerdmans, 1980.

Johnson, Vivian L. *David in Distress: His Portrait Through the Historical Psalms*. Library of the Hebrew Bible/Old Testament Studies 505. London: T&T Clark, 2009.

Keel, Othmar. *The Symbolism of the Biblical World: Ancient Near Eastern Iconography and the Book of Psalms*. Translated by Timothy J. Hallett. New York: Seabury, 1978.

Kidner, Derek. *Genesis: An Introduction and Commentary*. Tyndale Old Testament Commentaries. Downers Grove, IL: InterVarsity Press, 1967.

Kim, Uriah Y. "Postcolonial Criticism: Who Is the Other in the Book of Judges?" In *Judges and Method: New Approaches in Biblical Studies*, edited by Gale A. Yee, pp. 161-82. 2nd ed. Minneapolis: Fortress, 2007.

Knight, George A. F. *Ruth and Jonah: Introduction and Commentary*. Torch Bible Commentaries. London: SCM Press, 1950.

Kugel, James L. *The Idea of Biblical Poetry: Parallelism and Its History*. New Haven: Yale University Press, 1981.

Landy, Francis. *Paradoxes of Paradise: Identity and Difference in the Song of Songs*. Bible and Literature Series 7. Sheffield: Almond Press, 1983.

Lee, Kyung Sook. "Neo-Confucian Ideology in the Interpretation of the Book of Ruth." In *Korean Feminists in Conversation with the Bible, Church and Society*, edited by Kyung Sook Lee and Kyung Mi Park, pp. 1-13. Bible in the Modern World 24. Sheffield: Sheffield Phoenix Press, 2011.

Levenson, Jon D. *The Death and Resurrection of the Beloved Son: The Transformation of Child Sacrifice in Judaism and Christianity*. New Haven: Yale University Press, 1993.

Lewis, C. S. *Reflections on the Psalms*. New York: Harcourt, Brace, 1958.

Lowth, Robert. *Lectures on the Sacred Poetry of the Hebrews*. Translated by George Gregory. 2 vols. London: J. Johnson, 1787.

Mazar, Amihai, ed., *Studies in the Archaeology of the Iron Age in Israel and Jordan*. Journal for the Study of the Old Testament: Supplement Series 331. Sheffield: Sheffield Academic Press, 2001.

Mendenhall, George E. "The Biblical Conquest of Palestine." *Biblical Archaeologist* 25, no. 3 (1962): 68-87.

———. "The Monarchy." *Interpretation* 29 (1975): 155-70.

Metz, Johannes Baptist. "The Courage to Pray." In Karl Rahner and Johannes Baptist Metz, *The Courage to Pray*. New York: Crossroad, 1980.

Moberly, R. W. L. *Genesis 12–50*. Old Testament Guides. Sheffield: JSOT Press, 1992.

Moltmann, Jürgen. *Experiences of God*. Translated by Margaret Kohl. Philadelphia: Fortress, 1980.

Mowinckel, Sigmund. *The Psalms in Israel's Worship*. Translated by D. R. Ap-Thomas. 2 vols, in 1. Biblical Resource Series. Grand Rapids: Eerdmans; Dearborn, MI: Dove Booksellers, 2004.

Nicholson, E. W. *Deuteronomy and Tradition*. Oxford: Blackwell, 1967.

———. *Preaching to the Exiles: A Study of the Prose Tradition in the Book of Jeremiah*. Oxford: Blackwell, 1970.

Nissinen, Martti. *Prophets and Prophecy in the Ancient Near East*. Edited by Peter Machinist. Society of Biblical Literature Writings from the Ancient World 12. Atlanta: Society of Biblical Literature, 2003.

Noth, Martin. *The Deuteronomistic History*. Journal for the Study of the Old Testament: Supplement Series 15. Sheffield: JSOT Press, 1981.

———. *The History of Israel*. 2nd ed. New York: Harper, 1960.

Nussbaum, Martha C. *Poetic Justice: The Literary Imagination and Public Life*. Boston: Beacon, 1995.

Olson, Dennis T. "Negotiating Boundaries: The Old and New Generations and the Theology of Numbers." *Interpretation* 51 (1997): 229-40.

Petersen, David L., and Kent Harold Richards. *Interpreting Hebrew Poetry*. Guides to Biblical Scholarship: Old Testament. Minneapolis: Fortress, 1992.

Peterson, Eugene H. *Five Smooth Stones for Pastoral Work*. Grand Rapids: Eerdmans, 1992.

———. *Where Your Treasure Is: Psalms That Summon You from Self to Community*. Grand Rapids: Eerdmans, 1993.

———. *Working the Angles: The Shape of Pastoral Integrity*. Grand Rapids: Eerdmans, 1987.

Pope, Marvin H. *Song of Songs: A New Translation with Introduction and Commentary*. Anchor Bible 7C. Garden City, NY: Doubleday, 1977.

Pritchard, James B., ed. *Ancient Near Eastern Texts Relating to the Old Testament*. 3rd ed. Princeton, NJ: Princeton University Press, 1969.

Propp, Vladimir. *Morphology of the Folktale*. Translated by Laurence Scott. Austin: University of Texas Press, 1968.

Quinn-Miscall, Peter D. *Reading Isaiah: Poetry and Vision*. Louisville: Westminster John Knox, 2001.

Reid, Stephen Breck. *Experience and Tradition*. Nashville: Abingdon, 1990.

Rendtorff, Rolf. *Canon and Theology: Overtures to Old Testament Theology*. Translated and edited by Margaret Kohl. Overtures to Biblical Theology. Minneapolis: Fortress, 1993.

Richardson, Alan. *Genesis I–XI*. London: SCM Press, 1953.

Ross, Maggie. *Pillars of Flame: Power, Priesthood, and Spiritual Maturity*. San Francisco: Harper & Row, 1988.

Rushdoony, Rousas J. *The Institutes of Biblical Law: A Chalcedon Study*. Nutley, NJ: Craig Press, 1973.

Schaeffer, Francis A. *Genesis in Space and Time: The Flow of Biblical History*. Downers Grove, IL: InterVarsity Press, 1972.

Schiffman, Lawrence. Participant in a dialogue reported in "Losing Faith," *Biblical Archaeology Review* 33, no. 2 (March–April 2007): 50-57.

Slackman, Michael. "Did the Red Sea Part? No Evidence, Archaeologists Say." *New York Times*, April 3, 2007.

Stager, Lawrence. "The Archaeology of the Family in Ancient Israel." *Bulletin of the American Schools of Oriental Research* 260 (1985): 1-35.

Tamez, Elsa. *When the Horizons Close: Rereading Ecclesiastes*. Translated by Margaret Wilde. Maryknoll, NY: Orbis, 2000.

———. "The Woman Who Complicated the History of Salvation." In *New Eyes for Reading: Biblical and Theological Reflections by Women from the Third World*, edited by John S. Pobee and Bärbel von Wartenberg-Potter, pp. 5-17. Quezon City: Claretian Publications, 1987.

Thompson, J. A. *Deuteronomy*. Tyndale Old Testament Commentaries. Downers Grove, IL: InterVarsity Press, 1974.

Tollefson, Kenneth D., and H. G. M. Williamson. "Nehemiah as Cultural Revitalization." *Journal for the Study of the Old Testament* 56 (1992): 41-68.

Vanderkam, James C. *From Revelation to Canon: Studies in the Hebrew Bible and Second Temple Literature*. Supplements to the Journal for the Study of Judaism 62. Leiden: Brill, 2000.

van der Toorn, Karel. "The Exodus as Charter Myth." In *Religious Identity and the Invention of Tradition: Papers Read at a NOSTER Conference in Soesterberg, January 4–6, 1999*, edited by Jan Willem van Henten and Anton Houtepen, pp. 113-27. Studies in Theology and Religion 3. Assen: Van Gorcum, 2001.

Vischer, Wilhelm. "The Book of Esther." *Evangelical Quarterly* 11 (1939): 3-21.

von Rad, Gerhard. *Genesis: A Commentary*. Translated by John H. Marks. Old Testament Library. Philadelphia: Westminster, 1961.

Weinfeld, Moshe. *Social Justice in Ancient Israel and in the Ancient Near East*. Minneapolis: Fortress, 1995.

Weippert, Manfred. *The Settlement of the Israelite Tribes in Palestine: A Critical*

Survey of Recent Scholarly Debate. Translated by James D. Martin. London: SCM Press, 1971.

Wenham, Gordon J. *Genesis 1–15*. Word Biblical Commentary 1. Waco, TX: Word, 1987.

———. *Genesis 16–50*. Word Biblical Commentary 2. Nashville: Thomas Nelson, 1994.

Westermann, Claus. *Basic Forms of Prophetic Speech*. Translated by Hugh Clayton White. Philadelphia: Westminster, 1967.

———. *Isaiah 40–66: A Commentary*. Translated by D. M. G. Stalker. Old Testament Library. Philadelphia: Westminster, 1969.

———. *Praise and Lament in the Psalms*. Translated by Keith R. Crim and Richard N. Soulen. Atlanta: John Knox, 1981.

White, Sidnie Ann. "Esther." In *Gender and Difference in Ancient Israel*, edited by Peggy L. Day, pp. 161-77. Minneapolis: Fortress, 1989.

Wines, Michael. "In the Land of Homemade Names, Tiffany Doesn't Cut It." *New York Times*, October 1, 2007.

Wright, Christopher J. H. *Walking in the Ways of the Lord: The Ethical Authority of the Old Testament*. Downers Grove, IL: InterVarsity Press, 1995.

Yoo, Yani. "Han-Laden Women: Korean 'Comfort Women' and Judges 19–21." *Semeia* 78 (1977): 37-46.

Name Index

Subject Index

Scripture Index

Finding the Textbook You Need

The IVP Academic Textbook Selector
is an online tool for instantly finding the IVP books
suitable for over 250 courses across 24 disciplines.

---

ivpacademic.com
